The Grammar of Expressivity

OXFORD STUDIES IN THEORETICAL LINGUISTICS

GENERAL EDITORS: David Adger and Hagit Borer, Queen Mary University of London

ADVISORY EDITORS: Stephen Anderson, Yale University; Daniel Büring, University of Vienna; Nomi Erteschik-Shir, Ben-Gurion University; Donka Farkas, University of California, Santa Cruz; Angelika Kratzer, University of Massachusetts, Amherst; Andrew Nevins, University College London; Christopher Potts, Stanford University; Barry Schein, University of Southern California; Peter Svenonius, University of Tromsø; Moira Yip, University College London

For a complete list of titles published and in preparation for the series, see pp. 288–90.

The Grammar
of Expressivity

DANIEL GUTZMANN

OXFORD
UNIVERSITY PRESS

OXFORD
UNIVERSITY PRESS

Great Clarendon Street, Oxford, OX2 6DP,
United Kingdom

Oxford University Press is a department of the University of Oxford.
It furthers the University's objective of excellence in research, scholarship,
and education by publishing worldwide. Oxford is a registered trade mark of
Oxford University Press in the UK and in certain other countries

First Edition published in 2019

Impression: 1

Published in the United States of America by Oxford University Press
198 Madison Avenue, New York, NY 10016, United States of America

British Library Cataloguing in Publication Data
Data available

Library of Congress Control Number: 2018951740

ISBN 978-0-19-881212-8 (hbk.)
     978-0-19-881213-5 (pbk.)

Printed and bound by
CPI Group (UK) Ltd, Croydon, CR0 4YY

To my kids—the most expressive features of my life

Contents

General Preface

The theoretical focus of this series is on the interfaces between subcomponents of the human grammatical system and the closely related area of the interfaces between the different subdisciplines of linguistics. The notion of 'interface' has become central in grammatical theory (for instance, in Chomsky's Minimalist Program) and in linguistic practice: work on the interfaces between syntax and semantics, syntax and morphology, phonology and phonetics, etc. has led to a deeper understanding of particular linguistic phenomena and of the architecture of the linguistic component of the mind/brain.

The series covers interfaces between core components of grammar, including syntax/morphology, syntax/semantics, syntax/phonology, syntax/pragmatics, morphology/phonology, phonology/phonetics, phonetics/speech processing, semantics/pragmatics, and intonation/discourse structure, as well as issues in the way that the systems of grammar involving these interface areas are acquired and deployed in use (including language acquisition, language dysfunction, and language processing). It demonstrates, we hope, that proper understandings of particular linguistic phenomena, languages, language groups, or inter-language variations all require reference to interfaces.

The series is open to work by linguists of all theoretical persuasions and schools of thought. A main requirement is that authors should write so as to be understood by colleagues in related subfields of linguistics and by scholars in cognate disciplines.

David Adger
Hagit Borer

Acknowledgments

Being rooted in pragmatics and a semanticist at heart, I nevertheless had a soft spot for syntax, even though I couldn't put it to much use in my own work. But that changed when I, together with Katharina Turgay, submitted an article on German intensifiers to the *Journal of Comparative Linguistics* and Susi Wurmbrand, the editor-in-chief, and especially one of the anonymous reviewers sent us down the path of features and agreement, which helped us tremendously to get a grip on the quirky behavior of these expression. This paper, which, with some adaptations, will resurface here as one of the three major case studies, was my first foray in actually employing modern syntactic tools in my own work and it made me want to do that more. Hence, it followed naturally that I wanted to go after some syntactic problems for my second book (my so-called "Habiltationsschrift").

This was the first source of inspiration for this work. The second one came from a long talk with Daniel Hole, on the southbound train from the 2014 DGfS meeting in Marburg, who told me about his idea of an agreement-based, distributed analysis of the evaluative reading of German *nur* ('only'), which seemed to be a good way to tackle some particular problems raised by expressive adjectives. Although I was very inspired by these ideas, I mentally filed them away for the time being, but when I came to Cologne in Spring 2015 and had to give a lecture series, I decided to devote it to the more grammatical side of expressivity and this is where I developed the core ideas of the syntactic analysis of expressive adjectives that I will present in this book.

There are many people who supported and inspired me during this project and who indirectly influenced the final product. First, my colleagues in Cologne provided me with a great working environment. Thanks to Susanne Couturier for helping me to get through every bureaucratic jungle, especially before I even came to Cologne. The team I had in my first two years was a blast to work with, special thanks to Cedric Lawida, Frank Kirchhoff, Ilka Huesmann, Karin Barber, Martin Evertz, and Yamina Miri, and to Beatrice Primus for letting me borrow them for her for that time. Tim Graf deserves many thanks for helping me with the small experiment in Chapter 4, especially with the statistics. Petra Schumacher was always a pleasure to co-exam students with, inspiring to co-teach with, and very efficient to co-author a paper with (hopefully, there will be more to come). Since I came to Cologne, Stefan Hinterwimmer has become one of my closest academic friends, not just for talking about all things linguistics in our office and at the many conferences and workshops we have attended together, but also for going out for dinner and to the movies.

Outside of Cologne, I am especially thankful to my Accidental Tex(as) Posse—Chris Davis, Elin McCready, and Robert Henderson. I had the joy of working with all of them independently on all things expressive and I think at some time we should go for the big win and write a paper together.

I am grateful to David Adger and Hagit Borer for having included this work for publication in their series. To have my own book in the OSTL series was a little academic dream of mine, ever since I got my hands on #7 of this series—Chris Potts's 2005 book on the logic of conventional implicature. I had two reviews on my proposal for this book, which were very constructive and helpful in getting a better picture of what I think this book should be.

I thank Julia Steer and Vicki Sunter, my editors at OUP, who were a pleasure to work with and were very helpful, as I already knew from my previous book. The typesetters of OUP did a terrific job in creating a pretty book out of the quirkily customized LaTeX source I provided them with. Many thanks to Martin Noble and Hayley Buckley for getting the mess that is my English into good shape.

At various stages of my work on this book, I have profited in many ways from the input, inspiration, support, and conversations with, or general friendliness of, Andreas Trotzke, Angelika Kratzer, Antonio Fortin, Berit Gehrke, Carla Umbach, Chiara Gianollo, Cécile Meier, Daniel Hole, Emar Maier, Elena Castroviejo Miró, Erik Stei, Fabian Bross, Frank Sode, Gisbert Fanselow, Hans-Martin Gärtner, Hedde Zeijlstra, Henk Zeevat, Horst Lohnstein, Hubert Truckenbrodt, Josef Bayer, Katharina Hartmann, Katja Jasinskaja, Katie Frazier, Kilu von Prince, Lisa Matthewson, Malte Zimmermann, Manfred Krifka, Marco García García, Maribel Romero, Markus Steinbach, Martin Becker, Michael Franke, Regine Eckardt, Sascha Fink, Sophie Döring, Sophie Repp, Stanley Donahoo, Sven Lauer, Susi Wurmbrand, and Volker Struckmeier. Needless to say, this list is by no means exhaustive and I hereby grant the right to throw some 'damn' slurs at me to everyone I forgot to mention who deserved it.

My biggest thanks go to Ede Zimmermann and Klaus von Heusinger. To Ede for being a constant inspiration and for supporting me through all these years, even when I decided to leave Frankfurt in order to accept a position in Cologne. To Klaus for getting me to Cologne in the first place and for supporting me ever since during my post doc life.

As with my previous book, I do not even attempt to thank my family here, because even the longest and most elaborate "Thank you!" in an acknowledgment section will not be able to express how grateful and humbled I am to have these wonderful people in my life. But *damn it*: THANK YOU!

List of Tables and Figures

Tables

Figures

List of Abbreviations, Symbols, and Typographic Conventions

Abbreviations

A	adjective
ABS	absolutive
ACC	accusative
addr	adressee head
addrP	adressee phrase
Adr	adressee head
AdrP	adressee phrase
Adv	adverb
ALLOC	allocutive
AP	adjective phrase
AP	articulatory-perceptual system
C	complementizer
CI	conceptual-intentional system
COMP	comparative
CP	complementizer phrase
D	determiner
DA	descriptive adjective
DAT	dative
Deg	degree element head
DegP	degree phrase
Deg_N	adnominal degree element
$Deg_N P$	adnominal degree phrase
DP	determiner
EA	expressive adjective
EDC(s)	external degree modification construction
EI	expressive intensifier
ERG	ergative
eVoc	expressive vocative
F_L	faculty of language
FAMILIAR	familiar form (of pronouns)
FEM	feminine
FORMAL	formal form (of pronouns)
GEN	genitive
INTJ	interjection

IP	inflection phrase
IPX	intensifying prefixoid
LF	logical form
MASC	masculine
MP	minimalist program
N	noun
NEUT	neuter
NOM	nominative
NP	noun phrase
OC	occasional construction
P&P	principles and parameters
PART	particle
past	past tense
PF	phonological form
PL	plural
SA	(big) speech act head
sa	(little) speech act head
SAP	(big) speech act phrase
saP	(little) speech act phrase
SG	singular
Sp	speaker head
SpP	speaker phrase
SUP	superlative
T	tense
TP	tense phrase
v	little v head
vP	little v Phrase
V	verb
VP	verb phrase
V_{fin}	finite verb
VOC	vocative
VocP	vocative phrase

Syntactic and semantic symbols

c	context
c_S	speaker of context c
c_A	addressee of context c
c_L	location of context c
c_W	world of context c
w	world
CNU	contexts of non-defective use
Ø-you	covert 2nd person pronoun

P$_\varnothing$	phonologically empty preposition
Λ_A	logophoric agent
Λ_P	logophoric patentient
φ	φ-features (case, number, gender)
$[* X *]$	selectional feature: selecting for X
$[iF]$	feature, interpretable
$[uF]$	feature, uninterpretable
$[iDef]$	definiteness feature, interpretable
$[uGen]$	gender feature, uninterpretable
$[iNum]$	number feature, interpretable
$[uNum]$	number feature, uninterpretable
$[iT]$	tense feature, interpretable
$[uT]$	tense feature, uninterpretable
$[iEx]$	expressivity feature, interpretable
$[uEx]$	expressivity feature, uninterpretable
☹	negative attitude (value or operator)
INT	intensification (value of *Ex*-feature)
prop	a proposition
emo	emotive evaluation
INT	intensification function
$\llbracket \cdot \rrbracket$	interpretation function
$\llbracket \cdot \rrbracket^u$	interpretation function for use-conditional content
$\llbracket \cdot \rrbracket^t$	interpretation function for truth-conditional content
$\bullet$	separator of use-conditional content
$\blacklozenge$	separator for mixed content
$\neg$	logical negation
$\wedge$	truth-conditional conjunction
$\exists$	existential quantifier
$\forall$	universal quantifier
$\notin$	semantic (type) clash
$!$	expressive type shifter
$\uparrow^=$	type lifter (for e to $\langle e,t \rangle$)
γ	example found by googling
λ	lambda operator
π	projection function
$\cup$	set union
$\subseteq$	subset relation
$\in$	element relation
$\wp$	powerset
$+ >$	implicates
$\rightsquigarrow$	abbreviation function

Typographic conventions

In linguistic examples, I use **bold face** to highlight relevant expressions, and SMALL CAPS to indicate focus accent on an expression. In semantic formulas, **bold face** marks logical constants. In the main text and in quotations, I use *italics* to give emphasis. *Italics* in the main text are also used for expressions in the object language. I use "quotation marks" for translations of object expressions, verbatim quotes, as well as scare quotes.

1

Introduction

1.1 Descriptive and expressive language

Language can be used for a lot of different purposes. For instance, you can use it to advertise products.

(1.1)   Manufactured in Europe, the Virtuoso's 40 mm conical burrs grind coffee at 1.5 to 2.4 g/sec. depending on the setting. But what really sets the Virtuoso burrs apart is that these burrs can do a very uniform grind, with a distinct lack of fines across its grinding range. So the Virtuoso burrs are exceptional for espresso, drip, manual brewing methods and Press Pot. These conical burrs are durable and will remain sharp for many years. The burrs have a precision mounting system to ensure a stable platform for accurate grinding.
[https://www.baratza.com/grinder/virtuoso/]

Language can also be used to rant about something you are frustrated with or that makes you angry.

(1.2)   USPS, please just shut down your worthless fucking operation. You are a waste of space and oxygen. You couldn't deliver your booger hook to your own fucking nose hole if your life depended on it. You are so fucking worthless that you couldn't even do the only job that you have in delivering a package to my door. [...] So the fucking name of the road that's in my address that is also part of your route, wasn't a big enough fucking hint? Its not that fucking hard. Shit, even if you cant memorize every address on your route then just fucking google map it or some shit. Do you have a GPS? God damn. I google map my address and it pops right the fuck up. IF you have ANY fucking doubt, why not double check? No fuck that.
[https://www.ar15.com/forums/general/Dear-USPS--you-had-one-job----rant-inside-/5-1942704/]

These two example texts have obviously quite a different feel to them, not just regarding their content, but also regarding their form and the kinds of expressions involved. The reason for these differences is rooted in the different functions that play

The Grammar of Expressivity. First edition. Daniel Gutzmann.
© Daniel Gutzmann 2019. First published in 2019 by Oxford University Press.

the major role in their texts. By function I do not mean advertising or venting off one's emotions, but a more basic distinction. On a fundamental level (1.1) is primarily used to *describe* an object in the world and the properties it has, whereas (1.2) is primarily used to *express* the emotions and attitudes of the speaker. These basic functions have been called the descriptive and expressive language functions in semiotic theories of language, as in Bühler's (1934/1982) or Jakobson (1960a) work. While the descriptive function involves the relation of the linguistic sign to objects or state of affairs in the extra-linguistic world, the expressive function involves the relation between the sign to the speaker and what it conveys about her. Even if there are rarely cases in which a linguistic expression purely fulfills one function, we can see that the text in (1.1) falls mostly on the descriptive side of this divide, while (1.2) mostly fulfills the expressive function.

It is important to note that the distinction is not so much about what content is communicated by a linguistic expression, but more about the "mode" or "channel" in which it gets conveyed. Many contents may be conveyed either in a descriptive way or by using the expressive language function. Consider, for instance, the following examples (Kaplan 1999).

(1.3)   a. Ouch!
        b. Oops!

(1.4)   a. I am in pain.
        b. I witnessed a minor mishap.

To a certain extent, utterances of the expressions in (1.3) convey the same information as utterances of those in (1.4). If you (correctly) utter *ouch*, you are in pain and if you (correctly) utter *oops* you witnessed a minor mishap. However what differs is what Kaplan (1999: 41), in his influential paper on *ouch* and *oops*, calls the "mode of expression." The expressions in (1.4) *describes* particular situation, while the correct use of the expression in (1.3) *express* or *display* that the speaker is in those situations.

The distinction between descriptive and expressive language also has deep ramification about how to approach the meaning of descriptive and expressive expressions. While the meaning of descriptive expressions can be captured by analyzing the contribution they make to the truth-conditions of a sentence, this does not hold up for expressive language. It does not even make sense to ask under what conditions an utterance of "Oops!" is true. Instead, as Kaplan (1999) argued, it makes much more sense to ask about the conditions under which *oops* can be felicitously used, picking up one of the main ideas of theories of "meaning as use" that sprung from Wittgenstein's late work (Wittgenstein 1953). So instead of think about the *truth-conditional* meaning, we are thinking about the *use-conditional* meaning of expressive items (Recanati 2004: 447). Comparing the truth-conditions for (1.4b) and the use-conditions for (1.3b) illustrates the parallels and differences.

(1.5)   1 "I observed a minor mishap"

   2 is **true**,

   3 iff the speaker observed a minor mishap.

(1.6)   1 "Oops!"

   2 is **felicitously used**,

   3 iff the speaker observed a minor mishap.

In both cases, we have a condition in the third line that is meant to capture the meaning of an expression in the object language in the first line. Since the two conditions in (1.5) and (1.6) are the same—at least, let us assume that for the sake of the present discussion—the two expressions convey the same semantic information. However, they differ in how the expression is connected to its information. It is truth that connects the expression and the content in the first case; it is felicitous use in the second. They have different modes of expression.

1.2 From semantics to syntax

The difference in mode of expression is one of the fundamental differences between the descriptive and expressive language function and, being inspired by the pioneering work by Kaplan (1999) and the later formalization by Potts (2005), I devoted much of my earlier work to flesh out the reflexes that the distinction between truth-conditional descriptive and use-conditional expressive aspects of meaning have for semantic composition, how these two "dimensions of meaning" interact with each other and how a suitable, compositional semantic framework can handle both sides (Gutzmann 2015b). Together with a huge body of other work on expressive content in various languages and many different kinds of expressions, it has been shown that the expressive language function finds widespread and diverse realization in natural language.[1] This makes it safe to assume that the following hypothesis is true.

(1.7) **Hypothesis of expressive language**   (SemPrag version)
      The expressive language function is reflected in specialized linguistic items and constructions that exhibit special semantic and pragmatic properties.

For instance, the literature has shown that expressive items cannot easily be denied in discourse and are hard to embed under higher semantic operators. I will return to these semantic and pragmatic properties later on. However, even if the special semantic and pragmatic properties of expressives received a lot of attention and, by now, are rather well-studied, the question of whether the expressive language function is reflected in the grammar has not really been asked in the semantic literature, my own work included. To the extent that expressive items that are attested to have special

---

[1] See, for instance, the contributions in Gutzmann & Gärtner 2013.

grammatical behavior, it is argued to be a feature of their expressive content. For instance, with respect to expressive adjectives like *damn*, to which I will devote an entire chapter later in this book, Potts (2005: 163–4) writes that expressive adjectives "are syntactically much like other strictly attributive adjectives" and that an expressive adjective "plays no special role in the syntax of a nominal it appears in, beyond simply adjoining as any modifier would." He concludes "that the contrasts between [expressive adjectives] and other attributive adjectives don't follow from properties of the structures they determine" (Potts 2005: 165). However, as I hope to show in this book, expressive language is not just special with respect to its semantics and pragmatics, but also regarding its grammar. Therefore, the stronger hypothesis that I aim to establish is the following.

(1.8) **Hypothesis of expressive language**   (stronger version)
The expressive language function is reflected in specialized linguistic items and constructions that exhibit special **grammatical**, semantic, and pragmatic properties.

This stronger version of the hypothesis of expressive language still may not look very strong. But keep in mind that the special grammatical features it refers to have to be understood as genuine grammatical features that cannot be traced back to their special semantics or pragmatics. For instance, I have argued in various places (Gutzmann 2009, 2015a,b, 2017) that the special grammatical behavior of so-called modal particles in German can be derived from their use-conditional nature. They have special grammatical properties, which, however, are based on their semantics. The hypothesis in (1.8) is stronger than that. And my aim for this book is to go a step further than (1.8). Instead of just assuming that expressive items show special grammatical behavior, I assume that the mere fact that they are expressive items is a grammatical property itself. In particular, I argue for the following hypothesis.

(1.9) **Hypothesis of expressive syntax**
Expressivity does not only play a role for semantics and pragmatics, but it is a syntactic feature.

When I say *syntactic feature* here, I mean this in the theoretical sense of the term *feature*. That is, I argue that expressivity is a syntactic feature like, for instance, tense or number or gender, and that this expressivity feature can be involved in syntactic operations like other syntactic features—it may partake in agreement relations, it may trigger other syntactic operations like movement, and may be selected for by other expressions.

I will argue for the hypothesis of expressive syntax in an indirect way. In three extensive case studies I will investigate special properties of three kinds of expressions: expressive adjectives, expressive intensifiers, and expressive vocatives. In each case, I will show how an analyses that is built on the hypothesis in (1.9), and which assumes that expressivity is a syntactic feature, can explain some of the puzzling grammatical properties of these expressions, which, as I will argue, do not follow from their special semantics alone. Hence, in a nutshell the plan for this book is as follows. In the next two chapters, I will provide the theoretical semantic and syntactic background that will be needed for the three case studies that I will carry out in Chapters 4–6 and which form the heart of this book. I will finish this brief introduction with an overview of the individual chapters, before giving a short outline of how to approach this book if you are only interested in a subset of what I will deal with.

1.3 Overview of the chapters

Chapter 2   In the second chapter, I go deeper into the expressive function of language, the expressions that realize it and how it has been approached in formal semantics. The chapter offers a very brief historical perspective on the notion of expressivity and introduces the general idea of hybrid semantics, before presenting various instances of expressions that can be viewed as fulfilling the expressive language function. During this, I will introduce the three main phenomena to be dealt with in this book: expressive adjectives, expressive intensifiers, and expressives. The data section also includes a discussion of specific semantic properties that are often associated with expressive meaning. In the second half of the chapter, I will give an overview of recent formal approaches to expressivity. I will sketch the main ideas put forward by Potts (2005) for a formal semantic approach to expressive meaning that is based on the idea of a multidimensional system, before presenting the specific system that I will use for the purposes of the case studies. This will be a variant of the system developed in Gutzmann 2015b, which I specifically cut down and streamlined for what will be needed in the remainder of this book.

Chapter 3   Having laid out the empirical domain and the semantic background of expressivity in the second chapter, the third chapter will provide the syntactic background and talk about syntax, features, and agreement. This will be necessary to spell out the hypothesis of expressive syntax more precisely. After a brief sketch of the architecture of a minimalist syntax, I will focus on the notion of syntactic features, which will be put to use in all three case studies. I especially focus on the notion of agreement, which will be the syntactic operation that is most crucial for the analyses in the case studies. Starting with Chomsky's (2000) original conception, which I call C-Agree, I discuss more recent approaches to agreement (like Pesetsky & Torrego 2007) which are simpler but less constrained than C-Agree, as they drop the biconditional between (un)interpretability and (un)valuedness (hence I call it "S-Agree"); something that will be crucial for the case studies carried out later. This will then lead to the even more recent debate regarding the direction of agreement. I will side with the view that agreement looks upwards (Zeijlstra 2012), which will prove to be a perfect fit for the data discussed in Chapter 4. I will conclude with a discussion of phases and their relevance for Agreement. Following Bošković (2003, 2007) as well as Zeijlstra (2012), I assume that only CP is a boundary for Agreement, while DP is not. I will also briefly discuss some approaches that attempt to represent certain aspects of the context in syntax and investigate if they can be put to use for the following case studies.

Chapter 4   Chapter 4 deals with a poster child for expressive language. As can be witnessed from the text in (1.2) at the beginning of this chapter, expressive adjectives (EAs) are common expressions of the expressive language function. They are also, from a semantic point of view, the best studied. Interestingly, expressive adjectives are also the most obvious case in which the semantic literature ignores the syntactic component completely and even assumes that expressive adjectives do not behave differently from ordinary attributive adjectives. However, if one digs just a little deeper, one can find many properties in which expressive adjectives differ from their descriptive counterparts in crucial ways. The biggest difference is that expressive adjectives have some intriguing scope- and argument-taking behaviors. On the one hand, they have the strong tendency to be linked to the speaker and thus express the speaker's attitude even if semantically embedded. This is a well known fact and semantic approaches along the lines of Potts (2005) directly implement this behavior in the semantic system. There is however another, not so well documented problem that expressive adjectives pose for the syntax–semantics interface. Their semantic argument does not have to be their syntactic sister, but may be some bigger constituent that contains the adjective itself. For instance, an expressive adjective inside an object DP can nevertheless be interpreted as expressing a negative speaker evaluation regarding the entire situation expressed by the sentence. A proper approach to expressive adjectives should not only be able to deal with speaker linking, but also provide an explanation of argument extension.

Having established that the existing semantic approaches (Gutzmann 2015b; McCready 2010; Potts 2005) and others do not offer an explanation of argument extension (even though they are more successful with regards to speaker linking), I turn to the radical pragmatic solution to this syntax–semantics mismatch put forward by Frazier, Dillon, & Clifton (2014). Their approach completely ignores syntactic structure and may thus be called an "anti-syntactic" approach. However, their suggestion can be rejected by showing that there indeed are syntactic constraints for the interpretation of expressive adjectives. I therefore present a new approach to the role syntax plays for the interpretation of expressive adjectives. For this, I employ the upwards looking agreement mechanism argued for in the previous chapter. Assuming an uninterpretable expressivity feature on the expressive adjective and a corresponding interpretable feature at the respective locus of interpretation, the mismatch between the syntactic placement of the expressive and its interpretation can be solved by agreement. As I will show, this approach not only gives us an explanation for the observed syntactic restriction, but also highlights some further interesting properties of expressive adjectives.

The upshot of this chapter for the hypothesis of expressive syntax is that expressivity as a syntactic feature can be involved in agreement.

Chapter 5   In contrast to the expressive adjectives from Chapter 4, the class of expressive intensifiers (EIs), as I call them, have received almost no attention in the literature. Under this label, I consider a special class of degree expressions in varieties of colloquial German, including expressions like *sau* 'lit.female pig', *voll* 'fully' and *total* 'totally', which are distinguished from ordinary degree intensifiers like *very* by several puzzling syntactic properties. Most importantly, they can appear in what I call the external degree modification construction (EDCs), a construction of the form [EI D (A) NP]. Despite preceding the determiner in these constructions, the EI still intensifies the adjective or noun inside the DP. In this sense, EIs give rise to the mirror problem of the one posed by expressive adjectives, as they occur above their semantic target. Besides this mismatch regarding syntactic position and semantic interpretation, there is another form–interpretation mismatch involved with EIs: its interpretation must be indefinite, irrespective of the definite determiner that is strongly preferred in this construction. In addition, there is a lot of variation going on between different EIs.

After presenting a detailed description of the behavior of EIs, both in internal and external positions and in adjectival and adnominal use, I develop an analysis of EDCs to address these issues. The main idea is that EDCs are derived from a canonical DP-structure by moving the EI with the determiner where they form a complex quantifier. Crucially, and this is where this chapter directly builds on the previous ones, this movement is triggered by an expressivity feature in D. The chapter concludes with some intervention effects that are directly predicted by the analysis and confirmed by the data. This chapter is a revision of Gutzmann & Turgay 2015. While adopting the main structure and arguments of that article, it updates the analysis presented therein to tools employed here and also investigates the semantic interpretation of EIs in more detail. Some aspects, which are discussed in Gutzmann & Turgay 2015, are missing from this chapter since they are dealt with elsewhere in this book.

The upshot of this chapter for the hypothesis of expressive syntax is that expressivity as a syntactic feature can trigger movement.

Chapter 6   In the third and final case study, I investigate what I call expressive vocatives. In contrast to the previous two cases, at least the ordinary variant of vocatives has received some attention in the syntactic literature (Haegeman 2014; Haegeman & Hill 2013; Hill 2007, 2014), even although the connection to semantic approaches (like those by Eckardt 2014; Portner 2007; Predelli 2008) is not made explicit. After a brief discussion of standard vocatives, their structure, and their functions, I turn to expressive vocatives (eVocs), which consist of a second person pronoun and an expressive nominal part. After discussing the special properties of eVocs in much detail, thereby identifying three structural subtypes (autonomous, parenthetical, and integrated ones), I discuss previous approaches to vocative semantics. However, since none of these had eVocs on their radar, it comes as no surprise that they are not able to deal with them. Taking the crucial insights of these approaches, I develop a new semantic approach to eVocs that builds on the idea that integrated eVocs are actually the most basic ones, consisting of a pronoun and expressive modification. Parenthetical and autonomous eVocs are then extensions of the integrated version, just adding an activational vocative function and an exclamational component respectively. However, since the semantic analysis leaves some crucial restriction unaccounted for, I assume that, syntactically, eVocs consist of a D-element—the pronoun—which has to select for an expressive complement.

The upshot of this chapter for the hypothesis of expressive syntax is that expressivity as a syntactic feature can be selected for by other expressions.

Chapter 7   The final chapter is about looking back and looking ahead. It concludes with a broad view of the topic dealt with in this book and summarizes the main findings. I will sketch what the main conclusion—that expressivity is represented in syntax—may mean for existing and future research on expressives and the syntax-semantics interface, before giving some concrete suggestions for future directions of investigations.

1.4 How to approach this book

Let me close this chapter with a note on how to read it. Of course, the ideal scenario is to read it from front to back, but since I know that this often does not necesssarily fit researchers' and students' time, I tried to set up the book in a rather modular way so that, depending on your previous knowledge and interests, you can read chapters more or less selectively.

For the semanticist   If you come from a place like the one from which I came when starting this project, you are a semanticist familiar with expressives and multidimensional semantic frameworks in the Kaplan/Potts tradition and you can safely skip Chapter 2, maybe only going back to check the compositions' rules, which (for expository reasons) deviate a bit from how they are set up in, say, McCready 2010 or Gutzmann 2015b. If you are also familiar with minimalist syntax and the various notions of agreement, you can then directly jump to the case studies in Chapters 4–6 and refer back to Chapter 3 when necessary.

For the syntactician   If you are a syntactician familiar with syntactic minimalism and wonder what expressivity has to do with syntactic features, you may just read

Chapter 2, before going to the case studies. Chapters 4 and 5 may be especially interesting here, as they make the most use of the syntactic machinery, while Chapter 6 on expressive vocatives is a bit lighter on syntactic aspects.

For the student   Both background chapters—Chapter 2 on expressivity and the semantics behind it and Chapter 3 on the syntactic background—should give you everything that is needed to follow the rest of the book, as long as you have some basic training in semantics (you should know what functional application and semantic types are) and syntax (you should know what CPs and DPs are).

"I am just interested in the data"   In case you just came here for the quirky data on expressives, you can start by just reading the case studies in Chapters 4–6. In each chapter, I present almost all of the important observations and generalizations before I discuss and develop their analyses. In case you then get interested and want to know more about the background of the analyses, you can refer back to the appropriate sections in Chapters 2 and 3.

2

The expressive function of language

2.1 Some historical background

The idea that there are different "functions" or "modes" of language is not a recent invention of modern linguistics, but has a longstanding tradition, not only in linguistics itself, but also in related fields. Maybe not the first, but from the perspective of linguistics, most influential use of the notion of expressivity can be found in semiotics, especially in Bühler's (1934/1982; 1934/1999) work in which he develops his so-called *Organon model* of language, as depicted in Figure 2.1. According to this model, the linguistic sign, as represented by the triangle in the center of the illustration, has three different *semantic functions of language*. These different functions are rooted in the connections the linguistic sign can have to different cornerstones of communicative acts.

First, there is the *representation* or *descriptive* function ("Darstellungsfunktion") which encompasses the relation of the sign to the objects or state of affairs to which it refers. Since this can be understood in a referential-semantic way, it is certainly the most studied of the three functions and the one that got most attention in formal linguistics. And while Bühler (1934/1982: 37) does "not dispute the dominance of the representational function of language", he argues that the full function of linguistic signs does not stop at their relation to objects and state of affairs. Crucially, Bühler views the linguistic sign as a "a mediator between the speaker and the hearer" and hence, it has functions beyond the pure representational, descriptive function.

Rather, each of the two participants has his own position in the make-up of the speech situation, namely the sender as the agent of the act of speaking, as the subject of the speech action on the one hand, and the receiver as the one spoken to, as the addressee of the speech action on the other hand. They are not simply a part of what the message is about, rather they are the partners in an exchange, and ultimately this is the reason why it is possible that the sound as a medial product has a specific significative relationship to each, to the one and to the other severally. (Bühler 1934/1982: 37–8)

While the *appealing* function includes the effects the use of a linguistic sign has (or is intended to have) on the hearer, it is the speaker about whom the *expressive* function encodes information. That is, while using a linguistic expression does not *refer* to the

The Grammar of Expressivity. First edition. Daniel Gutzmann.
© Daniel Gutzmann 2019. First published in 2019 by Oxford University Press.

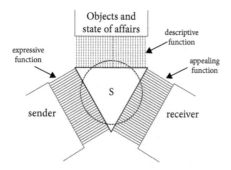

FIGURE 2.1 Bühler's (1934/1982: 35) Organon model of language

speaker's attitudes and, emotions (unless the utterance is about that), and so forth, it
nevertheless *reveals* or, to anticipate Kaplan's (1999) terminology, *displays* them.[1] That
is, every use of a linguistic sign may reveal something about the speaker's attitude.
For instance, if one uses a certain technical term over a descriptively equivalent, more
common term—like H_2O instead of *water*—one reveals a certain kind of knowledge
about water. However, in cases like this, what is revealed about the speaker is not
encoded in the linguistic sign itself but rather inferred from our knowledge about
context of uses and other conditions. Similarly, the manner in which a speaker utters
an utterance—with a sad or happy voice—may likewise display something about her
emotions and attitudes.

However, there are certain expressions that have the expressive function hardwired
into their lexical meaning. In his extension of Bühler's model, Jakobson (1960a)
mentions interjections as an example of expressions that encode the expressive
function in a very pure manner.

The purely emotive stratum in language is presented by the interjections. They differ from the
means of referential language both by their sound pattern (peculiar sound sequences or even
sounds elsewhere unusual) and by their syntactic role (they are not components but equivalents
of sentences).   (Jakobson 1960a: 354)

Since, by definition, expressive meaning does not belong to the descriptive realm of
language, it seems to escape the traditional Fregean method of formal semantics to
capture the meaning of a sentence by reference to its truth-conditions. This holds
even though the expressive meaning of interjections and other expressive items is
obviously conventionally encoded just like the descriptive meaning of an expression
like, say, *juice*.

---

[1] Similar remarks could be made regarding the appealing function, which, however, is not the topic of
this book.

That certain aspects of meaning fall by the wayside of truth-conditional semantics has been noted from its very beginnings; even before Bühler (1934/1982) drew his three-way distinction. Most famously, already Frege referred to the fact that the "coloring" of certain expressions convey an attitude of the speaker that however does not affect the truth-conditions of a sentence (cf. the discussion in Horn 2008b, 2013). That is, the difference between *dog* and *cur*, to use one of Frege's classic examples (Frege 1897/1979: 140), is not a difference in descriptive and thus truth-conditional relevant meaning, but a difference in the coloring.

(2.1)   a. This **dog** howled the whole night.
        b. This **cur** howled the whole night.

While (2.1a) and (2.1b) arguably have the same truth conditions—they are true if the dog in question howled the whole night—the use of *cur* in (2.1b) expressively displays a speaker's attitude that is not linguistically encoded in (2.1a).[2] In our terminology, *cur* also encodes expressive meaning on top of the descriptive meaning that it shares with *cur*. The distinction into descriptive, truth-conditional, and expressive use-conditional meaning can be illustrated by an informal tower notation, which I used in Gutzmann & Gärtner 2013, in which the descriptive content is written at the base level and the expressive content on top it.

(2.2)   *The cur howled the whole night* $= \dfrac{\text{The speaker feels negatively about the dog}}{\text{The dog howled}}$

Even if semanticists had expressive meaning as a non-truth-conditional yet conventional kind of meaning on their radar (see, e.g., textbooks by Cruse 1986, 2004), it didn't draw much attention in formal semantics. This changed with Kaplan's (1999) famous underground paper on "the meaning of *ouch* and *oops*" in which he argues that expressive meaning, contrary to common belief, can indeed receive a formal semantic treatment if one takes the fact seriously that they are non-truth-conditional, but instead are better captured by their *use-conditions*. That is, Kaplan says that one shouldn't ask what makes an utterance of *Goodbye!* true, since this does does not make any sense.

Instead, I ask, "What are the conditions under which the expression is *correctly* or *accurately* used?". This seems a much more fruitful line of inquiry for a word like "Goodbye". To the degree that such conditions reflect linguistic convention, the *information* that such conditions obtain is carried **in the semantics of the expression.**   (Kaplan 1999: 5; my emphasis, D.G.)

This later point is crucial. Even if expressive expressions resist a truth-conditional approach, the use-conditions they are associated with are based on the conventional, linguistic meaning of these expressions and thus should be considered to be semantic,

---

[2] This does not exclude the possibility that certain non-conventional aspects of an utterance of (2.1a) may reveal a similar attitude of the speaker. That is, if (2.1a) is uttered with an angry voice, the utterance may still reveal a negative speaker attitude even in the absence of any conventionally encoded expressivity.

rather than belonging to conversational pragmatics. This reflects an important point which has already been made by Jakobson (1960a).

> If we analyze language from the standpoint of the information it carries, we cannot restrict the notion of information to the cognitive aspect of language. A man, using expressive features to indicate his angry or ironic-attitude, conveys ostensible information.   (Jakobson 1960a: 354)

What is important about Kaplan's view, and what also shines through this quote by Jakobson, is that it does not lead to a radical departure from truth-conditional semantics. The point is just that truth-conditionally relevant aspects of meaning alone (the "cognitive aspect of language") are not sufficient to capture the full (conventional) meaning of natural language expressions. That is, Kaplan's suggestion is not to abandon truth-conditional semantics in favor of a radical theory of "meaning as use", but to enhance it by adopting a use-conditional perspective on certain linguistic expressions. That is, instead of letting linguistic expressions have a single denotation in form of their truth-conditional content, they have a second meaning dimension in form of use-conditional content as well. I call the general idea that expressions denote truth-conditional *and* use-conditional content *hybrid semantics* (Gutzmann 2015b). The following schema illustrates its basic concept, where $[\![\cdot]\!]$ gives the overall meaning of a natural language expression α, while $[\![\cdot]\!]^t$ and $[\![\cdot]\!]^u$ provide the truth- and use-conditional content of α (Gutzmann 2015b: 19).

(2.3)   **Hybrid semantics**
$$[\![\alpha]\!] = \langle [\![\alpha]\!]^t, [\![\alpha]\!]^u \rangle$$

Kaplan's insights as well as his conceptual suggestions for how to build a formal system for expressive or use-conditional content sparked a lot of subsequent work in semantics that elaborated on his ideas in order to deal with expressions that were previously more or less ignored by truth-conditional semantics.

However, before I give a brief overview of the formal approaches to expressive meaning developed in recent research and lay out the semantic tool I will employ in this book, let us first make a brief tour through the empirical variety of expressions that linguistically encode expressive meaning. I will mainly focus on the expressions that will be the topics of later chapters, but will also mention additional cases that I will not deal with in this book.

2.2 Expressive phenomena

Expressivity can and has been observed as a characteristic property of a huge variety of linguistic expressions. In this section, I will a give a brief overview of a selection of expressive items, without claiming that this is exhaustive. I start with the three phenomena that will be the main focus of this book, before mentioning some further cases to illustrate the diversity of the expressions that reflect the expressive language function.

2.2.1 *Expressive adjectives*

From a semantic point of view, the group consisting of expressives in the narrow sense received the most attention in the literature. Expressive nominal epithets like *bastard* and expressive adjectives like *damn* are already discussed by Kaplan (1999) and took a major part in Potts's (2005) book and subsequent work (Potts 2007).

(2.4) **Epithets**
    a. That **bastard** Kresge is famous.   (Potts 2007: 168)
    b. That **idiot** Kresge dropped the bottle again.

(2.5) **Expressive adjectives** (EAs)
    a. I hear your **damn** dog barking.   (Potts 2005: 18)
    b. My **friggin'** bike tire is flat again.

Let me focus on expressive adjectives here, as they will be the topic of the major case study in Chapter 4. Much has been said about their semantic properties, which served as a blueprint for a characteristic list of properties of expressive items (Potts 2007):

(2.6) **Properties of expressives**
    a. Independence
    b. Nondisplaceability
    c. Perspective dependence
    d. Descriptive ineffability
    e. Immediacy
    f. Repeatability

Let me briefly recapitulate them here, but without going into too much detail (see Gutzmann 2013 for a more in depth discussion).

Independence is the most characteristic property of expressive and use-conditional expressions, as it is based on the distinction between descriptive/truth-conditional and expressive/use-conditional content and simply states that expressives contribute content that is independent from the descriptive dimensions of meaning. Adding expressives to an utterance does not alter its truth-conditions, but imposes additional conditions on its felicitous use. That is, as long as the expression in question has only expressive content. In Potts's (2005, 2007) original work, there was no place for what I called hybrid expressions, like *cur*, that also have descriptive meaning, but subsequent modifications of Potts's framework opened it up for such (attested) possibilities (Gutzmann 2011, 2015b; McCready 2010).

Nondisplaceability is based on the independence of expressives and means that the interpretation of expressives cannot be displaced from being interpreted in the utterance situation by linguistic means such as negation, conditionalization, modalization, and the like. Consider the following examples, which are a slight modification from Potts 2007: 170.

(2.7) a. That damn Kresge isn't late for work. #He's a good guy.
    b. That damn Kresge was late for work yesterday. #But he's not damn today, because today he was on time.
    c. Sue says that that damn Kresge should be fired. #I think he's a good guy.
    d. Sue believes that that damn Kresge should be fired. #I think he's a good guy.
    e. Maybe that damn Kresge will be late again. #But if not, he's a good guy.
    f. #If that damn Kresge arrives on time, he should be fired for being so mean.

All these examples show that the negative attitude toward Kaplan that the speaker displays by her use of *damn* still holds, even if the rest of the propositional content does not (necessarily) do so. That is, even if an expressive seems to appear in the scope of such semantic contexts, it will still be interpreted in the expressive meaning dimension and therefore not be targeted by these operations. Semantic frameworks, that are built on the idea of multidimensionality, model this observation directly—as we will see below—but for now, the tower notation is already sufficient to illustrate the relation between the independence and nondisplaceability property. For instance, the modal operator in (2.7e) only resides in the lower descriptive dimension and therefore does not affect the expressive content that resides in the expressive dimension.

(2.8) *Maybe that damn Kresge will be late again.* =

                                The speaker feels negative about Kresge
                                  maybe(Kresge will be late again)

In this sense, expressive meaning is similar to presuppositions as it also projects out of embedding contexts, which is why both kinds of content are sometimes collectively referred to as *projective content*.

One very important property that also follows from nondisplaceability is the observation that, in may cases—we will come to the exceptions in a moment—the expressive speaker attitude expressed by expressive adjectives is attributed to the speaker, even when they are embedded in speech report or propositional attitude predicates. Consider example (2.7c) or the following variant.

(2.9) Sue said that Donna invited that damn Kresge to the party.

Even if the expressive adjective *damn* occurs inside the clausal argument of (2.9), it still seem to express the attitude of the speaker of (2.9). Even if this is just a special instance of the more general property of nondisplaceability, let me refer to this tendency of expressives to receive a speaker-oriented interpretation as **speaker linking**.

Speaker linking and the question of whether it is a hard fact about expressives (and use-conditional meaning in general) or merely a tendency is much discussed in the literature (Amaral, Roberts & Smith 2007). The emerging consensus seems to be that (i) expressives and other use-conditional items seem to differ with respect to their ability to be attributed to an attitude holder other than the speaker (Döring 2013; Gutzmann 2017), but (ii) at least some expressives can receive a non-speaker interpretation if the right circumstances hold (Harris & Potts 2009a,b; Kaiser 2015). The classic example to illustrate this comes from Kratzer (1999: 6). She used the epithet *bastard* in her example, but we can make the same point with an expressive adjective.

(2.10) My father screamed that he would never allow me to marry that **damn** Webster.

In this utterance, it is rather unlikely that the speaker intended to express a negative attitude toward Webster. Instead the expressive seems to be linked rather to the father. This illustrates the property of **perspective dependence.** In contrast to descriptive predicates, expressive always seem to be evaluate from the perspective of an attitude holder, which seems to default to the speaker but can also be instantiated by another salient attitude host, like the speaker's father in (2.10). Although this non-speaker attitude holder is linguistically realized in (2.10), this does not have to be the case, as discussed by Potts (2007) and Harris & Potts (2009a,b). Since a similar perspective-dependency can be attested for predicates of personal taste like *tasty* or *fun*, Potts (2007) assumes that expressives are, strictly speaking, not speaker-linked, but depend on the so-called contextual *judge* (i.e. they are rather "judge linked"), a contextual parameter introduced for a relativistic analysis of personal taste predicates by Lasersohn (2005). In many cases, the judge is the speaker and hence we get speaker orientation from that as well, but sometimes the judge is another salient individual, as in (2.10); a phenomenon that can also be observed for taste predicates. That is, if one assumes that some expressives are judge-linked in this way, while others are speaker-linked, we get an account of the observation that some expressives can get a non-speaker-linked interpretation—namely those that are judge-linked—and some cannot and always are interpreted from the speaker's perspective; namely those that are speaker-linked (see Döring 2013; Gutzmann 2017).

Descriptive ineffability refers to the observation that speakers "are never fully satisfied when they paraphrase expressive content using descriptive, i.e., nonexpressive, terms" (Potts 2007: 166). However, the status of this as a characteristic property of expressives has been challenged (Carston 2016; Drożdżowicz 2016; Geurts 2007; Gutzmann 2013; Mildenberger 2017). The problem is that it does not distinguish between descriptive and expressive language in a general way: many descriptive expressions cannot easily be paraphrased, irrespective of whether you do it with descriptive or expressive language. However, the core intuition that some of the special "mode of expression" gets lost, when you switch from expressive to descriptive language, seems true. That is, even if one could find the perfect descriptive paraphrase to capture the information expressed by an expressive, it would still not be expressed in the same way.[3] Conveying even the same information in descriptive and expressive language is just not the same thing. This is the basic insight behind Bühler's (1934/1982) and Jakobson's (1960a) ideas of different language functions.

With immediacy, Potts (2007) targets the performative-like character of expressive meaning. Behind this stands the idea that once an expressive is uttered, you basically performed an (expressive) speech act that cannot (or only with huge efforts and sometimes never) be successfully taken back. Potts's (2007: 167) characterization that expressives "do not offer content so much as inflict it" found a formal correspondence in the idea that in dynamic theories of conversational updates, expressive content is not put forward for discussion; it is not put "on the table", to use Farkas & Bruce's (2010) metaphor. Instead it directly affects the discourse context without awaiting further approval as ordinary asserted content does (AnderBois, Brasoveanu, & Henderson 2015; Gutzmann & Henderson 2015). This is also the reason why expressive content cannot be targeted by denials because it is not even *at issue* (Simons, Tonhauser, Beaver, & C. Roberts 2010).

Finally, repeatability means that expressives, in contrast to descriptive language, can often be repeated without redundancy (Potts 2007: 166). Again, the status of this as a *general* property of expressive/use-conditional meaning is not totally clear, since many expressive items cannot be repeated easily, like, for instance, modal particles as in (2.11) or interjections as in (2.12).

(2.11) #Gestern   ist   **ja**   Martin **ja**   mit   Ede **ja**   im   Kino
         yesterday *is* PART *Martin* PART *with* *Ede* PART *in.the* *cinema*
         gewesen.
         was

(2.12) #**Oops!** I forgot my keys. **Oops!** They are in the car. **Oops!**

However, for expressives in the narrow sense, repeatability seems to hit on something. Repeating the same expressive in an utterance at different positions does not feel redundant in the same way as repeating the interjection in (2.12) does.

(2.13) **Damn**, the **damn** dog peed on the **damn** couch again!

According to Potts (2007), each expressive in (2.13) contributes to narrowing down the expressive attitude the speaker displays by the utterance, leading to an expression of a more determined (and probably higher) emotional state than the same utterance with only one or two expressives would do.

This brief discussion already hints at an important property of expressive adjectives, which will play an important role in the case study in Chapter 4. Note that, in

---

[3] For a formal model to compare descriptive and expressive information, see Gutzmann 2015b: 22–7.

order to be surprised by the fact that the three instances of *damn* in (2.13) are not redundant, we have to assume that they all express an attitude toward the entire situation expressed by the sentence. That is, not the peripheral *damn* at the beginning, but also the two occurrences of *damn* that appear inside the subject and object DP respectively express a sentence-level interpretation. Consider the following variant of (2.13), in which there is only one expressive.

(2.14)   The dog peed on the **damn** couch!

An utterance of this sentence is ambiguous. The expressive adjective can have the couch as the target of its expressive attitude, but—and this is more likely with this sentence—it can also express negative feelings about the fact that the dog peed on the couch, without expressing any feelings regarding the couch itself. That is, (2.14) has a meaning that is pretty much the same as that of (2.15).

(2.15)   **Damn**, the dog peed on the couch!

I call this phenomenon in which an EA semantically reaches out of its host DP and takes a larger constituent as its argument **argument extension**. Note that already the reading of (2.14), in which *damn* targets the couch is a form of argument extension, since *damn* does not target its syntactic sister *couch*, but a larger constituent.

The ability to show this argument extension is a rather surprising behavior of EAs, given that it is not possible for ordinary descriptive adjectives, even if they are rather emotional. However, there is simply no way in which (2.16a) has a reading in which it approximates what (2.17b) expresses.

(2.16)   a.   The dog peed on the **awesome** couch!   ($\neq$)
         b.   **Awesome**, the dog peed on the couch!

Although the argument extension has implicitly been acknowledged in the semantic literature, it has not received a satisfying analysis. For instance, while Potts (2005: 18) observes that despite occurring "nominal-internal, EAs can take common nouns, full nominals, and full clauses as their arguments," he assumes that "we must call upon the semantics to ensure that the meaning of damn can apply to noun-phrase and clausal meanings (at least) despite its nominal-internal position in the syntax." However, he does not really address how this mismatch between where an EA appear syntactically and where it takes its semantic argument and just allows "that in these cases, the syntactic and semantic parsetrees have different shapes" (Potts 2005: 167). In Chapter 4 I will develop a syntactic solution to argument extension based on the main hypothesis of this book that expressivity is a syntactic feature and it is the mismatch between where this feature is morphologically realized (in the form of the adjective) and where it is interpreted (at the DP level or the sentence level) that leads to the impression that the adjective extends its argument.

Coming back from argument extension to repeatability, we can now see that (2.13) has a reading in which all three EAs receive a sentence-level interpretation and there is no specific emotion expressed toward the dog or the couch. This would then be the reading for which it may be surprising that the repetition of the EAs does not feel redundant.[4] Of course, there is then also a reading of (2.13) under which all three expressives target a different object: the sentence, the subject, and the object respectively; which then would not be an instance of *repeatability* in the first place.

To summarize, EAs adjectives show particular properties and while some of them seem to be a general hallmark of expressive language in general, like the independence of the expressive content from the truth-conditional content and the property of perspective dependence (and speaker linking), some properties like repeatability and argument extension are rather particular and are not even shared by closely related epithets such as *bastard* or *idiot*. While semantic approaches, as we will see further below, are built with the more general properties in mind, they more or less ignore argument extension (and thereby gloss over the underpinnings of repeatability). I aim to close this gap in Chapter 4.

2.2.2 Expressive intensifiers

The second case study that I will carry out later in this book deals with what can be called *expressive intensifiers* (Gutzmann & Turgay 2012, 2015). This label encompasses a small class of degree words in German that are mainly confined to informal varieties of German (like youth language or certain dialects), such as *sau* 'lit. female pig, sow,' *mords* 'lit. murder,' *krass* 'crass,' *total* 'totally,' and *voll* 'fully' (Androutsopoulos 1998) or *ur* in Viennese German (McCready & Schwager 2009).

(2.17)   **Expressive intensifiers (EIs)**
Du   hast   eine   **sau/mords/krass/voll/total**   schnelles   Auto.
you   have   a   EI   *fast   car*
'You've got a EI ($\approx$ totally) fast car.'

There are (at least) three important respects in which expressive intensifiers (EIs) differ from ordinary degree words like *sehr* 'very.' First, they are (mixed) expressives: truth-conditionally they are akin to ordinary intensifying degree words like *very*, while also expressing an additional expressive attitude about the fact that the object in question exhibits the property modified by the EIs to that high degree. That is, (2.17) does not just convey that the thing in question is very fast, but also expresses the speaker's excitement about that fact. Secondly, while prototypically, EIs modify adjectives, they can (under conditions to be discussed in Chapter 5) also modify nouns that are gradable along a salient dimension (Morzycki 2009), something that is impossible for *sehr* 'very':

---

[4] The syntactic approach to argument extension that I will develop in Chapter 4 will also address the issue of repeatability: when all EAs in an utterance like (2.13) receive a sentence-level interpretation, they are all a realization of the same feature, very much like in cases of negative concord all negation words are a realization of one negation feature (Zeijlstra 2004, 2012).

(2.18) Du hast eine **totale** Schrottkarre.
        you have a   EI   *junker*
        'You've got a total junker'

(2.19) *Du hast eine **sehr** Schrottkarre.
        you have a   *very* *junker*

The most surprising property of EIs, however, is a syntactic one. Besides occurring in the DP-internal position as in (2.17) and (2.18), EIs can also occur in a seemingly DP-external position in which the EI precedes the determiner. This holds both for the adnominal and the more usual "ad-adjectival" use.

(2.20) a. Das ist **sau** das schnelle Auto.
            that is   EI   *the fast   car*
            'That is a totally fast car.'

        b. Das ist **total** die Schrottkarre.
            that is   EI   *the junker*
            'You've got a total junker.'

This is a rather surprising fact about EIs and something that is again impossible for ordinary degree expressions.

(2.21) a. *Das ist **sehr** das schnelle Auto.
            that is   *very* *the fast   car*

        b. *Das ist **sehr** die Schrottkarre.
            that is   EI   *the junker*

Another puzzling aspect of EIs is that, when they occur in an external positions as in (2.20), they tend to occur with a definite article, which notably is interpreted like an indefinite article, as can be witnessed by the translation of these examples. That is, there are several mismatches between the syntax of the external EI-construction and its semantics. The article is interpreted as an indefinite despite surfacing as a definite one and the EI still interpreted as though it modified the adjective or noun inside the DP, not the entire DP itself. In a sense, we have the opposite picture of the EAs that extend their argument to the DP: the adjectives appear DP-internally, but (can) take the DP as its argument; the intensifiers (can) occur DP-externally, but are interpreted as being in an internal position.

As the case in Chapter 5 will show, the mismatch between syntax and semantics cannot be explained on semantic grounds alone, just as with EAs. Hence, even though the analysis will work differently for EIs than for EAs, the approach that I will argue for will also build on the idea of expressivity as a syntactic, thereby providing another case in point for the main hypothesis of this book.

2.2.3 Expressive vocatives

The final group of expressions that I will devote a detailed case study to are vocatives.

(2.22) **Vocatives**

    a. **Ede**, the pizza is ready.   (Eckardt 2014: 224)

    b. **Angelina**, the sky is on fire.   (Predelli 2008: 97)

This may seem to be a bit surprising, given that vocatives as in (2.22) are usually said to draw the addressee's attention and hence may rather be viewed as an instance of the appealing function of language. However, I will not focus on such ordinary vocatives, but will investigate the grammar and meaning of what I call *expressive vocatives* (eVocs) as in (2.23).

(2.23) **Expressive vocatives (eVocs)**

    a. **You idiot!**

    b. **You bastard!**

    c. **You linguist!**

    d. **You philosopher!**

These structures consist of a second person pronoun together with an expressive noun as in (2.23a) and (2.23b). What makes these structures even more interesting for the purposes of this book is that if the noun is usually a descriptive noun, it nevertheless receives an expressive interpretation, as in (2.23c) and (2.23d). That is, even if nouns like *linguist* or *philosopher* arguably do not convey a derogatory attitude lexically, they do so in the context of eVocs (d'Avis & Meibauer 2013).

In Chapter 6, I will show that eVocs can be used in three different structural contexts: in autonomous utterances, in parenthetical positions, and also in an integrated, argument position.

(2.24) **Autonomous eVocs**
Du Idiot!
'You idiot!'

(2.25) **Parenthetical eVocs**

Du	**Idiot,**	morgen	hat	die	Post	doch	geschlossen!
you	*idiot*	*tomorrow*	*has*	*the*	*post*	PART	*closed*

'You idiot, the post office is closed tomorrow!'

(2.26) **Integrated eVocs**

Du	**Arschloch**	hast	mir	mein	Frühstück	geklaut!
you	*asshole*	*has*	*me*	*my*	*breakfast*	*stolen*

'You asshole, you stole my breakfast!'

The challenge for an analysis of eVocs is to account for the similarities between these three structural variants of eVocs, but at the same time explain their differences. For instance, while integrated eVocs are mixed expressives—they not only express an attitude toward the addressee, but also refer to the addressee at the truth-conditional level—this does not hold for parenthetical or autonomous eVocs. In addition, we need a way to account for the shift in interpretation that neutral nouns have to undergo when used as eVocs.

The analysis that I will develop in Chapter 6 will again involve the hypothesis that expressivity is a syntactic feature. In contrast to expressive adjectives and intensifiers, where the mechanism of agreement plays an important role, eVocs show that expressivity is also a feature that can be selected for in syntax. In particular, I assume that second person pronouns can be used like determiners in German—an independently explored idea (Vater 1998, 2000)—which, however, select for expressive nominal arguments. As has been the case for EAs and even more for EIs, the study of eVocs again reveals a close connection between the syntactic category of D and expressivity.

2.2.4 *Further cases*

The three phenomena discussed so far will receive a major investigation in the three case studies that I will carry out later. However, expressive language is by no means confined to expressive adjectives, intensifiers, and vocatives. So let me briefly mention a few additional cases, which either were always viewed as prototypical cases of expressive language or have been analyzed as such in the literature. This already shows that the expressive language function is not confined to a handful of expression types but can be found across various kinds of expressions.

2.2.4.1 Interjections As mentioned in the brief historical introduction, perhaps the purest incarnation of the expressive function of language can be found with interjections. Examples like *ouch, oops,* and *oh* are stereotypical cases in point.

(2.27) **Interjections**
    a. **Ouch**, I've hit my thumb!   (Kaplan 1999)
    b. **Oops!**   (Kaplan 1999)
    c. **Oh**, I have another suit.   (Ameka 1992)

The use of such interjections directly displays the speaker's attitude. This is true even if they are used together with descriptive material, as in (2.27a) or (2.27c), where there is not much interaction between the interjection and the rest of the utterance. In fact, interjection, when occurring with other expressions, occurs in rather unintegrated positions; mostly at the right edge of the clause, but sometimes also in so-called parenthetical niches inside a clause (Altmann 1981). That is, there may be linear integration, but no hierarchical integration (Fries 1992: 317).

(2.28) a. Du bist—**ach**—viel   zu dumm dafür.
　　　　you are INTJ *much too dumb there.for*
　　　　'You are—gosh—way too stupid for that.'

　　　b. Ich habe mir—**autsch**—den Finger gequetscht.
　　　　I have me INTJ *the finger bruised*
　　　　'I—autch—bruised my finger.'

Due to their pure emotiveness and their "peculiar sound sequences" (Jakobson 1960b) and syntactic isolation, there has even been a long debate about whether interjections are even part of the language system at all or whether they are more akin to other non-linguistic signs, like gasps, moans, laughs, or other indexical signs (for an overview over the debate, cf. Burger 1980; Trabant 1983). However, in contrast to the aforementioned expressions of emotions, interjections are not natural signs in the sense of indices, but signs that are governed by the linguistic practices and conventions of the particular language at hand. Hence, different languages may have different interjections for the same emotions. For instance, for expressions of pain, we have the following interjections in four European languages.

(2.29) **Interjections of pain**
　　　a. *German:* autsch, aua
　　　b. *English:* ouch, ow
　　　c. *French:* aï, ouille
　　　d. *Spanish:* ay

In a similar vein, even if two interjections have the same form in two languages, their use-conditions may still differ in subtle ways conventionally determined by the language; see, for instance, Wierzbicka's (1992) discussion of *fu* in Polish and Russian.

Interjections played a crucial role for kicking of interest in expressivity in formal semantics and philosophy of language thanks to their prominent role in Kaplan's (1999) influential work. They serve as the poster child for conventional use-conditional meaning. However, they never attracted much interest beyond that, because, due to their autonomous and independent status, there is not much semantic composition going on.

However, even if there is not that much interaction going on semantically, there are some observations that may hint at more syntactic substance than meets the eye. For instance, there are constraints on the linearization of interjections with respect to each other. For instance, so-called primary interjections (like *autch*, *oh* and *uups*) precede secondary interjections that belong to or have a (semi-)transparent origin in other part of speeches (*damn, shit, fuck, jeez* etc.) if they co-occur together (see Nübling 2004: 31).

(2.30) a. **Oh Gott**, ich habe den Schlüssel vergessen!
        oh God   I   have the key   forgotten
        'Oh my god, I forgot the key!'

    b. *__**Gott oh**__, ich habe den Schlüssel vergessen!
        God   oh   I   have the key   forgotten

(2.31) a. **Oh nein**, wir verpassen den Anschlusszug!
        oh no   we miss   the connecting.train
        'Oh no, we will miss the connecting train!'

    b. *__**Nein oh**__, wir verpassen den Anschlusszug!
        no   oh we miss   the connecting.train

Similar linearization can also be observed between two primary interjections or between primary interjections (Nübling 2004: 31) and left-peripheral vocatives (Haegeman & Hill 2013).

(2.32) a. **Au   weia**, ich habe kein Geld   dabei.
        autch INTJ I   have no   money there.by
        'Oh no, I have no money with me.'

    b. *__**Weia au**__, ich habe kein Geld   dabei.
        INTJ autch I   have no   money there.by

(2.33) a. **Ach Kate**, wann sehen wir bloß uns wieder?
        INTJ Kate when see   we PART us again
        'Oh Kate, when will we see each other again?'

    b. *__**Kate ach**__, wann sehen wir bloß uns wieder?
        Kate INTJ when see   we PART us again

(2.34) Romanian   (Haegeman & Hill 2013: 380)

    a. **Vai Dane**   hai   că   nu   te   cred.
        INTJ Dan.VOC PART that not you believe.1SG
        'Ah, Dan, c'mon, I don't believe you.'

    b. *__**Dane**,   vai hai   că   nu   te   cred.
        Dan.VOC INTJ PART that not you believe.1SG

All this shows that syntax plays a role for interjections as well and accordingly, there have been some investigations into their syntactic properties (see, amongst others, Fries 1992; Haegeman & Hill 2013; Munaro 2010; Munaro & Poletto 2003, 2004), some of which we will examine in more detail later in this book. However, in these studies, interjections are not always clearly distinguished from particles, to which we now turn.

2.2.4.2 *Particles* Even though most particles do not seem to be expressive in the strong emotional sense, they have been connected to the resurgent semantic interest in expressivity thanks to Kratzer's (1999) comment on Kaplan's (1999) ideas, in which she suggests that German modal particles should be understood as conveying expressive/use-conditional meaning; an idea that by now is firmly established (Jacobs 2019; S. Müller 2017; M. Zimmermann 2012) and which influenced my own work on modal particles in German (Gutzmann 2009, 2015a,b, 2017).

Modal particles are special particles in some languages, like German, that occur in a sentence medial position and either express the speaker attitude or modify the sentence mood of the utterance (Doherty 1985; Jacobs 1991; Lindner 1991). Consider, for instance, the German modal particle *ja*, which expresses that the propositional content of the host clause may have already been known by the hearer.

(2.35) **Modal particles**

    Morgen   ist die Uni **ja**   zu.
    tomorrow *is*   *the* *uni* PART *closed*
    '(As you may know), the university is closed tomorrow.'

Crucially, the presence of the modal particle does not add anything to the descriptive content of the utterance. An utterance of (2.35) with or without *ja* is true if the university in question is closed on the next day. However, the presence of *ja* adds the additional use condition that this content may be known information. This part of the conventional meaning of *ja* can be witnessed by the infelicity of *ja* in breaking-news context (Gutzmann 2013: 12).

(2.36) [Context: A happy father rushes out of the delivery room]

    a. #Es ist **ja**   ein Mädchen!
       It   *is* PART *a*   *girl*
       'It's a girl!'

    b. Es ist ein Mädchen!
      It   *is* *a*   *girl*
      'It's a girl!'

Using the tower notation, we can depict the separation between descriptive and expressive meaning in case of (2.36a) as follows.

(2.37) *Morgen ist die Uni ja zu* =

$$\frac{\text{It may already be known that the university is closed tomorrow}}{\text{the university is closed tomorrow}}$$

Besides the semantic analysis of modal particles as conveying expressive meaning, there is a long and still ongoing debate about their syntactic status which mainly concerns the question of: i) what the syntactic status of modal particles are—are they heads or phrase—and ii) if and how the aforementioned interaction with sentence mood is reflected syntactically (Bayer 2012; Bayer & Obenauer 2011; Bayer & Trotzke ta; Coniglio 2011; Gutzmann & Turgay 2016; Struckmeier 2014; M. Zimmermann 2004a,b).

Besides modal particles, there are many other particles in almost every language that can be argued to be use-conditional in nature, for instance particles of epistemic bias in Japanese (Sudo 2013) or sentential particles in Eastern Veneto (Munaro & Poletto 2003, 2004).

2.2.4.3 *Pronouns*   I already alluded to the fact that the case studies in this book will hint at a close connection between expressivity and pronouns and determiners. Against this background, it is not surprising that pronouns themselves can also carry use-conditional meaning in many languages, in addition to their referential meaning. The prototypical example of pronouns that have an expressive function can be found in languages that have a distinction between formal and familiar pronouns. This is, amongst many others, the case in German and French.

(2.38)   **Formal vs. familiar pronouns**
    a. Ich rufe **dich/Sie**   an.
       I   *call* *you.*FAMILIAR/FORMAL *on*
       'I'll give you a call.'   (Potts 2007: 190)
    b. Tu   es / **Vous**   êtes soûl.
       *you.*FAMILIAR *are* / *you.*FORMAL *are* *drunk*
       'You are drunk.'   (Horn 2008a: 49)

Unlike interjections and (most) particles, such pronouns are hybrid or mixed expressives (Gutzmann 2011; McCready 2010) in the sense that they carry both descriptive and expressive meaning. On the truth-conditional layer, their meaning is just their referent, that is, the addressee of the context this case. The distinction between *formal* and *familiar* resides on the use-conditional layer, because choosing the wrong pronoun can never make an otherwise true sentence false, but it may result in a high degree of social infelicity.

$$(2.39) \quad du = \frac{\text{informal relationship between speaker and hearer}}{\text{the addressee}}$$

Another case of personal pronouns contributing use-conditional meaning are free personal dative pronouns that can have an expressive function in some languages. For English, Horn (2008a, 2013) argues that dative pronouns may have such an expressive use as in (2.40a). Other languages which have a more systematic system of free datives, like German (Gutzmann 2007; Lambert 2007; Wegener 1989) or Hebrew (Borer & Grodzinsky 1986), exhibit a pattern known as *ethical dative*.

(2.40)   **Personal datives**

    a. I want **me** an iPod.   (Horn 2008a: 175)

    b. Dass du   **mir**   ja   nicht zu spät kommst.
       *that you me.*DAT PART *not   too late come*
       'Don't you be late.'   (Lambert 2007: 5)

    c. hem kol ha-zman mitxatnim li
       they all the-time marry   to-me
       'They are getting married on me all the time (and it bothers me).'
                                 (Borer & Grodzinsky 1986: 179)

Common to these three free personal datives is that they all express some affection of the speaker toward the fact or event described by the sentence. That is, the speaker in (2.40a) expresses that she is somehow affected by her wanting an iPod. In a similar vein, the speaker in (2.40b) expresses that she has some personal interest in the hearer not being late (Gutzmann 2007: 277). In contrast, the Hebrew ethical dative in (2.40c) expresses the speaker's negative affection with all the marrying. However, all this is expressed solely in a use-conditional way. The presence of the personal datives does not alter the descriptive content of the sentence.

(2.41)   *I want **me** an iPod* = $\dfrac{\text{me(I want an iPod)}}{\text{I want an iPod}}$

This closes my brief discussion of further cases of expressive items that go beyond the three types of expressives items that I will study in more detail later. Let us now turn to some previous work on expressivity in semantics and how multidimensional systems have been employed to capture their special meaning and behavior.

2.3 Expressivity in multidimensional semantics

In his 2005 book, Potts developed the idea of a multidimensional system to what he called conventional implicatures. Deviating from Grice's 1975 original vision of this expression that involved—like *but* or *therefore*—which Grice basically viewed as "logical connectives plus additional stuff"—he included supplemental expressions like appositives, *as*-parentheses, or non-restrictive relative clauses under this label.

(2.42)   **Supplements**

    a. Ames, **who was a successful spy**, is now behind bars.   (Potts 2005: 90)

    b. Ames was, **as the press reported**, a successful spy.

    c. Ames, **a successful spy**, is now behind bars.

Intuitively, an utterance like (2.42a) that includes a non-restrictive relative clause, expresses two, rather independent propositions.

(2.43) a. Ames is now behind bars.

  b. Ames was a successful spy.

Therefore, such cases lead to some kind of multidimensionality as they express two contents that can be evaluated independently of each other.[5] However, in contrast to the multidimensionality induced by expressives, the multidimensionality induced by supplements is entirely truth-conditional. Just like the main content, the content of the non-restrictive relative clause or appositive can be judged as true or false (as long as it carries descriptive content). This shows that the issue of multidimensionality is not necessarily tied to expressivity or use-conditional content.[6] For our purposes it is therefore more important that the second class of expressions that Potts (2005) uses to make his point are expressive epithets and expressive adjectives as in (2.4) and (2.5). For this reason, his work played a major starting point for the development of multidimensional approaches to expressive meaning.

As already laid out at the beginning of this chapter in (2.3), the core idea of what I called hybrid semantics is that you have two independent meaning dimensions. This gives rise to a twofold question of compositionality (Gutzmann 2015b: 8):

  (i) How is the *truth*-conditional meaning of a complex expression calculated on the basis of the truth-conditional and use-conditional meaning of its parts and the way they are put together?

  (ii) How is the *use*-conditional meaning of a complex expression calculated on the basis of the truth-conditional and use-conditional meaning of its parts and the way they are put together?

Potts (2005) tries to address these question with his "logic of conventional implicature" (called $\mathcal{L}_{CI}$).

His system is based on the idea of distinguishing truth-conditional and use-conditional/expressive content on the level of semantic types. There are new basic semantic types for expressive content which then can be used to build complex, functional use-conditional/expressive types. Separating the two dimensions of content on the type level enables one to have dedicated application rules that reference whether the involved expression are truth-conditional or expressives. This in turn allows us to account for the fact that expressives behave differently with respect to how they compose with other expressions than ordinary descriptive expressions. The most important rule is the rule for what is called "CI application," which regulates how an expressive expression applies to a truth-conditional argument, and which is basically

---

[5] See Schlenker (2013) for an opposing view.

[6] For an overview of different notions of dimensions of meaning, see Gutzmann to appear.

the only way according to which expressive content composes with other content in $\mathcal{L}_{CI}$.[7]

(2.44) **CI application**   (Potts 2005: 223)

$$\beta : \sigma$$
$$\bullet$$
$$\alpha(\beta) : \tau^c$$

$$\alpha : \langle \sigma, \tau^c \rangle \qquad \beta : \sigma$$

What is crucial about this rule is that it passes back the truth-conditional argument, i.e. β here, unmodified, after the expressive function α has been applied to it. This ensures that it will be available for further semantic composition as if the expressive had never been there. The following example illustrates this.

(2.45) That damn Kermit is a frog.

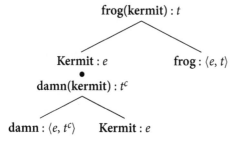

$$\text{frog(kermit)} : t$$

$$\text{Kermit} : e \qquad\qquad \text{frog} : \langle e, t \rangle$$
$$\bullet$$
$$\text{damn(kermit)} : t^c$$

$$\text{damn} : \langle e, t^c \rangle \qquad \text{Kermit} : e$$

Since the expressive content is left behind during the semantic composition and only the truth-conditional content is passed up the tree, Potts (2005: 224) then uses a mechanism called *parsetree interpretation* to ensure that the expressive content is also interpreted. The basic idea is simple: Instead of just interpreting the root node, we interpret the entire parsetree. The (interpretation of) the root node will become the truth-conditional content and the expressive dimension is given by (the set of interpretation of all) the isolated expressives left behind in the tree. That is, for (2.45), we get the following interpretation.

(2.46) $[\![(2.45)]\!] = \langle [\![\text{frog(kermit)}]\!], \{[\![\text{damn(kermit)}]\!]\} \rangle$

In this way, $\mathcal{L}_{CI}$ gives us a way to compose expressive and truth-conditional content during the semantic derivation and distribute that into two independent meaning dimensions. However, as has been discussed elsewhere (Barker, Bernardi, & Shan

---

[7] There are also the additional rules for isolated CIs and feature semantics (Potts 2005: 223–4), which I ignore here. The first does not do much except for isolating expressions that lexically already denote full use-conditional propositions (like *ouch* in *Ouch, I hit my thumb*). The second is problematic for the general position $\mathcal{L}_{CI}$ has on expressive composition. See Gutzmann 2015b: 57–9 for a discussion.

Problems

2010; Gutzmann 2015b), the mechanism of parsetree interpretation is problematic for conceptual reasons: i) it is not compositional in the strict sense that the meaning of a complex expression is determined by the meaning of its *immediate* parts (T.E. Zimmermann 2012); ii) it requires that the semantic parsetrees themselves are part of the semantic representation. In addition, the original version of $\mathcal{L}_{CI}$ has been shown to be too restrictive (Gutzmann 2011; McCready 2010) as it only allows for expressives like *damn* that do not affect the truth-conditional content at all. However, as already mentioned above, there are mixed expressives that carry both expressive and descriptive content, like the expressive intensifiers that I will study in Chapter 5. In addition, there are also so-called "shunting expressives" that do not pass their argument back after they applied to it (which I will not really make use of in this book). For this reason, I will not discuss Potts's original system and its stepwise extensions here and will instead directly present a reformulated system which is loosely based on the full system I developed in Gutzmann 2015b and which tries to keep the original spirit of $\mathcal{L}_{CI}$, while avoiding the mentioned problems.

Let us start with the semantic types. These definitions are pretty standard except for two new additions. Clause (2.47b) introduces type u as the new basic use-conditional type (it will be the type for use-conditional propositions) and clause (2.47d) states that we can have complex use-conditional types that have truth-conditional types in their input and use-conditional as their output. That is, we will only have expressions that map from truth-conditional content to use-conditional content, but not vice versa.[8]

(2.47) **Types**
   a. e, t are basic truth-conditional types.
   b. u is a basic use-conditional type.
   c. If σ and τ are truth-conditional types, $\langle \sigma, \tau \rangle$ and $\langle s, t \rangle$ are truth-conditional types.
   d. If σ is a truth-conditional type and τ is a use-conditional type, $\langle \sigma, \tau \rangle$ is a use-conditional types.
   e. Nothing else is a type.

Equipped with these types, which are basically like the type system of $\mathcal{L}_{CI}$, we can now build our semantic expressions. In contrast to $\mathcal{L}_{CI}$ though, I assume that very expression comes with a "store" for use-conditional proposition (i.e. expressions of type e) in order to solve the aforementioned compositionality problems. This second dimension is empty for most lexical expressions (except for isolated expressives like *ouch*). For every expression e, we there have T_e, the truth-conditional content of e, and U_e, the set of use-conditional propositions expressed by e (let us call this the *use set*).

---

[8] In contrast to Gutzmann 2015b, I will also not use types for use-conditional modification, since those will not be needed for the purposes of this book.

Technically, we are dealing with a tuple here, but I like to use the bullet "•" (to honor the notation used in $\mathcal{L}_{CI}$) to separate the two dimension, as in the following.

(2.48) $\langle T_e, U_e \rangle \rightsquigarrow T_e \bullet U_e$

I will simplify semantic expressions using some lazy shorthand. If the use set of an expression is empty, I will just omit the bullet and the set from its semantic representation as follows.

(2.49) **frog** : $\langle e, t \rangle \bullet \varnothing \rightsquigarrow$ **frog** : $\langle e, t \rangle$

In addition, if the expressive set just contains a single use-conditional proposition, I will omit the set parentheses.

(2.50) **kermit** : $e \bullet \{\text{damn}(\text{kermit}) : u\} \rightsquigarrow$ **kermit** : $e \bullet \text{damn}(\text{kermit}) : u$

With this in mind, we can now provide the necessary application rules. The first rule we need is what I call *generalized application*, which is applicable for both truth-conditional and use-conditional application, as long as the argument is a truth-conditional expression and the output is not a full use-conditional proposition of type u.[9]

(2.51) **Generalized application** (for $\tau \neq u$)

$$\alpha(\beta) : \tau \bullet U_\alpha \cup U_\beta$$

$$\alpha : \langle \sigma, \tau \rangle \bullet U_\alpha \qquad \beta : \sigma^t \bullet U_\beta$$

In contrast to $\mathcal{L}_{CI}$, the system used here will percolate all expressive content up the semantic tree. That is, both expressions in (2.51) may come with a set of use-conditional propositions that are just merged and carried along. The application rule is then for the special case that the application of a use-conditional function to its argument ends in an expression of type u, which I call *use-conditional saturation*.

(2.52) **Use-conditional saturation**

$$\beta : \sigma^t \bullet \{\alpha(\beta) : u\} \cup U_\alpha \cup U_\beta$$

$$\alpha : \langle \sigma, u \rangle \bullet U_\alpha \qquad \beta : \sigma^t \bullet U_\beta$$

In this case, the resulting use-conditional expression is "stored" into the expressive set (behind the bullet) and the argument is passed back, as was the case for Potts (2005) CI application. With this, we can provide the updated semantic derivation for the example in (2.45).

---

[9] In the following, I use superscripted t and u to indicate that a type is truth- or use-conditional.

(2.53)

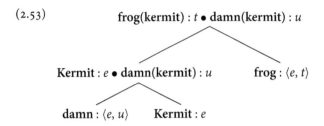

This looks pretty much like the semantic parsetree in (2.45) except for the fact that the saturated use-conditional content is carried to the top instead of being left behind at the lower node.

We also need two additional rules to deal with mixed content expressions. Again, I will split this up into an "application" and a "saturation" rule. In these rules, I use the diamond "♦" to separate the truth-conditional portion of an expression's meaning from its (not yet saturated) use-conditional content, being reminiscent of McCready's 2010 use of the diamond to build mixed expressives.

(2.54)   **Mixed application** (for $\rho \neq u$)

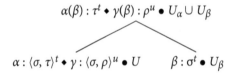

(2.55)   **Mixed saturation**

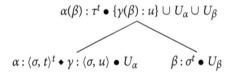

These two rules are very similar. In both cases, the two parts of the functional expression are applied to the truth-conditional content of the argument and possible already present use-conditional propositions are merged behind the bullet. The difference is that in the case of (2.54), the use-conditional content behind the diamond remains active and thus stays in front of the bullet so that another instance of (2.54) can be used with it. However, if a mixed expressive gets its last argument, (2.55) kicks in and the resulting use-conditional proposition is stored behind the bullet and merged into the set of use-conditional propositions.

Note that this set of application rules together with the type system does not account for various constellations of combining use-conditional expressions with other expression. But it covers everything that will be needed for the purposes of this book and hence I will leave it as it is. For the "official" and more general compositional system for multidimensional expressions, I refer the reader to Gutzmann 2015b.

With this set of composition rules in place, let us briefly look at how this system captures one of the important properties discussed above, namely nondisplaceability, which means that expressives cannot be subverted by semantic operators like negation, modalization, or embedding under attitude reports. Consider the following example.

(2.56)   Frederico believes that that damn Kermit is a frog.

To semantically parse this sentence, we start with the tree in (2.53), which corresponds to the local subtree for the embedded clause in (2.56). Note that the content of the application of *damn* to *Kermit* is already stored in the use set. And since the compositions rules introduced above always pass up and merge the use sets of two combining expressions, there is just no way in which the higher operator can get to it. It just combines with the truth-conditional content of the embedded clause.

(2.57)   believe (frog(kermit))(frederico) : ⟨e, t⟩ • damn(kermit) : u

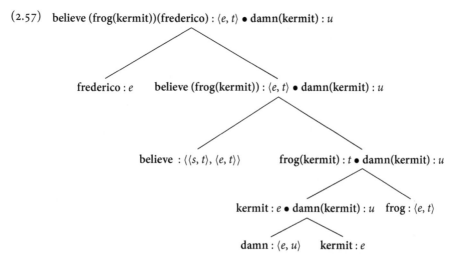

That is, even in an embedded context, the expressive attitude expressed by *damn* (when applied to its argument) is not interpreted below the attitude predicate but percolates up the tree. This is how the multidimensional system semantically derives what I called *speaker linking*. By default, the root node is interpreted with respect to the speaker of an utterance and since all expressive propositions in the use set will end up there, they will be ascribed to the speaker, if possible. This gives rise to the impression that expressive content always has wide-scope over all other semantic operators. In actuality they just do not interact with those operators at all.

Before we end this chapter on the expressive language function and how it is dealt with in the semantics, a short note on the semantic ontology of expressive content is in order. We saw that the basic use-conditional type is type *u*, the type of use-conditional propositions. But what are those propositions? Following my earlier work (Gutzmann 2015b), I assume that use-conditional propositions are like ordinary propositions but with one important difference. While ordinary propositions can be viewed as the set of *worlds* in which the propositional content expressed by a sentence is true, a use-conditional proposition is the set of *contexts* in which the sentence is felicitously used.[10] This directly reflects the core idea that we have truth conditions and use-conditions. We can therefore state the following parallel conditions.

(2.58) a. "α" is true in a world w iff $w \in [\![\alpha]\!]^t$.

       b. "α" is felicitously used in a context c iff $c \in [\![\alpha]\!]^u$.

I use $[\![S]\!]^t$ and $[\![S]\!]^u$ as a shorthand for the truth- respectively use-conditional content of S, which we get interpreting the first and second dimension of the semantic representation of S respectively.[11]

2.4 Summary

Even if the descriptive language function has been the main area of investigation of formal semantics, the expressive language function as a general aspect of the semiotic power of natural language has been on the radar of theories of meaning since early on. Starting with Kaplan's (1999) pioneering work that laid the foundations of what I call *hybrid semantics*, followed up by Potts's (2005) first attempt to develop a multidimensional semantic framework to deal with expressive content, the expressive language function has gotten much more attention in formally oriented semantic investigations. This chapter gave a glimpse at the vast diversity of expressions that can encode expressive content and introduced the topics of the three case studies that I will carry out in Chapters 4–6—expressive adjectives, expressive intensifiers, and expressive vocatives. I also introduced the semantic machinery that I will need for the semantic analyses of the three phenomena to be investigated. These will carry us a long way and for expressive adjectives I already have illustrated how the multidimensional approach can account for the property of speaker linking and nondisplaceability. However, as I will later show, in each of the three cases, semantics cannot explain everything. Instead, the case studies will show that there is more to expressive expression than their special semantics. They also have special syntactic properties as well that cannot be traced back to their multidimensional and non-truth-conditional meaning. In order to be able to tackle their special syntax as well, let us turn to the syntactic background in the next chapter.

---

[10] That is, if C is the set of context, the domain of type u is $D_u = \wp(C)$.

[11] Formally: If S has the semantic representation $T_\alpha \bullet U_\alpha$, then $[\![S]\!]^t = T_\alpha$ and $[\![S]\!]^u = U_\alpha$. Taking both dimensions, we then have again $[\![\alpha]\!] = \langle [\![\alpha]\!]^t, [\![\alpha]\!]^u \rangle$, the base formula of hybrid semantics given in (2.3).

3

Syntax, features, and agreement

3.1 Introduction

In this chapter, I will lay out the theoretical background of the framework of which terms the investigations in expressive grammar, that will be carried out later in this book, will be couched in. I will adopt many of the ideas that sprung from the *minimalist program* as kicked off by Chomsky (1992, 1995), but also make use of more recent suggestions put forward in the theoretical debates that differentiate various ways of elaborating a minimalist syntax. This will provide us with the tools and concepts needed to analyze the expressions that will be the topic of the next chapters. In order to do so, I will introduce all the necessary theoretical terminology and concepts and try to briefly motivate them independently from their application to expressivity. However, it should be clear from the outset that I can't do justice to the lively debates on many still unsettled issues in minimalist syntax. That is, the final reason why I pick one formulation of a syntactic component over an alternative one may just be that it is more applicable to the case studies that will follow this chapter.

3.2 Some basic ingredients of a minimalist syntax

The start of the so-called *minimalist program* (MP, Chomsky 1992, 1995, 2000, 2001) marked a turning point in generative grammar. In some sense, it can be viewed as a continuation and elaboration of the *principle and parameters* framework (P&P, Chomsky 1981); in another, it can be viewed as a de- and reconstruction of the theory. The P&P framework assumed that the capability of human language derives from a universal and innate grammatical system, the universal grammar (UG), with a universal set of specific rules and an accompanying set of variable parameters that can be valued differently during language acquisitions and which thereby lead to the linguistic variation between different languages. The minimalist program, which, instead of a *theory* really is more of a research *program*, takes an Ockam's razor-like view on the preceding theories of generative grammar and tries to dispense with all assumptions and components that could not be motivated externally. The core minimalist idea is that the so-called faculty of language (F_L), which generates

The Grammar of Expressivity. First edition. Daniel Gutzmann.
© Daniel Gutzmann 2019. First published in 2019 by Oxford University Press.

linguistic expressions, interacts with two other mental components: the articulatory-perceptual system (AP), which produces and processes the *form* of linguistic expressions, and the conceptual-intentional system (CI), which interprets the *meaning* of linguistic expressions.[1] The connection between the language faculty and these two systems is provided by two interfaces. The phonological form provides the interface to the articulatory-perceptual system, while the logical form provides the interface to the conceptual-intentional system. This model is illustrated in Figure 3.1.

One of the key assumptions that sets the MP apart from the P&P framework, is that these two interfaces are the only level of linguistic representation. That is, while the P&P framework involved a pure syntactic level of representation, this is not present anymore under this minimalist view. A minimalist grammar model consists of a lexicon consisting of a set of lexical items, which are often considered to be bundles of features (more on this below). If a linguistic expression is to be derived, selected lexical items are drawn from lexicon and enter the so-called numeration, which can be understood as the toolbox that contains all the ingredients from which the expression has to be built.[2] The lexical items then enter the syntactic derivation during which a set of syntactic operations can apply to them. At a certain point—the so-called spell-out—the expression so far derived is transferred to the two interfaces PF and LF. Crucially, the syntactic derivation may continue after spell-out on the way to PF and LF, but since the two straits are now divorced, operations that happen on the way to PF do not influence LF and operations applying on the way to LF have no effect on PF. This model of grammar is graphically illustrated in Figure 3.2 (Chomsky 1995).

Regarding the question of how syntactic structures are built during the syntactic derivation, there are basically two operations; both of which are variants of a syntactic operation called MERGE, which is a simple, recursive operation that allows us to build binary structures and which is often thought to be the one crucial operation that made human language possible in the first place in a biological sense. The first version, called *external merge*, builds a new, complex expression by putting two preexisting expressions together. In addition to just putting the expressions together,

FIGURE 3.1 The faculty of language and its interfaces with other components

---

[1] This is not meant to imply that these components necessarily only apply to linguistic form and linguistic meaning.

[2] Crucially, all elements of the numeration have to be used during the derivation and each item can only be used as often as it is in the numeration.

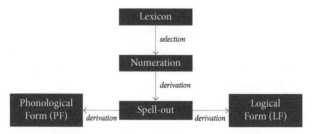

FIGURE 3.2 Model of a mimimalist grammar

the expression that results from external merge also has a so-called label that equals one of the two expressions and which determines which of the two inputs is the dominant one and thereby projects its properties to the entire new expression. That is, the label specifies the head.

(3.1)   MERGE$(\alpha, \beta) = \begin{cases} \{\alpha, \{\alpha, \beta\}\}, \text{ if } \alpha \text{ projects} \\ \{\beta, \{\alpha, \beta\}\}, \text{ if } \beta \text{ projects} \end{cases}$

The label is sometimes written as a subscript and the braces around the two constituents is dropped.

(3.2) $\{_{\alpha/\beta} \, \alpha \, \beta\}$

The two options for applying MERGE to an expression α and an expression β can also be illustrated by the following syntactic trees.

(3.3)   a.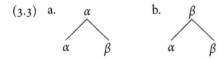

(3.3a) corresponds to the case in which α projects, while (3.3b) illustrates the case in which β does. These trees already illustrate an important difference between minimalist systems and the P&P framework which was based on X′-theory, according to which different projection levels are marked. This is thought unnecessary in minimalist syntax, since the projection level can easily be read of from the position of the labels in the tree. That is, even the two projection level X′ and XP in (3.4a) are absent in the minimalist variant in (3.4b), the intermediate and maximal projection level can still be identified by their relative position in the tree.

(3.4)   a.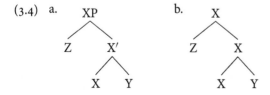

The second variant of MERGE is called *internal merge*. Alternatively, it is called MOVE, as it is the merge-based reimagination of the traditional *move α* operation known from the early days of generative grammar. In contrast to external merge where two independent expressions are merged, the internal variant merges an expression with one of its subparts (Zeijlstra 2004: 15).

(3.5)   MOVE: $L = \{_{\alpha/\beta} \{\alpha, K\}\}$, where $K = \{_{\beta} \{\ldots\alpha\ldots\}\}$

What internal merge basically does is to extract some subpart of an expression and re-merge it with the expression itself. Again, we can illustrate this with a tree.

(3.6)
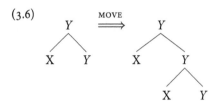

The thus "moved" expression hence shows up twice in the resulting complex expression; once as one of the two immediate constituents of the resulting expression and once as the original subpart of the input expression. We can illustrate this with a more concrete example. Consider the following case of a *wh*-question in German.

(3.7)   Was   hat   der   Hund   gefressen?
        what   has   the   dog   eaten
        'What did the dog eat?'

German, like English, is a language in which *wh*-expressions have to be fronted to a left peripheral position to mark a sentence as a *wh*-question. That is, the standard analysis of (3.7) is that the accusative *wh*-pronoun *was* ('what') originated in the VP and is moved to the sentence initial position (i.e., CP^{spec} in P&P terminology).

(3.8)   [hat der Hund was gefressen]
         ↑_____|

This movement is derived via internal merge of the entire sentence, in which the *wh*-expression is not yet fronted, with the *wh*-expression itself. That is, setting α in the definition in (3.5) to *was* and K to *hat der Hund was gefressen*, we can apply MOVE to extract the *wh*-expression.

                                  MOVE
(3.9)   [hat der Hund was gefressen] ⟹ [was [hat der Hund was gefressen]]
                          ↑_____|

Again, note that the moved expression, the *was* ('what') in this case, appears twice. Of course, the right-hand side is not what the sentence should look like in the end, since, obviously, only the moved version should be pronounced, but not the original version. Therefore, the idea is that the lower version is marked for deletion at PF and thus it will have no phonological realization and remains silent.

(3.10)   [was hat der Hund ~~was~~ gefressen]

Since MOVE leads to having a second version of any moved expression of which only one is phonologically realized, this implementation of movement operations is known as the *copy theory of movement*. This contrasts with the traditional understanding of movement in the P&P framework under which a moved expression leaves back a (co-indexed) trace.

(3.11)   [was$_1$ hat der Hund t_1 gefressen]

In some sense, the "trace theory of movement" does not only add the fronted *was* to the original expression but also changes the original expression as well. This is not the case for implementing movement via internal merge. In some sense, moving an expression via internal merge is not movement at all, but just a merge operation that applies to a complex expression and another expression that happens to be a subpart of the former. That is, under a minimalist view, movement is not a dedicated syntactic operation, but just a way of structure building. That is, "[i]nternal and external Merge both involve exactly the same operation. They differ only in where the argument [α] is found." (Collins & Stabler 2016: 55). Again, this contrasts with the traditional P&P (and earlier) understanding of movement where it was its own syntactic operation. Despite this, I follow the common practice and talk about expression moving, even if this should be understood as internal merge.

   Another important difference between the minimalist conception of movement and the old P&P view is that in the minimalist program, movement is highly restricted, while in the P&P framework it could apply rather freely, as long as it did not violate any constraints on possible movement operations. In a minimalist setting, movement is often considered to be some kind of "last resort" that only happens if it is actively triggered by some syntactic requirement. Those requirements are commonly formulated in terms of *syntactic features*, which hence play a major role in the formulation of minimalist approaches to various linguistic phenomena. This also holds for the investigations that I will carry out in the following chapters of this book, because I assume that expressivity is precisely one of those features. Therefore, let us have a more detailed look at syntactic features and their role in minimalist syntax.

3.3 Syntactic features

For the purposes of this book, syntactic features are properties of linguistic expressions that have shown some relevance for syntactic structure building and possibly a phonological and semantic reflex in form of morphological markup and interpretation. Obvious candidates for syntactic features can be found in categories like tense of verbs, case of determiners and nouns, or φ-features like person, number, and gender.

(3.12) a. *sagte* 'said'
        [Person: 3rd, Number: singular, Tense: past]

   b. *der Katze* 'the cat's'
        [Case: genitive, Number: singular, Gender: feminine]

   c. *der Katzen* 'the cats''
        [Case: genitive, Number: plural, Gender: feminine]

From a minimalist point of view, such syntactic features can be distinguished with respect to whether they are interpretable or not. For instance, the number feature on nouns is interpretable at LF, since it obviously has a semantic effect, as can be witnessed by the simple fact that the following two sentences, which form a minimal pair with respect to number, differ in their truth conditions (as well as their presuppositions).

(3.13) a. Maya liebt ihre **Katze-Ø**.
           Maya loves her   cat-SG
           'Maya loves her cat.'

   b. Maya liebt ihre **Katze-n**.
           Maya loves her   cat-PL
           'Maya loves her cats.'

We adopt the common convention to indicate that a syntactic feature F is interpretable by prefixing it with a small "*i*." That is, a noun like *Katze* ('cat') carries an *i*Num feature. This contrasts with the number features on (finite) verbs which does not have any effect on semantic interpretation and hence is considered to carry *u*Num: the analogous uninterpretable number feature.

(3.14) a. Livas   Tochter   **liebt**   Katzen.
           Liva.GEN *daughther*.SG *love*.SG *cats*
           'Liva's daughter loves cats.'

   b. Livas   Töchter   **lieben**   Katzen.
           Liva.GEN *daughther*.PL *love*.PL *cats*
           'Liva's daughters love cats.'

Of course, (3.14a) and (3.14b) differ in their truth conditions, but they are not minimal pairs, since in order to change the number feature of the verb, one also has to alter the subjects number feature, which, as seen above, receives a semantic interpretation. That is, the number feature on the verb does not change between (3.14a) and (3.14b) due to semantic reasons. Instead it is merely a reflection of the subject's number feature.

This later observation, that the verb gets its number feature from the subject, leads us to the next distinction that can be drawn between syntactic features. Besides distinguishing between interpretable and uninterpretable features, Chomsky (2000, 2001) also differentiates between features that already have a *value* when taken from the lexicon and those that do not have a specific value yet and only receive their value during the syntactic derivation. This can be illustrated using the same examples as before. A noun like *cats* will be inserted into the numeration already having a value for its number features. It is already lexically *valued*, as the parlance goes. We can write the value of a feature after the feature designator. For (3.13a) and (3.13b), we can notate this as follows.

(3.15)   a. *Katze*   [*i*Num: sg]
       b. *Katzen*   [*i*Num: pl]

As alluded to above, this contrasts with the verb which does not enter the derivation with a specific number: it is lexically *unvalued*. We indicate this by using an extended underscore as follows.[3]

(3.16)   LIEBEN   [*u*Num: __]

In the examples discussed, the properties of being (un)valued and (un)interpretable fall together, such that the noun has an interpretable, valued number feature, whereas the verb has an uninterpretable, unvalued number feature. According to Chomsky (2001: 5), this not an accident: uninterpretable features must be unvalued and interpretable ones must be valued. This is expressed in the following biconditional (Pesetsky & Torrego 2007: 266).

(3.17)   **Valuation/interpretability biconditional**
       A feature F is uninterpretable iff F is unvalued.

Chomsky's rationale for this strict correlation between valuation and interpretability lies in the assumption that the question of whether a feature is interpretable in the semantics or not should not be visible to the narrow syntactic system. However, whether a feature has a certain value or not is a syntactic matter and thanks to the biconditional in (3.17), valuation can function as "a lexical encoding of interpretability" (Pesetsky & Torrego 2007: 266). This is important because most theories within the minimalist program assume—following (Chomsky 2000, 2001)—that uninterpretable features somehow must be dealt with during the syntactic derivation, because, so the assumption goes, if an uninterpretable feature reaches LF, the derivation will crash, since the conceptual system will not be able to deal with it. In the words

---

[3] I adopt the convention here to use small caps to mark the fact that a verb does not enter the derivation as a fully specified morphological form, precisely because it is not yet valued for all features. That is, depending on which values the verb's features will be output by the derivation, the verb receives its different morphological realizations at PF. Strictly speaking, the same should be done for *Katze* as well.

of Preminger (2014), uninterpretable features are "derivational time bombs" that must "better be defused by the end of the derivation" in order for the derivation to not explode (Preminger 2014: 7). The basic idea of Chomsky 2000 is that the deactivation of these time bombs is connected to them receiving a value. Pesetsky & Torrego (2007: 266) give a concise formulation of this idea.

(3.18)   **Deletion of uninterpretable features**
Once an uninterpretable feature is valued, it can and must delete.

Unvalued features are valued during the syntactic derivation by a syntactic operation called Agree, which will be discussed in more detail in Section 3.4. However, before we turn to this operation, let us first discuss the proposed biconditional in (3.17), as it has recently been called into question.[4] If the two notions are divorced from each other and allowed to combine freely, we expect four possible types of syntactic features.

(3.19)   a. $[uF:$ __$]$ unvalued and uninterpretable feature
         b. $[uF: val]$ unvalued and interpretable feature
         c. $[iF:$ __$]$ unvalued and interpretable feature
         d. $[iF: val]$ valued and interpretable feature

And indeed, considerations on morpho-syntactic properties of various lexical items and their semantic interpretation also make the two new combinations in which valuedness and interpretability do not match up as conceptually plausible. An illustrative case, discussed by Pesetsky & Torrego (2007), is the syntax of tense. As commonly assumed, tense is semantically interpreted in a projection of a functional T-head that dominated the verb phrase. This can be motivated by semantic considerations about the relative scope of tense. However, in spite of the rather high locus of interpretation, most languages realize the different values of tense not in T, but at the level of the finite verb, which is located lower in the syntactic structure. That is, following Pesetsky & Torrego (2007: 270) and others, one can assume that T° hosts an interpretable yet unvalued tense feature, whereas the tense feature of the finite verb is valued but cannot be interpreted at that position (Zeijlstra 2012: 508).

(3.20)   ...weil   Maya   schlief.
         *because Maya   sleep.*PAST
         ... because Maya was sleeping.

         a.   T: $[iT:$ __$]$
         b. V_{fin}: $[uT:$ past$]$

Another case where interpretability and valuedness do not go hand in hand is constituted by gender features. In languages that have a true grammatical gender system, the gender features on nouns do not have any semantic effect and

---

[4] Amongst many others, see Baker 2008; Pesetsky & Torrego 2007; P. W. Smith 2015; Wurmbrand 2012; Zeijlstra 2012.

hence are arguably uninterpretable. Consider, for instance, the following pairs from German.

(3.21) a. *Couch:* fem – *Sofa:* neut 'couch'
        b. *Joghurt:* masc – *Joghurt:* neut 'yogurt'

The pair in (3.21a) differs in its gender. While *Couch* is feminine, *Sofa* is neuter. Crucially, the two expressions are synonymous in German, which shows that the gender features do not have any semantic effect. Example (3.21b) illustrates this even more clearly. Even though most nouns have one, lexically fixed gender, for certain nouns there is some variation. This variation is sometimes regionally determined, but some constitute genuine intra-speaker variation. (3.21b) is a case in point. Many speakers, myself included, can use *Joghurt* ('yogurt') as a masculine or as a neuter noun. Again, this has no effect on semantic interpretation. Similar examples can be given for other languages that exhibit grammatical gender. For instance, Bošković (2011) provides the following examples from Serbo-Croatian.

(3.22) *kola:* fem – *auto:* neut – *automobil:* masc 'car'

Again no effect of gender features on interpretation. We can therefore conclude that (grammatical) gender on nouns in languages like German or Serbo-Croatian is lexically valued, but uninterpretable.

(3.23) N: [*u*Gen: *val*]

Compare this with the gender of adjectives and determiners. In languages that have grammatical gender and show gender agreement on adjectives and determiners in the DP, the gender of those expressions is certainly not lexically fixed because the value of their gender depends on the syntactic context; i.e. on the noun.

(3.24) a. Maya liebt die   kleine   Katze.
        Maya loves the.FEM *small*.FEM *cat*.FEM
        'Maya loves the small cat.'

        b. Maya liebt das   kleine   Kätzchen.
        Maya loves the.NEUT *small*.NEUT *kitten*.NEUT
        'Maya loves the small kitten.'

        c. Maya liebt den   kleinen   Kater.
        Maya loves the.MASC *small*.MASC *tomcat*.MASC
        'Maya loves the small tomcat.'

In these sentences, both the definite determiner as well as the adjective receive their gender feature from the noun they occur with. An analogous example from Serbo-Croatian is again provided by Bošković (2011).

(3.25) a. Zelena   kola   su   kupljena.
        green.FEM *car*.FEM *are bought*.FEM
        'The green car was bought.'

    b. Zeleno   auto   je kupljeno.
       green.NEUT   *car*.NEUT *is* *bought*.NEUT

    c. Zeleni   automobil je kupljen.
       green.MASC   *car*.MASC   *is* *bought*.MASC

These considerations lead to the conclusion that, in contrast to the gender features on nouns, those on adjectives and determiners are not lexically valued. And since they do not have any semantic effect either, they are an instance of unvalued, uninterpretable features.

(3.26)   a. D: [uGen: __]
         b. A: [uGen: __]

As for the last remaining kind of feature—valued, interpretable features—there do not seem to be many clear cases, once Chomsky's (2001) biconditional in (3.17) is dropped. Depending on specific analyses of various phenomena, there are nevertheless some good candidates. First, depending on how number in DPs is treated syntactically, the number feature on the noun may be still thought to be valued and interpretable (even though it is often thought to be interpreted in a special number phrase on top of the NP). Moreover, Pesetsky, & Torrego2007 (2007: 272) suggest that elements like *if* or *whether* in embedded interrogatives are interpretable, valued interrogative features because they on their own can provide the interrogative interpretation of the clause while they do not need any assistance of *wh*-words to be valued; in contrast to the abstract features that are usually assumed to trigger *wh*-movement in interrogatives. Another instance may be constituted by negation. A negation expression can be viewed as carrying a syntactic negation feature, because it may license negative polarity items or lead to negative concord (Kuno 2011; Zeijlstra 2013). Clearly, the negation itself is semantically interpretable and, arguably, is lexically valued and does not receive its value from its syntactic context.

As mentioned above, the distinction between interpretable and uninterpretable features plays an important role, because most approaches in the minimalist tradition assume that uninterpretable features should not reach LF, because this would lead the derivation to crash.[5] Likewise, even if not as much emphasis is put onto this in the literature, unvalued features should be valued during the derivation because for many expressions, the values of all features must be known in order for the phonological component to be able to choose the concrete form of the expression (see Pesetsky & Torrego 2007: 274, fn. 17).[6] The mechanism by which unvalued features get valued and uninterpretable features get deleted is called Agree, which besides

---

[5] A notable, recent exception to this is Preminger 2014.

[6] There are exceptions to this. For instance, one could argue that adjectives in predicative use are equipped with gender and all their other φ-features, but, in contrast to the attributive use, these features remain unvalued in predicative positions in languages like German that do not show any φ-inflection for predicatively used adjectives. An alternative assumption would be that they do not come equipped with φ-features in the predicative position.

internal and external merge, constitutes the third important syntactic operation in recent implementation of minimalism. Since this operation will play a crucial role for the analyses of expressive phenomena that I will carry out in this book, let us investigate this mechanism more closely.

3.4 Varieties of Agree

The notion of *agreement* is first and foremost a traditional descriptive term that describes a certain relation between two (or more) linguistic expressions. However, as discussed by Corbett (2006) in his comprehensive monograph on agreement, it is not easy to define it precisely and definitions in the literature, if given at all, are sometimes even somewhat conflicting. In Anderson's words, it is an "intuitive notion which is nonetheless surprisingly difficult to delimit with precision" (Anderson 1992: 103, quoted after Corbett 2006: 4). For the present purposes, we can use the definition that Corbett (2006: 4) quotes from Steele 1978:

The term *agreement* commonly refers to some systematic covariance between a semantic or formal property of one element and a formal property of another.   (Steele 1978: 610)

Sometimes, *agreement* is used synonymously with *concord*. For instance, the wikipedia article on *agreement* states: "Agreement or concord happens when a word changes form depending on the other words to which it relates."[7] Similar quotes from the linguistic literature are given by Corbett (2006: 5, fn. 3). Sometimes, the two terms are used differently such that one is the cover term and the other a special case or that both do not even overlap. If the terms are used differently, the tendency—though not the rule, as Corbett (2006) shows—is to reserve concord for "agreement" pattern within the DP and use *agreement* either as the cover term or reserve it for the "morphologically overt covariance in φ-features between a verb-like element and one or more nominal arguments" (Preminger 2014: 6). For the descriptive terminology, I follow Corbett and just adopt the use of *agreement* as the most general term so that it includes both agreement between verbs and nominal arguments, between nouns, modifiers, and determiners, as well as other forms like complementizer agreement (Fuß 2014; Haegeman & Koppen 2012).

From the theoretical point of view of minimalism, *agreement* denotes the relation between two expressions as it is established by the formal syntactic operation of Agree. This operation is what enables the valuation of a yet unvalued feature by a corresponding valued feature. That is, Agree allows to pass the value of one feature to another. Without going into the details (yet), this can be illustrated as follows, using agreement in number ϕ-features between a determiner and a noun as an example.

(3.27)   die   Katzen $\overset{\text{AGREE}}{\Longrightarrow}$ die   Katzen
       [*u*Num: __] [*i*Num: **pl**]   [*u*Num: **pl**] [*i*Num: **pl**]

---

[7] https://en.wikipedia.org/wiki/Agreement_(linguistics) (retrieved March 26, 2016).

Even if the general idea of an Agree operation is broadly accepted in recent minimalist approaches, the actual implementation is very much in dispute right now. On the one hand, these current controversies target the definition of the structural configurations that must hold in order for two expressions to stand in an Agree relation to each other. In particular, the direction of Agree is currently being debated. On the other hand, is it being discussed whether the Agree operation is triggered by a feature being unvalued or by the uninterpretability of a feature.

3.4.1 C-Agree

In Chomsky's (2001) conception, Agree is driven by the need for an unvalued expression to be assigned a value. This expression, called the *probe*, searches its c-command domain for another feature of matching category, called a *goal*. If that feature has a value, it assigns its value to the probe. Using Pesetsky & Torrego's (2007: 265) formulation, this conception of Agree, which I label *C-Agree* ("C" for "Chomsky") can be defined as follows.

(3.28) **C-Agree**   (Chomsky 2000, 2001)
      a. An unvalued feature F (a *probe*) on a head H scans its c-command domain
         for another instance of F (a *goal*) with which to agree.
      b. If the goal has a value, its value is assigned as the value of the probe.

Now, recall that according to Chomsky's biconditional, every unvalued feature is also uninterpretable. Therefore, if a feature gets valued by the operation of C-Agree, that feature must be uninterpretable and hence, as it now gets valued, it can be marked for deletion in accordance with the principle in (3.18). We thus just add (3.17) to the definition of C-Agree in order to make the discussion of alternative conceptions of Agree in the remainder of the section more explicit.

(3.28) **C-Agree** (*cont.*)
      c. A feature F is uninterpretable iff F is unvalued.   = (3.17)

Turning back to our simple example in (3.27), we can illustrate the application of C-Agree in a bit more detail.

(3.29)

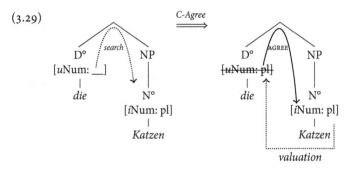

A few points to note here. First, as illustrated by the curved line in (3.29) and made explicit in (3.28a), C-Agree is a downward-looking operation. The probe that triggers C-Agree to apply must c-command the goal and thus the probe has to be in a higher position than the goal (given that they cannot be direct sisters). Furthermore, what drives the probe's search for a goal to agree with is its lack of value. That is, unvaluedness is the trigger of C-Agree. Given the valuation/interpretability biconditional in (3.17), we only have two kinds of features and thus four possible configurations between two features (where one c-commands the other).

(3.30)   **Agreement relation licensed by C-Agree**
  a. $*[uF: \underline{\quad}] \ldots [uF: \underline{\quad}]$
  b. $*[iF: val] \ldots [iF: val]$
  c. $*[iF: val] \ldots [uF: \underline{\quad}]$
  d. $[uF: \underline{\quad}] \ldots [iF: val]$

The two "pure" cases in (3.30a) and (3.30b) in which two features of the same kind encounter each other are not valid C-Agree configurations. The higher uninterpretable unvalued feature in (3.30a) may function as a probe and search for a goal, but the lower uninterpretable unvalued feature cannot function as such, because it is unvalued itself and hence is unable to value the probe according to (3.30). Hence, the higher feature will remain unvalued and hence not be marked for deletion. In fact both features are in a configuration in (3.30a); barring any lower, valued features. The second case in (3.30b), in which two interpretable, valued expressions encounter each other does (necessarily) not lead to a ungrammatical structure, but the configuration just does not trigger C-Agree. Given that the higher feature is valued, it does not probe for another valued feature. However, since it is also interpretable, it does not matter that it is not deleted because it does not pose a problem of semantics in the first place. The same holds for the lower interpretable and valued feature in (3.30b). Now consider case (3.30c). Here, we have the right combination of one uninterpretable unvalued feature and one interpretable valued feature. However, they do not stand in the right configuration for C-Agree to do its magic. The unvalued will act as a probe and search its c-command domain for a valued counterpart. However, it cannot find its feature mate there, since the valued feature is in a higher position in (3.30b). Given that there are no other matching valued features below uF, it cannot be valued and thus not be deleted, thereby leading the derivation to crash. Finally, consider (3.30d), which now is the right configuration for C-Agree. There is an unvalued feature that c-commands a corresponding valued feature. Hence, uF in (3.30d) can establish a C-Agree relation with iF and receive its value from iF. This will mark it for deletion and, therefore, no uninterpretable feature will survive on LF and hence it will pose no danger to crash the derivation anymore.

3.4.2 S-Agree

In (3.30), there are only four cases because it is based on the strict correlation between (un)valuedness and (un)interpretability as stated above in (3.17). However, as I already briefly discussed in the previous section, there seem to be many good reasons to decouple these two notions; the most pressing being to avoid being forced to assume that every lexically valued feature has to be interpretable, which does not make much sense, for instance, for grammatical gender features (Bošković 2011). In addition, it allows for a dissociation between the morpho-syntactic realization of a feature and its locus of interpretation, which also seems to be a not uncommon case; consider, as a case in point, again the relation between tense marking in V^0 and tense interpretation in T^0. It hence seems to be desirable to drop the biconditional from the definition of C-Agree, which would lead us to the following redefinition of the Agree operation, which I label S-Agree, ("S" for *simple*).[8]

(3.31)   **S-Agree** $= (3.28)–(3.17)$
    a. An unvalued feature F (a *probe*) on a head H scans its c-command domain
       for another instance of F (a *goal*) with which to agree.
    b. If the goal has a value, its value is assigned as the value of the probe.

Once the strict correlation between valuedness and interpretability is dropped, we get more possible combinations beyond the four cases illustrated in (3.30). To be precise, we get a total of sixteen possible configurations, which are presented in Table 3.1.

TABLE 3.1 All features combinations and configurations

1. [uF: ___]…[uF: ___]	9. [iF: ___]…[uF: ___]
2. [uF: ___]…[uF: *val*]	10. [iF: ___]…[uF: *val*]
3. [uF: *val*]…[uF: ___]	11. [iF: *val*]…[uF: ___]
4. [uF: *val*]…[uF: *val*]	12. [iF: *val*]…[uF: *val*]
5. [uF: ___]… [iF: ___]	13. [iF: ___]… [iF: ___]
6. [uF: *val*]… [iF: ___]	14. [iF: ___]… [iF: *val*]
7. [uF: ___]… [iF: *val*]	15. [iF: *val*]… [iF: ___]
8. [uF: *val*]… [iF: *val*]	16. [iF: *val*]… [iF: *val*]

---

[8] I did not go for "PT-Agree," since Pesetsky & Torrego (2007) deviate from C-Agree not only with respect to solving the tie between interpretability and valuedness, but also introduce what they call the *feature sharing* version of Agree Pesetsky & Torrego (2007: 268), according to which the goal does not just pass its value to the probe, but instead the probe feature is substituted by the goal feature, such that both become one *instance* of the same feature.

Only the four combinations from (3.28a), which correspond to 1, 15, 11, and 7 in Table 3.1 respectively, are possible under the biconditional (3.17), and only combination 7 is licensed under C-Agree as defined in (3.28). Now, if the correlation between interpretability and valuedness is dropped and we get the sixteen possibilities in Table 3.1, we maybe have to reconsider the notion of Agree, in order to incorporate the new possibilities provided by the new features. And indeed, there are many suggestions for how to (re)define agreement on the marked. In the following, I will consider a small subset of them (Bošković 2011; Pesetsky & Torrego 2007; Wurmbrand 2012; Zeijlstra 2012). To spoil some of the results of the discussion, we will see that all of them have some shortcomings.

In order to discuss the different redefinitions of Agree, let us first become clear about the axes along which the proposals to be discussed differ from each other. The following list highlights the two main differences between the approaches (there are some others to be discussed below).

(3.32) a. **Trigger of Agree**
      (i) *Valuedness:* The probe searches for a goal because it is unvalued.
      (ii) *Interpretability:* The probe searches for a goal because it is uninterpretable.

  b. **Directionality of Agree**
      (i) *Downward:* The probe is above the goal.
      (ii) *Upwards:* The probe is below the goal.
      (iii) *Bidirectional:* The probe can be above or below the goal.

The definition of C-Agree combines a valuation trigger (3.32a-i) with a downward search (3.32b-i). That is, the probe is unvalued and searches for a valued goal below. In addition to the one possible configuration in (3.30), this constraint allows for three other configurations, after the biconditional is given up.

(3.33) **Agreement relations licensed by S-Agree**
    a. $[uF: \underline{\quad}] \dots [iF: val]$ (Table 3.1: 7)
    b. $[iF: \underline{\quad}] \dots [uF: val]$ (Table 3.1: 11)
    c. $[uF: \underline{\quad}] \dots [uF: val]$ (Table 3.1: 1)
    d. $[iF: \underline{\quad}] \dots [iF: val]$ (Table 3.1: 14)

The configuration in (3.33a) obviously is the only one that respects the biconditional and thus is the one that was originally the sole licensed arrangement for C-Agree. The new case in (3.33b) can account for the case we discussed above, in which a feature that is marked in a low position nevertheless receives a high interpretation. An example that was mentioned above is the tense marking at the verb, which gets interpreted in T^0 (3.20).

(3.34)

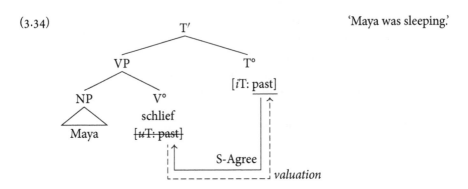

'Maya was sleeping.'

Interestingly, as noted by Kuno (2011), under the more liberal notion of S-Agree, not only is it just the goal that can be interpreted (as it is the case under C-Agree), but also the probe may be interpreted. That is, the difference between the first two configurations in (3.33) lies in the locus of interpretation. In the first case, the lower goal will be interpreted, while in the second case, the probe is what is interpreted (see Kuno 2011: 24).

(3.35) a. $[uF:$ __$]$ $[iF: val]$ $\Rightarrow$ ~~$[uF: val]$~~ $[iF: val]$

                       S-Agree   *interpretation*

     b. $[iF:$ __$]$ $[uF: val]$ $\Rightarrow$ $[iF: val]$ ~~$[uF: val]$~~

                       S-Agree   *interpretation*

Regarding the third case in (3.33), there are some conflicting opinions as to whether this constitutes a valid case for S-Agree. Of course, configuration-wise, the case where an uninterpretable, unvalued probe c-commands an uninterpretable, valued goal fulfills the requirements of S-Agree. However, depending on your specific background assumption about interpretation and deletion, such a configuration may be worrisome. Consider a first option according to which the same process applies as if the goal were interpretable. That is, the goal values the probing feature which, because it is uninterpretable, gets marked for deletion in accordance with the principle stated in (3.18).

(3.36) $[uF:$ __$]$ $[uF: val]$ $\Rightarrow$ ~~$[uF: val]$~~ $[uF: val]$

                       S-Agree   *remaining uF*

The problem with this interpretation of this particular configuration is that, with the goal, an uninterpretable feature remains which will make the derivation crash if it reaches LF. In order to circumvent this, we can follow Bošković (2011), who assumes that valued uninterpretable features can delete without participating in an Agree relation. Such an assumption was not possible in Chomsky's (2000) orginal conception of C-Agree, because there were no uninterpretable yet valued features. But since adopting S-Agree over C-Agree allows for this, this assumption of a second deletion process becomes viable.

(3.37) **Deletion of valued, uninterpretable features**
A lexically valued, uninterpretable feature may delete.

Equipped with this additional deletion option for valued, uninterpretable features, the configuration in (3.36) can now be restated.

(3.38) $[uF:\_\_]$ $[uF: val]$ $\Rightarrow$ $[uF: val]$ $[uF: val]$

S-Agree   no interpretation

What is noteworthy about this outcome is that neither the probe nor the goal receives an interpretation. Here is where the approaches found in the literature actually diverge from each other. While for Bošković (2011) this is exactly what should be the case in face of grammatical gender features which genuinely do not seem to have a semantic effect. In contrast, Pesetsky & Torrego (2007) and Kuno (2011) follow Brody's (1997) thesis of *radical interpretability* (after Pesetsky & Torrego 2007: 273).

(3.39) **Thesis of radical interpretability**   (Brody 1997)
Each feature must receive a semantic interpretation in some syntactic location.

Obviously allowing valued, uninterpretable features to delete can lead to situations as in (3.38) in which a feature does not receive any interpretation, which is at odds with the principle in (3.39). Of course, one may ask how well motivated the thesis of radical interpretability actually is. Conceptually, it seems to be desirable as it constrains the use of uninterpretable features as a means to just steer the syntactic derivation. Furthermore, as forcefully argued by Zeijlstra (2008), genuinely uninterpretable features pose a serious challenge to language acquisition and hence should be discarded from the inventory of possible features. However, in light of phenomena like grammatical gender, it seems equally undesirable to just posit an interpretable counterpart for such semantically vacuous features. Even though this is an interesting and important issue for a theory of agreement, it will not be a problem for the plans of this book, since all the expressive features that I will make use of have a clear semantic effect (somewhere), so that radical interpretability will always be met. I therefore leave this issue for others to solve.

The last remaining configuration in (3.33) contains an interpretable probe as well as an interpretable goal. This can be illustrated as follows.

(3.40) $[iF:\_\_]$ $[iF: val]$ $\Rightarrow$ $[iF: val]$ $[iF: val]$

S-Agree   two interpretation

This also seems a bit problematic because it would mean that the feature in this configuration is interpreted twice. As long as we are not talking about two completely distinct occurrences of the same features (like two number features of two nouns), it is very unlikely that such a double interpretation makes sense. At least not without further stipulations.[9]

3.4.3 ↑Agree

Besides the two somewhat troublesome cases, the definition of S-Agree received criticism from a completely different direction. Recall that S-Agree as definied in (3.28), just like the orginal version of C-Agree in (3.28), is a downward looking operation. That is, the needy element (the probe) searches its c-command domain to find a goal downstream. And since S-Agree, as well as C-Agree, are driven by valuation, it follows that the unvalued feature has to be above the valued one. In contrast to this tradtional position, there are recent pleas for a reversal of the direction in which the Agree mechansim operates. Wurmbrand (2012, 2014) and Zeijlstra (2012) make the most forceful proposals for a reverse definition of Agree, even though suggestions into this direction have been made elsewhere before.[10] As this line of research will prove useful for the purposes of this book, let us have a closer look at the idea of an upwards Agree relation. This is the common idea of the proposals put forward by Wurmbrand (2012, 2014) and Zeijlstra (2012); namely that the probing element is c-command by the goal. That is, they both choose option (3.32b-ii) from the list of possible options above. For obvious reasons, I will call such approaches to the agreement operation ↑Agree$_i$. However, even if Wurmbrand and Zeijlstra both argue for an upwards-looking definition of Agree, they differ with respect to what the driving factor is; that is, they choose different options from (3.32a). For Wurmbrand (2012, 2014), the trigger of Agree is valuation, while for Zeijlstra (2012), it is interpretability. Let us briefly compare these two views.

For Wurmbrand (2012, 2014), what triggers a probe to search upwards for a goal is that the probe is unvalued. An unvalued probe can get valued if it finds a matching valued goal under an upwards-looking agree relation.

(3.41)   ↑**Agree**$_v$ (valuation-driven version)   (cf. Wurmbrand 2012: 132)
A feature F: ___ on α is valued by a feature F: *val* on β, iff
a. β asymmetrically c-commands α and
b. There is no γ ($\neq \beta$), with a valued interpretable feature F such that γ commands α and is c-commanded by β.

---

[9] One possible stipulation could be that of two instances of the same interpretable feature that have the same value, only one (e.g. the higher one) gets interpreted.

[10] See, for instance, Merchant 2011; Stechow 2009, 2003, 2004. See Wurmbrand 2014: 132 for more references. In addition, there have been proposals for a bidirectional Agree operation that may look up or down (Adger 2003; Baker 2008) or having a probing direction differ with respect to what features are involved (P. W. Smith 2015).

That is, while the direction of agree is upwards under Wurmbrand's conception, the valuation that results from ↑Agree$_v$ happens downwards. That is, the value of the goal is passed downwards to the probe after the ↑Agree$_v$-relation is established.

Interestingly, one of the main examples Wurmbrand uses to illustrate the need for an upwards-looking, valuation driven notion of Agree is case assignment. Following the usual asumption that case is assigned by T, a valuation-based verison of ↑Agree$_i$ can directly establish a link between T and the DP, so that the tense feature of T can value the tense feature of the DP, which is then realized as nominative case on PF (Wurmbrand 2012: 133).

(3.42)

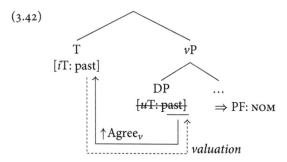

What is also noteworthy in this case is that Wurmbrand diverges from the assumption that the T-feature in T is an instance of an interpretable but unvalued feature, something we also assumed above. Instead, she treats the T-feature in T as being valued and it is the T-head that values the tense feature of the verb and thus selects for the specific morpho-logical markup of the verb, something that enables, so she argues, a proper treatment of the morphology in Germanic verb clusters (Wurmbrand 2012). That is, the ↑Agree$_v$-based derivation of the relation between the TP and V is, so to speak, the mirror image of the derivation in (3.43).

(3.43)   'Maya was sleeping.'

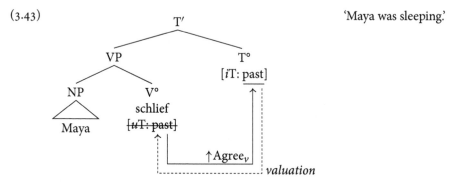

It is also important to point out that under Wurmbrand's analysis of tense agreement and case assignment, valued interpretable features are very common. However, note that ↑Agree$_v$ does not specify whether the interpretable feature is above or below the uninterpretable one, just that the unvalued probe is below the valued goal. This is the most important difference between Wurmbrand's (2012; 2014) approach and the one championed by Zeijlstra (2012) which I turn to now.

While Wurmbrand's ↑Agree$_v$ is driven by the need for an unvalued feature to find a valued counterpart at a higher position, Zeijlstra (2012) takes a different route. Even though he also argues for a "reverse" upwards-looking version of Agree, he suggests it is not the probe's unvaluedness that establishes its need to enter into an Agree relation. Instead, it is its uninterpretability. That is, the probe is an uninterpretable feature that looks upwards for a matching interpretable feature. A definition for this interpretation-driven notion of ↑Agree can be given as follows.

(3.44) **↑Agree$_i$** (interpretation-driven version)   (Zeijlstra 2012: 514)
        α can ↑Agree$_i$ with β iff:
        a. α carries at least one uninterpretable feature and β carries a matching interpretable feature.
        b. β c-commands α.
        c. β is the closest goal to α.

The main difference between the valuation-driven version of ↑Agree given in (3.41) and this interpretation-driven version is that according to the former, the relative position of the valued and unvalued features is fixed and the relative positions of the interpretable and uninterpretable features is unrestricted, the latter fixes the relative position of the interpretatable and uninterpretable features but does not specify the order between the valued and unvalued features.

The following list compares the possible feature configurations as licensed by ↑Agree$_v$ and ↑Agree$_i$.

(3.45) **Agreement relations licensed by ↑Agree$_v$**
        a. $[uF: val] \ldots [iF:\ \_\_]$ (Table 3.1: 6)
        b. $[iF: val] \ldots [uF:\ \_\_]$ (Table 3.1: 11) ◁
        c. $[uF: val] \ldots [uF:\ \_\_]$ (Table 3.1: 3)
        d. $[iF: val] \ldots [iF:\ \_\_]$ (Table 3.1: 15)

(3.46) **Agreement relations licensed by ↑Agree$_i$**
        a. $[iF:\ \_\_] \ldots [uF:\ \_\_]$ (Table 3.1: 9)
        b. $[iF:\ \_\_] \ldots [uF: val]$ (Table 3.1: 10)
        c. $[iF: val] \ldots [uF:\ \_\_]$ (Table 3.1: 11) ◁
        d. $[iF: val] \ldots [uF: val]$ (Table 3.1: 12)

Since the two approaches each require a certain configuration for either (un)interpretable and (un)valued features, they overlap just in one case (as indicated by the little triangle), name case 11 from Table 3.1, in which an interpretable and valuable goal c-commands an uninterpretable, unvalued probe. Interestingly, this configuration, in which the two variants of upwards-looking Agree overlap, is the reversed image of the single configuration that was licensed under the original definition of C-Agree as given in (3.28), that still respected the biconditional in (3.17).[11] Due to this overlap, the ↑Agree$_i$ can handle the case-assignment configuration in (3.42) just like ↑Agree$_v$. The difference, however, concerns how the agreement of the verbal and nominal ϕ-features are handled. According to Zeijlstra (2012) T carries uninterpretable ϕ-features like number that must be checked by the interpretable ϕ-features of the subject. To establish a ↑Agree$_i$-configuration, the subject DP must move to a position that immediately c-commands T°. Under ↑Agree$_i$, subject-to-T° movement is thus not triggered for case-assignment requirements, but is necessary in order to provide a goal for the uninterpretable ϕ-feature carried by T°. That is, under ↑Agree$_i$, T° first checks and values the uninterpretable T-feature of the subject DP (which will surface as nominative), just as in (3.42).

(3.47)

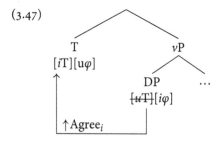

In a second step, the subject DP moves to (or: is externally merged) TP^{spec} so that the uninterpretable φ-feature of T can be checked by the subject's φ-feature.

(3.48)

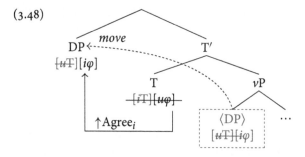

Crucially, this second step is possible under ↑Agree$_i$ irrespective of the question of whether one thinks that the ϕ-features of the DP (or, more correctly, the head noun) comes already valued and values T° or whether one thinks it is the T° that carries a value and selects for a certain DP/noun. Both options are possible under ↑Agree$_i$. In contrast, under ↑Agree$_v$, subject-movement is triggered if it is assumed that it is the subject that values the ϕ-features of T° (Wurmbrand 2014: 139).

---

[11] See the list in (3.30).

I am not going into the discussion of whether the valuation or the interpretation-based understanding of upwards-looking Agree is overall better suited to cope with all the different data. For the purposes of this work, however, I will adopt Zeijlstra's (2012) interpretation-driven version, because the feature configuration that we will encounter repeatedly in the case studies in the later chapters involves an uninterpretable yet valued probe that is c-commanded by an interpretable and, crucially, unvalued goal (that is, configuration 10 in Table 3.1). While this configuration falls under the scope of $\uparrow\text{Agree}_i$, it is not covered by $\uparrow\text{Agree}_v$; compare (3.45) and (3.46).

Let me close this section on varieties of Agree by mentioning that there are also bidirectional approaches (Adger 2003; Baker 2008) that allow for Agree to work both in an upwards and downwards fashion. In addition, there are also mixed approaches in which different directions of Agreement hold for different kinds of features (for instance, P. W. Smith 2015). However, since $\uparrow\text{Agree}_i$ includes all the configurations I will need in this book and the alternatives license more, I will stick to the more restricted version.

3.5 Phases

Another ingredient of many conceptions of minimalist syntax is the so-called *phase theory* as first put forward by Chomsky (2000, 2001).[12] The core idea behind this approach to syntactic derivation is that the minimalist T-model of grammar, as illustrated in Figure 3.2, is split up into smaller increments. That is, instead of deriving an entire sentence in the narrow syntax and then shipping the output to the two interfaces, Chomsky's proposal is that the derivation is chunked into smaller partial steps, called *phases*, where each phase has access to a subset of the lexical material (called "lexical subarrays"). The main consequence of phase theory is that at specific points of the derivation (the precise point of which is up for dispute), a phase is transferred to the interface(s). The resulting model is illustrated in Figure 3.3 (see Citko 2014: 42).

Conceptually, this phase-wise transfer of syntactic material is supposed to lessen the memory load the derivational system needs. From a more grammatical perspective, the consequence of this assumption is that the material of a phase that is already transferred to the interfaces becomes inaccessible for further syntactic derivations (Boeckx & Grohmann 2007: 205). This restriction is formulated in Chomsky's

---

[12] Citko (2014) offers a comprehensive, book-length introduction into phase theory. The collections by Gallego (2012); Grohmann (2009) provide a lot of discussion. Related to phase theory is the multi spell-out theory developed by Uriagereka (1999, 2012).

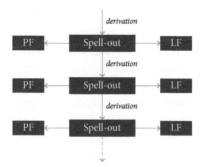

FIGURE 3.3 Multiple spell-out model

(2001:13) *Phase Impenetrability Condition* (PIC), according to which the so-called "domain" of a phase head—basically the head's complement—is not accessible to operations from outside the phase; only to itself and its "edge"—basically the specifier of H and possible adjuncts—remain accessible. The following schematic tree illustrates this (cf. Citko 2014: 32).

(3.49)

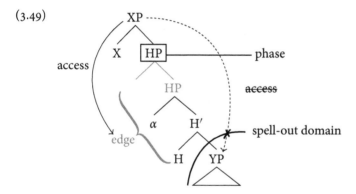

In this tree, H is a phase head and α is a specifier, while the gray part signifies possible, optional adjuncts. Together, they constitute the edge of the HP-phase. All three parts, the head, the specifier, and all possible adjuncts are accessible from the higher XP. In contrast, the complement of H—the YP in (3.49)—is inaccessible for XP.

Phase theory in itself is not uncontroversial (see, e.g., the important critique by Boeckx & Grohmann 2007), but even amongst its proponents, there are a lot of open questions, as explicitly discussed in detail by Citko (2014). I will briefly address three of them, as they will be relevant for certain aspects of this book.

(3.50) a. Which phrases are phases?
      b. What is the timing of transfer?
      c. For what do phases matter?

The first question concerns the question of how many phases are there. Basically, this boils down to the question of which categories constitute phase heads and which phrases thus can be considered to be a phase. In Chomsky's (2000) original conception, in which he likened phasehood to "integrity" at the interfaces, phases should semantically be complete and hence propositional. Therefore, Chomsky assumed vP (as the propositional core) and CP (as the proposition together with force indicators) to be phases. Since then, other phrases have been argued to be (or not to be) phases. A common addition to the inventory of phases, also hinted at by Chomsky (2001), is the DP (see, amongst others, Bošković 2012; Heck, G. Müller, & Trommer 2009; Kramer 2009; Svenonius 2004; for a contrary position see Matushansky 2005). Other suggestions go over PPs (Bošković 2004; Drummond, Hornstein, & Lasnik 2010; Kayne 2005) and predication phrases (Bowers 2002; Matushansky 2000) to the radical position that all phrases constitute phases (Epstein & Seely 2006; Lahne 2008; Müller 2004; G. Müller 2011).

The second question in (3.50) targets the issue of when exactly the (spell-out) *domain* of a phase—its non-edgy part, that is—becomes inaccessible. The illustration in (3.49) suggests that this happens when the phase HP is merged with the X of the next phrase. This idea, that the domain of a phase HP cannot be accessed by anything outside HP, corresponds to Chomsky's (2000) first definition of the PIC, the strong version.

(3.51)   The domain of H is not accessible to operations **outside HP**; only H and its *edge* are accessible to such operations. (Chomsky 2001: (7), p. 13; my emphasis, D.G.)

For a variety of reason, one of which I will discuss below, Chomsky provides the following weaker version of the PCI as well, where ZP is the next higher phase.

(3.52)   The domain of H is not accessible to operations **at ZP**; only H and its *edge* are accessible to such operations. (Chomsky 2001: (11), p. 14; my emphasis, D.G.)

The difference between (3.51) and (3.52) concerns, so to speak, the timing of the phasal spell-out. According to the strong version in (3.51), once a phase is merged with something else, the domain is shipped to the interfaces. In contrast, the weaker version is relativized to the presence of the next phase; the ZP in (3.52). That is, if a phase is immediately merged with another phase head, both versions amount to the same (e.g. if the X in (3.49) is a phase head). However, if the phase HP is merged with a non-phase, the domain of HP remains accessible until the entire structure is at some point merged with the next phase. The following configuration illustrates this.

(3.53)

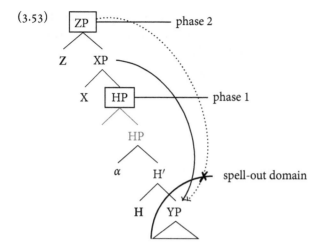

If the XP in (3.53) were a phase as well, the configuration would just look like the one in (3.49). It is only in cases like (3.53) where the strong and weak version of the PIC differ, since the weak version makes the domain of HP accessible to the (non-phasal) XP in (3.53), whereas under the strong PIC, this access would be blocked even in (3.53). Note that under both versions, the (phasal) ZP in (3.53) is unable to access YP.

I do not want to go into the intricate debate about which definition fares better—see G. Müller 2011 or Richards 2001 for more detailed discussions—but let me mention one empirical argument that favors the weak version. Inspecting the schematic illustration in (3.53) again, note that this corresponds to the common CP-TP-vP-VP configuration, where CP and vP are phases, but TP is not. Recall from the section on agreement, that T° and V° have to enter an Agree relation. Now under the strong PIC, such an agreement would never be possible, since as soon as vP, as a phase, is merged with T°, the VP, as the domain of vP, is spelled out. That is, the lower V° in the spell-out domain of the vP-phase cannot interact and hence not agree with T° which is *outside* of the phase.

(3.54)   **Strong PIC: agreement between T° and V° is blocked**

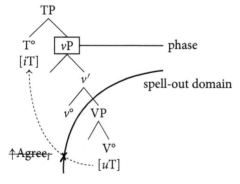

In contrast, under the weak version of the PIC, T° has access to the VP, since because TP is not considered to be a phase, the domain of vP is not yet transferred when vP and T° are merged, as indicated by the dotted spell-out border.

(3.55) **Weak PIC, step 1: agreement between T° and V° is possible**

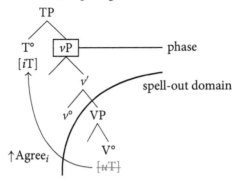

It is only after TP merged with C°, the next phase head, that the domain of vP is spelled-out and thus becomes inaccessible (for CP). However, agreement between T° and V° already took place at this point and thus the VP can be transferred with no harm.

(3.56) **Weak PIC, step 2: merging with C°, spell-out of VP**

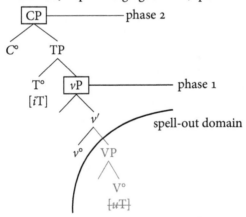

That is, the relation between T° and V°, which was one of the major discussion points in the section on agreement, provides some arguments in favor of the weak PIC, even though there are solutions to overcome these problems (see Citko 2014: 33–7, for an overview of this discussion).

One possible answer to cases like the agreement between T° and V° is tied to the third question raised in (3.50). The question is are phases relevant for all syntactic operations or just a subset thereof? To be more precise, the question arises if the PIC holds for both kinds of merge as well as for Agree. And indeed, there have been various suggestions to the point that the PIC only constrains merge but does not effect the establishment of agreement relations. For instance, Bošković (2003, 2007) argues on the basis of various empirical observations "that phases and the Phase Impenetrability Condition (PIC) do not constrain Agree" (Bošković 2007: 591). For instance, there are languages in which long distance agreement into an embedded finite clause is possible, something that violates (both versions of) the PIC. Bošković (2007) discusses, for instance, Chukchee, a Palaeosiberian language, in which the main predicate in a matrix sentence can agree with an object in an embedded clause.

(3.57) ənan qəlɣiḷu ləŋərkə-nin-et [iŋqun Ø-rətəmŋəv-nen-at qora-t]
      he   *regrets-3-PL*   *that*   *3SG-lost-3-PL*   *reindeer-PL*
      'He regrets that he lost the reindeer.'   (Bošković 2007: 613)

Such agreement into an embedded clause clearly disregards the PIC, as the embedded object is separated by at least two phases (CP and *v*P) from the matrix verb. Similar examples are discussed for Tsez (Polinsky & Potsdam 2001), Blackfoot (Legate 2005) and Hindi–Urdu (Bhatt 2005). Based on such data, Bošković (2007) concludes that the PIC does not hold for agreement.[13]

However, if one gives up phases as an instrument to put constraint on the establishment of agreement relations, one needs other ways to prohibit unattested agreement patterns. Consider for instance the aforementioned long distance agreement into a finite clause. While the argument for the irrelevance of the PIC for agreement is based on such agreement relations crossing the sentential border, this is something that many, if not even most, do not allow. For instance, neither in English nor in German is it possible for a matrix predicate to agree with a DP inside an embedded CP. So how can this be prohibited? Bošković (2003) suggests that agreement into a finite clause is prohibited if a finite clause carry N-features and hence act as interveners for agreement with the matrix verb. For the purposes of this work, I will leaves these issues unsettled. Instead, I will assume that the PIC does not effect agreement but that CPs seems to block agreement in languages like German and English.

3.6 Syntax meets speech acts

Before we end this presentation of the syntactic toolbox that I will employ in this work, let have a brief look at syntactic approaches that attempt to build "discourse"

---

[13] See also Fox & Pesetsky 2005 who argue that, in general, the PIC *as a syntactic constraint* should be abandoned altogether. Instead it can be derived from considerations about linearization at PF insofar as merge operations that would violate a syntactic PIC cannot be properly linearized at PF. Hence, there is no need to replicate the PIC in the syntax and, therefore, it does not effect pure syntactic operations of Agree. See also Stjepanović & Takahashi 2001 (cited in Bošković 2007) and Bošković (2003).

into syntax. By this, I mean approaches that structurally represent elements of the utterance context, like the speaker or addressee, in the syntax. Since many of them address some of the phenomena that I will deal with in the following chapters, they are particularly relevant for the main thesis of this book. If these approaches have the means to deal with the special syntactic properties of expressive adjectives, expressive intensifiers, and expressive vocatives without referring to their expressivity (for instance by assuming dedicated expressivity projections or, as I will suggest, syntactic expressivity features), this would mean that the hypothesis of expressive syntax should be dropped. So let us discuss a selection of these approaches to be able to refer back to them later on and maybe already estimate whether they might be useful for the endeavors to follow.

One influential line of proposals to give aspects of discourse a representation in syntax was sparked by Speas & Tenny (2003) idea to have dedicated speech act-related projections in the clausal periphery, an idea that is inspired by the gist of Ross's (1970) performative hypothesis that tried to build speech acts into syntax. They assume that, at the highest level of the CP, there is a speech act phrase, consisting of two shells, the "big" (SAP) and "little" (saP) speech act phrase, in analogy to the VP and vP shells in the verbal domain.[14] Both are headed by a functional head (SA° and sa° respectively)[15] that take the so-called pragmatic or P-roles as their arguments, which encode the conversational participants. Again, this is analogous to the verbal domain, where θ-roles encode the participants of the event described by the VP. This gives us the following structure.

(3.58)

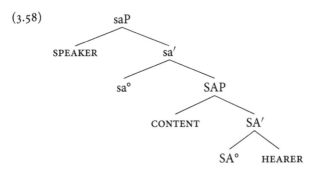

The big SA takes the HEARER P-role as its first argument and the utterance content (like the TP) as its second argument (similar to datives and accusative objects of a ditransitive verb). This big SAP is then the argument of the sa° head (the "subject" of the entire phrase), which also hosts the SPEAKER P-role in its specifier. That is, "the

---

[14] See Hill (2007: 2100, Table 4) for an overview over the parallel between the vP and saP.

[15] In their original 2003 paper, Speas & Tenny call them *sa** and *sa* respectively, but I follow here the more recent convention of having a little and big speech act phrase, which highlights the relation to the VP shells.

relations among the roles are asymmetric" and, in analogy to (structural) case, the roles "are not primitives, but are defined in terms of their structural position" (Speas & Tenny 2003: 320).

The syntactic structure in (3.58) is the structure Speas & Tenny assign to declaratives clauses and they assume that other sentence moods, like interrogative or imperative, are derived from this this structure.[16] For instance, they assume that in interrogatives, the hearer role moves to a higher position above the utterance content adjoining SAP (thereby resembling a movement similar to dative-shift).

(3.59)

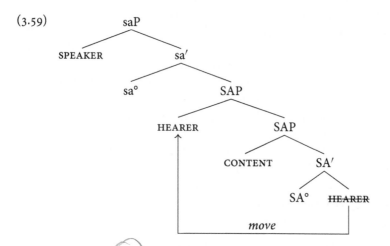

This will model that observation that "a question, it is the hearer who possesses the knowledge relevant to evaluating the UTTERANCE CONTENT" (Speas & Tenny 2003: 321). This can, for instance, model the "epistemic flip" that can be observed with some epistemic expressions. For instance, the function German modal particle *wohl* can be thought of as lowering the speaker's confidence threshold for a felicitous assertion (e.g. by changing a *believe* requirement into an *assume* requirement), whereas in question, it is the hearer's confidence threshold for her possible answer that is lowered (M. Zimmermann 2004a,b).

(3.60) Martin ist **wohl** zum dem Markt   gegangen.
        Martin is PART *to*   *the* *market* *gone*
        'Martin went to the market, I assume.'

---

[16] For an alternative view on sentence mood that does not build on speech act phrases but assumes that sentence mood (at least in German) is composed of various syntactic factors of a sentence, like presence of [wh]–features or verb movement, see Truckenbrodt 2006 and my reformulation in Gutzmann 2015b.

(3.61) Ist Martin **wohl** zum dem Markt gegangen?
     is   Martin PART *to   the   market gone*
     'Do you assume: Martin went to the market?'

Similar behavior can be observed for many evidentials (Faller 2002; Garrett 2001; Murray 2017).

The data that Speas & Tenny refer to in order to motivate the existence of their speech act phrases and P-roles is quite diverse. Let me mention just two data points,. First, they discuss the behavior of first and second person pronouns in Slave, a Northern Athabaskan language, which in speech reports may refer to the matrix subject or object instead of indexically referring to the speaker (or hearer) of the current context. Crucially, whether a first or second person pronoun does this depends on whether the embedding clause contains an overt subject (or object) or not (Speas & Tenny 2003: 325, who refer to Rice 1986 for their data). This can be captured by the assumption that Slave first person pronominals are bound by the most local SPEAKER, whereas Slave second person pronominals are bound by the most local HEARER.

Besides many other phenomena, Speas & Tenny also discuss expressive adjectives like *damn*, which will be the main topic of the chap:EAs. They assume that, since the negative attitude expressed by EAs is usually that of the speaker's, expressive adjectives are bound by the SPEAKER role. This actually looks like the default speaker linking I mentioned in Chapter 2. However, since in speech reports there is another "speaker," the expressive may also express his attitude (Speas & Tenny 2003: 328).

(3.62) a. John phoned his *damned* cousin/the bastard.   (damned by speaker)
     b. John said he phoned his *damned* cousin/the bastard.

                                        (damned by speaker, or subject)

However, as observed by Potts (2007), expressives can also express the attitude of someone other than the speaker outside of speech reports (that provide an additional speaker), so that the generalizations taken from Speas & Tenny cannot be the last word.

Building on these ideas, others have extended or modified the structure in (3.59). For instance, Hill (2014) and Haegeman & Hill (2013) adopt a slightly modified version of Speas & Tenny's structure, in which the utterance content is also c-commanded by the big SA.[17] This gives us the following structure, in which I adopt Zu's (2018) notational variant of writing SAP as Adr(essee)P and saP as Sp(eaker)P to make the connection to the speaker and the addressee more obvious.

---

[17] I refer the reader to Zu 2018 for a good overview of this discussion and the differences between the original Speas & Tenny proposal and the modification by Hill and others.

(3.63)

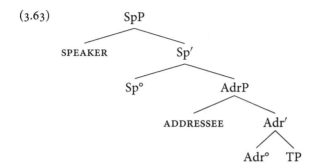

With this structure, Hill (2007, 2014) and Haegeman & Hill (2013) analyze various observations about the syntax of discourse particles and, relevant for the purposes this book, vocatives. For instance, they can capture syntactic constraints on ordering of vocatives and some other discourse particles. Since vocatives are the head of the addressee projection, speaker-related discourse particles are predicted to precede vocatives. I will come back to this in more detail in Chapter 6.

The modification in (3.63) is also employed by Miyagawa (2012) in order to analyze so-called *allocutive agreement* in Souletin, an eastern dialect of Basque (Miyagawa (2012) refers to Oyharçabal 1993 for the data). Allocutive agreement is a phenomenon, in why the verb agrees not also with the subject of the clause, but also—in cases in which the subject is not first or second person—varies according to who the addressee of the utterance is. For instance, in the following example, only the addressee changes and the verbal inflexion changes with it (Miyagawa 2012: 83).

(3.64)   [to a male friend]
    a. Pettek   lan   egin
        *Peter.*ERG   *work.*ABS   *do.*PRF
        dik.
        AUX-3.SG.ABS-<u>2.SG.C.MASC.ALLOC</u>-3.SG.ERG
        'Peter worked.'

    b. Pettek   lan   egin   **din.**
        *Peter.*ERG   *work.*ABS   *do.*PRF   AUX-3.SG.ABS-<u>2.SG.C.FEM.ALLOC</u>-3.SG.ERG
        'Peter worked.'

Begin inspired by Oyharçabal (1993), and Miyagawa (2012: 85) assumes the allocutive agreement is induced by an allocutive probe in C (even if it is pronounced in T). Since Miyagawa assumes a downward-looking version of agreement, this probe has to move to the higher SA position (via the lower) in order to c-command its goal, the Adr-head.

A related but different approach is presented by Sigurðsson (2004, 2011), who also argues for the representation of the speaker and addressee or, as he calls it, the *logophoric agent* (Λ_A) and *logophoric patentient* (Λ_P), which are hosted in the high left periphery, but below Force (I am ignoring possible topic, focus, and other projections from Luigi Rizzi 1997 here).

(3.65)

This ~~is~~ looks rather similar to the representation of speaker and addressee in the syntactic speech act approach sketched above. However, there are some differences. First, Λ_A and Λ_P are not necessarily the contextual speaker and addressee but can be some other entities; for instance in direct quotation (Sigurðsson 2004: 236).

(3.66)   **He said to me: "I love you."**

Here, the logophoric agent of the embedded quoted clause is not the contextual speaker (which would equal the logophoric agent of the matrix clause), but the subject of the matrix clause. This, in Sigurðsson's (2004: 35) approach, takes care of the shifted interpretation of indexical pronouns in direct quotation, which, for him, shows that direct quotation "is not an extra-syntactic phenomenon."

(3.67)   [$_{CP}$ ... {Λ_A}$_i$ ... {Λ_P}$_k$ ... [$_{IP}$ ... he$_j$ ... me$_i$ ... [$_{CP}$ ... {Λ_A}$_j$ ... {Λ_P}$_i$ ... [... you$_i$ ...]]]]

This helps to highlight another important aspect of Sigurðsson's work. What he proposes is that there is a general relation between basic syntactic layers in which what he calls speech features, grammatical features, and event features are linked to each other. Syntactically, these are hosted in the CP, the IP, and the vP domain respectively (Sigurðsson 2004: 242).

(3.68)   [$_{CP}$ ... Speech Features [$_{IP}$ Grammatical Features [$_{vP}$ Event Features ...]]]

Now, according to Sigurðsson, this is not just a relation between syntactic domain, but crucially the corresponding syntactic features are also correlated in a similar way. He illustrates this, for instance, with person features. On the event level, these correspond to θ-features, on the grammatical level to ϕ-features, and on the speech level to the logophoric features.

(3.69) θ-features $\leftrightarrow$ ϕ-features $\leftrightarrow$ Λ-features

In general, Sigurðsson (2004: 226) assumes, "θ-features are interpreted in relation to ϕ-features, which in turn are interpreted in relation to Λ-features." With this, he tries to capture the relation between contextual discourse participants, other possible logophoric entities, and the person features on pronouns.

This should round-up our quick look at various proposals on how to represent aspects of the discourse on syntax. So, how useful are they for the purposes of this book? Without giving too much away about the three phenomena I will deal with, we can already conclude from this brief presentation of such syntactic speech act approaches that they are not sufficient to deal with the most pressing problems they give rise to. For expressive adjectives, which I will study in the next chapter, they at least offer a place to deal with speaker-linking (and when there is no speaker-linking). However, the approaches presented here are too restrictive, because without further assumptions, they predict that a non-speaker-linked reading should only be possible if there is an overt "speaker" present in the syntax, something that is not confirmed by the data. Moreover, these approaches do not give us a handle on the more challenging phenomenon of argument extension, which is the observation that an expressive adjective does not have to take its syntactic sister as its semantic argument, but can apply to a larger constituent. Since this is not related to the conversational participants and is still confined to the content level, the syntactic speech act approaches have no direct way to account for them. Similar considerations apply to the topic of Chapter 5, expressive intensifiers. Since all of their special syntactic behavior is confined to the DP, the higher speech act layer that is the innovation of the speech act approaches does not help us here. However, I will employ the extended structure that the syntactic speech act approaches offer when dealing with expressive vocatives in Chapter 6. All this, however, does not imply that the sketched approaches (or similar other ones) are unjustified; they are just not designed to handle the problems I will be concerned with. However, consolidating the findings of this work and the analyses I will develop with the core ideas of these approach could be a fruitful area of further research.

3.7 Summary

This concludes the brief presentation of the syntax-theoretic machinery that I will employ in the remainder of this book. Before jumping into the first case study of expressive syntax, let me make explicit the three main assumptions I will build upon. First, I do not adopt the biconditional correspondence between (un)valuedness and (un)interpretability and instead assume that all four combinations of (un)valuedness and (un)interpretability are possible. Secondly, for the purposes of this book,

I subscribe to the upwards-looking, interpretability-driven view of agreement from Zeijlstra 2012, which I labeled ↑Agree$_i$ and according to which and uninterpretable probe searches for an interpretable goal, by which it is c-commanded. Finally, I assume that only CP is a 'barrier' for agreement. I also briefly discussed some approaches that attempt to represent certain aspects of the context in syntax and estimated that their use for the analyses to follow will be rather low. However, equipped with the three core assumptions from this chapter, we can now dive deeper into the syntax of expressives and explore the hypothesis of expressive syntax in three detailed case studies.

4

Expressive adjectives

4.1 Introduction

When introducing the notion of expressive meaning to students and contrasting it with descriptive meaning, expressive adjectives (EAs) are—besides interjections and some slurs that are nouns—the first thing they come up with as examples of expressive language. Standard cases for English, taken from Potts's (2005) monograph, are given in (4.1); (4.2) shows authentic examples from German.[1]

(4.1) a. I have seen most **bloody** Monty Python sketches! (Potts 2005: 18)
  b. Nowhere did it say that the **damn** thing didn't come with an electric plug! (Potts 2005: 6)
  c. I have to mow the **fucking** lawn. (Potts 2005: 60)
  d. My **friggin'** bike tire is flat again! (Potts 2005: 6)

(4.2) a. *ʸ*Jetzt suche ich den **verdammten** Hund von der Händlerin in
     *Now search I the damn dog of the dealer.*FEM *in*
     der Westwehr.
     the Westguard
     'Now I am searching for the damn dog of the dealer in Westguard.'
     [http://forum.spellforce.com/showthread.php?t=69609]

  b. *ʸ*Sollt ihr doch das **verfickte** Nestlé-Logo direkt in eure
     should you PART *the fucking Nestlé-logo diretcly in your*
     Fahne mit aufnehmen.
     flag with on.take
     'You should directly implement the fucking Nestlé logo into your flag!'
     [http://tommiboe.com/2014/03/]

---

[1] I follow the Horn-style convention and use a prefixed "*ʸ*" to mark examples were found by googling (see, e.g., Horn 2013). If it is a common and not specific example with a lot of hits, I will not provide a URL for it.

The Grammar of Expressivity. First edition. Daniel Gutzmann.
© Daniel Gutzmann 2019. First published in 2019 by Oxford University Press.

c. ᵞDeutsche Sprache, schwere Sprache; Der **verflixte** Buchstaben
   German   language, difficult language the   damn   letter
   H   machte tatsächlich Probleme
   H actually makes   problems
   'German language, difficult language. The damn letter *H* actually makes
   problems.'
   [http://www.bote.ch/nachrichten/bilder/leserbilder/Verschiedenes;cme934,923389]

d. ᵞEinmal war es sehr gruselig, da   hab ich gerade
   one.time was it   very scary   there have I   just
   Paranormal Activity geguckt,   und dann geht die **verfluchte**
   Paranormal Activity watched   and then goes the damn
   Tür auf,   das war echt   ein Schock.
   door open   that was really a   shock
   'Once it was very scary. I was just watching *Paranormal Activity* and then
   the damn door opens; that was really a shock.'
   [http://www.gespensterweb.de/wbb2/thread.php?threadid=11446]

And indeed, expressive adjectives—or EAs, for short—are also the standard case used
to illustrate expressive meaning in the literature, which may be the reason why they
received the most attention during the recent spark in interest in expressivity. This
interest, which mainly concerns their expressive semantics, lead to the development of
elaborated formal analysis that seeks to account for the particular semantic properties
exhibited by EAs.[2] However, this strong focus on semantic issues left the grammatical
side of EAs more or less unilluminated. If current work on EAs mentions their syntax
at all, it is merely stated that EAs behave just like other attributive(-only) adjectives,
deeming their syntactic behavior rather uninteresting.[3] For instance, in his extensive
case study of expressives, Potts (2005: 163) argues that "neither EAs nor epithets
display syntactic properties that suggest a nonstandard syntax" and "that EAs are
syntactically much like other strictly attributive adjectives." He concludes that "an EA
plays no special role in the syntax of a nominal it appears in, beyond simply adjoining
as any modifier would" and that "the contrasts between EAs and other attributive
adjectives don't follow from properties of the structures they determine" (Potts 2005:
164f.). In a similar vein, Frazier, Dillon, & Clifton (2014: 291) state that the syntax of
EAs is that of normal attributive adjectives. But how great is the similarity between
EAs and other standard attributive adjectives actually? Indeed, in many respects, they

---

[2] For instance, beside type-based multidimensional systems like the one used in this book (Gutzmann
2015b; McCready 2010; Potts 2007), there are frameworks that use continuations (Barker, Bernardi, & Shan
2010; Kubota & Uegaki 2011) or monads (Giorgolo & Asudeh 2011, 2012).
[3] One exception is, of course, the mismatch between their syntactic position and where they are
semantically interpreted. More on this below in § (5.76).

behave completely the same. However, there are many aspects in which EAs differ from ordinary descriptive adjectives in interesting ways that warrant a closer look at their syntactic properties. The most important observation we will make is that EAs license non-local readings in which they target some constituent greater than the nominal in which they occur. The following examples illustrates this.

(4.3) ^{y}I lost my **damn** watch and I need to buy another one soon!
        [http://forums.redflagdeals.com/mens-timex-indiglo-watch-404088/]

(4.4) ^{y}Ich hab   meine **verdammte** Uhr   verloren.
        I   have   my   damn   watch lost
        'I lost my damn watch.'
        [http://www.randomhouse.de/leseprobe/Fallen-Angels-Die-Versuchung-Fallen-
        Angels-5/leseprobe_9783453267961.pdf]

As is already observed by Potts (2005: 18) and will be detailed below, examples like (4.3) and (4.4) have a reading in which the EA expresses the speaker's negative attitude toward the entire proposition; that is, the speaker is angry that they lost their watch, not about their watch. Given that in (4.3) and (4.4) the EA is part of the NP, it is rather surprising that it can scope over the entire sentence. Crucially, ordinary descriptive adjectives do not allow for such extended readings when they are nominal attributes. That is, (4.5) does not have a reading in which the adjective *wunderbar* ('wonderful') expresses an attitude toward the entire proposition.

(4.5) ^{y}Du hast   Dir   eine **wunderbare** Uhr   gekauft.
        you have   yourself a   wonderful   watch bought
        'You've bought yourself a wonderful watch'
        [http://uhrforum.de/hentschel-hamburg-der-hafenmeister-t158813-2]

The major aim of this chapter is to get a better understanding of this mismatch between the syntactic occurrence of the EA in (4.4) and its place of interpretation, especially what constrains the scope of interpretation and how it can be analyzed. In order to achieve those goals, we will have to study the conditions under which non-local readings of EAs are possible and under which they aren't and how they compare to other known kinds of non-local reading of adjectives.

However, the availability of non-local readings, even though the most prominent, is not the only respect in which EAs behave differently from descriptive adjectives. In the following, I will therefore dive into a detailed discussion of the grammatical behavior of EAs, starting with those aspects in which they indeed behave like their descriptive sisters, before we uncover many respects in which they behave differently. As we will see, most of the noteworthy behavior can be derived from the syntactic mechanism regulating their non-local interpretation, once the necessary machinery is in place.

4.2 The grammar of EAs

4.2.1 Standard syntax

As reported in the introduction, the majority of recent work on EAs does not really delve into their grammatical properties and simply assumes that they behave like ordinary descriptive adjectives ("DAs," henceforth). And indeed, *prima facie*, EAs behave just like attributive DAs. First of all, they seem to occur in exactly the same attributive position inside the DP in which DAs occur. The following English examples illustrate this.

(4.6)

a. [$_{DP}$ The $\left\{ \begin{array}{l} \text{bloody} \\ \text{damn} \\ \text{friggin'} \\ \text{fucking} \end{array} \right\}$ dog] barked the whole night.

b. [$_{DP}$ The $\left\{ \begin{array}{l} \text{aggressive} \\ \text{big} \\ \text{new} \\ \text{young} \end{array} \right\}$ dog] barked the whole night.

Regarding the position of EAs, German EAs are mostly deverbal adjectives (or, more accurately: verbal past participles which are converted into adjectives) involving the verbal prefixes *ver-* or *be-*, as in the following cases.

(4.7) a. verdammt, verfickt, verflucht, ...
        damn   *fucking*   *cursed*

    b. bekloppt, bescheuert, beschissen, ...
       cuckoo   *daft*   *shitty*

Between the members of the *ver-* and *be-*EAs themselves, there is not a huge difference between the individual items: they mainly differ in register and expressive strength. However, there is a difference between the EAs in (4.7a) and (4.7b). The former are purely expressive adjectives, while the latter have mixed content as so far, as they also carry descriptive content. The two kinds of EA will thus be called **pure** and **mixed** EAs respectively. I will come back to this difference later in Section 4.2.3.

Regarding the position of EAs, German patterns with English, as EAs occur in the same prenominal attributive position as DAs.

(4.8) a. [$_{DP}$ Der {verdammte, verfickte, verflixte, verfluchte} Hund] hat
          the *damn*   *damn*   *fucking*   *dog*   *has*
       die   ganze Nacht lang   gebellt.
       whole night long   barked
       'The damn dog barked the whole night.'

b. [DP Der {große, **junge, neue, aggressive**} Hund] hat die ganze
    the   big   young new aggressive   dog   has the whole
Nacht lang gebellt.
night long barked
'The {big, young, new, aggressive} dog barked the whole night.'

As is the case for the majority of DAs, EAs are banned from occurring postnominally.[4]

(4.9) a. *Hund **verdammt**
         dog   damn

     b. *Katze **verflixt**
         cat   damn

     c. *Uhr **verflucht**
         watch damn

Additional evidence for the assumption that DP-internal EAs really are syntactically part of the DP is that in languages like German, that morphologically mark DP-internal agreement, EAs partake in agreement phenomena just like DAs do. In general, the morphological markup of prenominal attributive adjectives in German adapts in case, gender, number, and inflexion class to the φ-features of the noun and determiner.

(4.10) a. Gestern hat **der**   **jung-e**
        *yesterday has a.*NOM.SG.MASC *young-*NOM.SG.MASC
        Hund   die ganze Nacht gebellt.
        *dog.*NOM.SG.MASC *the whole night barked*
        'Yesterday, a young dog barked the whole night.'

     b. Gestern hat **ein-Ø**   **jung-er**
        *yesterday has a.*NOM.SG.MASC *young-*NOM.SG.MASC
        Hund   die ganze Nacht gebellt.
        *dog.*NOM.SG.MASC *the whole night barked*
        'Yesterday, a young dog barked the whole night.'

     c. Gestern hat **ein-e**   **jung-e**   Katze
        *yesterday has a-*NOM.SG.FEM *young-*NOM.SG.FEM *cat.*NOM.SG.MASC
        die ganze Nacht miaut.
        the whole night meowed
        'Yesterday, a young cat meowed the whole night.'

---

[4] There are some special exceptions to this in German, like *Wahlkampf pur* ('election campaign pure'), which, however, are very restricted (see Dürscheid 2002).

d. Gestern   haben **die**   jung-**en**
   *yesterday has   the.*NOM.PL.MASC *young-*NOM.PL.MASC
   Hund-**e**   die ganze Nacht gebellt.
   *dog-e*NOM.PL.MASC *the whole night   barked*
   'Yesterday, the young dogs barked the whole night.'

e. Ich bin genervt von **dein**-em   jung-**en**
   *I   am annoyed by your-*DAT.SG.MASC *young-*DAT.SG.MASC
   Hund.
   *dog.*DAT.SG.MASC
   'I am annoyed by your young dog.'

In all variants of (4.10) the DA *jung* ('young') reflects changes in case, gender, number or the kind of determiner used. Exactly the same pattern holds for EAs, as the following variants of (4.10) show.

(4.11) a. Gestern   hat **der**   verdammt-**e**
           *yesterday has a.*NOM.SG.MASC *damn-*NOM.SG.MASC
           Hund   die ganze Nacht gebellt.
           *dog.*NOM.SG.MASC *the whole night   barked*
           'Yesterday, the damn dog barked the whole night.'

        b. Gestern   hat **ein**-Ø   verdammt-**er**
           *yesterday has a.*NOM.SG.MASC *damn-*NOM.SG.MASC
           Hund   die ganze Nacht gebellt.
           *dog.*NOM.SG.MASC *the whole night   barked*
           'Yesterday, a damn dog barked the whole night.'

        c. Gestern   hat **ein**-e   verdammt-**e**   Katze
           *yesterday has a-*NOM.SG.FEM *damn-*NOM.SG.FEM *cat.*NOM.SG.MASC
           die ganze Nacht miaut.
           the whole night   meowed
           'Yesterday, a damn cat meowed the whole night.'

        d. Gestern   haben **die**   verdammt-**en**
           *yesterday has   the.*NOM.PL.MASC *damn-*NOM.PL.MASC
           Hund-**e**   die ganze Nacht gebellt.
           *dog-e*NOM.PL.MASC *the whole night   barked*
           'Yesterday, the damn dogs barked the whole night.'

        e. Ich bin genervt von **dein**-em   verdammt-**en**
           *I   am annoyed by your-*DAT.SG.MASC *damn-*DAT.SG.MASC
           Hund.
           *dog.*DAT.SG.MASC
           'I am annoyed by your damn dog.'

If the features of the attributive adjective and the noun and determiner do not match up, the result is ungrammatical. Again, this is true for both DAs and EAs.

(4.12) a. *Gestern   hat **der**   **jung-em**
          *yesterday has the.*NOM.SG.MASC *young-*DAT.SG.MASC
          Hund   die ganze Nacht gebellt.
          *dog.*NOM.SG.MASC *the whole night barked*

     b. *Gestern   hat **der**   **verdammt-em**
          *yesterday has the.*NOM.SG.MASC *young-*DAT.SG.MASC
          Hund   die ganze Nacht gebellt.
          *dog.*NOM.SG.MASC *the whole night barked*

According to this data, the most straightforward syntactic analysis for EAs would be the same as for attributive DAs. That is, they can be assumed to be simple adjuncts to the NP (see Potts 2005: 164).

(4.13)

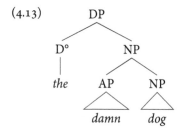

Beyond these standard syntactic properties that EAs indeed share with ordinary DAs, there many respects—as the next section will reveal—in which EAs seem to be much more restricted than their descriptive counterparts. However, before doing that, let us first have a look at how EAs and DAs interact with each other. In sentences in which an EA co-occurs with a DA, the EA tends to precede the DA (Jay & Janschewitz 2007), even if a preceding DA is not ungrammatical.

(4.14) a. der **verdammte** neue Hund
     b. ??der neue **verdammte** Hund

(4.15) a. that **damn** new dog
     b. ??that new **damn** dog

However, as observed by Jay & Janschewitz, EAs that appear closer to the noun have a tendency to receive the 'literal,' non-expressive reading.

Therefore, the *shitty little boy* is more likely to be understood as a "bad" little boy, while the *little shitty boy* is more likely to be understood as a boy who needs his diaper changed (see Jay & Danks, 1977).   (Jay & Janschewitz 2007: 218f.)

In a similar vein, if an EA co-occurs with more than one DA, having it taking up the middle slot is much more marked and a surface linearization that does not mix up the EA with the DAs is clearly preferred.[5]

(4.16) a. Der **verdammte**, aggressive, junge Hund hat die ganze
            the damn   aggressive young dog has the whole
            Nacht gebellt.
            night barked
            'The damn, aggressive, young dog barked the whole night.'

        b. ?Der aggressive, junge, **verdammte**, Hund hat die ganze Nacht
            the aggressive young damn   dog has the whole night
            gebellt.
            barked

        c. ??Der aggressive, **verdammte**, junge Hund hat die ganze
            the aggressive   damn   young dog has the whole
            Nacht gebellt.
            night barked

    In a similar vein, if there is more than one EA in addition to one or possible more DAs, the EA tend to be clustered together.

(4.17) a. Der **verdammte**, **verfluchte** neue Hund hat die ganze Nacht
            the damn   damn   new dog has die ganze night
            gebellt.
            barked
            'The friggin', damn new dog barked the whole night.'

        b. ?Der neue, **verdammte**, **verfluchte** Hund hat die ganze Nacht
            the new damn   damn   dog has the whole night
            gebellt.
            barked

        c. ??Der **verdammte**, neue **verfluchte** Hund hat die ganze
            the damn   new damn   dog has the whole
            Nacht gebellt.
            night barked

However, that fact that EAs preferably precede DAs like *new* or *aggressive* and that EAs tend to be clustered together is in itself not surprising, given that similar observations can be made regarding different groups of DAs anyway. For instance, Laenzlinger,

---

[5] Potts (2005: 163) provides examples that should show that EAs "freely intermingle with other adjectives." I am not sure about the English data, but find intermingling EAs and DAs in German rather marked, though clearly not ungrammatical. Moreover, Potts only showcases examples in which an EA follows a DA; so we are really talking about the linearization of one EA and one DA.

following Cinque 1994, assumes the following semantic hierarchy of adjectives for object-denoting nouns (Laenzlinger 2010: 59, 76).

(4.18) $A_{quantification} \prec A_{quality} \prec A_{size} \prec A_{shape} \prec A_{color} \prec A_{nationality}$

According to this hierarchy, a quality denoting-adjective should, for instance, precede a size-denoting one, which in turn should tend to precede a nationality-denoting adjective. This seems to be on the right track both for English and German, as the permutations in (4.19) and (4.20) illustrate.

(4.19)   a.   a good big German beer
        b.   ??a German good big beer

(4.20)   a.   ein gutes, großes deutsches Bier
        b.   ??ein deutsches, großes gutes Bier

As we observed above for EAs and DAs, DAs from the same category tend to band together and separating them with DAs from a different category is marked.

(4.21)   a.   a good tasty big beer
        b.   ??a good big tasty beer

(4.22)   a.   ein gutes, leckeres, großes Bier
        b.   ??ein gutes, großes, leckeres Bier

Given that such linearization patterns hold for different kinds of DAs, it is not really surprising that there is a similar constraint regarding the co-occurrence of EAs and DAs. In view of the data discussed above, it seems that EAs have a default position above descriptive quality-denoting adjectives like *neu* ('new'). However, they still are ranked below quantificational adjectives, as shown by the following contrasts.

(4.23)   a.   many **damn** dogs
        b.   *__damn__ many dogs

(4.24)   a.   viele **verdammte** Hunde
        b.   *__verdammte__ viele Hunde

Hence, it seems as if EAs take up an additional slot in the adjective hierarchy depicted in (4.25), just between quantificational and quality-denoting adjectives.[6]

(4.25) $A_{quantification} \prec A_{expressive} \prec A_{quality} \prec A_{size} \prec A_{shape} \prec A_{color} \prec A_{nationality}$

Of course, this suggestion shouldn't be taken too seriously at this point, since it is only based on my intuitions about German and English and is not meant to present a

---

[6] An alternative would be to subsume EAs under quality-denoting adjectives and have a closer look at the relative ordering of the different subclasses of those adjectives.

cross-linguistic tendency; even though it wouldn't surprise me at all if it actually does. It is only meant to show that the ordering constraints between EAs and DAs are nothing particular and are just one case of the bigger puzzle of adjective ordering.[7]

After having discussed the similarities between EAs and DAs and their linearization, it is now time to move to the, for the purposes of this book, more important questions, namely where the grammatical differences between them lie. This will help us in our goal of approaching the grammar of expressivity.

4.2.2 *Special syntax*

Given the amount and scope of the differences between EAs and DAs that we will discuss in this section, it is a bit surprising that so little of them are even mentioned in the literature—not to speak of being looked at more closely—and that most work assumes, without further ado, that the grammar of EAs equals that of DAs. As I will argue, the fact that EAs diverge in their grammatical behavior from DAs in so plentiful and different ways renders any attempt of treating them just the same as ordinary attributive DAs very suspicious, especially if considered in conjunction with their special expressive semantics. Of course, it is not a trivial task to decide for each of the grammatical properties to be discussed below whether it is really a genuine grammatical property or whether it is a consequence of the expressive, use-conditional semantics of EAs. But let us put that question aside for the moment and have a quick run through the distinguishing behavior of EAs. One caveat though: most of the properties to be discussed hold only for pure EAs, but not for mixed EAs. I will pick up and explain this difference at the end of this chapter.

A first observation that we can make regarding the grammar of EAs is that they are restricted to the positive form. That is, neither can they surface in the comparative nor superlative form.[8]

(4.26) a. Der verdammte Hund hat die ganze Nacht gebellt.
            the   damn   dog   has the whole night barked
            'The damn dog barked the whole night.'

     b. *Der verdammt-er-e Hund hat die ganze Nacht gebellt.
            the   damn-COMP-φ   dog   has the whole night barked

     c. *Der verdammt-est-e Hund hat die ganze Nacht gebellt.
            the   damn-SUP-φ   dog   has the whole night barked

EAs in English show the same restrictions.

---

[7] That this is still an issue is witnessed by the fact that the 2016 annual meeting of the German Linguistics Society (DGfS) at Konstanz hosted a workshop on *Adjective Order: Theory and Experiment* (organized by Eva Wittenberg and Andreas Trotzke).

[8] As we will see later, there is a second class of EAs, mixed ones that also have some descriptive content, for which many of the observations in this section now hold. I will come back to them in Section 4.2.3.

(4.27) a. The damn dog howled the whole night.
  b. *The {damn-**er**, **more** damn} dog howled the whole night.
  c. *The {damn-**est**, **most** damn} dog howled the whole night.

This is an obvious contrast to ordinary DAs, which mostly can appear in all three forms.

(4.28) a. der aggressive Hund
      'the aggressive dog'
  b. der aggressiv-**er**-e Hund
      'the more aggressive dog'
  c. der aggressiv-**est**-e Hund
      'the most aggressive'

Comparative and superlative morphemes are of course not the only kinds of degree morphology in German, nor are they in English. Instead of using these suffixes, degree expressives like *sehr* ('very') can also be used to saturate the degree argument of a gradable adjective.

(4.29) Der {**sehr**, **äußerst**, **arg**} aggressive Hund hat die ganze Nacht gebellt.

(4.30) The {**very**, **extremely**, **utterly**} aggressive dog barked the whole night.

As is the case for the comparative and superlative degree suffixes, those degree expressions can also not be used with EAs.

(4.31) *Der {sehr, äußerst, arg} **verdammte** Hund hat die ganze Nacht gebellt.

(4.32) *The {very, extremely, utterly} **damn** dog barked the whole night.

What is surprising and, for the purposes of the present discussion, crucial is that the impossibility to be graded or intensified cannot be traced back to an underlying ungradabilty and hence non-intensiviability of the expressive content of an EA. Intuitively, the (mostly) negative expressive attitudes conveyed by the use of EAs are scalar in nature. One can be in a more emotionally charged state of mind than another person or than one was at other times. I surely can have a negative attitude toward your dog, but also have an even more negative attitude to your neighbor's dog, for instance.

Besides resisting intensification by degree morphology or other degree expressions, EAs can also not be the target of adverbial modification which, again, is possible with DAs. This is true for German and English again.

(4.33) a. *Der {vermutlich, wahrscheinlich, tatsächlich} **verdammte** Hund hat die ganze Nacht gebellt.
  b. Der {vermutlich, wahrscheinlich, tatsächlich} **aggressive** Hund hat die ganze Nacht gebellt.

(4.34) a. *The {presumably, probably, actually} **damn** dog barked the whole night.

b. The {presumably, probably, actually} **aggressive** dog barked the whole night.

Such adverbial modification is possible with the majority of DAs, even those with a non-scalar semantics that are therefore nongradable, like, for instance, *schwanger* ('pregnant'), *arbeitslos* ('unemployed'), or *viereckig* ('quadrangular').

(4.35) a. Die {vermutlich, wahrscheinlich, tatsächlich} **schwangere** Hündin
      the presumably probably   actually   pregnant   dog
      hat die ganze Nacht gebellt.
      has the whole night barked
      'The {presumably, probably, actually} pregnant dog barked the whole night.'

b. Ich habe gestern   einen {vermutlich, wahrscheinlich,
      I have yesterday a   presumably probably
      tatsächlich} **arbeitslosen** Linguisten kennengelernt.
      actually   unemployed linguist   got.to.know
      'I met a {presumably, probably, actually} unemployed linguist yesterday.'

c. Der Platz ist von {vermutlich, wahrscheinlich, tatsächlich,
      the square is by presumably probably   actually
      überraschenderweise} **viereckigen** Skulpturen umgeben.
      quadrangular   sculptures   surrounded
      'The square is surrounded by {presumably, probably, actually} quadrangular sculptures.'

This suggests that the fact that EAs resist degree intensification is not caused by a possible non-degree semantics of EAs, but must have some deeper roots.

 Another common property of standard DAs is their ability to occur in constructions with *wirken* ('seem'). It is not sensitive to gradability, such that both gradable and nongradable DAs can function as the argument of *wirken* or *seem*.

(4.36) a. Der Hund wirkte **aggressiv**.

b. Der Linguist wirkte **arbeitslos**.

(4.37) a. The dog seemed **aggressive**.

b. The linguist seemed **unemployed**.

Since other parts of speech or phrasal types are impossible in these structures, the ability to occur in such constructions is actually assumed to be a classic test for adjective-hood.

(4.38) a. *Der Hund wirkte **bellen**.   (V)

b. *Der Hund wirkte **Kampfhund**.   (NP)

    c. *Der Hund wirkte **ein Kampfhund**.   (DP)

    d. *Der Hund wirkte **wahrscheinlich**.   (AdvP)

(4.39) a. *The dog seemed **bark**.   (V)

       b. *The dog seemed **fighting dog**.   (NP)

       c. *The dog seemed **a fighting dog**.   (DP)

       d. *The dog seemed **likely**.   (AdvP)

In contrast to DAs, EAs are ungrammatical in these otherwise adjective-licensing environments.

(4.40) *Der Hund wirkte {**verdammt, verflucht, verfickt**}.

(4.41) *The dog seemed {**damn, friggin', fucking**}.

To be clear, the impossibility to occur in these contexts does not distinguish between EAs and DAs in general, since there are also DAs that resist such *wirken*-constructions. Examples for such exceptions are DAs with temporal or modal restricting semantics.

(4.42) a. der {**ehemalige, zukünftige**} Finanzminister

      b. der {**angebliche, scheinbare, vermutliche**} Täter

(4.43) a. the **former, future** minister of finance

      b. the {**alleged, seeming, supposed**} offender

The reason why such adjectives cannot be used here is due to the fact that these attributive-only adjectives cannot be used predicatively, as the following examples illustrate.

(4.44) a. *Der Finanzminister ist {**ehemalig, zukünftig**}.

      b. *Der Täter ist {**angeblich, scheinbar, vermutlich**}.

(4.45) a. *The minister of finance is {**former, future**}.

      b. *The offender ist {**alleged, seeming, supposed**}.

The idea is that *wirken-* and *seem*-constructions do not actually select simple adjectives but rather small clauses in which the adjective is used predicatively. Therefore, those adjectives that cannot be used predicatively are blocked from occurring in such constructions. The fact for EAs to be used in these syntactic contexts therefore is only indirectly related to their expressive nature; the main reason being that they are attributive-only adjectives for the most part.[9]

---

[9] Obvious exceptions are again the mixed EAs, mentioned in footnote 8 on page 78. I will turn to those in Section 4.2.3.

(4.46) *Der Hund ist {**verdammt, verflucht, verfickt**}.[10]

(4.47) *The dog is {**damn, friggin', fucking**}.

Another dividing line between EAs and DAs is that EAs, even if they may come close in terms of the attitude they express to the meaning of some DAs, cannot be used adverbially, whereas ordinary DAs can.

(4.48) a. *Helge singt {**verdammt, verflucht, verfickt**}.
      b. Helge singt {**schlecht, katastrophal, grauenhaft**}.

(4.49) a. *Helge sings {**damnly, blastedly, fuckingly**}.
      b. Helge sings {**badly, abysmally, horribly**}.

Leaving the word level even more and switching completely to syntactic restrictions, another grammatical difference between EAs and DAs is that it is impossible to coordinate the former. While SAs can be coordinated with other SAs without problem—given that no specific semantic restriction speaks against it—EAs neither coordinate well with other EAs nor with SAs. The order between EA and DA does not matter here.

(4.50) a. Der **junge und aggressive** Hund hat die ganze Nacht gebellt.
      b. *Der **verdammte und junge** Hund hat die ganze Nacht gebellt.
      c. *Der **junge und verdammte** Hund hat die ganze Nacht gebellt.
      d. *Der **verdammte und verfickte** Hund hat die ganze Nacht gebellt.

(4.51) a. The **young and aggressive** dog barked the whole night.
      b. *The **damn and young** dog barked the whole night.
      c. *The **young and damn** dog barked the whole night.
      d. *The **damn and fucking** dog barked the whole night.

Given all these grammatical differences between EAs and DAs, it is rather surprising that EAs didn't receive more interest from a syntactic point of view; and statements saying that they do not show any remarkable syntactic properties are even more surprising. However, it is a non-trivial question whether these properties are merely a reflection of their special, expressive semantics, or whether they are genuine grammatical differences between EAs and DAs. Therefore, we will briefly discuss their semantic particularities, which squarely fit into the semantic ideas sketched in

---

[10] Note that example (4.46) is grammatical under the non-expressive, descriptive use of *verdammt*, which corresponds to using *damned* over *damn* in English. The same holds for *fucking* in the English example in example (4.47) in the main text. Here and anywhere else, we are only interested in the expressive reading and hence disregard the grammatical, though unexpressive readings of examples like (4.46) and (4.47).

Chapter 2. After that, we will turn to the most surprising property of EAs, which we haven't even discussed yet, namely the observable mismatch between their syntactic position and their semantic scope.

4.2.3 Semantics and two kinds of EAs

As alluded to in the introduction, the semantics of EAs received a lot of attention in the formal semantics literature since the influential work by Potts (2005, 2007) and various formal frameworks have been developed to model the composition of EAs and other expressions (Barker, Bernardi, & Shan 2010; Giorgolo & Asudeh 2011; Gutzmann 2015b; Kubota & Uegaki 2011; McCready 2010). The uniting idea of these frameworks is that expressive content resides in a separate meaning dimension, which is independent of the ordinary truth-conditional dimension. Against this theoretical background, EAs can be classified into two different categories, depending on which meaning dimensions they contribute to. In the parlance of Gutzmann 2013, the majority of EAs belong to the class of so-called *functional, expletive* expressives. That is, they are functions that take an argument toward which they express a negative speaker attitude. They are expletive insofar as they do not contribute anything to the ordinary descriptive content. They only have expressive, use-conditional content.[11] Hence, I call them *pure EAs* for the purposes of this book. Using the informal fraction notation introduced in Chapter 2, the contribution by a pure EA like *verdammt* ('damn') as in (4.52) can be given as in (4.53), where the "frownie operator" functions as a shorthand for whatever the concrete semantic contribution of the expressive may be.

(4.52) Der **verdammte** Hund hat die ganze Nacht gebellt.
        the   damn   dog has the whole night barked
        'The damn dog barked the whole night.'

(4.53) *The damn dog barked the whole night* = $\dfrac{\text{☺(the dog)}}{\text{The dog barked the whole night}}$

That is, the presence of *verdammt* ('damn') does not affect a sentence's descriptive, truth-conditional layer, which is given by the lower level in the fraction notation. In (4.53), the descriptive level of the sentence is the same as for the *damn*-less minimally different example. The-conditional content, with is the only meaningful content provided by *verdammt* resides at the upper level in the fraction notation.

From these two levels of meaning, we can get both the truth-conditions of the sentence as well as its use-conditional content.

---

[11] The suggestion to call such expressives *expletive* comes from Cruse (2004: 57). It should not be confused with *expletives* in the syntactic sense.

(4.54)   a. "Der **verdammte** Hund hat die ganze Nacht gebellt" is true, if the dog
             howled the whole night.

b. "Der **verdammte** Hund hat die ganze Nacht gebellt" is felicitously used, if
             the speaker has a negative attitude toward the dog.

Examples for such expletive, functional expressives can be given as in (4.55).[12]

(4.55)   verdammt, verfickt, verflixt, verflucht, vermaledeit, …

Interestingly, all of them have the somewhat negative verbal prefix *ver-* attached to a
verbal base; the base not always being transparent. However, in addition to the cases in
(4.55) and several others, there are also EAs that are not expletive, but also contribute
something to the descriptive dimension as well. Such kinds are called *functional mixed
expressives* in Gutzmann (2013). Examples for these are given in (4.56).

(4.56)   bekloppt, beknackt, bescheuert, beschissen, …

Grammatically, the examples are united by the fact that they feature a common verbal
prefix *be-* together with a more or less transparent base.[13] The important aspect of
these EAs in contrast to those given in (4.55) is that they have a reading in which
they contribute truth-conditional descriptive content besides the expressive speaker
attitude. This descriptive component consists in some kind of speaker judgment or
evaluation of some inherent quality feature of the argument. The following example
illustrates this.

(4.57) ^{y}Ich schreib   eine **beschissene** Note   nach der anderen. …
         I   write   a   shitty   grade   after the   other
         'I am writing one shitty grade after the other …'
         [http://hoywoy.myblog.de]

Crucially, the expressive *beschissen* ('shitty/crappy') in (4.57) is not expletive. If it
were, (4.57) would descriptively mean that the speaker is writing one grade after the
other. This would be rather trivial and clearly is not what (4.57) means. Instead, it
descriptively conveys that the speaker is writing one *bad* grade after the other. In
addition, there is the expressive attitude toward that bad grade. Using the fraction
notation gain, we can illustrate the contribution of *beschissen* to the two meaning
dimension informally as follows:

$$(4.58) \quad \textit{I wrote a crappy grade} \; = \; \frac{\text{☺(bad grade)}}{\text{I wrote a bad grade}}$$

In case of grades, the "target" of the negative evaluation in the descriptive dimension,
comes from the scale on which grades are naturally ordered from good to bad. In other

---

[12] I do not even bother to try to give glosses for them at this point.

[13] Even if it is a very curious fact, I will not investigate here why the expletive EAs are prefixed with *ver-*
and the mixed ones with *be-*.

cases, the quality that is judged as bad by the use of a mixed EA has to be inferred from context. In this sense, the descriptive dimension of mixed EAs works just like other quality-targeting adjectives like *bad*.

The fact that mixed EAs also have descriptive content contrasts with expletive EAs. In the following examples, in which it is the expletive *verdammt* ('damn') that is an attribute to *Note* ('grade'), the use of the EA does not give rise to the implication that the grade is bad.

(4.59) a. $^\gamma$Ich will   endlich diese **verdammte** Note! Ist meine letzte
  I   want finally   that   damn   grade is   my   last
  für den 1.   Abschnitt!!
  for the first phase
  'I finally want this damn grade! It's the last one for the first section!!'
  [http://www.psychologieforum.at/diskussion-nach-der-pruefung-t8260-25.html]

  b. $^\gamma$Warte schon seit 3   Wochen auf die **verdammte** Note,
  waiting already since three weeks   for the damn   grade
  dann sowas?
  then   such.thing
  'I have been waiting since 3 weeks for the damn grade, and then that?'
  [http://board.gulli.com/thread/1330881-schlechte-note-geschrieben-was-tun/]

In (4.59a), the grade is not yet known to the speaker and in (4.59b), the speaker was certainly not waiting for a *bad* grade. The following example demonstrates the fact that *verdammt* ('damn') does not contribute anything to the descriptive dimension from another angle.

(4.60) $^\gamma$Jede **verdammte** Note zählt voll in   die Endnote   ein.
  every damn   grade counts fully into the final-grade in
  'Every damn grade counts for the final grade.'
  [http://www.studis-online.de/Fragen-Brett/read.php?3,773959,page=2]

Certainly, the presence of *damn* does not introduce a negative evaluation into the descriptive dimension, because if it would, it would be part of the restrictor of the universal quantification and hence (4.60) would state that all bad grades matter for the final grade, which is true, but clearly not the intended reading of (4.60).

It should be noted that mixed expressives like *beschissen* sometimes may have a pure, that is, expletive reading in which they do not convey anything descriptively. Therefore it is sometimes possible to use mixed EAs in contexts like (4.59) and (4.60) that do not require a descriptive evaluation besides the expressive attitude. However, the other direction—using expletive EAs as mixed EAs—is not as easily possible. For instance, in cases in which one contrasts the descriptive dimension of *beschissen* with another evaluative adjective, the use of expletive EAs like *verdammt* is rather marked.

(4.61) a. Lena hat eine gute und Lukas eine **beschissene** Note
            Lena has a   good and Lukas a   shitty   grade
            gekriegt.
            gotten
            'Lena got a good and Lukas a crappy grade.'

        b. #Lena hat eine gute und Lukas eine **verdammte** Note
            Lena has a   good and Lukas a   damn   grade
            gekriegt.
            gotten

In the remainder of this section, I will focus on pure, expletive EAs and put the mixed cases aside. The motivation is that due to their double-faced nature, mixed EAs do not display all aspects of the special grammar of expressivity that we are searching for. However, they will serve as a good test pattern in order to decide which properties of (expletive) EAs are of semantic or grammatical nature and thus I will come back to mixed EAs at the end of the chapter. Now, however, it is time to turn to the most important of the special properties of EAs, their scoping behavior.

4.2.4 Syntax–semantic mismatches

Probably the most interesting and puzzling property of EAs is one that we have not explicitly discussed yet. In many if not in the majority of cases, we can observe a mismatch between the syntactic realization of an EA as a DP-internal attribute to a noun and its scope of semantic interpretation (see Potts 2005: 18). This is already the case for the examples discussed so far. Despite its attributive position, EAs are not interpreted intersectively with the noun.

(4.62) a. *der **verdammte** Hund* $\not\approx$ das *x*, das verdammt und ein Hund ist
        b. *the **damn** dog* $\not\approx$ the *x*, which is damned and a dog

This obviously contrasts with ordinary, attributively used DAs, many of which give rise to such an intersective interpretation.

(4.63) a. *der braune Hund* $\approx$ das *x*, das braun und ein Hund ist
        b. *the **brown** dog* $\approx$ the *x*, which is **brown** and a dog

To be sure, the fact that EAs are not interpreted in this way in itself is not that special, as there obviously are many DAs which are not intersective as well, like the modal or temporal adjective discussed in (4.42).

(4.64) a. *der **angebliche** Täter* $\not\approx$ *das *x*, das angeblich und ein Täter ist
        b. *the **alleged** offender* $\not\approx$ *the *x*, which is alleged and an offender

Instead, such DAs give rise to an interpretation in which the predicate denoted by the noun is restricted to specific temporal or, in the case of (4.64), modal domains.

(4.65)   a. *der **angebliche** Täter* ≉ *das x, das angeblich ein Täter ist*
   b. *the **alleged** offender* ≉ *the x, which allegedly is an offender*

Crucially for our purposes, this is also not a way in which EAs can be interpreted.

(4.66)   a. *der **verdammte** Hund* ≉ **das x, das verdammterweise ein Hund ist*
   b. *the **damn** dog* ≉ **the x, which damnedly is dog*

Instead, EAs can receive a reading in which they take the entire DP as their argument—which they are a constituent of—instead of the sister NP, like ordinary DAs do.

(4.67)   *der verdammte Hund* $= \dfrac{\odot(\text{der Hund})}{\text{der Hund}}$

What is even more surprising is that such non-local interpretations are not confined to the DP-level; EAs can semantically be applied to even bigger constituents. Most interestingly, they may target the entire sentence, as in the following examples.

(4.68)   Der **verdammte** Hund hat den Kuchen gefressen.

(4.69)   The **damn** dog ate the cake.

That is, instead of only expressing a negative attitude toward the dog, an utterance of (4.69) also has a reading in which the speaker is just upset about the entire situation. Setting aside the descriptive content (that the dog ate the cake) for a moment, (4.69) is therefore ambiguous between (at least) the following two readings.

(4.70)   Der **verdammte** Hund hat den Kuchen gefressen.
   ≈ 'I feel negatively about the dog!'
   ≈ 'I feel negatively about the fact that the dog ate the cake!'

Of course, these two readings are a bit hard to disentangle since they seem to be closely entwined, but if we alter the example such that the EA sits on the direct object, the two readings become more distinct.

(4.71)   Der Hund hat den **verdammten** Kuchen gefressen.
   the   dog   has   the   damn   cake   eaten
   'The dog ate the damn cake.'
   ≈ 'I feel negatively about the cake!'
   ≈ 'I feel negatively about the fact that the dog ate the cake!'

Taking into account the descriptive meaning and using the fraction notation, a sentence like (4.71) thus can give rise to (at least) the following two combinations of meaning dimensions, which differ in the size of the argument of the frownie-operator in the expressive dimension.

(4.72) $\dfrac{\odot(\text{the dog})}{\text{the dog ate the cake}}$
        (4.73) $\dfrac{\odot(\text{the dog ate the cake})}{\text{the dog ate the cake}}$

It is clear that these two readings are felicitous in different situations, sometimes even opposite ones. For instance, it could be the case that the speaker dislikes the cake in question so much that she is actually happy that the dog ate it because now she does not have to eat it anymore. In such a context, only the DP-reading is felicitous, while the sentence reading is blocked. This can be made explicit by a positive evaluation that targets the proposition.

(4.74) Hurrah! Der Hund hat den **verdammten** Kuchen gefressen.
        hurray the dog has the damn   cake   eaten
        'Hurray! The dog ate the damn cake.'
        ≈ 'I feel negatively about the cake!'
        ≉ 'I feel negatively about the fact that the dog ate the cake!'

We describe this behavior by saying that EAs allow what can be called *argument extension,* which basically means that they extend their scope to bigger constituents, which contain themselves. This could be, for instance, the DP or the CP.

The availability of these different interpretation points for nominal-internal EAs leads to the interesting observation that sentences that differ with respect to their EA placement nevertheless share a common reading. That is, regardless of whether the EA is used inside the subject- or object-DP, it can take sentential scope so that the following two sentences can be synonymous (under this one reading), despite the different placement of the expressive (see Frazier, Dillon, & Clifton 2014).

(4.75) a. Der **verdammte** Hund hat den Kuchen gefressen.
           the damn   dog has the cake   eaten
           'The damn dog ate the cake!'

        b. Der Hund hat den **verdammten** Kuchen gefressen.
           the dog has the damn   cake   eaten
           'The dog ate the damn cake!'

        ≈ 'I feel negatively about the fact that the dog ate the cake' (available reading for both).

In this sense, the attribute use of EAs can lead to interpretations that are very similar to the stand-alone, interjection-like use of EAs before another utterance. That is, (4.75a) and (4.75b) mirror (4.76) in their sentential reading.

(4.76) **Verdammt!** Der Hund hat den Kuchen gefressen.
        damn   the dog has the cake   eaten
        'Damn! The dog ate the cake.'

As long as we assign a standard attributive syntactic structure to cases like *der verdammte Hund* ('the damn dog'), as is suggested in (4.13), following Potts 2005, these observations imply a mismatch between the syntax and semantics of EAs. The fact that an expression takes scope over a bigger constituent (of which itself is a part of) on itself is not that special though. Such behavior can be observed with other phenomena as well, quantified DPs being the most obvious case.

(4.77) Your dog ate every cake.
 ≈ 'For every cake x, your dog ate x.'

What is puzzling about the EA case though, is that such behavior is rather unheard of for attributive adjectives. To quote Potts (2005: 18) here, "syntactic movement of English attributive adjectives is contraindicated by all known syntactic tests." The same can be said for German. Moreover, most DAs certainly do not display this kind of behavior. For instance, (4.78) does not have a reading in which the DA *großartig* ('awesome') targets the entire proposition.

(4.78) Der Hund hat den **großartigen** Kuchen gefressen.
 the dog has the awesome cake eaten
 'The dog ate the awesome cake.'

That is, (4.78) cannot have a reading under which it is synonymous with (4.79).

(4.79) **Großartig**! Der Hund hat den Kuchen gefressen.
 awesome the dog has the cake eaten
 'Awesome! The dog ate the cake.'

Therefore, the question arises how EAs get their non-local readings and why ordinary DAs cannot receive the same range of interpretations. Or can they? Despite the unavailability of non-local readings for most DAs, there are actually a bunch of adjectives that show a seemingly similar ability to generate non-local readings. These include, for instance, different adjectives like *occasional, unknown,* or *wrong*. Even though I can already spoil that their behavior is only superficially similar to that of EAs and thus, the analyses that have been proposed for them cannot be transferred to EA, let us nevertheless make a small detour and have a closer look at them. This will not only get us a better understanding of what properties EAs do *not* have, but these other non-local adjectives or, more correctly, how they are analyzed, will also be important for the next chapter, in which we are dealing with expressive intensifiers.

4.3 Excursus: comparison to other non-local adjectives

Beside the general inability of DAs to be interpreted outside of their attributive position, there are various examples of adjectives that have been shown to feature non-local (Schwarz 2005, 2006) or so-called adverbial interpretation (Bolinger 1967; Stump 1981).[14]

---

[14] For a concise discussion of the varieties of non-local adjectives and their analysis, see Morzycki 2013: § 2.5, from where most of the data and discussion in the main text is drawn.

4.3.1 *The* occasional-*construction*

The best-known and most studied class of examples are constructions involving an infrequency adjective inside a DP which is interpreted like the corresponding, DP-external adverbial (see, amongst others, Gehrke & McNally 2010; Larson 1999; Stump 1981; M. Zimmermann 2003). Due to the examples used in Stump's (1981) influential paper on this topic—one of which he in turn attributes to Bolinger (1967: 5)—such constructions are known as *occasional constructions* (OCs).

(4.80)   An occasional sailor strolled by.

Besides the ordinary attributive interpretation that there is a person who sails occasionally, (4.80) also offers an alternative reading in which *occasional* is not interpreted locally as an attributive adjective, but like an adverb scoping over the entire event. That is, (4.80) has a reading that makes it synonymous to (4.81).

(4.81)   Occasionally, a sailor strolled by.

Such constructions are also available in German, where they have pretty much the same structure.

(4.82)   Ein **gelegentlicher** Segler kam   vorbei.
         an   occasional   *sailor came by*
         'An occasional sailor strolled by.'

That the adverbial reading is available is most clearly shown in cases in which an attributive reading is ruled out, as in the following case.

(4.83)   Nächste Woche erwartet uns ein **gelegentliches** Gewitter.
         next   week   await   us a   occasional   thunderstorm
         'An occasional thunderstorm is awaiting us next week.'
         ≉ #'Something that occasionally is a thunderstorm is awaiting us next week.'
         ≈ 'Occasionally, a thunderstorm is awaiting us next week.'

An interesting observation about *occasional*-constructions, which leads to many of their analyses involving some kind of movement, is that in the presence of other scope-taking expressions like quantifiers, OCs lead to the usual scope ambiguities one also expects from the corresponding adverbial version.

(4.84)   Jeder Tourist sah   einen **gelegentlichen** Segler.
         every tourist saw   a   occasional   sailor
         'Every tourist saw an occasional sailor.'
         ≈ 'For every tourist *x*: *x* occasionally saw a sailor.'
         ≈ 'Occasionally it is true that every tourist saw a sailor.'

The *occasional*-construction, even if is the most prominently discussed case, is not the only instance of an attributive (descriptive) adjective that receives a non-local interpretation.

4.3.2 Other non-local adjectives

Besides these well-known cases, Morzycki (2013: § 2.5), who provides an overview over the landscape of what he calls *non-local adjectives*, presents many other cases. For instance, *average* or *wrong* feature adverbial-like readings as well (Schwarz 2005, 2006).

(4.85) Ein **durchschnittlicher** Student braucht elf Semester.
   a average student needs eleven semesters
   'An average student needs eleven semesters.'
   a. 'A student, who is average, needs elven semesters.'
   b. 'On average, a student needs eleven semesters.'

(4.86) Frida öffnete eine **falsche** Flasche.
   Frida opened a wrong bottle
   'Frida opened the wrong bottle.'
   $\not\approx$ #'Frida opened a bottle, that was wrong.'
   $\approx$ 'Frida opened a bottle, for which it was wrong to open it.'

Other cases of non-local interpretation of seemingly attributive adjectives are epistemic adjectives like *possible* (Leffel 2014; Romero 2013; Schwarz 2005) or modal adjectives like *unknown* (Abusch & Rooth 1997).

(4.87) Doktor X wohnt in einem unbekannten Hotel.
   Doctor X stays in an unknown hotel
   'Doctor x stays in an unknown hotel.'
   $\approx$ 'Doktor X stays in a hotel that is unknown.'
   a. 'Doktor X stays in some hotel, but it is unknown in which hotel he stays.'

(4.88) Die Polizei befragte jeden möglichen Zeugen.
   the police interrogated every possible witness
   'The police interrogated every possible witness.'
   a. 'The police interrogated every person who was possibly a witness.'
   b. 'The police interrogated every witness that is was possible to interrogate.'

As the presentation in Morzycki 2013 shows, there are many other cases so that non-locally interpreted attributive adjectives do not seem to be such an exception anymore. Therefore, we will have a closer look at their interesting properties to see whether they behave in other ways like EAs.

4.3.3 *Syntactic and semantic particularities of non-local adjectives*

Besides their adverbial-like interpretation, non-local adjectives share a lot of interesting features. And in order to compare them to EAs (and to work out their relevance for the next chapter), it is helpful to briefly look at them.

One important constraint that holds for the non-local reading of the discussed adjectives is that it is restricted to specific determiners. It is only possible with indefinite and definite articles, but neither with cardinal or strong quantifiers, nor with demonstratives (M. Zimmermann 2003: 252).[15]

(4.89) a. **Zwei** gelegentliche Segler kamen vorbei.
        Two   occasional   sailors strolled by
        ≉ 'Occasionally, two sailors strolled by.'

   b. **Jeder** gelegentliche Segler kam   vorbei.
      every occasional   sailor strolled by
      ≉ 'Occasionally, every sailor strolled by.'

   c. **Dieser** gelegentliche Segler kam   vorbei.
      This   occasional   sailor strolled by
      ≉ 'Occasionally, this sailor strolled by.'

Another, rather puzzling aspect of the non-local reading is that the kind of determiner chosen does not matter much for the interpretation. That is, regardless of whether it is the definite or indefinite determiner that heads the DP that houses the adjective, the DP itself is interpreted as being indefinite (M. Zimmermann 2003).

(4.90) **Der** gelegentliche Segler kam   vorbei.
        the occasional   sailor came by
        ≈ 'Occasionally, **a** sailor strolled by.'
        ≉ 'Occasionally, **the** sailor strolled by.'

Another restriction that holds for the external, non-local reading is that the adjective in question must be adjacent to the determiner and hence must take the highest position with respect to other kinds of adjectives in the DP. Other adjectives that intervene between the non-local adjective and the noun block the external reading (see M. Zimmermann 2003: 252).

(4.91) Ein **gelegentlicher**, begeisterter Segler kam   vorbei.
        a   occasional   enthusiastic sailor strolled by
        ≈ 'Occasionally, an enthusiastic sailor strolled by.'

---

[15] M. Zimmermann (2003) also mentions bleached 2nd person singular possessive pronouns as another possibility for the external reading, as in *Well, your occasional sailor would also show up.*

(4.92) Ein begeisterter, **gelegentlicher** Segler kam   vorbei.
an   enthusiastic   occasional   sailor strolled by
≉ 'Occasionally, an enthusiastic sailor strolled by.'

In a similar vein, there is also the restriction that adjectives with a non-local reading cannot be coordinated with other ordinary adjectives.

(4.93) Ein gelegentlicher **und** begeisterter Segler kam   vorbei.
a   occasional   and enthusiastic sailor strolled by
'An occasional and enthusiastic sailor strolled by.'
≉ 'Occasionally, an enthusiastic sailor strolled by.'

Finally, under the external reading, these adjectives resist degree modification. That, using degree expression like *sehr* ('very') or comparatives morphemes block the non-local interpretation (see Morzycki 2014).

(4.94) Ein **sehr** seltener   Segler kam   vorbei.
a   very infrequent sailor strolled by
'A very infrequent sailor strolled by.'
≉ #'Very infrequently, a sailor strolled by.'

(4.95) Ein selten-er-er   Segler kam   vorbei.
a   infrequent-COMP-φ   sailor strolled by
'A more infrequent sailor strolled by.'
≉ #'More infrequently, a sailor strolled by.'

Since we are just starting to get a sense of how widespread non-local adjectives are, there may be more special features to be discovered. For the purposes of our investigation of EAs, this is more than enough though. So let us check which of the properties of non-local adjectives are shared by EAs and which are not.

4.3.4 Comparing non-local adjectives and EAs

Most importantly, both EAs and non-local adjectives have a NP-external reading, which is why we are comparing them in the first place. Both EAs as well as non-local adjectives resist coordination with other adjectives and do not license degree expressions. Regarding the linearization in the attributive domain with respect to other adjectives, they both clearly prefer to precede other ordinary DAs. For non-local adjectives, this seems to be a very hard restriction as the non-local reading gets lost and only the ordinary internal reading remains, whereas for EAs this restriction does not seem to be as hard. EAs can appear after other DAs, as shown in (4.14), even though that may be rather marked (or the EA receives a non-expressive reading).

When it comes to the remaining special properties, EAs and non-local adjectives start to diverge more clearly. First, as Potts (2005: 164) already notes, the external

TABLE 4.1 Comparison between non-local
adjectives and expressive adjectives

	NLAs	EAs
external reading	✓	✓
coordination	✗	✗
degree expressions	✗	✗
before other adjectives	✓	✓
after other adjectives	✗	?
all determiners	✗	✓
always indef. interpretation	✓	✗

reading of EAs is not limited by the choice of the determiner, while the adverbial reading of the discussed adjectives is restricted to the simple articles, and, marginally, possessives. Secondly, as this seems to be even more important, the interpretation of non-local adjectives is *prima facie* non-compositional as the choice of the determiner does not matter: even if the DP involves a definite article, its interpretation is nevertheless indefinite. Not so with EAs, where the determiner seems to make its usual contribution. Table 4.1 summarizes the comparison between non-local adjectives and EAs.

Unfortunately for our purposes, all approaches to non-local adjectives are tailor-made to account for exactly those last two properties in which EAs and non-local adjectives differ completely, which, admittedly, are the most interesting features of infrequency adjectives and their other non-local friends. However, this means that the hope of adopting an available approach to non-local adjectives for an analysis of EAs is a non-starter, since they will make wrong predictions in these crucial aspects. This does not mean that the foregoing discussion was fruitless. As the next chapter will show, expressive intensifiers are more akin to non-local adjectives and hence we will revisit them there. But for now, we have to set them aside and turn back to our original question of how to build an analysis of EAs that can account for their properties without aligning them with non-local adjectives.

4.4 Just pragmatics?

Despite the special syntactic properties discussed so far, Potts (2005) concludes—see the quotes given on pages 4 and 18—that the syntax of EAs like *damn* plays no special role and "we must call upon the semantics to ensure that the meaning of *damn* can apply to noun-phrase and clausal meanings (at least) despite its nominal-internal position in the syntax" (Potts 2005: 18). However, Potts does not really provide a story of how this is supposed to work in his book. However, with Frazier, Dillon, & Clifton 2014, there is one sole approach available that tries to account for the non-local interpretation of EAs. Instead of relying on special semantic mechanisms, it is a purely pragmatic approach, without any regard to the syntax of EAs. In some sense to be elaborated below, their approach can be said to be anti-syntactic. Therefore, let us discuss their proposal in more detail so see if their approach is adequate.[16]

4.4.1 An anti-syntactic approach

The basic idea of Frazier, Dillon, & Clifton's (2014) approach is that EAs are, for compositional reasons, not part of the sentence they occur in at all. Rather, they base their analysis of what they dub the "speech act hypothesis" (Frazier, Dillon, & Clifton 2014: 294).[17]

> [The speech act hypothesis] claims that an expressive like *damn* constitutes a speech act separate from the speech act of the at-issue content conveyed by the rest of the sentence (Potts, 2005, 2007), and permits the expressive to be interpreted with respect to portions of the utterance (including the entire utterance) other than its syntactic sister.
>
> (Frazier, Dillon, & Clifton 2014: 299)

That is, instead of being integrated into the sentence, EAs behave as if they were uttered independently and search their target from that unintegrated position in a purely pragmatics way. This can informally be illustrated as follows.

(4.96)

```
        ┌─────────── verdammt
        │              │
        └→ [CP Der Hund hat └→ [DP den Kuchen] gefressen]]
```

For this reason, their approach can be called an "anti-syntax approach."

From the sketched core assumption they derive the prediction that a sentence-internal EA gives rise to the same reading as if an EA is uttered independently before or after the sentence. At first sight, this prediction corresponds to the observation we made in (4.75) and (4.76): minimal pairs that differ only with respect to the question of whether the EA is in subject position, object position, or used in an unintegrated, interjection-like manner all share the reading in which the EA targets the entire sentence. For convenience, I repeat the example here, but drop the detailed glosses.

(4.97) a. Der **verdammte** Hund hat den Kuchen gefressen.
   b. Der Hund hat den **verdammten** Kuchen gefressen.
   c. **Verdammt!** Der Hund hat den Kuchen gefressen.

(4.98) a. The **damn** dog ate the cake.
   b. The dog ate the **damn** cake.
   c. **Damn!** The dog ate the cake.

---

[16] Spoiler: it isn't.

[17] Their approach should not be confused with syntactic approaches along the lines of Speas & Tenny (2003), which in some sense, are the complete opposite because they argue for a syntactic approach to certain pragmatic aspects, whereas Frazier, Dillon, & Clifton 2014 argue for a pragmatic approach to the syntactic (semantic) problem of argument extension.

That is, all three variants in (4.97) and (4.98) allow for the reading in which the argument is the entire CP, even the two cases in which the EA is embedded in the subject or object DP.

$$(4.99) \quad \frac{☺(\text{the dog ate the cake})}{\text{the dog ate the cake}}$$

However, so far, we only observed this synonymy with respect to the sentence-level interpretation of the EA. What Frazier, Dillon, & Clifton's purely pragmatic speech act hypothesis allows as well is an interpretation that may completely disregard the syntactic placement of the EA, which pragmatics allow for it. That is, Frazier, Dillon, & Clifton (2014: 295) predict that the variants should not only share the sentence interpretation, but also the subject and object interpretation. That is, an EA in subject position should be able to target just the object and *vice versa*. In addition, an EA in an unintegrated position, as in (4.97c) and (4.98c) respectively (let's call this *sentence position* henceforth), does not have to be interpreted with respect to the entire sentence, but is supposed to be able to target just the subject or object (or any other relevant constituent for that matter). This seems to be a very strong claim and we will evaluate it in more detail below, but let us first see what evidence Frazier, Dillon, & Clifton put forward for it. As it happens, they present an empirical study that investigates the readings that are available for the different positions.

4.4.2 Culprit hypothesis

In their study Frazier, Dillon, & Clifton (2014: 294) investigate not only the speech act hypothesis, but also what they call the "culprit hypothesis." By this, they mean the hypothesis that considerations about what may construed as a "causal agent" influence the likelihood of a subject to be chosen as the target of an EA. If the subject is an animate entity and could be construed as causing the situation described by the sentence, so their reasoning goes, it should attract subject readings from non-subject positions. For instance, they predict that (4.100a) should be more often interpreted as involving a negative attitude toward the subject than (4.100b), which involves an inanimate subject that cannot easily be interpreted as a causal agent (Frazier, Dillon, & Clifton 2014: 295f.).

(4.100) a. Damn. The dog is on the couch.
         b. Damn. The holiday is on the weekend.

In addition, they assume that even though embedded EAs are supposed to perform an independent speech act, the position in which an EA is used may nevertheless have an impact on the interpretation. This effect, however, is hypothesized to be a pragmatic one, since "the reader will wonder why the speaker/author placed the expressive where she did" (Frazier, Dillon, & Clifton 2014: 296). That is, they predict that an EA in subject position as in (4.97a) gets more subject than object reading, whereas (4.97b) gets more object than subject readings.

4.4.3 *Experimental data*

Frazier, Dillon, & Clifton (2014: 296) test their predictions in an experiment involving 48 undergraduate students, who had to read a sentence on a computer terminal and, after they confirmed comprehension by pressing a keyboard key, answer a question about the test sentence. The test items differed with respect to the position of the EA (subject, object, or sentence position) and whether the subject could be construed as a causal agent. For the thirty critical test items (which were mixed with ninety-six items from unrelated experiments), the subjects were asked about the most likely target of the EA. The following examples illustrate this (Frazier, Dillon, & Clifton 2014: 302f.).

(4.101)   **Non-causal items**
      a. The house is filled with damn stinkbugs.
         (object position)
      b. The damn house is filled with stinkbugs.
         (subject position)
      c. Damn. The house is filled with stinkbugs.
         (sentence position)

      Question: *Which is the speaker most likely to have a negative attitude toward?*
        i. the house
        ii. the stinkbugs
        iii. the house being filled with stinkbugs

(4.102)   **Causal items**
      a. The dog is on the damn couch.
         (object position)
      b. The damn dog is on the couch.
         (subject position)
      c. Damn. The dog is on the couch.
         (sentence position)

      Question: *Which is the speaker most likely to have a negative attitude toward?*
        i. the couch
        ii. the dog
        iii. the dog being on the couch

The results of (Frazier, Dillon, & Clifton 2014: 297–9) experiment seem to support their two hypothesis. First, they clearly show that EAs have a sentence-level interpretation, even if they are in object or subject position. On average, the subjects chose a sentence-level interpretation in 39% of the subject conditions and in 42% of the object conditions. However, they also observe a transfer in the other direction. In only 63% of the cases in which the EA was in sentence position, it actually received a sentence level interpretation. That is, in 37% the negative attitude expressed by the EA was interpreted as targeting the subject or object.[18] This seems to support the speech act hypothesis, since the position of the EA does not strictly determine its place of interpretation. However, as we will discuss below, there is an alternative and, as I will argue, more adequate explanation of this which does not rely on assuming a non-integrated status of the EA.

Frazier, Dillon, & Clifton (2014: 299) also see support for the culprit hypothesis in their data. First, when the mean proportions for the sentence-level interpretation reported above are split according to the causality condition, it can be observed that the causality has an effect on the likelihood of a sentence-level interpretation when the EA occurs sentence-internally. In subject position, 50% of the non-causal examples received a sentence-level interpretation, while only 28% of the causal cases received a sentence-level interpretation. In object position, 46% of the non-causal examples and 38% of the causal cases received a sentence-level interpretation. This is graphically illustrated in Figure 4.1.

Looking at how many subject interpretations were chosen *given that the sentence interpretation was not chosen*, Frazier, Dillon, & Clifton (2014: 297f.) report that in the causal condition, the subject position leads to 98% subject interpretation, while it is only 62% in the non-causal case. For the object position, they find 51% subject interpretations in causal and 29% in non-causal cases. Finally, when the EA is in

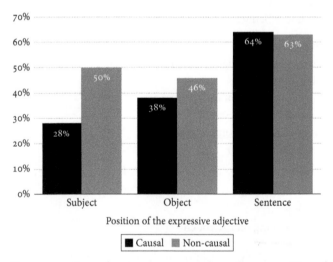

FIGURE 4.1 Mean proportions of sentence responses depending on position of the EA and causality of subject

Source: Data from Frazier, Dillon, & Clifton (2014).

---

[18] Frazier, Dillon, & Clifton (2014) do not specify how many of those target the subject and how many the object.

sentence position, the subjects give 86% subject responses in causal and 42% in non-causal cases. This is illustrated in Figure 4.2.

Having presented Frazier, Dillon, & Clifton (2014) experiment and their main results, it is now time to discuss whether their findings really support their two hypothesis. I think, the culprit hypothesis makes sense insofar as it is highly plausible that considerations about whether the subject may be considered a causal agent or not may very well influence the construal of the target of an EA, if the speech act hypothesis were actually true. But I think that it is exactly this hypothesis that is, on the one hand, not entirely supported by their data, insofar as their results are perfectly compatible with an alternative hypothesis to be discussed soon. On the other hand, the speech act hypothesis just makes wrong empirical predictions. Let us first explore this second criticism, based on which we will develop an alternative approach, after which we check how the data presented by Frazier, Dillon, & Clifton (2014) can be accounted for by that alternative approach.

4.5 The role of syntax

The speech act hypothesis leads to a purely pragmatic approach to the interpretation of EA which is almost completely free from structural considerations (only the pragmatic reasoning about why the speaker chose to put an EA where she put it keeps some structural aspects). This is pretty powerful and unconstrained. But is the interpretation of EAs really that free and independent of their syntactic environment?

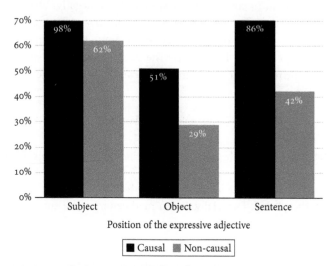

FIGURE 4.2 Proportion of subject responses *given that sentence response was not given,* depending on position of the EA and causality of subject

Source: Data from Frazier, Dillon, & Clifton (2014).

I think it is not and that there are actual structural aspects that constrain the interpretation of EAs.

4.5.1 *Syntactic constraints*

First note that Frazier, Dillon, & Clifton (2014) only test EAs in rather simple syntactic context. In order to see the problem the speech act hypothesis faces, consider the following example in which an EA occurs in an embedded clause.

(4.103) Peter hat erzählt, dass der Hund den **verdammten** Kuchen
        Peter has told that the dog the damn cake
        gefressen hat.
        eaten has
        'Peter said that the dog ate the damn cake.'

What readings does an utterance of (4.103) give rise to? First, we can observe that inside the embedded clause, the EA can either target the object DP in which it occurs or the entire embedded clause itself. Speaking informally and ignoring the descriptive dimension, we can say that (4.103) can express a negative attitude toward the cake itself or to the fact that the dog ate the cake.[19]

(4.104) a. ☹(the cake)
       b. ☹(the dog ate the cake)

These are two different readings which, again, are felicitous in most likely different contexts. For instance, if the speaker dislikes the cake, she may be happy about the fact that the dog ate it. In contrast, if the speaker has a negative attitude toward the fact that the dog ate the cake, she may have a very positive picture of the cake.

The fact that an utterance of (4.103) allows for these two readings is very much in line with the speech acts hypothesis. The EA, performing a speech act that is independent of the remainder of the utterance, can freely target the object DP or the entire embedded sentence.

(4.105)   — verdammt

Peter hat erzählt ↳ [CP dass der Hund ↳ [DP den Kuchen]gefressen hat]]

However, and this is the crucial observation, the EA inside the embedded clause cannot target everything. Especially, it can neither target the subject of the matrix

---

[19] There is the question of whether the negative attitude is the speaker's attitude or Peter's; i.e. whether we have speaker linking or not. I think both readings are available, but I leave that discussion unaddressed at this point. It does not bear anything on the point I am making in the main text. For a discussion of the (semantic) embeddability of expressives, see Gutzmann 2017; Harris and Potts 2009a,b.

clause nor the entire sentence itself. That is, an utterance of (4.103) *does not* have the following two readings.

(4.106)   a. *☺(Peter)
          b. *☺(Peter said that the dog ate the cake)

That is, (4.103) cannot be used to express a negative attitude just toward the fact that Peter said that the dog ate the cake. Nor can it be used to express one's own disregard of Peter. If this is true, then there is a constraint at work to the effect than an EA cannot target something outside the embedded sentence. This, of course, would be a structural constraint, which in turn would mean that syntactic aspects are relevant for the calculation of the interpretational target of an EA. This is at odds with the speech act hypothesis. Moreover, the purely pragmatic approach, while perfectly able to generate the readings in (4.104), is unable to exclude readings like (4.106); it even predicts that they are available.

4.5.2 *Experimental evidence for syntactic barriers*

Even though my intuitions—which I checked with a lot of informants—are pretty clear in this respect, I conducted a small empirical pilot study in order to check whether syntactic embedding actually has a kind of blocking effect on the semantic interpretation of EAs. We tested sixty undergraduate students using a Latin square design with four lists, each containing fifteen critical items, along with thirty-two fillers. The design is similar to the one used by Frazier, Dillon, & Clifton (2014), but we use simple questionnaires instead of reading at a computer terminal. The items vary along two factors: embedding (EA in embedded or unembedded clause) and position (EA in subject or object position).[20] The following examples illustrate the four variants of one item.

(4.107)   **Simple items**
          a. Heute Nacht hat der **verdammte** Nachbar den Rasen gemäht.
             (subject position)
          b. Heute Nacht hat der Nachbar den **verdammten** Rasen gemäht.
             (object position)
          'Last night, the ⟨damn⟩ neighbor mowed the ⟨damn⟩ lawn.'

          Question: *Was bewertet der Sprecher am wahrscheinlichsten negativ?* 'What does the speaker most likely judge as negative?'

---

[20] Because there is no sentence position available for the embedded cases, we did not test the sentence position.

    i. *den Nachbarn* ('the neighbor')
    ii. *den Rasen* ('the lawn')
    iii. *dass der Nachbar den Rasen gemäht hat*
        ('that the neighbor mowed the lawn')

(4.108) **Embedded items**

    a. **Susanne hat gesagt**, dass der **verdammte** Nachbar den Rasen gemäht hat.
       (subject position)
    b. **Susanne hat gesagt**, dass der Nachbar den **verdammten** Rasen gemäht
       hat.
       (object position)
       'Susanne said that the ⟨damn⟩ neighbor mowed the ⟨damn⟩ lawn.'

    Question: *Was bewertet der Sprecher am wahrscheinlichsten negativ?* 'What
    does the speaker most likely judge as negative?'

    i. *den Nachbarn* ('the neighbor')
    ii. *den Rasen* ('the lawn')
    iii. *dass Susanne gesagt hat, dass der Nachbar den Rasen gemäht hat*
        ('that Susanne said that the neighbor mowed the lawn')

We investigated the collected responses with respect to the question of whether syntactic embedding has an effect on the likelihood that the subjects choose the sentence interpretation. The prediction is that syntactic embedding should lead to a significant decrease in sentence interpretation. This prediction is confirmed by our data. In the unembedded case, the EA in subject position received 95 sentence responses compared to 120 subject or object responses. When in object position, the EA got 77 sentence responses compared to 113 subject or object responses. This is illustrated in Figure 4.3(a). Compare this to the embedded case. Here, the sentence responses for the subject position dropped down to 23, while the subject/object interpretation was chosen 182 times. A similar picture arises for EAs in object position, for which 29 sentence responses were given, compared to 176 subject/object interpretations. See Figure 4.3(b).

We analyzed the results using a mixed-effects logistic regression model. The model computes the likelihood for a switch from a non-sentence position to a sentence-level interpretation. It contains random intercepts for subjects and items in order to "correct" for possible different preferences of subjects and items, since the data points are not completely separate from each other as several data points come from the same source. The results are given in Table 4.2.

The intercept represents the starting level (subject position, unembedded). We find an effect for embedding: syntactically embedding an EA significantly reduces the likelihood of a sentence-level interpretation (beta $= -2.2536$, SE $= 0.2916$; $p < 0.001$). In addition, we also find an effect for position: if the EA is part of the syntactic

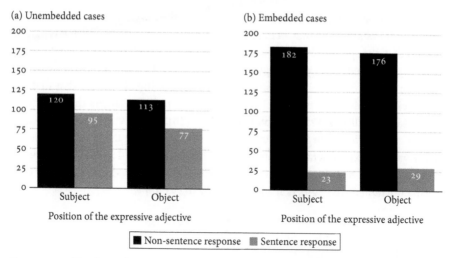

FIGURE 4.3 Number of sentence vs. non-sentence responses depending on embedding and position

TABLE 4.2 Parameters of mixed model, situation responses, syntactic embedding

	Estimate	*Std. error*	*z value*	*Pr(> |z|)*	
(Intercept)	−0.2627	0.2515	−1.045	0.296	
syn.embedded	−2.2536	0.2916	−7.728	1.09e−14	***
object	0.8819	0.2252	3.916	9.02e−05	***
syn.embedded : object	−0.4547	0.3860	−1.178	0.239	

object, the likelihood of a sentence-level interpretation rises significantly (beta = 0.8819, SE = 0.2252; $p < 0.001$). The interaction between embedding and position is not significant though (beta = −0.4547, SE = 0.3860, $p = 0.23$), which can be interpreted such that the blocking effect of embedding does not differ for the two positions. Overall, we can conclude that the syntactical embedding of an EA has a very strong blocking effect. The experiment thus confirms the intuitive assessment of the (un)available readings for examples like (4.103).

4.5.3 No argument lowering

The fact that syntactic embedding poses a barrier for getting the widest-scope reading of an EA contradicts the speech act hypothesis. If anything, the main-clause level interpretation should be the easiest to get if the EA really did perform an independent speech act. However, there is an additional, also severe problem for the speech act hypothesis. Recall that in our original investigation of the readings an EA can give rise to, we attested that they can lead to what we called *argument extension*, which described the observation that an EA can target a larger constituent which it is part of. Beyond that, the speech act hypothesis would also let us predict cases of what may be called *argument narrowing* and *argument hopping*. The former would be the case if an EA in sentence position targets only the subject (or the object, for that matter). The latter would be the case if an EA in, say, object position targets the subject; or vice versa. According to Frazier, Dillon, & Clifton (2014) these two processes are also possible, in addition to argument extension. But is this really the case? At least the data from their experiment seems to support this assumption. However, let us again go through some reasoning to see whether the conclusion they draw from their data is really warranted. To begin, consider the following example.

(4.109)   **Verdammt!** Der Hund hat den Kuchen gefressen!
   damn   *the*   *dog*   *has*   *the*   *cake*   *eaten*
   Damn! The dog ate the cake.

At first sight, an utterance of (4.109) has a reading under which the EA in sentence-external position targets *the dog*, in addition to the reading under which it targets the entire proposition.

(4.110)   a.   ☹(the dog ate the cake)
   b.   ☹(the dog)

The second reading would then be a case of *argument narrowing*, since an EA in a higher position targets only a subpart of its argument. Nevertheless, the important intuition is that, even if one interprets (4.109) in a way in which *verdammte* ('damn') expresses a negative attitude toward the dog, the sentence-level interpretation is nonetheless still active. This can be tested by building a variant of (4.109) in which the sentence-level reading is excluded. This can be achieved, for instance, by inserting a sentence adverb of positive evaluation into the clause that would block a sentential reading. If a pure below-sentence-level interpretation of the EA were possible, such a sentence would be felicitous. However, if the sentence-level interpretation is still active, then the resulting sentence should be infelicitous or even sound contradictory. And this is indeed the case.

(4.111)   #**Verdammt.** Zum Glück hat der Hund den Kuchen gefressen.
   damn   *to.the* *luck*   *has*   *the*   *dog*   *the*   *cake*   *eaten*
   '# Damn. Luckily, the dog has eaten the cake.'

What is important here is that, according to the speech act hypothesis, (4.111) should have readings under which it is felicitous, namely those in which the EA targets just the subject or just the object, but not the entire sentence. For instance, if somebody dislikes the dog and has a vicious plan which involves the dog eating the cake so that the dog gets into trouble, then an utterance of (4.111) should be felicitous, just as (4.112) would be where the EA actually appears on the object.

(4.112) Zum Glück hat der **verdammte** Hund den Kuchen gefressen.
         to.the luck has the damn dog the cake eaten
         'Luckily, the damn dog ate the cake.'

However, given a special context like the one just mentioned, (4.112) does not sound contradictory at all, in contrast to (4.111). Similar considerations apply to the alternative of having the EA targeting the object. Under the speech act hypothesis, an utterance of (4.111) should not only have a felicitous subject-related reading, but also the corresponding object reading. This time, assume a context in which the speaker feels negatively about the cake; maybe it is really big and she is eating from it for the last three days and wants to be done with it. In such a context, an object-internal EA is perfectly acceptable, as witnessed by the following example.

(4.113) **Zum Glück** hat der Hund (endlich) den **verdammten** Kuchen
         to.the luck has the dog finally the damn cake
         gefressen.
         eaten
         'Luckily, the damn dog (finally) ate the cake.'

I added *endlich* ('finally') to make the intended reading stronger, but it can be left off easily. What is crucial again is that an utterance of (4.111) does not have a reading like (4.113), where the EA targets just the object. That is, in both cases, the sentence-level interpretation is still active. This provides a direct explanation for why (4.111) is infelicitous: the sentence-external EA evaluates the proposition as negative, while the speaker adverbial *zum Glück* ('luckily') does evaluate it as positive. Hence the feeling of contradiction.[21] The conclusion, hence, is that cases in which an EA in sentence position seems to take scope inside the sentence and seem to target only the subject or only the object are not really cases of argument narrowing. Instead, they still receive a sentence-level interpretation that remains active all the time. However, this does not exclude the possibility that due to the sentential reading of the EA, a pragmatic inference is drawn that the speaker has a negative attitude toward the subject, or object, as well. A strong argument in favor of this is the observation that such additional inferences also happen with non-expressive evaluative expressions. For instance, with *leider* ('unfortunately') in the following example.

---

[21] It should be noted that I use the term "contradiction" here in a loose, non-technical sense, since we are talking about one descriptive and one expressive content here. And if expressive content is non-truth-conditional, as I argued in Gutzmann 2015b, following Kaplan (1999), we cannot use standard definitions of contradiction. Conceptually, the case is clear: a descriptive and an expressive proposition contradict each other, if in all contexts, in which the former is true, the latter is infelicitous and vice versa.

(4.114) **Leider**   hat der Hund den Kuchen gefressen.
      unfortunately has the dog   the   cake   eaten
      'Unfortunately, the dog ate the cake.'

First note that such descriptive adverbs cannot be used with DPs at all, as they are adverbs and hence cannot be used as nominal attributes. And even if one uses an expression that has an attributive counterpart, like *unglücklich* ('unlucky'), it does not get the intended reading as expressing a negative evaluation of the situation.[22]

(4.115) a. *der **leider**   b. %der **unglückliche**
        the unfortunately   *the unhappy*
        Hund   Hund
        dog   *dog*

Despite the inability of *leider* to target the subject, or object, an utterance of (4.114) may give rise to the implicature that the speaker feels negatively about the dog, likely because it was the dog who ate the cake and thus caused the situation. This would actually be very much in accordance with the culprit hypothesis. Therefore, it may very well be the case that subjects, if asked, focus on this derived inference, especially if allowed only a single choice. That is, if subjects were asked questions like those in Frazier, Dillon, & Clifton (2014) experiment for a test item like (4.114), one would likely get a mix of sentence- and subject-level interpretation, which would be just the same as for the original case that involved an EA instead of an ordinary adverb.

To sum up these observations, alleged cases of argument lowering from sentence-level position to subject or object interpretation really is not a case of a high EA targeting some subpart of its argument, but rather it is a pragmatic inference drawn *in addition* to a still active sentence-level interpretation. But what is it about what I called argument hopping? These are cases in which an EA targets a different constituent that neither dominates the EA nor is dominated by it. Cases like these are seemingly observed in Frazier, Dillon, & Clifton (2014) experiment. For instance, they attest cases in which subjects interpret an EA in object position to nevertheless target the subject of the sentence (see Figure 4.2). This can again be illustrated by our standard example.

(4.116) Gestern   hat der Hund den **verdammten** Kuchen gefressen.
      yesterday has the dog   the   damn   cake   eaten
      'Yesterday, the dog ate the damn cake.'

That is, a sentence like (4.116) does not only have the local object and global sentence-level interpretation of the EA, as in (4.117a) and (4.117b), but also seems to allow for the subject-related reading in (4.117c).

---

[22] I use the "%" here to indicate that the sentence cannot have the relevant reading.

(4.117) a. ☺(the cake)
      b. ☺(the dog ate the cake)
      c. ☺(the dog)

Again, we should ask ourselves if an interpretation of (4.116) along the lines of
(4.117c) really is a case of argument hopping or whether it is rather an indirect
reinterpretation, like I argued to be the case for argument lowering. I think the general
gist is the same for argument hopping, but the derivation of the hopped interpretation
involves one step more. I assume the following derivation of the subject interpretation
of (4.116). The EA in object position receives a sentence-level interpretation (which is
a case of argument extension). From this sentence-level interpretation, which remains
active, the subject interpretation is then derived pragmatically. That is, semantically, a
sentence like (4.116), where the EA is in object position, only has the object (4.117a)
and the sentence-level reading (4.117b). If the sentence-level reading is chosen, the
subject reading in (4.117c) may be derived additionally. Schematically:

(4.118)   *Yesterday, the dog ate the damn cake.*
      ≈ ☺(the dog ate the cake)   (argument extension)
      +>The speaker is angry about the dog.   (implicature)

That is, the argumentation is almost the same as for an EA in sentence position, expect
that the EA starts out in object position and receives the sentence-level interpretation
via argument extension, before the implicature targeting the subject is derived. As in
the case of argument lowering, this way of thinking predicts that argument hopping
should be hard to get if the sentence-level interpretation is semantically blocked. This
can be tested with examples like the one we mention in (4.113), which I repeat here
for convenience.

(4.119) **Zum Glück** hat der Hund (endlich) den **verdammten** Kuchen
      to.the luck   *has the dog*   *finally*   *the*   *damn*   *cake*
      gefressen.
      eaten
      'Luckily, the damn dog (finally) ate the cake.'

The addition of the adverbial *zum Glück* ('luckily') semantically blocks the sentence-
level interpretation. Crucially, an utterance of (4.113) only has the local object interpretation. It cannot be interpreted as expressing just a negative attitude toward the
dog. This is a prediction from the argumentation given above, namely that a subject
interpretation of an EA in object position is only possible via argument extension to
the sentence-level. However, this is blocked in (4.119) and thus only the object reading
remains as a viable interpretation. To conclude, what appears to be argument hopping
is a pragmatic inference based on a (still active) sentence-level interpretation of a
DP internal EA. However, the speech act hypothesis predicts real cases of argument

hopping and hence, (4.119) should have a reading under which it is synonymous to (4.112), which I repeat here as well.

(4.120) Zum   Glück hat der   **verdammte** Hund den Kuchen gefressen.
         to.the has   the damn dog   luck the cake   eaten
         'Luckily, the damn dog has eaten the cake.'

This, however, is not the case and the alleged cases of argument hopping do not provide support for the speech act hypothesis. Quite the contrary. The fact that argument hopping is blocked if the sentence-level reading is not viable show that EAs are not as independent as the speech act hypothesis assumes them to be. Instead, the observed constraints on the displaced interpretation of EAs shows that there are structural restrictions at work. There is only one way in which EAs can look for a place to be interpreted. Up. Let us call this the HEADS UP! generalization.

(4.121) HEADS UP!
         a. EAs have to look for a place to be interpreted.
         b. They can only look up.

Together with the syntactic blocking effect we observed when EAs are put into embedded clauses, this speaks against a completely free and structurally unconstrained, purely pragmatic approach, like the one suggested by Frazier, Dillon, & Clifton (2014). Instead, the data hints at a syntactic underpinning of the mechanism that drives the interpretation of EAs. Can the syntactic approaches that attempt to represent aspects of the utterance context in the syntax, which are briefly discussed at the end of Chapter 3, capture these syntactic constraints? I do not think so, because they can only capture the relation certain expressions can have to the discourse participants. That is, maybe they can provide an approach to speaker linking. But in case of argument extension, the relevant syntactic relation holds between the EA and some larger, overt constituent that contains the EA and does not represent the speaker or addressee. Therefore, we need to develop a new syntactic approach to argument extension, which is the aim of the next section.

4.6 A syntactic approach to the interpretation of EAs

The key to get a grip on the flexible though not completely unconstrained interpretation of EAs lies in the observation that the flexibility regarding their target only goes in one direction, namely upwards. That is, we can get a sentence-level interpretation from the subject or object position, but not vice versa. Nor can an EA in object position semantically be interpreted as just targeting the subject nor can an EA in subject position just target the object. In order to account for this restriction in direction, I employ the syntactic mechanism of agreement laid out in Chapter 3. After introducing the necessary assumptions to make the agreement work for our purposes, I will show how an agreement-based approach to the mismatch between where an ES is realized and where it gets interpreted can also account for the observed structural restrictions. In addition, it makes further empirical predictions that seem to pan out.

4.6.1 An agreement-based solution

As discussed in Chapter 3, I adopt the unidirectional, upward-looking version of agreement championed by Zeijlstra (2012), which I labeled ↑Agree$_i$.

(4.122) **↑Agree$_i$:**   (Zeijlstra 2012: 514)
      α can ↑Agree$_i$ with β iff:
      a. α carries at least one uninterpretable feature and β carries a matching interpretable feature.
      b. β c-commands α.
      c. β is the closest goal to α.

In the context of the HEADS UP! generalization from (4.121), the definition of upward-looking ↑Agree$_i$ is a perfect fit, as it involves uninterpretable stuff (the α) that looks up for some place of interpretation (the β). It is therefore rather straightforward to employ the ↑Agree$_i$-mechanism for the case of EAs by making the following assumptions. First, I assume that the actual interpretation of the EA is not provided by the EA itself. Rather it is a syntactic *expressivity feature, Ex,* which is what is actually is semantically interpreted. However, the operator only provides the place of interpretation, so to speak, rather than the content. The content itself is instead realized by the EA. This renders the case of EAs parallel to various cases discussed in Chapter 3. Consider, for instance, the interpretation of tense in German again. In this case, the interpretation of tense happens at the TP-level in T°. However, how tense is interpreted is not determined by T°, but rather by the features of the finite predicate in V°, which is located lower in the syntactic structure. To use more formal syntactic parlance, it is assumed that T° carries an interpretational tense feature, iT, which does not, however, come with a value. In contrast, V°, as the place of the finite verb, does carry a morpho-syntactic tense feature, like past tense, for instance. However, this feature is not interpreted at the lower VP-level.

(4.123)   'Maria slept.'

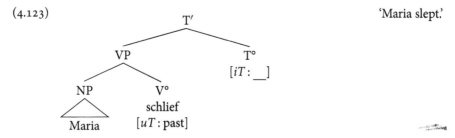

This configuration—an interpretable, unvalued feature in T° and a matching uninterpretable, but valued feature in V° which is c-commanded by T°—matches the requirement of ↑Agree$_i$ment as defined in (5.125). Hence, T° and V° can ↑Agree$_i$

with each other, which leads to sharing the tense feature of V° with T° and marking the uninterpretable tense feature of V° for deletion under ↑Agree$_i$ment.

(4.124)   'Maria slept Maya was sleeping.'

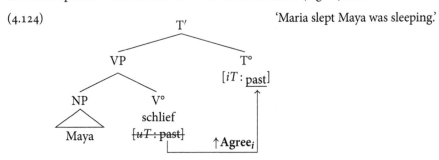

What is crucial here is that with respect to tense, we can observe a similar mismatch between syntactic realization (at the finite verb) and semantic interpretation (at the TP-level) as we saw for EAs. And given the assumptions made above, EAs and the assumed expressivity feature are in a completely analogous configuration. Therefore, just like ↑Agree$_i$ helps us to connect the place of realization with the place of interpretation in case of tense, ↑Agree$_i$ gives us a way to connect the EA to its locus of interpretation. For this, I assume that the expressivity feature, *Ex*, can appear in different head positions where it is interpreted, but not yet valued. It is the EA, which appears in a lower position, that provides a valued version of the expressivity feature, which cannot be interpreted though. To see how this works, let us begin with the case in which an EA in subject position targets the subject. For this, it is sufficient to just look at the DP.

(4.125)   der verdammte Hund
        'the damn dog'

For a DP like this, we get the configuration in (4.126). Consulting the definition in (5.125) again, we see that the two *Ex*-features in (4.126) fulfill the conditions for ↑Agree$_i$. Therefore, as illustrated in (4.127), the interpretable version of the expressivity feature in D° can receive its value from the EA, whereas the feature, which is uninterpretable at the EA, is marked for deletion.

(4.126)

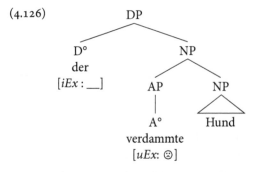

(4.127)

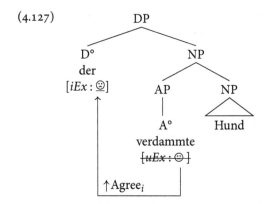

The mechanism of ↑Agree$_i$ment thus provides us a means to link the EA, which realizes the expressive attitude, and the higher place of interpretation. Assuming that the expressivity feature cannot only be present in D°, but also in C°, we can get a sentence-level interpretation in a similar way. That is, for a sentence like (4.128), we get the ↑Agree$_i$ment configuration in (4.129).

(4.128)   Gestern   hat   der   verdammte   Hund   den   Kuchen   gefressen.
         yesterday   has   the   damn   dog   the   cake   eaten
         'Yesterday, the damn dog ate the cake.'

(4.129)

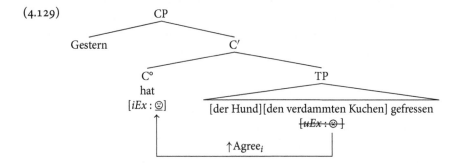

If we compare the two structures in (4.126) and (4.129), we notice that the only difference between them is the placement of the interpretable *iEx* feature that matches the *uEx* feature of the EA. In the case of the subject interpretation, *iEx* is in the corresponding D°, whereas it is C° in the case of the sentence-level interpretation.

(4.130)   [$_{CP}$ Gestern hat der Hund [$_{DP}$ den$_{[iEx]}$ verdammten$_{[uEx]}$ Kuchen] gefressen]

(4.131)   [$_{CP}$ Gestern hat$_{[iEx]}$ der Hund [$_{DP}$ den verdammten$_{[uEx]}$ Kuchen] gefressen]

Under this agreement-based approach to the interpretation of EAs, the difference between the subject and sentence-level interpretation of (7.2) comes down to a syntactic ambiguity, since the different placement of the *iEx* feature has to be considered to be two distinct syntactic configurations, which, however, do not lead to any detectable difference in overt structure.

Now that we have seen an approach based on the syntactic mechanism of ↑Agree$_i$ment, let us investigate this approach in more detail and see how it can account for the structural constraints on the interpretation of EAs, which lead us to consider a syntactic approach in the first place.

4.6.2 EAs can only look up

The discussion regarding the mismatch between the syntactic placement of an EA and its semantic interpretation carried out in this chapter revealed that this mismatch is not of the "anything goes" kind (as assumed by Frazier, Dillon, & Clifton (2014) speech act hypothesis), but that it is rather constrained. This was formulated in the informal HEADS UP! generalization in (4.121). The ↑Agree$_i$ approach directly accounts for this restriction. Recall that in the definition in (5.125), only one configuration licenses ↑Agree$_i$; namely precisely that in which the interpretable feature c-commands the uninterpretable feature and thus is in a higher position. In case of EAs, this leads to what I called argument extension, as it is already illustrated in the two configurations in (4.130) and (4.131). In contrast, argument lowering, which would correspond to an agreement configuration in which the interpretable feature is below the uninterpretable one, is not a viable configuration for ↑Agree$_i$. Similar considerations apply to cases of argument hopping in which the interpretable and uninterpretable features do not stand in a c-command relation, irrespective of whether the hopping is supposed to be to the left (4.132c) or right (4.132d).

(4.132) a. $[iF \ \ldots \ [uF]]$ *argument extension* ✓
         b. $[uF \ \ldots \ [iF]]$ *argument lowering* ✗
         c. $[iF] \ \ldots \ [uF]$ *left-hopping* ✗
         d. $[uF] \ \ldots \ [iF]$ *right-hopping* ✗

That is, the employment of ↑Agree$_i$ as the basis for building the link between the EA and its place of interpretation directly captures the uni-directionality of the syntax–semantics mismatch.

4.6.3 Syntactic blocking

One of the main arguments against Frazier, Dillon, & Clifton (2014) pragmatics-only approach, according to which EAs basically ignore the syntactic structure of the sentence they occur in altogether, was the observation that EAs cannot scope out of an embedded clause. That is, if occurring in a DP in an embedded clause, they can neither target a DP in the main clause nor the entire sentence itself. To repeat the data, an utterance of (4.103), which I repeat here with a new number, does not have all the reading in (4.133).

(4.133) Peter hat erzählt, dass der Hund den **verdammten** Kuchen
Peter has told that the dog the damn cake
gefressen hat.
eaten has
'Peter said that the dog ate the damn cake.'

(4.134)   a. ☺(the cake)
      b. ☺(the dog ate the cake)
      c. *☺(Peter)
      d. *☺(Peter said that the dog ate the cake)

The impossible reading in (4.134c) is ruled out by the constraint that EAs can search for their locus of interpretation in a strictly upwards fashion, as defined in the conditions for ↑Agree$_i$ in (5.125). However, the reading in (4.134d) under which the EA targets the entire utterance, is unavailable as well, but the configuration of features that would lead to such an interpretation concurs with the definition of ↑Agree$_i$. The EA in the embedded clause carries an uninterpretable *Ex*-feature that is matched by an interpretable feature in the left periphery of the main clause.

(4.135)   [$_{CP}$ Peter hat$_{[iEx]}$ erzählt, [$_{CP}$ dass der Hund den **verdammten**$_{[uEx]}$ Kuchen gefressen hat]]

However, this configuration nevertheless does not seem to license ↑Agree$_i$ment between the higher *iEx* in C° and the EA in the embedded clause. So how can this reading then be blocked? Given that accounting for this structural blocking effect was one of the major reasons to develop the syntactic approach in the first place, there should be some better solution that is not just stipulated. Such an explanation is indeed available. As laid out in Chapter 3, CPs are relevant for agreement and that they constitute "barriers" for agreement phenomena. Following this line of thinking, the intervening CP-boundary thus is the reason for why the EA in the embedded clause cannot ↑Agree$_i$ with an assumed *iEx*-feature in the main clause.

(4.136)   [$_{CP}$ Peter hat $_{[iEx]}$ der erzählt, [$_{CP}$ dass der Hund den verdammten$_{[uEx]}$

Kuchen gefressen hat.]]

In a configuration like (4.136), the embedded CP is shipped to the interfaces before it is merged with the embedding predicate and thus the uninterpretable *uEx* in the embedded CP remains unchecked and thus violates the principle of radical interpretability discussed in Chapter 3.

4.6.4 *Multiple agreement*

Another interesting prediction made by the ↑Agree$_i$ment analysis of EAs is that it lets us expect that there are instances of multiple agreement with EAs. Recall from the discussion in Chapter 3, that multiple agreement phenomena happen if an expression bearing an interpretable feature agrees with multiple expressions downstream that all carry the corresponding uninterpretable feature. For illustration, consider the following example from Italian given by Zeijlstra (2012: 519).

(4.137) Gianni non ha   detto   niente a   nessuno
         Gianni NEG *said* *n-thing* *to*   *n-body*
         'Gianni didn't say anything to anybody'   (Italian)

(4.138) [Gianni non$_{[iNeg]}$ -ha [ditto niente$_{[uNeg]}$ a nessuno$_{[uNeg]}$]]

The crucial observation is that only the highest negation bears the interpretable negative feature, while the lower n-words are all uninterpreted.

   A very similar configuration can be built with EAs. Assume that we have an EA in subject as well as in object position, but no interpretable *iEx*-feature in the respective D-heads. Instead, we only have an *iEX* in C^0. Such a configuration would lead to a case of multiple agreement where both *uEx*-features of the two EAs agree with the higher, interpretable feature.

(4.139) a. Gestern   hat der **verdammte** Hund den **verdammten** Kuchen
            yesterday *has* *the* *damn*   *dog*   *the*   *damn*   *cake*
            gefressen.
            eaten
            'Yesterday, the damn dog ate the damn cake.'

(4.140) [$_{CP}$ Gestern[hat $_{[iEx]}$ [$_{DP}$ der verdammte$_{[uEx]}$ Hund] [$_{DP}$ den verdammten$_{[uEx]}$

         Kuchen] gefressen.]]

Given this possible configuration, the ↑Agree$_i$ment-based approach predicts that a sentence like (4.139) has a reading under which it only expresses a negative attitude toward the fact that the dog ate the cake, and no such attitude toward the dog or the cake. And there is such a reading. Maybe it is not that easy to get with the chosen example, since one tends to infer a negative attitude toward the dog, but that there is such a reading can be highlighted by using a different example which is completely analogous to (4.139) in its syntactic configuration, but does not have a "causal" subject.

(4.141) Gestern   ist mir die **verdammte** Flasche auf meinen
         yesterday *is* *me* *the* *damn*   *bottle*   *on* *my*
         verdammten Fuß   gefallen.
         damn   *foot* *fallen*
         'Yesterday, the damn bottle fell on my damn foot.'

For this sentence, the reading in which the DP-internal EAs are both interpreted at the CP-level is actually the most likely one. That is, the predication that followed from the ↑Agree₁ment approach is confirmed. Interestingly, the possibility to have more than one EA which all contribute to the sentence-level interpretation perfectly fits the common assumption, sketched in Chapter 2, that expressives are *repeatable* (Potts 2007: 167, 182f.).

Before we go on to another prediction, let me stress that the sentence-only interpretation is of course not the only reading of (4.139a), nor of (4.141). The approach developed so far predicts that there are at least three more readings (ignoring any intermediate TP-level interpretations). Both EAs may be interpreted in their local DP, or the EA in subject position is interpreted at the sentence-level and the EA in object is interpreted at its local DP, or vice versa. These differences all come down to the question of where the interpretable *iEx*-features are located. The following three examples illustrate this. Below each one, I give the two resulting expressive attitudes that the structures respectively give rise to.

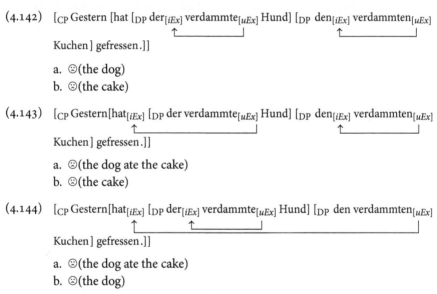

(4.142)   [CP Gestern [hat [DP der[iEx] verdammte[uEx] Hund] [DP den[iEx] verdammten[uEx]

Kuchen] gefressen.]]

   a. ☺(the dog)
   b. ☺(the cake)

(4.143)   [CP Gestern[hat[iEx] [DP der verdammte[uEx] Hund] [DP den[iEx] verdammten[uEx]

Kuchen] gefressen.]]

   a. ☺(the dog ate the cake)
   b. ☺(the cake)

(4.144)   [CP Gestern[hat[iEx] [DP der[iEx] verdammte[uEx] Hund] [DP den verdammten[uEx]

Kuchen] gefressen.]]

   a. ☺(the dog ate the cake)
   b. ☺(the dog)

All these configurations seem to be actual readings of (4.139a) and thus the predictions of the theoretical analysis are confirmed by the data.

4.7 Semantic interpretation

Up to this point, I did not really show how the expressive meaning of EAs composes with the rest of the sentence. Now that we have the syntactic approach in place,

I can get more explicit about that. One important advantage of the agreement-based analysis presented here is that we do not have to just take the mysterious syntax-semantics mismatch as a given (as I did in Gutzmann 2015b). Instead we can have a more transparent and direct mapping between the syntax and semantics of EAs. In order to spell this out explicitly, I assume that checked uninterpretable features are just ignored in the semantics; that is, they receive no semantic value.[23] In contrast, interpretable features receive a semantic counterpart, which in turn depends on the value the features have or did receive during the derivation. Let us start with the DP-level interpretation of a DP-internal EA. After ↑Agree$_i$ between D and the EA, we arrive at the following syntactic structure.

(4.145)   [$_{DP}$ [$_{D°}$ der$_{[iEx:☺]}$] [$_{NP}$ verdammte$_{[uEx:☺]}$ Hund]]

In the following, I will sketch how pure EAs are interpreted and how this can help to derive some of the particular syntactic properties discussed in Section 4.2.2. After that, I will turn to mixed EAs, as discussed in Section 4.2.3. As we will see, they do not behave as strangely as their pure sisters, which can be traced back to the fact that they do have actual semantic content.

4.7.1 *The interpretation of pure EAs*

I assume that the semantic content of a pure EA like *verdammt* ('damn') as in (4.145) is an identity function on properties, while the uninterpretable feature is simply ignored at the semantic level. That is, for the NP, we get the following semantics, which is just the same as for the bare *dog*.

(4.146)

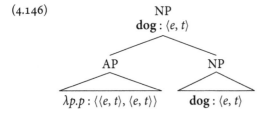

For the interpretation of the interpretable Ex-feature, I have to make a few decisions for how to represent it in the semantics. We know that the expressive feature has to take the entire DP as its argument, since, under the reading we are after, the expressive targets the individual dog as referred to by the DP. That is, the definite article must first combine with the NP in order to provide the correct result. There are various ways to achieve this. First, we can just assume that the expressivity feature actually applies to the DP, so that it effectively acts as an adjunct on the semantic level.

---

[23] An alternative implementation would be that checked uninterpretable features are represented by identity functions in the semantics.

(4.147)

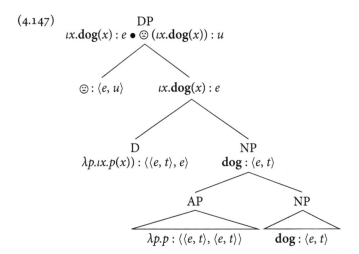

However, this would lead to a somewhat dissatisfying mismatch between the syntactic structure and its semantic interpretation, because the definiteness feature of D and the expressivity feature that is also located there are split into two non-sister nodes, while in the syntax, they belong closer together. An alternative that respects the syntactic structure more closely is to assign a type-raised type to the expressivity feature so that it combines with the determiner first, but still gives the desired output. The problem with this "solution" is that it would be rather arbitrary. Instead, a more general and straightforward solution is to use functional composition as a mode of composition.

(4.148) **Functional composition**

If $\alpha : \langle \sigma, \tau \rangle$ and $\beta : \langle \tau, \rho \rangle$, then $\lambda x_\sigma.\beta(\alpha(x)) : \langle \sigma, \rho \rangle$

What functional composition does is chaining two functions together if the output of the first function matches the input of the second one. With this, we can combine the definiteness function with the expressive function while keeping the type of the expressive function at type $\langle e, u \rangle$.

(4.149)

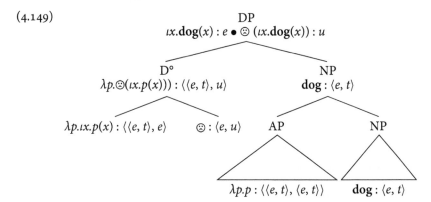

Regardless of whether we chose this semantic representation or the one from (4.147), the interpretation of the DP would be the same. On the truth-conditional level it refers to an individual dog, while on the use-conditional level, it expresses a negative attitude toward that dog. If we compose this with the rest of the sentence, we get truth- and use-conditions along the following lines, which is what we were after.

(4.150)   a. $[\![$*Gestern hat der verdammte Hund auf das Sofa gepinkelt*$]\!]^t$
              $= 1$, if the dog peed on the couch yesterday.
          b. $[\![$*Gestern hat der verdammte Hund auf das Sofa gepinkelt*$]\!]^u$
              $= \checkmark$, if the speaker has a negative attitude toward the dog.

For the sentence level interpretation, the derivation proceeds very similarly. The crucial difference is that the expressivity feature in C^0 is represented by an expressive function that takes a propositional argument instead of an individual. That is, the [*iEx*]-feature in C^0 is of type $\langle\langle s,t\rangle, u\rangle$ instead of type $\langle e, u\rangle$.

The semantic analysis of the proposed syntactic structure can explain many of the observed non-standard properties of EAs that were mentioned in Section 4.2.2. First, recall from example (4.26) and (4.27), that pure EAs seem to appear in the positive form only: comparative and superlative morphology is excluded. This also holds for degree words like *sehr* ('very'). This is directly implemented by the assumption made above that pure EAs receive a semantic representation as an identity function on properties. Since degree morphemes usually are assigned a semantic representation of type $\langle\langle d, \langle e, t\rangle\rangle, \langle e, t\rangle\rangle$, they cannot take the EA as their argument, because it is of type $\langle\langle e, t\rangle, \langle e, t\rangle\rangle$.[24] Therefore, if we try to combine a pure EA with a degree expression like *sehr*, this will lead to a type clash in the semantics.[25]

(4.151)   *sehr   verdammt
          very   damn

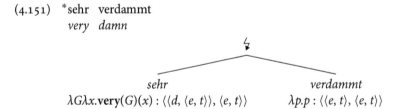

sehr   verdammt
$\lambda G\lambda x.\mathbf{very}(G)(x) : \langle\langle d, \langle e, t\rangle\rangle, \langle e, t\rangle\rangle$ $\lambda p.p : \langle\langle e, t\rangle, \langle e, t\rangle\rangle$

---

[24] See, for instance, Kennedy & McNally 2005; Stechow 1984. Alternatively, if adjectives are treated as measure functions of type $\langle e, d\rangle$, they are assigned type $\langle\langle e, d\rangle, \langle e, t\rangle\rangle$. See e.g. Kennedy 2007. For a recent overview, see the handbook article by Beck 2012. I will go a bit more into the details of the semantics of gradable adjectives in the next chapter.

[25] Of course, with functional composition, it would be possible to combine the two expressions into a function, which, however, would be of type $\langle\langle e, d\rangle, \langle e, t\rangle\rangle$ again and would essentially have the same meaning as the degree expression. Crucially, this resulting expression then could not be combined with the noun, so that the type clash occurs just one step later.

Interestingly, this problem arises not only with degree words and comparative and superlative morphology, but also with the (covert) positive morpheme, which is obviously of the same type as the other kinds of degree expressions.

(4.152)

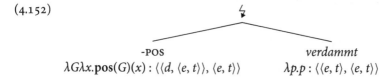

$\lambda G \lambda x.\mathbf{pos}(G)(x) : \langle\langle d, \langle e, t\rangle\rangle, \langle e, t\rangle\rangle$ —POS   verdammt $\lambda p.p : \langle\langle e, t\rangle, \langle e, t\rangle\rangle$

That is, the generalization made above, that EAs can only occur in the positive form is not even strong enough, as they do not license even this degree expression. For this reason, I assume that EAs are not selected by degree phrases and that they just project simple APs. Similar considerations apply to the restriction against the modification of pure EAs by other modifiers. Since they are not predicates, they cannot be targeted by such operators.

The present analysis can also derive the inability to be used predicatively. Since both the copula *ist* ('is') and the EA *verdammt* ('damn') are both identity functions on type $\langle e, t\rangle$ expressions, they can be combined via functional composition. However, the resulting expression—again an identity function—then cannot be combined with the subject of the sentence.

(4.153) *Alex ist verdammt.
      Alex is damn

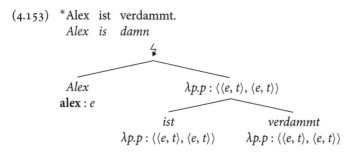

Alex $\mathbf{alex} : e$ $\lambda p.p : \langle\langle e, t\rangle, \langle e, t\rangle\rangle$

ist $\lambda p.p : \langle\langle e, t\rangle, \langle e, t\rangle\rangle$ verdammt $\lambda p.p : \langle\langle e, t\rangle, \langle e, t\rangle\rangle$

To sum up, we can trace back many syntactic restrictions that hold for pure EAs to the fact that they are semantically empty. Their only interpretational effect is contributed by the interpretable expressivity feature, which is located at some higher position and which they have to agree with. This contrasts with mixed EAs, to which we now turn.

4.7.2 *The interpretation of mixed EAs*

Recall from the discussion c that there are two kinds of EAs. On the one hand there are pure or expletive EAs, which do not contribute anything to the truth-conditional content. They are the main focus of this chapter. The other kind are *mixed* EAs since they come with some evaluative though descriptive content besides their expressive content. How can they be analyzed using the tools developed so far? The basic idea is just the same as before: their expressive content, which is introduced by an expressive feature, is not interpreted on the adjective itself but on an interpretable counterpart that is located at a higher head position. In contrast to pure EAs, a mixed EA itself carries descriptive content and hence it receives an ordinary semantic interpretation like other degree adjectives; in contrast to denoting just an identity function, as we assumed for pure EAs.[26]

(4.154)   *beschissen* ('shitty') $\rightsquigarrow \lambda d \lambda e.\textbf{bad} : \langle d, \langle e, t \rangle \rangle$

Crucially, the assumption that mixed EAs have descriptive and, more importantly, a degree based semantics predicts that most of the restrictions that we observed for pure EAs do not hold for mixed EAs. For instance, mixed EAs combine naturally with degree morphology and degree expressions.

(4.155) $^{\gamma}$eine **beschissenere** Antwort, als   die von   Frank, hätte es
           a   *shitty*.COMP   *answer*   *than the from Frank   could it*
           gar   nicht geben können
           even not   given can
           'There couldn't be a more shitty answer than the one from Frank at all.'
           [http://www.unfallopfer.de/forum/showthread.php?t=12857&page=2]

(4.156) $^{\gamma}$Das hier ist so   ziemlich die **beschissenste** Idee, von der ich
           that here is   like rather   the   shitty.SUP   *idea   of   that I*
           jemals gehört habe
           ever   heart   have
           'This here is pretty much the shittiest idea I've ever heard of.'
           [http://csgo.99damage.de/de/forums/591-sonstiges/597-off-topic/421136-esl-
           one-cologne-2016]

(4.157) $^{\gamma}$Da   momentan   noch **sehr beschissenes** Wetter   ist, kann
           because momentarily still   very shitty   *weather is,   can*
           ich leider   nicht draussen üben
           I   unfortunately not   outside   practice
           'Since at the moment there still is very shitty weather, I unfortunately cannot practice outside.'
           [https://www.grower.ch/forum/threads/poweriser-sprungstiefel.22869/]

We hence can assume that mixed EAs, in contrast to pure EAs are selected by degree expressions that project degree phrases. The syntactic structure for a DP-level

---

[26] I use **bad** to stand for the evaluative (descriptive) content of mixed EAs.

interpretation of a mixed EA hence is as in (4.158), while the corresponding semantic structure is given in (4.159).[27]

(4.158) das beschissene Auto
        the shitty   car

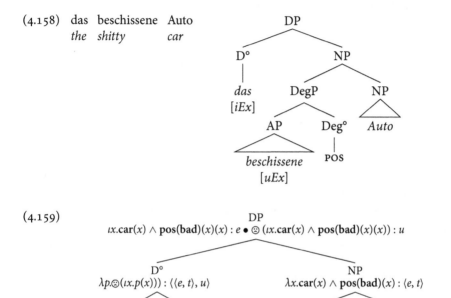

(4.159)

Since the mixed EA comes with actual (gradable) semantic content, it is no problem at all to combine it with degree expression. Similar considerations apply to other modifiers that target the adjectival content.

As we saw in (4.160), pure EAs cannot be used predicatively. Again this does not hold for mixed EAs since they do not denote an identity function on predicates.

---

[27] In order to avoid some type-shifting acrobatics, I treat the descriptive component of *beschissen* as an intersective adjective in (4.159), which is certainly not correct. This simplification does not effect the point being made in the main text though.

(4.160)   Das Auto ist beschissen.
　　　　　 the   car   is   shitty

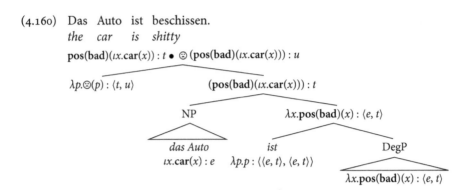

$\mathbf{pos(bad)}(\iota x.\mathbf{car}(x)) : t \bullet \odot (\mathbf{pos(bad)}(\iota x.\mathbf{car}(x))) : u$

Interestingly, since the only available interpretable expressive feature that can be the goal for the uninterpretable one is in C, the predicative use of a mixed EA should only have a sentence-level interpretation which seems to be right.

To sum up the preceding elaborations, the crucial difference between pure EAs and mixed EAs is that the former do not have non-trivial adjectival content, while mixed EAs have. This is responsible for the differences with regards to their abilities to be semantically modified. Mixed EAs more or less behave like ordinary descriptive adjectives, while in the case of pure EAs, there is not much to be modified in the first place.

Interestingly, the split into a local descriptive component and an expressive part that is interpreted at a higher node makes the employment of actually mixed expressive types, which is argued for by McCready (2010) and Gutzmann (2011), unnecessary for the analysis of mixed EAs. That is, the present syntactic split analysis, which is used to deal with the strange scoping possibilities of EAs, frees the semantics from some of its burden to cope with mixed content expressions as well.[28]

4.8 Summary

Expressive adjectives are a poster child for expressive items and therefore they have received a lot of attention from the semantic literature. However, the vast majority of this work (my own included) more or less ignored the syntactic side of EAs and treated them on par with descriptive adjectives. This chapter has shown that this is unwarranted and that EAs differ in many and crucial ways from descriptive ones. The most interesting observation is that EAs lead to a mismatch between their syntactic placement and semantic interpretation, as they tend to take a much larger expression as their argument than the one they occur in. With the approach suggested by Frazier,

---

[28] This does not mean, though, that semantic mixed types are completely unnecessary. It may well be the case that there are actual mixed expressions for which the syntactic analysis proposed in this chapter is not very plausible. A case in point may be provided by racist slurs like *Kraut* (Williamson 2009) or verbal pejoratives (Gutzmann & McCready 2016).

Dillon, & Clifton (2014), there is a first proposal how to deal with this mismatch: it is just pragmatics. However, experimental data as well as an investigation of more data using intuitions suggests that their purely pragmatic approach is way too liberal and overgenerates. Looking at more complex data shows that there are structural constraints on the syntax–semantics mismatch. It only goes up insofar as EAs can only be interpreted at a higher position, but neither at a lower one nor another non-c-commanding position. This leads us to a direct adoption of the upwards-looking agreement mechanism from the previous chapter. Assuming that the EA comes with an uninterpretable expressivity feature it has to look for a matching interpretable feature at a higher node, which it can valuate. This not only captures the directionality restriction but, in conjunction with a now direct mapping from syntax to semantics, can also account for many of the special properties. In addition, it also explains why mixed EAs, that have both descriptive and expressive content, behave more like descriptive adjectives. To conclude, with respect to the main hypothesis of this book—the hypothesis of expressive syntax—the upshot of this chapter is that expressivity as a syntactic feature can be involved in agreement.

5

Expressive intensifiers

5.1 Introduction

Like other languages, German exhibits different possibilities for intensifying the meaning of gradable adjectives. The most obvious way to intensify an adjective like *fast* in (5.1) is by means of the overt comparative morpheme *-er* as in (5.2), or by using degree words like *sehr* ('very'), *überaus* ('acutely') and other 'intensity particles' (Breindl 2009), as illustrated in (5.3). There are also syntactic ways to express that a certain property holds to a high degree, for instance exclamative sentences (5.4). Under certain circumstances, intonation can also be used to express intensification as in (5.5).

(5.1) Piet ist schnell.
       *Piet is fast.*POS
       'Piet is fast.'

(5.2) Sophie ist schnell-**er**.
       *Sophie is fast-*COMP
       'Sophie is faster.'

(5.3) Sophie ist **sehr** schnell.
       Sophie is DEG *fast*
       'Sophie is very fast.'

(5.4) Wie schnell Sophie ist!
       how fast Sophie is
       'How fast Sophie is!'

(5.5) Piet ist groooß!
       Piet is big
       'Piet is huuuge!'

Chapter adapted with permission from SpringerScience+Business Media: *The Journal of Comparative Germanic Linguistics*, "Expressive intensifiers and external degree modification", Daniel Gutzmann & Katharina Turgay © 2015. I thank Susi Wurmbrand, who was the editor in charge of that paper, and the anonymous reviewers who helped to shape the ideas developed in that paper and presented here. Many thanks also to my co-author Katharina Turgay, who gave her permission to reuse the paper as part of this book.

What I am interested in in this chapter, however, is a special subclass of degree expressions. Beside the standard degree words like *sehr* in (5.3), German exhibits a number of special intensity particles, which I call *expressive intensifiers* (EIs). These are mainly confined to informal varieties of German like youth language, where they are very frequent: expressions like *sau*, which is (diachronically) derived from the homophone expression for 'female pig, sow', *mords* (lit. 'murder'), *krass* ('crass'), *total* ('totally'), and *voll* ('fully') (Androutsopoulos 1998).[1]

(5.6)   *ʸ*Das Ding ist {**sau, voll, total**} schnell.[2]
       the   thing is EI   *fast*
       'That thing is EI (≈ totally) fast.'

EIs are distinguished from ordinary degree items by particular syntactic properties which, as I will show in this chapter, pose some challenging puzzles for their syntactic analysis. However, despite or because of that, EIs have received almost no attention in the literature. Even from a descriptive point of view, these elements are not well documented. Only in Androutsopoulos's comprehensive reference work of German youth language are they described in a bit more detail in the general context of intensification strategies (Androutsopoulos 1998: 345–57). From a more theoretical point of view, Meinunger (2009) provides the only serious investigation of EIs I am aware of. However, he leaves out a lot of important data about EIs and, as a consequence, draws inadequate conclusions, as I will discuss below.

The most interesting fact about EIs, also discussed by Meinunger, is that beside the standard adjectival position in which EIs precede the adjective they intensify, as in the predicative constructions in (5.6) or the attribute use in (5.7), they can also appear in a DP-peripheral position in which the entire DP follows the EI, as in (5.8).

(5.7)   **DP-internal position**
       *ʸ*Du bekommst [**eine sau** coole party] ABER deine eltern
       *you get   a   *EI *cool party but   your   parents*
       finden raus, dass du   eine feierst, weil   die   das   net wussten
       find   out   that you one   throw   because they that not known
       und schmeißen alle raus.
       and throw   all   out
       'You're getting/having a EI cool party but your parents find out that you are throwing one, because they didn't know that, and kick everybody out.'
       [http://www.iphpbb.com/foren-archiv/25/1590400/1589280/die-boese-fee-39872219-79563-323.html]

---

[1] See Kirschbaum (2002) for an overview of the metaphoric patterns according to which intensifiers evolve, both conceptually and diachronically. For further patterns of adjective intensification, cf. Claudi 2006. A general overview of the aspects of intensification in German is provided by van Os (1989).

[2] As before, I follow the Horn-style convention and use a prefixed "*y*" to mark examples that were found by googling (cf., e.g., Horn 2013). If it is a common and not specific example with a lot of hits, I will not provide a URL for it.

(5.8) **DP-external position**
   $^\gamma$Es ist [**sau die** coole Party], und Sinus, Cosinus und Tangens
   It   is   EI   the cool   party   and sine   cosine   and tangent
   hüpfen im Kreis.
   jump in circle
   'There is a EI cool party and sine, cosine and tangent are jumping in circles.'
   [http://www.lachschon.de/item/18377/]

When talking about constructions like (5.8), I will say that the EI is in an *external position* in order to contrast them with examples like (5.7) in which the EI resides in a position that is *internal* to the DP. Accordingly, let us call the pattern in (5.8) an *external degree modification construction* or EDC for short. However, this is rather descriptive terminology and is not meant to imply that *sau* in (5.8) does not belong to the DP. In fact, as I will show below, external EIs still remain inside the DP.

   Besides these two variants of EI-constructions just discussed, both of which seem to target an adjective, there is also an adnominal use in which an EI directly modifies a noun rather than an adjective. In this case, the EI must carry the appropriate inflection for ϕ-features.

(5.9) $^\gamma$die {**krass-e,   total-e**} Party
   the   EI-NOM.SG.F   party.NOM.SG.F
   'the total party'

This adnominal use of EIs extends to the external position so that there are EDCs without adjectives as well. In such cases, the EI remains uninflected.

(5.10) $^\gamma${**total, krass**} die Party
   EI   *the party*
   'EI a party'

Crucially, while the internal adnominal use is only available for a subset of EIs, namely those that can carry inflectional morphology, the external adnominal use is licensed for all of them.[3]

---

[3] Note that *sau+N* is grammatical for many speakers if *sau* is interpreted as a noun and the linear string is understood as a compound structure (in this case N+N: *Sau.idiot*; see also the discussion of prefixoids around (5.61) below). We hence use a prefixed '%' to mark strings that are ungrammatical for adnominal EIs, but okay under a compound reading. The two structures can be distinguished by adding an intervening modification of the noun, which blocks the compound reading (5.i). If *sau* is taken to modify just the adjective, the string is of course fine, but has a different reading (5.ii).

(i) *der **sau** [soziale Idiot]
      the   EI   social   idiot
      intended: ≈ 'a big idiot in social matters'

(ii) der [**sau** soziale] Idiot
      the   EI   social   idiot
      ≈ 'an idiot, but a highly social one'

(5.11) a. der {**totale**, %**sau**} Idiot
    the EI   *idiot*
    'the EI idiot'

   b. {**total**, **voll**, **sau**} der Idiot
    EI   *the idiot*
    'EI an idiot'

The adnominal use and the availability of the external position are defining characteristics of EIs, and distinguish them from ordinary degree items like *sehr* ('very'), which can neither be used adnominally (5.12) nor occur in the external position (5.13).

(5.12) Du hast gestern die {**totale**, *****sehr**} Party verpasst.
   you have yesterday the EI   *very party missed*
   'Yesterday, you missed the EI party.'

(5.13) Du hast gestern {**sau**, *****sehr**} die coole Party verpasst.
   you have yesterday EI *very the cool party missed*
   'Yesterday, you missed EI/*very a cool party.'

Besides its particular syntactic structure, the EDC is connected with an interesting "indefiniteness effect" (Wang & McCready 2007). The external position is perfectly fine if the DP is headed by a simple definite article, but impossible with indefinite articles for almost all speakers (in the case of *sau*) or, at least, for some speakers (e.g. with *voll*).

(5.14) a. ʸ**sau** die coole Party
    EI *the cool party*
    'a EI cool party'

   b. *****sau**/ʔ**voll** eine coole Party
    EI   *a cool party*

As expected, such intervening modification is possible for those EIs that can be used adnominally.

(iii) ʸEin Forum ist in gewisser Weise auch eine soziale Gemeinschaft, da
   a forum is to certain extend also a social community there
   bekommt man Eigenschaften bestimmter Poster doch schon mit, wenn man
   gets one character certain post.er PART *already with if one*
   nicht der **totale** soziale Idiot ist.
   not the EI *social idiot is*
   'To a certain extent, a forum is also a social community; even there, you can come to know
   the character of a contributor, if you aren't a EI social idiot.'
   [http://www.heise.de/foren/S-Nutzungsprofil/forum-10541/msg-12513526/read/ flatviewforum/]

What is even more curious is that, in spite of this preference, even an EDC with a definite article is interpreted as being indefinite. That is, the interpretation of (5.14a) corresponds to the internal construction in (5.15a), which involves the indefinite article, and not, as may be expected, to (5.15b).

(5.15)   a. ^Yeine **sau** coole Party
               a   EI *cool   party*
               'a EI cool party'

         b. ^Ydie **sau** coole Party
               the EI *cool   party*
               'the EI cool party'

A last observation regarding the external position is that it can be blocked by different structures inside the DP. First, an internal adnominal EI or adnominal size adjective blocks the external degree modification construction.

(5.16)   a. *****sau der **totale** reiche Idiot
               EI   *the* EI   *rich   idiot*

         b. *****sau der **große** reiche Idiot
               EI   *the big   rich   idiot*

Secondly, constructions with complex quantifiers like *die+ganzen* ('all the') also block EIs in external position. The same holds for so-called *occasional* constructions—DPs containing an infrequency adjective—which block external EIs under the relevant DP-external adverbial interpretation of the adjective.

(5.17)   a. *****sau die **ganzen** reichen Kunden
               EI   *the whole   rich   customers*
               intended: 'EI all the rich customers'

         b. *****Sau der **gelegentliche** Idiot betrat   den Laden.
               EI   *the occasional   idiot entered the shop*
               intended: 'Occasionally, EI the idiot entered the shop.'

The aims of this chapter are twofold. First, I will provide a detailed description of the behavior of EIs, because, as stated above, it is hardly studied at all. Secondly, I would like to present an approach that accounts for the obstacles that are raised by EDCs for their syntactic analysis. The following questions are what we take to be the main hurdles.

(Q1)   **Relation between internal and external EIs**
       How is the external position related to the internal one? That is, is it derived by movement or are external EIs base-generated?

(Q2)   **Position**
       What is the position in which external EIs reside and why can they appear there in the first place?

(Q3)   **Definiteness mismatch**
Why are EDCs with definite articles nevertheless interpreted as indefinite?
See (5.15).

(Q4)   **Constraint on EIs**
Why can EIs occur DP-externally, but not ordinary degree items like *sehr*
('very')? See (5.13).

(Q5)   **Different classes of EIs**
Given that in external position, all EIs can be used adnominally, why are some
EIs blocked from the internal adnominal position? See (5.11).

(Q6)   **Intervention effects**
Why do a variety of constructions, like complex quantifiers or even other EIs
or adnominal size adjectives, block EDCs? See (5.16) and (5.17).

The main clue to answering these questions lies in the expressive nature of EIs and
the assumption that expressivity is a syntactic feature, as stated in the hypothesis
of expressive syntax. As we will see, expressive intensification can alternatively be
expressed by the determiner alone, which leads us to the assumption of an expressivity
feature that can be marked in D. This feature is what can trigger the movement of an EI,
leading to the external degree modification construction. In addition, the observation
that not all EIs behave the same will lead us to distinguish between three different
subclasses of EIs that exhibit different degrees of grammaticalization and differ in their
ability to carry inflection morphology and thereby express φ-features.

In a nutshell, our analysis works as follows. Internal EIs move to D, where they
incorporate with the determiner to form a complex quantifier, following M. Zimmermann's (2003) analysis of the adverbial reading of the *occasional* construction. This
movement is triggered by an expressivity feature in D which must be phonologically
expressed.

(5.18)   [$_{DP}$ [$_{D^\circ}$ sau$_{[iEx:\ \text{INT}]}$+die$_{[uEx:\ \_][iDef:\ -][\phi:\ \text{NOM.SG.F}]}$] [$_{NP}$ [$_{DegP}$ [$_{Deg^\circ}$ ~~sau~~] [$_{AP}$
coole]] [$_{NP}$ Party]]]

This answers (Q1) and (Q2). The definiteness mismatch then is assumed to be a PF
effect that is based on the morphological realization rules of expressive determiners
in German. Furthermore, the fact that ordinary degree items like *sehr* ('very') do
not exhibit the expressivity feature, provides a direct answer to (Q4), as there is
nothing that would drive their movement. Furthermore, a side effect of EI-movement
is that after incorporation, the determiner can serve as a kind of ersatz inflection,
thereby licensing otherwise uninflectable EIs in external position that would be
ungrammatical when in internal position, which answers (Q5). Finally, the observed
intervention effects are directly accounted for by the fact that the adnominal degree
position c-commands the adjectival one, allowing the head movement constraint to
block the raising of adjectival EIs. Likewise, if another element has to incorporate with
the determiner, EI-movement is also blocked (Q6).

TABLE 5.1 Four cases of EI-constructions

	POSITION	TARGET	EXAMPLE	SECTION
(IA)	internal	adjective	*eine total coole Party*	Section 5.2.1
(IN)	internal	noun	*eine totale Party*	Section 5.2.2
(EA)	external	adjective	*total die coole Party*	Section 5.2.3
(EN)	external	noun	*total die Party*	Section 5.2.4

The structure of this chapter is as follows. In Section 5.2, I will give a detailed description of the behavior of the four EI-constructions. We argue that internal EIs behave like degree elements and that they are the head of the extended degree projection of the adjective or noun they modify. However, only a subclass of EIs can be used adnominally. Then I discuss the external degree modification construction and present the puzzling mismatch between the syntax and semantics that they involve. After this first part, I will then present the analysis of EDCs in Section 5.3, where I first give an outline of the approach, before motivating it in more detail by addressing the questions outlined above. Section 5.4 concludes and provides some outlook for open questions and further research.

5.2 Expressive intensifiers and external intensifying constructions

In this section, I provide an empirical description of the properties of EIs and EDCs. Given that EIs can be used adnominally or to intensify adjectives and that they can either appear in internal or external position, we are dealing with four interrelated constructions, summarized in Table 5.1.

In the following, let us go through these four cases in detail. This will not only move us toward the goal of a proper documentation of these understudied constructions, but will provide us with some first constraints in the distribution of EIs and EDCs that will guide our analysis later parts of this chapter. We will begin with the internal position before addressing EDCs. In both cases, we start with the adjectival variant.

5.2.1 *Expressive intensifiers in internal adjectival position*

When used with an adjective, EIs and ordinary degree items have the same range of uses. Common intensity particles like *sehr* ('very') can occur with gradable adjectives regardless of whether the adjective is used attributively, predicatively or adverbially. As the following examples show, this also holds for EIs.[4]

---

[4] In addition, both ordinary degree words and EIs can also occur in some adverbial contexts, even if their distribution is not completely the same.

(i) Es hat **sau/sehr** geregnet.
     It *has* EI/*very* *rained*
     'It rained a lot.'

(5.19) ᵞDas Ding ist **sau/sehr** cool.
     the thing is EI/very cool
     'The thing is EI/very cool.'

(5.20) ᵞDas Ding läuft **sau/sehr** schnell.
     the thing runs EI/very fast
     'The thing runs EI/very fast.'

(5.21) ᵞWar eine **sau/sehr** coole Party!
     was a   EI/very cool party
     'That was a EI/very cool party!'

However, it is only in the attributive position where the important difference between EIs and standard degree items can be observed. This is because only in that syntactic context of a DP can there be an external position at all.

Further similarities between EIs and *sehr* ('very'), that also point toward their categorial status, are provided by their behavior with respect to other means of degree expression. As is well known, degree words like *sehr* ('very') are incompatible with other overt degree morphology (cf., among many others, Kennedy & McNally 2005). This holds for the comparative morpheme *-er* in (5.22a), as well as for the superlative morpheme *-st* in (5.22b). The same is true for EIs as the examples in (5.23) show.

(5.22) a. *Unsere Party ist **sehr** cool-er als   eure.
       our   party is very cool-er than yours

      b. *Unsere Party ist die **sehr** cool-ste von allen.
        our   party is the very cool-est of all

(5.23) a. *Unsere Party ist **sau** cool-er als   eure.
       our   party is EI   cool-er than your

      b. %Unsere Party ist die **sau** cool-ste von allen.
        our   party is the EI   cool-est of all

A further fact that illustrates that EIs and expressions like *very* both function as degree elements is that EIs and standard degree words cannot co-occur. This holds irrespectively of the particular ordering of an EI and *sehr*.

(5.24) a. *Die Party ist **sau sehr** cool.
       The party is EI   very cool

      b. *Die Party ist **sehr sau** cool.
       The party is very EI   cool

From these various observations, we can conclude that EIs are in fact degree expressions, just like *sehr* ('very') or the comparative morpheme *-er*. We presuppose a standard syntactic analysis of adjective phrases, according to which gradable adjectives are dominated by an extended functional projection, a so-called degree phrase or DegP (cf. e.g. Abney 1987; Corver 1997; Kennedy 1999). EIs are the head of this phrase, just like degree elements such as comparative morphemes, intensifiers or the positive morpheme, which is covert in languages like German or English (Kennedy 2007: 5).

(5.25)

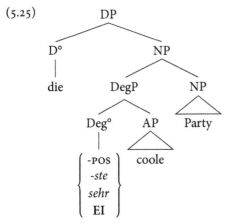

'the {cool-POS, cool-est, very cool, EI cool} party'

While this structural analysis of internal EIs is relatively uncontroversial and rather conservative, it cannot be the entire story, because we also have to address the adnominal use of EIs, to which I will turn later.

5.2.1.1 The semantics of internal EIs   Semantically, EIs increase the degree that is expressed by their adjective argument just like common intensifiers do. According to the "standard theory" (Beck 2012), an adjective like *cool* denotes a relation between a degree *d* and an entity *x* such that the coolness of *x* equals *d* (cf. e.g. Kennedy & McNally 2005; Stechow 1984). Therefore, adjectives are of type $\langle d, \langle e, t, \rangle \rangle$.[5]

(5.26) $[\![cool]\!] = \lambda d \lambda x.x$ is cool to degree *d*   ("*x* is *d*-cool")

Degree expressions like measure phrases (*1.83 meter, 190 kilometers per hour*), degree morphology (comparative *-er*, superlative *-est*) or degree words (*very*) all can occur in the head position of DegP. Semantically, they determine the degree argument of the adjective. For instance, many adjectives—especially those with concrete measurements like speed, weight, or height—license explicit measure phrases, as in (5.27), which saturate the degree argument directly and turn an adjective into a property.

---

[5] An alternative view perceives adjectives as expressions of type $\langle e, d \rangle$, so-called measure phrases that map entities onto degrees (cf., e.g., Kennedy 2007). Degree expressions then turn these measure functions into properties. Nothing in this chapter hinges on choosing one approach over the other.

(5.27) a. $[\![1.83m \text{ tall}]\!] = \lambda x.x$ is $1.83m$-tall
     b. $[\![190\frac{km}{h} \text{ fast}]\!] = \lambda x.x$ is $190\frac{km}{h}$-fast

Degree morphology and degree expressions work differently. Instead of determining the adjective's degree argument by providing a value for it, they quantify over it (Kennedy & McNally 2005: 350). The meaning of the superlative, for instance, can be rendered along the following lines (Heim 2001).

(5.28) $[\![\text{-est}]\!] = \lambda G_{\langle d,\langle e,t,\rangle\rangle}\lambda x_e$. there is a degree d, such that x is G to degree d and that for all y, if $y \neq x$, then y is not G to degree d.

In case there is no overt degree word or morphology, the standard theory assumes a covert positive morphem *pos* which heads the DegP. Its function is to relate the degree argument of the adjective to a proper comparison class for the adjective (Kennedy & McNally 2005: 350). In most cases the comparison class C remains free such that its value must be fixed by the context.

(5.29) $[\![\text{pos}]\!] = \lambda G\lambda x$. there is a degree d, such that d meets the standard given by the comparison class C and x is G to degree d.

The restriction imposed by intensifiers like *very* is such that relative to a comparison class, the degree must be higher than it should be the case if the positive adjective were used. That is, while for the positive, the comparison class has to be extracted from the context, the comparison class for *very G* is given by the objects that have the property denoted by the positive adjective G in that context (Kennedy & McNally 2005: 370).

(5.30) $[\![\text{very}]\!] = \lambda G\lambda x$. there is a degree d, such that d meets the standard given by the comparison class $\lambda y. [\![\text{pos}(G)(y)]\!]$ and x is G to degree d.

Now, one semantic difference between *very* and *sau* is that *sau G* expresses an even higher degree of G-ness than *very G*. That is, while *very cool* is cooler than just *cool*, *sau cool* is even cooler. We therefore have the following ordering.[6]

(5.31) sau cool $\succ$ sehr cool $\succ$ (pos) cool

The comparison class for *sau* thus should not be given by the objects that fulfill the positive case, but by the class of objects that exhibit the property expressed by the adjective as intensified by *very*.

(5.32) $[\![\text{sau}]\!] = \lambda G\lambda x$. there is a degree d, such that d meets the standard given by the comparison class $\lambda y. [\![\text{very}(G)(y)]\!]$ and x is G to degree d.

If this would be all there was to say about the semantics of EIs, this would hardly be interesting. However, the more important semantic difference between *sau* and

---

[6] This ordering is confirmed by our questionnaire study.

common intensifiers, is that—beside their intensifying function—EIs convey an additional expressive speaker attitude, which is why I have called them expressive intensifiers in the first place. That is, an utterance containing an EI is a hybrid expression and conveys (at least) two kinds of contents: (a) the ordinary descriptive meaning, and (b) an expressive attitude displayed by the EI in question which comments on the descriptive content. For an utterance of (5.33), the two levels of meaning are given paraphrases in (5.34).

(5.33)   Du   hast   gestern   eine   **sau**   coole   Party   verpasst.
         you   has   yesterday   a   EI   cool   party   missed
         'Yesterday, you missed a EI cool party.'

(5.34)   a. Descriptive meaning of (5.33): "Yesterday, you missed a very very cool party."
         b. Expressive meaning of (5.33): "The speaker is emotional about how cool the party was."

That this attitude is not part of the truth-conditional content of the utterance can be shown, for instance, by the denial-in-discourse test (cf. e.g. Jayez & Rossari 2004). The descriptive content of an EI can be denied directly, as in (5.35B), where B denies that the party was cool to the high degree expressed by *sau cool* but grants that it reaches the standard for being very cool.

(5.35)   A: Die Party war **sau** cool.
           'The party was EI cool'

         B: Nee,   so   cool   war   die   Party   nicht,   auch   wenn   sie   sehr   cool
            no   so   cool   was   the   party   not   even   if   it   very   cool
            war.
            was
            'No, the party wasn't that cool, even if it was very cool.'

In contrast, the expressive attitude conveyed by *sau* behaves differently. Denying an utterance on the basis that the attitude expressed by the EI does not hold is not felicitous, as witnessed by the following example.

(5.36)   A: Die   Party   war   **sau**   cool.
            the   party   was   EI   cool
            'The party was EI cool.'

         B: #Nee,   das   ist   dir   doch   egal.
            no   that   is   you   PART   equal
            'No, you don't care.'

A dialog as this one, however, should be perfectly fine if the evaluative component of *sau* were part of its truth-conditional content. If you nevertheless want to deny the expressive attitude, you can do so, but you first have to make clear that you do not challenge the descriptive content.[7]

(5.37) A: Die Party war **sau** cool.
'the party war EI cool.'

B: Ja,   stimmt,   aber   das   ist   dir   doch   eigentlich   egal.
yes   right   but   that   is   you.DAT   PART   PART   *equal*
'Yes, right, but you don't actually care about that.'

That you can only deny them if you make use of special means is typical for non-truth-conditional content (cf. e.g. Fintel 2004; Horn 2008b). Semantically, EIs are therefore mixed expressives that contribute to both dimensions of meaning (cf. McCready & Schwager 2009).

In all examples presented thus far, the expressive meaning of *sau* was a *positive* emotional attitude. However, I have not included the positive polarity of the attitude into the paraphrase in (5.34b). This is because whether the attitude is a positive or negative evaluation depends on the context. This is illustrated by the following two examples.

(5.38) Mann,   es   ist   wieder   **sau**   kalt.
man   *it*   *is*   *again*   EI   *cold*
'Man, it's EI cold again.' (negative attitude)

(5.39) Bei   dieser   Hitze   kommt   das   **sau**   kalte   Bier   genau   richtig.
at   *this*   *heat*   *comes*   *the*   EI   *cold*   *beer*   *exactly*   *right*
'In this heat, the EI cold beer comes just right.' (positive attitude)

In order to account for this, let us follow McCready (2009: 681) and define a function E that takes the utterance context as an argument and maps it on a function that, when applied to the propositional content of the sentence, delivers one of emotional predicates **good** or **bad**, corresponding to the positive and negative attitude respectively.

(5.40) $E : c \mapsto (\wp(W) \mapsto A)$, where $A \in \{\textbf{bad}, \textbf{good}\}$

That is, instead of directly expressing **good** or **bad**, the expressive meaning of *sau* is given by this function E which yields one of those predicates depending on the context. This emotional predicate can in turn be applied to the propositional content to yield an expressive proposition. However, in what follows, I will ignore this, and just write **emo** for the underspecified emotional attitude expressed by EIs.

---

[7] Without the particles *doch* and *eigentlich*, which signal contrast or correction, such a reply becomes less acceptable. The following example also shows how hard it is to cancel the evaluative component, even if the descriptive content is affirmed:

(i) B: ?Ja,   stimmt,   aber   das   ist   dir   egal.
yes,   right   but   that   is   you.DAT   *equal*
'Yes, right, but you don't care about that.'

EIs like *sau* are mixed expressive, because they combine a degree intensifying function in the descriptive dimension with an expressive attitude, we need the corresponding composition rules for mixed expressions from Chapter 2, which I repeat here.

(5.41)   **Mixed application** (for $\rho \neq u$)

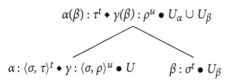

$$\alpha(\beta) : \tau^t \bullet \gamma(\beta) : \rho^u \bullet U_\alpha \cup U_\beta$$

$$\alpha : \langle \sigma, \tau \rangle^t \bullet \gamma : \langle \sigma, \rho \rangle^u \bullet U \qquad \beta : \sigma^t \bullet U_\beta$$

(5.42)   **Mixed saturation**

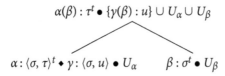

$$\alpha(\beta) : \tau^t \bullet \{\gamma(\beta) : u\} \cup U_\alpha \cup U_\beta$$

$$\alpha : \langle \sigma, \tau \rangle^t \bullet \gamma : \langle \sigma, u \rangle \bullet U_\alpha \qquad \beta : \sigma^t \bullet U_\beta$$

Against the backdrop of these two rules, let us now give a lexicsl semantics for an EI like *sau*.

(5.43)   **sau** $= \lambda G \lambda x.\mathbf{int}(G)(x) : \langle \langle d, \langle e, t \rangle \rangle, \langle e, t \rangle \rangle \blacklozenge \lambda G \lambda x.\mathbf{emo}(G)(x) : \langle \langle d, \langle e, t \rangle \rangle, \langle e, u \rangle \rangle$

We have two parts here, the intensifying aspect in the truth-conditional dimension (**int**) and the expressive attitude in the second dimenions (**emo**). We can then give the following interpretation to these components.

(5.44) $[\![\mathbf{int}]\!] = \lambda G \lambda x.$ there is a degree d, such that d meets the standard given by the comparison class $\lambda. [\![\mathbf{very}(G)(y)]\!]$ and x is G to degree $d : \langle \langle d, \langle e, t \rangle \rangle, \langle e, t \rangle \rangle$.

(5.45) $[\![\mathbf{emo}]\!] = \lambda G \lambda x.$ the speaker c_S is emotional about the fact that there is a degree d such that d meets the standard given by the comparison class $\lambda. [\![\mathbf{very}(G)(y)]\!]$ and x is G to degree. $d : \langle \langle d, \langle e, t \rangle \rangle, \langle e, u \rangle \rangle$.

Equipped with this lexical meaning for *sau*, we now compose a sentence containing *sau*.

(5.46)   Die Party is **sau** cool.

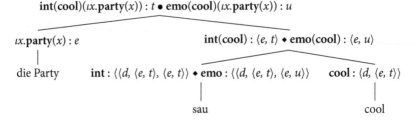

$$\mathbf{int}(\mathbf{cool})(\iota x.\mathbf{party}(x)) : t \bullet \mathbf{emo}(\mathbf{cool})(\iota x.\mathbf{party}(x)) : u$$

$\iota x.\mathbf{party}(x) : e$ 　　　　　　 $\mathbf{int}(\mathbf{cool}) : \langle e, t \rangle \blacklozenge \mathbf{emo}(\mathbf{cool}) : \langle e, u \rangle$

die Party 　　 $\mathbf{int} : \langle \langle d, \langle e, t \rangle, \langle e, t \rangle \rangle \blacklozenge \mathbf{emo} : \langle \langle d, \langle e, t \rangle, \langle e, u \rangle \rangle$ 　　 $\mathbf{cool} : \langle d, \langle e, t \rangle \rangle$

　　　　　　　　　　　　　　 sau 　　　　　　　　　　　　　 cool

The first application here, the one that applies *sau* to *cool*, is an instance of mixed application. The second step (combining the result with the subject), involves the proceeds via mixed saturation, so that the resulting use-conditional proposition is stored in the use set.

The meaning of the entire sentence therefore consists of two independent parts. First, it says that the party in question had a degree of coolness that was higher than the threshold as set by the comparison class of very cool parties (i.e., the expression to the left of the diamond). Secondly, it displays the expressive attitude that the speaker is emotional about the party's high degree of coolness.

Before we now turn to the syntax and semantics of EIs in the external position, note that what I have said with regards to the semantics of the internal position also holds for the external position. That is, external *sau* intensifies the adjective by imposing a higher restriction on the degree argument of the adjective and conveys an expressive speaker attitude toward the propositional content. However, as we will see in the following section, the semantics of the external position is connected with additional indefiniteness effects that are absent when the EI is in the DP-internal position.

5.2.2 *Expressive intensifiers in internal adnominal position*

As we have seen above in (5.9), EIs can also be used adnominally, directly modifying a noun instead of an adjective.

(5.47) $^\gamma$total   die   Party
      EI   *the*   *party*
    'EI a party'

Similar to the analysis of gradable adjectives as arguments of degree expressions, a degree based analysis has also been proposed more recently for certain nouns (Matushansky & Spector 2005; Morzycki 2009, 2012).[8] The basic observation is that some nouns are associated with a gradable property that licenses degree morphology pretty much like gradable adjectives do. For instance, (5.48a) reads like a nominal variant of the comparative construction in (5.48b).

(5.48)   a. Clyde is more of an idiot than Floyd.   (Morzycki 2012: 189)
      b. Clyde is more idiotic than Floyd.

Furthermore, some seemingly adjectival expressions do not modify a noun in a simple intersective way, but rather target the degree that is associated with a gradable noun.

(5.49)   a. the big idiot
      b. the real idiot

---

[8] See Constantinescu 2011 for an opposing view.

These DPs have two readings. First, the adjective can be interpreted as a proper adjective modifying the noun. (5.49a) then refers to a person that is both an idiot and big, while (5.49b) refers to a person that is both an idiot and real (as opposed to imaginary). The most likely reading for (5.49b), though, which is also available for (5.49a), is the one in which it refers to an object that is an idiot *to a high degree*, that is, somebody whose idiocy is even higher than that of a plain idiot.

That the degree function is syntactically distinct and not just a pragmatic reinterpretation of the adjectives is shown by the fact that the degree reading disappears in predicative position. That is, the following examples only exhibit the adjectival interpretation.

(5.50)   a. This idiot is big.
         b. This idiot is real.

In addition, the degree function is only available for certain adjectives and not for others, even if they are close in their meaning, which also supports the degree element being actually different, not just derived by a general pragmatic reinterpretation.[9] For instance, while *big* allows the degree reading, *tall* does not, so (5.51) lacks the relevant intensification and just has the size reading.

(5.51)   the tall idiot

Another crucial observation is that such adnominal degree elements are not licensed by all nouns, but only by those that have a very salient dimension of gradability. An important difference between adjectival and nominal gradability is that gradable adjectives are associated with a single dimension, whereas many nouns are complex bundles of semantic features that do not necessarily have a prominent dimension that can be targeted by degree expressions. Therefore, "gradable nouns are those for which a single criterion can be distinguished from the others as the most salient" (Morzycki 2009: 186). This explains the different levels of acceptability in the following minimal pairs.[10]

(5.52)   a. *ein   totales Auto
             a   EI   *car*

         b. ?eine   totale Schrottkarre
             a   EI   *junker*
             'a total junker'

---

[9] Of course, some kind of pragmatic mechanism, like metaphorical transfer, most certainly had been the start for the grammaticalization of an adjective like *big* into an adnominal degree expression.

[10] I do not understand "salience" here in the standard pragmatic sense, because using, say, *Auto* ('car') in a context in which velocity is salient does not increase the acceptability of *ein totales Auto*. Instead, the gradable dimension of a gradable noun must be lexically delivered and thereby be 'salient' for the adnominal intensifier.

(5.53)   a. *ein totaler Film
         a   EI   *movie*

   b. ᵛein totaler Horrorfilm
      a   EI   *horror.movie*
      'a total horror movie'

(5.54)   a. *ein totales Haus
         a   EI   *haus*

   b. ᵛeine totale Villa
      a   EI   *villa*
      'a total villa'

(5.55)   a. *totales Wasser
         EI   *water*

   b. ᵛtotales Eiswasser
      EI   *ice.water*
      'total ice water'

To account for this kind of degree modification in the nominal domain, Morzycki (2009: 188) proposes to extend the structure of the NP by an adnominal degree phrase Deg_NP, in analogy to the extension of adjective phrases to DegPs. This analysis seems to be an adequate analysis of internal adnominal EIs as well.

(5.56) Deg_NP
            ⁀⁀⁀⁀⁀⁀⁀⁀
      $Deg_N°$ NP
         | △
      ⎡ -POS ⎤   idiot
      ⎪ more ⎪
      ⎨ real ⎬
      ⎪ EI ⎪
      ⎣   ⎦

It should be noted that the analysis of size adjectives in adnominal degree phrases is more complicated, as it is assumed that they are not the head of Deg_NP, but are viewed as measure phrases that are selected for by an abstract morpheme MEAS$_N$.

   There is, however, a complication to be noted, as the internal adnominal use is not licensed for all EIs. For instance, *sau, mords* and *voll* cannot be used in this way.[11]

(5.57)   ⎡ %mords ⎤
      ein ⎨ %sau   ⎬ Idiot   intended: 'an EI idiot'
              ⎣ ?voll-er ⎦

---

[11] However, note that even those EIs can intensify a bare, i.e. adjectiveless, NP if they occur in external position. We will come back to this issue in subsection Section 5.2.4. Also note that *voll* is not as restricted as *sau* and *mords* and can be used with certain nouns, even though it is a bit marked.

There are, as I argue, two reasons why certain EIs cannot be used in such adnominal contexts, allowing them to be divided further into two subclasses. First, note that the $\text{Deg}_N{}^\circ$-position takes part in the agreement chain between the determiner and the noun, so that the adnominal degree element has to agree with the determiner (and the NP) with respect to its case and φ-features. Without inflection, the construction is ungrammatical.

(5.58) a. ein-e   total-e   Katastrophe
            a-NOM.SG.F *total*-NOM.SG.F *catastrophe*.NOM.SG.F
            'a complete catastrophe'

     b. mit ein-em   total-en   Idiot-en
         with *a*-DAT.SG.M *total*-DAT.SG.M *Idiot*-DAT.SG.M
         'with a total idiot'

     c. *mit ein-em   total Idiot-en
         with *a*-DAT.SG.M *total* *Idiot*-DAT.SG.M

Now, in contrast to *total*, EIs like *sau* and *mords* are uninflectable expressions and cannot bear any case- or φ-morphology. Trying to inflect them, as *total* in (5.58b), is ungrammatical.

(5.59)

$$*\text{mit ein-em} \left\{ \begin{array}{l} \text{sau} \\ \text{mords} \end{array} \right\}\text{-en Idiot-en.}$$

However, not inflecting them is not an option either, as shown by (5.57). Hence, we can conclude that EIs like *sau* and *mords* cannot be used purely adnominally due to their inability to express the necessary case- and ϕ-morphology that seems to be required in this syntactic position.

For the other group of EIs, instantiated by *voll*, things are different, at least superficially. As shown in (5.57), *voll* cannot be used adnominally either, even if it is inflected (as it is in that example). Therefore, it may seem as if we needed an alternative explanation for this restriction. However, I think that the difference is only superficial and *voll*, as an EI, actually cannot be inflected. What can be inflected is the homonymous adjective *voll* ('full'), not the EI. That is, in an ordinary non-degree reading, *voll* can occur attributively, and also (uninflected) predicatively. However, the homophone adjective lacks the intensification reading altogether (Meinunger 2009).

(5.60) a. mit ein-er   voll-en   Flasche
            with *a*-NOM.SG.F *full*-NOM.SG.F *bottle*.NOM.SG.F
            'with a full bottle';   *not* 'with a total bottle'

     b. Die Flasche ist voll.
         the *bottle*   *is* *full*
         'The bottle is full.'

That is, the main difference between *sau* or *mords* on the one hand, and *voll* on the other, is most likely a diachronic one regarding the different sources from which the EIs were grammaticalized. Let us address these differences in a bit more detail. However, I shall note that the following remarks on the development of EIs are rather speculative, since actual diachronic studies of the development of such elements are yet to be done, and an endeavor like that is beyond the scope of this chapter. Hence, the assertions in the following should be considered more as hypotheses, rather than statements of matters of fact. That being said, it seems highly plausible that the EI *voll* originated from the still existing homophone adjective (Claudi 2006: 354). While adjectives in general seem to be the most frequent source of EIs, this is, however, not the case for *sau* and *mords*, which developed out of nouns. An intermediate stage, which also supports at least an adnominal component, is the use of these nouns in nominal word formation.

(5.61) a. **Sau**wetter,   **Sau**regen,   **Sau**karre
             sow.weather,   sow.rain,   sow.junker

   b. **Mords**party,   **Mords**spaß,   **Mords**sound
             murder.party,   murder.fun,   murder.sound

Interestingly, this use as first elements in nominal compounds seems to have developed into so-called prefixoids in adjectival intensifying word formation (R. J. Pittner 1991, 1996; Stevens 2005). In such cases, *sau* and *mords* are already pretty close to being EIs, the major difference being that they are not entirely independent words yet and, given the orthographic conventions of written German on word formation, hence are written without a separating space between prefixoid and base.[12]

(5.62) **mords**dumm,   **sau**dumm
             murder.dumb,   sow.dumb
             'very stupid'

For these constructions, I assume, it is a small step to a reanalysis as independent degree expressions, in which case they have to be considered as proper independent words and are also written as such. In the case of EIs, the availability of the external position is the perfect diagnostic for this because elements of derivational morphology, prefixes, and prefixoids alike cannot be separated from their bases. Furthermore, note that not all intensifying prefixoids underwent this kind of grammaticalization. That is, while EIs can occur in external position, this is impossible for the majority of other elements R. J. Pittner (1996) lists. For instance, while *stock* (lit. 'stick') or *stroh* (lit. 'straw') combine naturally with *dumm* ('stupid'), they cannot do so in external position like *sau* and *mords* can (we use 'IPX' to gloss the intensifying prefixoids).

---

[12] See R. J. Pittner 1996 for more criteria to distinguish the first elements of intensifying word formation from independent words.

(5.63) a. **stockdumm, strohdumm**
           IPX.*stupid,*   IPX.*stupid*
           'very stupid'

       b. *{**stock, stroh**} die   dumme   Idee
              IPX   *the   stupid   idea*

       c. {**sau, mords**} die   dumme   Idee
              EI   *the   stupid   idea*
           'EI a stupid idea'

What we can conclude from this excursus into the diachronics of *sau* and *mords* is that they had a development path different from *voll*, and this is what makes them behave superficially differently. However, as already noted above, the sole reason is that *voll* has a homophone adjective (which is its historical source). What unites them is that they are unable to carry inflectional morphology, in contrast to *total, komplett* and the like, which can (still?) be inflected like adjectives, even in their EI function. As summed up in Table 5.2, we therefore end up with two to three different classes of EIs, depending on whether you want to count the *voll* group as its own class or not.

The important difference is that only members of the *total* group can actually surface in adnominal position. However, as I will explicate below, it has to be assumed that the other EI classes can function as adnominal degree elements as well, but due to their inability to bear φ-features, they cannot stay in that position. It can be argued, then, that—as EIs—the *voll* group exhibits a greater degree of grammaticalization because they have lost the ability for inflection of their adjectival source items, while EIs like *total* still retain them.

Despite the differences between the three groups, what they all have in common—in addition to the availability of the external position—is that none of them, not even those of the inflectable *total*-group, can bear comparative or superlative morphology, which further supports the assumption that they are the head of the Deg$_N$P and not adjectives.[13] This contrasts, for instance, with size adjectives such as *groß* ('big'),

TABLE 5.2 Classes of EIs

		internal Deg$_N{}^o$	φ on EI	source
(I)	*total* group	✓	✓	ADJ
(II-a)	*voll* group	✗	✗	ADJ
(II-b)	*sau* group	✗	✗	N

---

[13] Further arguments against an analysis of EIs as adjectives will be presented further below.

which, even in the adnominal degree reading, are still APs viz. DegPs. But, as mentioned briefly above, rather than modifying the noun directly as attributive adjectives do, they are selected for by the abstract MEAS-morpheme which itself takes up the Deg$_N$P head position.

Having discussed EIs in the two DP-internal variants, let us now turn to the external degree modification construction. As before, we start by discussing the adjectival use first, before turning to the adnominal case.

5.2.3 Adjectival external intensifying constructions

The fact that EIs can occur in DP-external position, in which they precede the entire DP, sets them apart from the well studied ordinary degree expressions like *sehr* 'very'. Since those cannot occur in the external position (van Os 1989: 16), it is a rather surprising position for a degree expression to appear in.

(5.64) Du hast gestern {sau, *sehr} die coole Party verpasst.
          you have yesterday EI   very the cool party missed
          'Yesterday, you missed EI/*very a cool party.'

The external position is by a large margin the most prominent feature of EIs and what sparked our interest in them in the first place. As we will see, this position is associated with some puzzling syntactic and semantic aspects that are in need of an explanation. In the following sections, we will give an overview of the behavior of the external degree modification construction (EDC). In doing so, I will especially concentrate on features that will point us toward an appropriate analysis of EDCs.

5.2.3.1 EDCs are DPs

A first important observation about EDCs is that, despite having the degree expression outside of the DP, they nevertheless behave like DPs and not like DegPs. As shown by (5.64) and many other examples, the external EI-construction can serve as an argument for predicates like *verpassen* 'to miss' that take DPs but not DegPs. Replacing the EDC in (5.64) with a proper degree phrase clearly leads to ungrammaticality, as in (5.65).

(5.65)

$$
\text{Du hast gestern} \left\{ \begin{array}{l} [_{DP} \textbf{ sau } \text{die coole Party}] \\ [_{DP} \text{ eine Party}] \\ {}^{*}[_{DegP} \text{ sehr cool}] \end{array} \right\} \text{verpasst.}
$$

$$
\text{'You missed} \left\{ \begin{array}{l} [_{DP} \text{ EI a cool party}] \\ [_{DP} \text{ a party}] \\ {}^{*}[_{DegP} \text{ very cool}] \end{array} \right\} \text{yesterday.'}
$$

That EDCs are DPs and not DegPs is also shown by the fact that they can be freely coordinated with other DPs, as witnessed by the following example.

(5.66) Du   hast   [DP **sau** die coole Party] und [DP ein tolles Konzert]
        you have   EI *the cool   party   and   a   great   concert*
        verpasst.
        missed
        'You missed EI a cool party and a great concert.'

The previous example also illustrates that the entire structure [EI DP] forms a single constituent. This conclusion is also reached by Meinunger (2009), who provides the sole theoretical discussion of the external degree modification construction I am aware of. He presents further arguments that show that external EIs indeed belong to the DP they precede. If they did not form a constituent, they should be able to be split apart. This, however, is impossible (cf. Meinunger 2009: 124).

(5.67) a. *Sau hast du   die coole Party verpasst.
           EI *have you the cool   party missed*

        b. *Die coole Party hast du   sau verpasst.[14]
           the cool   party have you EI *missed*
           Both intended: 'You missed EI the cool party.'

These examples illustrate that splitting an EDC apart leads to ungrammaticality, regardless of the order of the splitting.

5.2.3.2 EDCs are degree expression (not adjectives)   In contrast to our analysis of internal EIs as degree expressions that occupy the head position of DegP, Meinunger takes external *voll* and *total*, as well as some other examples, to be adjectives. He calls them *left-most adjectives* and argues for an analysis that treats them parallel to some special adverbials that occur in the left-most periphery of the CP, thereby giving more support for the thesis of the parallelism between CP and DP (Abney 1987; Laenzlinger 2010). The adverbials Meinunger studies are speaker-orientated adverbs that can even precede the so-called prefield, the otherwise first position in German main clauses, leading to a seemingly verb third constellation, something which is otherwise mostly excluded in German. An illustrative example is given in (5.68), while (5.69) shows that other elements from inside the clause cannot occur in that left-most position.

---

[14] Note that using *voll* or *total* instead of *sau* in (5.67b) makes the sentence grammatical.

(i) Die coole Party hast du   **total** verpasst.
     the cool   party have you   totally   missed
     'You totally missed the cool party.'

However, in that case we are not dealing with EIs but with ordinary adverbs modifying the VP. As indicated by the translation, this leads to a different reading. To avoid such issues, I prefer to use *sau* in our examples whenever the difference between the EI classes do not matter, because *sau* is unambiguously an EI, except for the homophone noun, with which it can hardly be confused.

(5.68) **Offen gesagt**, ich fand   die Party ziemlich langweilig.
          openly said   I   found the party pretty   boring
          'Frankly speaking, I think the party was pretty boring.'

(5.69) *Die Party, ich fand   **offen   gesagt** ziemlich langweilig.
          the party I   found openly said   pretty   boring

While such adverbials occur in an orphaned position preceding even the specifier position of C (the otherwise highest projection of the clause), Meinunger argues that external *voll* and *total* take up the same position with respect to the DP. In particular, he assumes that external EIs or—this is also his terminology—"outer adjectives," are base-generated in the external position (Meinunger 2009: 132). Accordingly, he assumes, they are not inflected because they are not derived from relative clauses like attributive adjectives under a Kayne-style analysis (Kayne 1994) of attributive adjectives, which he adopts, following Struckmeier (2007). Because of that, they are not in a position in which they receive inflection and, therefore, they remain uninflected when in external position.

However, without needing to go into the details of Meinunger's analysis, I think that it cannot be correct. First, while there are homophone adjectives for the EIs from the *voll* or *total* group, which may have lead Meinunger to his adjectival analysis, this does not hold for EIs from the *sau* group, which are derived from nouns. As we have seen, EIs like *sau* cannot be used as adjectives, regardless of whether they are inflected (which is impossible) or remain uninflected. The fact that this holds not only for supposedly attributive uses, but also for predicative positions, shows that *sau* cannot even be considered an uninflectable adjective.

(5.70) a. %die **sau** Party
            the EI *party*

      b. *die **sau-e**   Party
          the EI-NOM.SG.F *party*.NOM.SG.F

      c. *Die Party ist **sau**.
          the party is EI

A second argument against an adjectival treatment of EIs comes from the fact that it loosens the connection between external and internal EIs. As for internal EIs, it is even more evident that they cannot be adjectives, simply because of the fact that they are used to modify adjectives, which is not generally possible for adjectives in German. This is true, even if the adjective in question would semantically be well suited for an intensifying function, shown by its felicity in adnominal degree phrases.[15]

---

[15] Again, recall that adjectives like *big*, when used in adnominal degree phrases, are not the head, but are selected for by a MEAS function. This contrasts with EIs and other adnominal degree elements, which can directly occur in $Deg_N P^0$.

(5.71)   *eine {groß, stark} coole Party
        a   *big*   *strong* *cool*   *party*

In addition, the problem regarding additional degree elements also holds for internal EIs, see example (5.23) above. That is, an analysis of external EIs as adjectives is unlikely on its own merits, but it is even more unlikely given that such an analysis of internal EIs faces additional problems. In light of the discussed data, we therefore conclude that an analysis of EIs, regardless of whether they are internal or external ones, as adjectives is inadequate. However, as I will show later below, some aspects of Meinunger's (2009) approach will still carry over to our own proposal, even if I reject the adjectival basis of his approach.

5.2.3.3 *The "definite" article*   Further elaborating on the question of what construc-
tions allow EIs in external position, it is important to note that the presence of a gradable target inside the DP is not the only factor licensing EDCs. It depends also on the syntactic form of the DP, especially on the determiner. First, while EIs can occupy an external position if the DP is headed by a definite article, this is marked if the DP is a projection of an indefinite article (Androutsopoulos 1998: 353). The following examples illustrate this contrast.

(5.72)   ?Du hast gestern   **sau eine** coole Party verpasst.
       you have yesterday EI   *a*   *cool*   *party* *missed*

(5.73)   Du hast gestern   **sau die** coole Party verpasst.
       you have yesterday EI *the* *cool*   *party* *missed*
       'You missed a totally cool party yesterday.'

Contrasting this restriction with the *definiteness effect*, which can be observed in existential constructions (Milsark 1977) or possessive constructions with *have* (Bach 1967), EDCs could be said to be connected with an *indefiniteness* effect (Wang & McCready 2007).

However, this constraint does not seem to be absolute, because there actually seem to be two speaker groups. One group, in which I count myself, goes with Androutsopoulos's judgment and generally rejects external EIs with indefinites, while the other group seems to accept them generally. I will later come to implement this micro-variation into our analysis.

Despite this variation, there seems to be a preference for definite articles in EDCs that is shown by corpus data. Unfortunately, though, there is no openly available corpus of informal varieties of German (nor youth language) and since the two major corpora of German, *cosmas 2* and *DWDS*,[16] are mainly based on newspaper articles and therefore, EDCs cannot be expected to occur there. Thus, we have to rely

---

[16] The corpora are accessible under http://www.ids-mannheim.de/cosmas2 and http://www.dwds.de.

TABLE 5.3 Total Google hits for EDCs

EI	[Def: +]	[Def: −]
		#y
sau	30,308	1
total	44,128	376
voll	715,146	2,173

on Google searches. However, even this method can illustrate the contrast between the definite and indefinite article in EDCs. We searched for the following variations of the EDC.

(5.74)

$$[\text{EI}]\ [\text{D}] \left\{ \begin{array}{l} \text{coole(r) 'cool'} \\ \text{geile(r) 'wicked'} \\ \text{gute(r) 'good'} \end{array} \right\} \left\{ \begin{array}{l} \text{Band 'band'} \\ \text{Freund 'friend'} \\ \text{Freudin '(girl)friend'} \\ \text{Idee 'idea'} \\ \text{Party 'party'} \end{array} \right\}$$

For [D], I used the simple definite or indefinite article—*der/die* ('the') and *ein/eine* ('a') respectively while for [EI], I used *sau, total* and *voll*. Cumulating the results for each variant in Table 5.3, the number of google hits, #y, for the definite article is #y = 715,146. In contrast, for the indefinite article, we end up with #y = 2,173. Since the frequency for the various is quite different, depending on the adjective and noun involved, I give the numbers of hits for each variant in Table 5.5 in the appendix.

We take these results as empirical support for the preference of definite determiners in EDCs, even for those speakers that accept indefinite EIs. As an interesting side note, the fact that *voll* is much more frequent than *total* matches the conjecture made above that *voll* is more grammaticalized and hence has lost its ability to be inflected (as an EI), while *total* still inherits this property from its adjectival source.

However, besides the preference for definite articles, there are some hard constraints on the syntax of EIs, since it does not allow other definite determiners. For instance, demonstrative pronouns, which are definite, are also impossible with external EIs. The same holds for possessive pronouns and possessive genitives.

(5.75) *Heute steigt **sau** {diese, ihre, Ronjas}   coole Party.
        today goes.on EI   *that   her Ronja.*GEN *cool party*

Furthermore, EIs cannot occur in the external position of quantified DPs irrespective of whether the quantifier is strong or weak.

(5.76) *Heute steigen **sau** {alle, einige, die meisten, höchstens drei}
        Heute goes.on EI *all some the most at.most three*
        coole(n) Partys.
        cool parties

All these examples illustrate that the syntactic structures that license EDCs are very specific and highly restricted. Furthermore, only EIs are allowed in this position, while ordinary degree words like *sehr* ('very') are not, as has been shown in (5.64). This contrasts with the DP-internal position, in which EIs are much less restricted and exhibit the same behavior as their non-expressive counterparts.

5.2.3.4 Definiteness mismatches   Besides their syntactic constraints, EDCs also involve a curious semantic effect. Even EDCs with definite determiners are nevertheless interpreted as indefinite. The EDCs in (5.77a) therefore correspond to the internal variant in (5.77b) and not, as would be expected, to (5.77c).

(5.77) a. Heute steigt   **sau** die coole Party.
           today goes.on EI   *the cool   party*
           'Today, EI a cool party is going on.' $(5.77a) = (5.77b) \neq (5.77c)$

        b. Heute steigt   eine **sau** coole Party.
           today goes.on a   EI   *cool   party*
           'Today, a EI cool party is going on.'

        c. Heute steigt   die **sau** coole Party.
           today goes.on the EI   *cool   party*
           'Today, the EI cool party is going on.'

The following example nicely illustrates the indefinite interpretation of the entire EDC.

(5.78) ^{y}Boah ist der Vater sch****!!!! ich dachte,   da   kommt jetzt
        *whoa is   the father sh****   I   thought there comes   now*
        voll der coole Typ (der Rufus vlt   möglicherweise auch
        EI   *the cool   guy   that Rufus perhaps possibly   also*
        noch ähnlich sieht...) und dann schiebt sich   so   ein
        even alike   look   and then wheel   himself such a
        Drecksack ins   Bild!!!
        scumbag   into.the picture
        'Man, is the father sh****!!!! I thought, now there comes EI a cool guy (that perhaps possibly even looks like Rufus) and then such a scumbag wheels itself into the picture!!!'
        [http://www.youtube.com/watch?v=m3szYNo8cZk]

Replacing the EDC in this context by a internal variant with definite article is clearly illicit. As predicted, one needs to use an indefinite article to preserve the intended reading.[17]

---

[17] Stress on the determiner renders (5.79a) fine again. We will come back to this later in Section 5.3.4.

(5.79) a. #da   kommt jetzt **der** **voll** coole Typ
            there comes   now   the   EI   cool   guy

   b. da   kommt jetzt **ein** **voll** cooler Typ
            there comes   now   a   EI   cool   guy
            'there comes a EI cool guy'

That this mismatch between definite syntactic form and indefinite interpretation is
a semantic effect and not a pragmatic one can be illustrated by the fact that the
DP-external use is incompatible with phenomena that require a definite interpretation, like explicit contrast constructions or adding the demonstrative *da/dort* ('there')
in post-nominal position.

(5.80) *Ich habe **voll** den coolen Typen geküsst, nicht den langweiligen.
          I   have EI   the cool   guy   kissed   not   the   boring
          intended: 'I kissed EI the cool guy, not the boring one.'

(5.81) *Ich kenne **voll** den coolen Typen da   von einer Party letzte
          I   know EI   the cool   guy   there from a   party last
          Woche.
          week
          intended: 'I know EI the cool guy over there from a party last week.'

Further evidence for the indefinite interpretation of EDCs is provided by the classical
test for indefinites, namely, the ability to occur in existential or *have* constructions,
which are impossible with definites (Bach 1967; Milsark 1977). External EIs pass
this test, whereas definite DPs with internal EIs show the common definiteness effect
associated with these constructions.

(5.82) a. Es gibt **sau** den coolen Typen auf meiner Schule.
             it gives EI   the cool   guy   at   my   school
             'There is EI a cool guy at my school.'

   b. *Es gibt den **sau** coolen Typen auf meiner Schule.
             it gives the EI   cool   guy   at   my   school.

(5.83) a. Ich habe **sau** den coolen Freund.
             I   have EI   the cool   boyfriend
             'I've got EI the cool friend.'

   b. *Ich habe den **sau** coolen Freund.
             I   have the EI   cool   boyfriend

An additional piece of evidence for the definiteness mismatch is provided by proper
names. In their ordinary use, proper names are always definite. Even if they do not
require a determiner in standard German in order to have referential force, they
combine freely with definite articles in many variants of German. When they do so,
they are, however, impossible with EDCs, but fine with internal EIs.

(5.84) a. *Ich treffe heute **sau** den coolen Peter.
          I   meet   today EI   the cool   Peter

      b. Ich treffe heute den **sau** coolen Peter.
          I   meet   today the EI   cool   Peter
      'I'll meet the EI cool Peter today.'

Note that (5.84a) is only unacceptable when *Peter* is used as a real proper name. In cases in which a proper name is used to denote a property instead of an individual, external EIs are possible. For instance, *Einstein* can be used to express a property that is saliently associated with Einstein, like being a genius or having a bad grade in math.[18] If used in this way, which is indefinite, proper names license the use of EDCs.[19]

(5.85) [ɣ]Der David is son   kleines Genie, **voll** der EINSTEIN...
          the David is such.a small   genius EI   the Einstein
      'David is such a genius, a total Einstein.'
      [http://joylaura.homepage24.de/Friends]

(5.86) [ɣ]Jeah **voll** der Einstein. Nein du   hast sogar recht, in Mathe
          yeah EI   the Einstein   no   you have even right in math
      hatte ich eine 5
      had   I   a   5
      'Yeah, a total Einstein. No, you're actually right, I had a 5 in math.'
      [http://forums.d2jsp.org/topic.php?t=33449169&f=149&o=130]

Taking the discussed data together, I take this as conclusive evidence that EDCs really behave like indefinite DPs, in spite of the required definite article.

Table 5.4 summarizes the discussion of the definiteness mismatch, adding internal EIs to the picture as well. In contrast to EDCs, internal EIs do not exhibit a similar mismatch between the syntactic form and semantic interpretation. The choice of the determiner is not restricted at all, and the interpretation of the entire DP compositionally reflects which determiner is used. Only in EDCs can we detect the definiteness mismatch. First, indefinite articles (as well as many other kinds of determiners) are

---

[18] The latter property wasn't actually true for Einstein. This widespread popular myth is based on the fact that the grade system in Switzerland, where Einstein went to high school, is the mirror image of the German one. That is, 6 is the worst and 1 the best grade in Germany, while in Switzerland at that time, 6 was the best. See http://commons.wikimedia.org/wiki/File:Albert_Einstein%27s_exam_of_maturity_grades_%28color2%29.jpg.

[19] Example (5.85) contains a curious exception to the bigness generalization that seems to be particular to German. As Morzycki (2009: 181) observes, "[a]djectives that predicate bigness systematically license degree readings. Adjectives that predicate smallness do not." But, as he addresses in a footnote, *klein* in German provides a curious exception to this otherwise widely held generalization (Morzycki 2009: 181). We think it is not really problematic. First, it is not clear that it expresses a small degree: rather it seems to act upon the dimension expressed by the noun itself. That is, a *kleines Genie* is not necessarily somebody that has a small degree of being a genius, but is a genius in not all the major respects, which is akin to Morzycki's significance reading. Secondly, even if it allowed a true degree reading, it seems to be an idiosyncratic property of German, as in general, adjectives of smallness do not give rise to degree readings in German.

TABLE 5.4 Syntax–semantics (mis)matches with EIs

	syntax	←match→	semantics
internal	indefinite	✓	indefinite
	definite	✓	definite
external	indefinite	(✓)	indefinite
	definite	✗	indefinite

marked in EDCs, whereas the (required) definite article is nevertheless interpreted as indefinite.

5.2.4 *Nominal external intensifying constructions*

Let us now turn to the EI-construction that is still missing, namely the one in which an external EI intensifies the degree associated with a DP-internal noun instead of the degree of an adjective. We gave an example for this in (5.10), and more examples of such adnominal EDCs can easily be found.

(5.87) $\gamma \left\{ \begin{array}{l} \text{mords} \\ \text{sau} \\ \text{total} \\ \text{voll} \end{array} \right\} \left\{ \begin{array}{l} \text{der Idiot} \\ \text{die Party} \\ \text{die Stimmung} \end{array} \right\}$ 'EI the {idiot/party/atmosphere}'

Like their internal kin, adnominal EDCs are only licensed by particular, gradable nouns. Hence, the contrasts observed in (5.52)–(5.55) for internal adnominal EIs carry over to the external variants.

(5.88) a. *total   das   Auto
          EI   the   car
       b. $^\gamma$total   die   Schrottkarre
          EI   the   junker
          'EI a junker'

(5.89) a. *total   das   Haus
          EI   the   haus
       b. $^\gamma$total   die   Villa
          EI   the   villa
          'EI a villa'

Adnominal EDCs also share properties with the external adjectival variants. In particular, they exhibit the same definiteness mismatch, as the definite article is interpreted as indefinite.

(5.90)   *Ich habe **total** die Schrottkarre da   gekauft.
          I   have   EI   the junker   there bought
          intended: 'I've bought EI the junker over there.'

The important observation about adnominal EDCs is that they are possible with all
EIs, even those from the *voll* or *sau* group, which, as I have shown in the discussion
around (5.57), cannot be used in the internal adnominal position. That is, in contrast
to (5.57), which I repeat here for convenience, the variants in (5.91) are all possible.

(5.57) $*$ein $\left\{ \begin{array}{l} {}^{\%}\text{mords} \\ {}^{\%}\text{sau} \\ {}^{?}\text{voll} \end{array} \right\}$ Idiot

(5.91) $\gamma \left\{ \begin{array}{l} \text{mords} \\ \text{sau} \\ \text{voll} \end{array} \right\}$ der Idiot   'EI the idiot'

That, of course, does not mean that the external position in adnominal EDCs is an
anything-goes position; ordinary degree items like *sehr* are still excluded from that
position, just as they are impossible in internal adnominal contexts.

(5.92)   a. *sehr der Idiot   b. *ein sehr Idiot
             very the idiot   *a   very idiot*

Any approach to EDCs therefore must tell something about why EIs which seem
to have the same internal distribution as ordinary degree items—being licensed in
adjectival contexts, but excluded from adnominal ones—can nevertheless occur in
external adnominal and adjectival EDCs, while *sehr* and its kin cannot.

    Before going on, let us briefly address an interaction between adnominal and
adjectival use, especially in EDCs. The important observation is that EDCs seem
to be possible even with non-dimensional adjectives that do not combine well with
degree modifiers (van Os 1989), at least not without coercion. Consider, for instance,
adjectives like the following.

(5.93)   a. sechsbeinig 'with six arms'
          b. letzt 'last'
          c. unlösbar 'unsolvable'
          d. arbeitslos 'unemployed'
          e. schwanger 'pregnant'

As these adjectives are not connected to a dimensional scale, they are marked, if not
unacceptable, with ordinary degree expressions. The same holds for EIs in internal
position.

(5.94) a. *ein {**sehr** / **sau**} sechsbeiniges Monster
    a *very* EI *six.legged* *monster*

  b. *ein {**sehr** / **sau**} arbeitsloser Mann
    a *very* EI *unemployed man*

  c. *ein {**sehr** / **sau**} unlösbares Problem
    a *very* EI *unsolvable problem*

In contrast to this restriction, such non-dimensional adjectives can, however, co-occur with external EIs under certain circumstances.

(5.95) a. **sau** das sechsbeinige Monster[20]
   EI *the six.legged* *monster*

  b. ᵞdas war **voll** das unlösbare problem [...]
   that was EI *the unsolvable problem*
   'That was a totally unsolvable problem.'
   [http://www.bym.de/forum/welt/437314-hallo-80-print.html]

  c. ᵞGerade bin ich **voll** der arbeitslose Penner [...]
   currently am I EI *the unemployed bum*
   'Currently, I am a totally unemployed bum.'
   [http://www.tagesspiegel.de/berlin/ich-bin-ein-berliner-63-ich-bin-gerade-penner/8226140.html]

However, I think that such examples constitute only superficial evidence against the generalization that EIs can only be used with gradable expressions. The EDCs in (5.95) do not target the adjective directly, but instead are used adnominally and intensify the complex NP containing the attributive adjective as well as the noun. There are two arguments in favor of this assumption. First, all of the examples in (5.95) are still grammatical if the adjective is omitted.

(5.96)

  a. ᵞ $\left\{ \begin{array}{l} \text{sau} \\ \text{voll} \\ \text{total} \end{array} \right\}$ das Monster 'EI a monster'

  b. ᵞ $\left\{ \begin{array}{l} \text{sau} \\ \text{voll} \\ \text{total} \end{array} \right\}$ das Problem 'EI a problem'

  c. ᵞ $\left\{ \begin{array}{l} \text{sau} \\ \text{voll} \\ \text{total} \end{array} \right\}$ der Penner 'EI a bummer'

This shows that the adnominal use is available for the EDCs in (5.95). The availability of the internal adnominal degree reading for the following examples further confirms this.

(5.97) a. ein {totales, großes} Problem
        a   EI   *big*   *problem*
        'a EI/big problem'
    b. ein {totaler, großer} Penner
        a   EI   *big*   *bum*
        'a EI/big bum'

The second argument for an adnominal analysis of the cases in (5.95) comes from the observation that the examples become bad if the noun is substituted by a non-gradable one.

(5.98) a. *sau das sechsbeinige Insekt
        EI   *the* *six.legged*   *insect*
    b. *sau die arbeitslose Person
        EI   *the* *unemployed* *person*

These considerations support an analysis in which EDCs that involve non-gradable adjectives are actually modifying a complex NP which happens to contain an adjective as well. That is, as long as at least one component inside the DP is gradable, the noun or the adjective, an EDC should be available.

5.3 Toward a syntactic analysis of EDCs

Having described in detail the behavior of expressive intensifiers in both internal and external position, we can now tackle the questions raised at the beginning of this chapter, and which I repeat here.

(Q1) **Relation between internal and external EIs**
How is the external position related to the internal one? That is, is it derived by movement or are external EIs base-generated?

(Q2) **Position**
What is the position in which external EIs reside and why can they appear there in the first place?

(Q3) **Definiteness mismatch**
Why are EDCs with definite articles nevertheless interpreted as indefinite? See (5.15).

(Q4) **Constraint on EIs**
Why can EIs occur DP-externally, but not ordinary degree items like *sehr* ('very')? See (5.13).

(Q5) **Different classes of EIs**
Given that in external position, all EIs can be used adnominally, why are some EIs blocked from the internal adnominal position? See (5.11).

(Q6) **Intervention effects**
Why do a variety of constructions, like complex quantifiers or even other EIs or adnominal size adjectives, block EDCs? See (5.16) and (5.17).

Before I am going to answer these questions one by one, we will first outline our syntactic analysis and then show what answers it provides to the six questions, which in turn will give us the opportunity to motivate the approach in more detail.

5.3.1 *The syntactic structure of EDCs*

Our analysis of the EDC is based on two main hypotheses. The first one concerns the relation between the internal and external position, the second one makes assumptions about the relation between the determiner and the expressive nature of EIs.

(H1) **The external position is derived by complex quantifier formation**
From the adnominal degree position, EIs are moved to D and form a complex quantifier with the determiner.

(H2) **Expressivity is a synactic feature**
D can come with an expressivity feature that must be realized phonologically.

Taken together, these two hypotheses lead to a syntactic analysis of EDCs which, I think, is able to account for the major empirical observations regarding EIs and the EDC as detailed in this chapter.

As summarized in Table 5.1, the two factors POSITION (*internal* vs. *external*) and TARGET (*adjective* vs. *noun*) lead to four different cases of EI-constructions. For each of these we need a slightly different analysis, although all of them are directly based on the two hypotheses just introduced.

The basic syntactic grid on which I base our analysis of all four cases combines the two degree projections that I outlined in Sections 5.2.1 and 5.2.2. We have the adjectival degree phrase as an extension of the AP (5.99) and the adnominal degree phrase as an additional functional layer for gradable NPs (5.100).

(5.99) $[_{DP} D^{0} [_{NP} [_{DegP} Deg^{0} [_{AP} \ldots]] [_{NP} \ldots]]]$

(5.100) $[_{DP} D^{0} [_{Deg_{N}P} Deg_{N}^{0} [_{NP} \ldots]]]$

For internal use of EIs, i.e., the (IA) and (IN) case in Table 5.1, the structures are the ones already sketched in (5.25) and (5.56): internal adjectival EIs are the head of the adjectival degree phrase, just like ordinary degree items such as *very*, whereas internal adnominal EIs take up the head position of the adnominal degree phrase.

(5.101)   a. [$_{DP}$ eine [$_{NP}$ [$_{DegP}$ [$_{Deg^0}$ total] [$_{AP}$ coole]] [$_{NP}$ Party]]]
              'a EI cool party'

          b. [$_{DP}$ eine [$_{Deg_NP}$ [$_{Deg_N^0}$ totale] [$_{NP}$ Party]]]
              'a EI party'

From these internal structures, the external variant is derived, according to (H1), by moving the EI into D^0, where it forms a new complex quantifier with the definite determiner.[21]

(5.102)   a. [$_{DP}$ [$_{D^0}$ total+die] [$_{NP}$ [$_{DegP}$ [$_{Deg^0}$ ~~total~~] [$_{AP}$ coole]] [$_{NP}$ Party]]]
          b. [$_{DP}$ [$_{D^0}$ total+die] [$_{Deg_NP}$ [$_{Deg_NP^0}$ ~~total~~] [$_{NP}$ Party]]]

Keeping this basic analysis in mind, we can now provide answers to the four questions outlined above and explore the motivation for and consequences of (5.101) and (5.102) in more detail.

5.3.2 *EDCs are derived by movement*

Our analysis of EDCs is based on the basic idea that EDCs are derived by movement from the internal EI-constructions. However, I should briefly consider the alternative that external EIs are independent from the internal position and are base-generated in their external surface position.

A first challenge for the base-generation approach is that it must tell a story about why EDCs are only possible if there is actually a gradable target inside the DP, that is, if the DP contains an adjectival or adnominal degree phrase (5.103a). Also, as shown by (5.103b), if there is a degree phrase, its degree argument must not already be satisfied by a measure phrase.

(5.103)   a. ****sau** der   Liter   Saft
               EI   *the   liter   juice*

          b. ****sau** die   2   Meter   langen   Bretter
               EI   *the   2   meters   long   planks*

Since it should not be possible for an external EI to look inside a DP, there must be a mechanism to ensure that the information about gradability percolates up to the DP level. This is not to say, of course, that this cannot be done, but that it involves additional assumptions that are not necessary for a derivational approach, and which

---

[21] Except for the landing site and the incorporation, this analysis of adjectival EDCs follows Matushansky's (2002) analysis of "degree movement" in English.

(i)   [$_{NumP}$ [$_{AP}$ so capable]$_1$ [$_{Num'}$ [$_{Num}$ an] [$_{NP}$ t_1 [$_{NP}$ assistant]]]].

The important difference between constructions like this and the EDC is that they involve phrasal movement as the adjective is commonly pied-piped. Therefore, Matushansky assumes the specifier position as the landing site. See also Kallulli & Rothmayr 2008 for a similar construction in German.

go beyond what is needed to account for internal EIs, something that is not necessary for the derivational approach.

A more severe challenge is provided by the blocking examples I discussed in the introduction. What is relevant here is the case in which an internal adnominal EI blocks an external use of an adjectival EI.

(5.104)   *sau der **totale** reiche Idiot
        EI   *the*   EI   *rich*   *idiot*

The problem with this construction is that the impossibility of having *sau* in external position solely depends on the presence of the adnominal EI, which has nothing to do with the gradability of the adjective which *sau* is supposed to target. We do not see a reasonable explanation for this blocking effect under a base-generation approach, whereas the derivational account does not need any additional assumptions, as I will show in Section 5.3.7. We therefore conclude that a derivational relation holds between the internal and external position. We will discuss the reasons that drive this movement in the next sections.

5.3.3 *External EIs undergo complex quantifier formation with the determiner*

Besides derivationally relating external EIs to internal ones by movement, the main component of the proposed analysis is the idea that EIs undergo complex quantifier formation with the determiner. The inspiration for this move is drawn from M. Zimmermann's (2003) analysis of constructions involving an infrequency adjective inside a DP which is interpreted like the corresponding DP-external adverbial. Such *occasional constructions* (OCs) (Bolinger 1967; Stump 1981), which are one of the non-local adjectives discussed in the previous chapter.

(5.105)   Ein **gelegentlicher** Segler kam vorbei.
        an   *ocassional*   *sailor came by*
        "An occasional sailor strolled by."

As shown in Chapter 4, besides the ordinary internal interpretation that there is a person who sails occasionally, OCs allow an alternative reading under which *occasional* is not interpreted as an attributive adjective, but like an adverb scoping over the entire event, as in (5.106).

(5.106)   Gelegentlich kam ein Segler vorbei.
        occasionally   *came a*   *sailor*   *by*
        Occasionally, a sailor strolled by.

As already noted by Stump (1981: §2.2), but discussed in more detail by M. Zimmermann (2003), OCs are also possible with definite determiners. Crucially, as shown in Chapter 4, even such seemingly definite OCs are interpreted like the indefinite adverbial counterpart in (4.81). Let me repeat the relevant example from 109.

(5.107)   **Der** gelegentliche Segler kam   vorbei.
　　　　　the   occasional   sailor   came   by

　　　　　≈ 'Occasionally, a sailor strolled by.'
　　　　　≄ 'Occasionally, the sailor strolled by.'

In this regard, OCs exhibit a definiteness mismatch similar to the one involved in EDCs, even if it is not as strong, because OCs are also possible with indefinite articles, something that has been rejected by many (but not all) speakers for EDCs.

　　The non-local reading (Morzycki 2013), as the adverbial reading of OCs can be called, is not freely available, but obeys some syntactic restrictions, both of which are similar to what we observed for EIs. First, the non-local reading is only possible with simple indefinite and definite articles; other "meaningful" expressions in D exclude it (M. Zimmermann 2003: 252). For instance:

(5.108)   {**Jeder, dieser**} gelegentliche Segler kam   vorbei.
　　　　　every   that   occasional   sailor   strolled   by
　　　　　≄ 'Occasionally, {every, that} sailor strolled by.'

Secondly, as already observed by Stump (1981), the non-local reading requires adjacency of the determiner and the adjective, so that it is blocked if there is an intervening element (M. Zimmermann 2003: 252). That is, of the following examples—repeated from Section 4.3.3—only the first one allows the non-local reading of the adjective, while in the second one, it gets blocked by the presence of the ordinary adjective that intervenes between the determiner and the frequency adjective.

(5.109)   Ein **gelegentlicher,** begeisterter Segler kam   vorbei.
　　　　　a   occasional   enthusiastic   sailor   strolled   by

　　　　　≈ 'Occasionally, an enthusiastic sailor strolled by.'

(5.110)   Ein begeisterter, **gelegentlicher** Segler kam   vorbei.
　　　　　an   enthusiastic   occasional   sailor   strolled   by

　　　　　≄ 'Occasionally, an enthusiastic sailor strolled by.'

While not exactly the same, quite similar constraints hold for EDCs. First, recall from the last section that EDCs are also impossible with quantifiers and demonstratives. Secondly, an additional adnominal EI blocks a reading in which an external EI intensifies a lower adjective.

(5.111)   *Heute steigt   voll die große, ~~voll~~ coole Party.
　　　　　today   goes.on EI   *the   big   cool   party*
　　　　　intended: 'Today an important, totally cool party goes on'

OCs are related to EDCs in another important aspect. Since OCs are interpreted as in (4.81), the infrequency adjective somehow must be raised into a position from which it can take scope over the event denoted by the VP, even if this raising happens covertly. Therefore, any analysis of OCs must provide a proper landing site (at LF) for the infrequency adjective. Without committing to any particular analysis, similar things hold for the EDC and therefore the analysis of OCs may cast some light on what a syntactic analysis of EDCs may look like. M. Zimmermann (2003: 250, 254) discusses three potential analyses for the external reading of OCs.

(5.112)   **LF-extraction out of the DP**
A ...[$_{DP}$ D [A̶ NP]]

(5.113)   **Complex quantifier formation by incorporation into the determiner**
[$_{DP}$ D+A [A̶ NP]]

(5.114)   **LF-movement to the specifier position of DP**
[$_{DP}$ A [D [A̶ NP]]]

After discussing the alternatives, M. Zimmermann (2003) settles on (5.113), complex quantifier formation (CQF), as the proper analysis. The main reasons are (i) that the CQF analysis can account for the observed syntactic restrictions and (ii) the shift in interpretation, while (iii) not violating general syntactic constraints. First, the blocking effect of an intervening adjective can be explained by Travis's (1984) head movement constraint or its minimalist successors like relativized minimality (Chomsky 1995; Rizzi 1990), according to which a head can only be moved to its next suitable head position and cannot skip an intervening head position (see M. Zimmermann 2003: 258, for this argument; cf. also I. Roberts 2001). In addition, since the infrequency adjective and the determiner form a new, complex quantifier, it is not necessarily the case that what surfaces as a definite article really is a definite article and hence the shift in interpretation can be accounted for. That is, "compositionality does not extend into the complex quantifier," but this is to be expected as "choosing the indefinite or the definite article as part of the complex quantifier does not make a difference for the overall meaning of OCs" (M. Zimmermann 2003: 257). In contrast, LF-extraction out of the DP and LF-movement to DP^{spec} cannot account for the definiteness mismatch as easily. In addition, the LF-extraction approach faces the problem that definite DPs are islands for both overt and covert extraction (Fiengo & Higginbotham 1981) and therefore, without further motivation, it is unclear why extraction should be possible in this case.

Let us see how these arguments transfer to external EIs. First, note that movement to DP^{spec} is not a viable option for EIs, which are heads and hence cannot end up in that position due to the standard structure preservation requirement that "the landing site of head movement must always be another head" (I. Roberts 2001: 113). Extraction out of DP is not an option either, as the head movement constraint prohibits an EI from skipping an intervening head, which is D^0 in this case. Hence, as for OCs, complex quantifier formation is the only option left for EDCs as well. Note that in contrast to the occasional constructions, CQF happens overtly in the case of EDCs and not just at LF.

Basically, I follow M. Zimmermann's (2003) argumentation and adopt his analysis of OCs and assume that EDCs are derived by moving an EI into D^0, where it undergoes incorporation with the determiner.

(5.115)

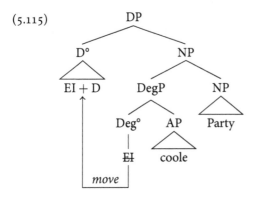

In addition to these more theoretically driven arguments for a CQF-based approach to EI-raising, it is also supported by some empirical considerations. First, it allows us to adopt M. Zimmermann's (2003: 258) reasoning regarding the observation that EIs are impossible with quantifiers, demonstrative or possessive pronouns—see (5.75) above—namely that they "cannot take part in CQF because their inherent semantics must not be overwritten." In addition, it offers a place to account for the observed interpretational shift of the determiner. Similar to the interpretational effects observed in the complex quantifier *occasional+the* in OCs, a complex quantifier like *sau+die* 'EI+the' is not expected to necessarily have compositional meaning. That is, I assume that what occurs as EI plus definite article after CFQ is actually not a definite article, but rather an indefinite one.

Similar considerations apply to the preference for definite articles in EDCs, a problem which the CQF analysis allows us to address The comparison to the OC again helps. While, as we have seen, the OC equally allows both definite and indefinite articles to incorporate with the infrequency adjective, the definite one is preferred with EDCs. The crucial difference between the two constructions is that OCs only involve CQF at LF, while EDCs also show it on PF. Hence, the preference for the definite article may best be expressed as a PF-constraint. That phonological factors are relevant is supported by the following considerations. As as illustrated by the google-data in 5.3, *sau* is almost impossible with indefinite articles, while *total* and *voll* occur more frequently with them. It is likely that this is due to a phonological constraint against the vowel hiatus that occurs with *sau+ein* 'EI+a'. Also, if the indefinite article is used in its reduced form *'n-*, it occurs more frequently with EDCs than the full form *ein-* ('a'). For instance, a Google search for *voll eine coole* yields $\#y = 887$, whereas for *voll ne coole*, the variant with the reduced article, we get $\#y = 37{,}600$ (and $\#y = 145{,}000$ for the definite variant *voll die coole*). For *sau ne coole* we get $\#y = 10$ compared to $\#y = 0$ for *sau eine coole*.

5.3.4 *Expressivity is a feature of D*

As to the question of *why* the article should form a complex quantifier with an EI, there are two different factors that I would like to address. The first is based on the morphological properties of EIs and will be detailed in Section 5.3.6. The more important one involves the connection between the expressive character of EIs and the determiner. Before I can tackle EI-movement in the next section, let us start our approach with the assumption of having expressivity as a feature of D. We already saw in the previous chapter, that D can host interpretable, though unvalued, expressivity features that provide the interpretational counterpart to the valued expressivity feature of a DP-internal expressive adjective. Now, there is another connection between expressivity and D in German: it can come the interpretable and valued variant as well. As discussed by Androutsopoulos (1998: 353f.), the definite article itself can be used to express an EI-like function, when it receives heavy stress.

(5.116) a. Gerhard ist DER Fußballexperte.
  Gerhard is the football.expert
  'Gerhard is THE football expert.'

 b. Heute steigt DIE Party.
  today goes.on the party
  'Today, THE party is going on.'

Constructions like those are also what Androutsopoulos assumes to be the historical source for EDCs. The two relevant observations are that the heavily accented article is (i) interpreted as indefinite and (ii) expresses an intensification of the content of the NP. Following Androutsopoulos, we can hence paraphrase the meaning of constructions like (5.116a) with an indefinite DP with an adnominal degree element.

(5.117) Gerhard ist ein besonders großer Fußballexperte.
  Gerhard is an exceptional big football.expert
  'Gerhard is an exceptionally big soccer expert.'

Androutsopoulos's (1998) idea is that using intensifiers with full DPs is related to such heavily accented determiners. If a heavy accent is a means to give an expressive interpretation to a DP and change its interpretation from definite to indefinite, it does not seem implausible that other expressions like EIs can express this function, when they incorporate with the determiner, so that the heavy accent becomes superfluous. Androutsopoulos's considerations, if correct, fit our approach perfectly. Note, for instance, that a heavy accent on an indefinite DP does not give rise to the same interpretation.

(5.118)   #Gerhard ist EIN Fußballexperte.
           Gerhard is   a   football.expert
           intended: 'Gerhard is an exceptionally big soccer expert.'

In addition, using the intensifying accent together with an external EI is also infelicitous under the intended reading, which further supports the conjecture that the two phenomena are closely related (cf. also Androutsopoulos 1998: 352).

(5.119)   #Gerhard ist **sau** DER Fußballexperte.
           Gerhard is   EI the football.expert

Let us spell out this connection in a bit more detail.[22] As shown by the accented cases, an accented definite determiner can function as an expressive intensifier. Building on the ideas from the previous chapter, I again assume that there is an interpretable expressivity feature in D. In contrast to the one used for the analysis of argument extension of expressive adjectives, the expressivity feature for cases like (5.116) already seems to be valued, as it does not depend on another expression. And since the effect of the accentuation of the determiner results in expressive intensification, let us write that feature as [*iEx*: INT].

Moreover, as we also saw, the constructions in (5.116) are interpreted as indefinite. Hence, I assume that [*iEx*:INT] always co-occurs with a negative definiteness feature, which I write as [*iDef*: –]. As (5.116) shows, this feature combination of [*iEx*: INT] [*iDef*: –] in D° must be spelled-out as a definite article plus phonological emphasis in German.[23] For instance:

---

[22] Many thanks to the Susi Wurmbrand for the inspiration for an approach along the lines developed here.

[23] The fact that it must be the definite determiner that realizes this feature combination in German, and that it cannot be the indefinite one, probably results from a conspiracy of various factors. First, there seems to be a blocking effect, as stress on the indefinite *ein-* ('a') results in a numerical interpretation.

(i)   Heute steigt EINE Party! (Nicht zwei.)
       today goes.on a   party not two
       'Today, A party goes on (not two).'

Secondly, as suggested by Regine Eckardt (p.c.) such use of definite DPs may have started from a proper definite, but modal-like reading of the definite article induced by the stress. Under such a reading, (5.116a) could be paraphrased by (5.ii).

(ii)   In the given comparison class, if you called anyone *the soccer expert*, it would be Gerhard.

(5.120) D[*iEx*: INT][*iDef*: –][ϕ: NOM.SG.F] $\Longrightarrow$ DIE

Obviously, I assume that EIs are [*iEx*: INT] as well. When they incorporate with D°, we then get the same set of features in D. In contrast to the case without an EI in D, there is no need to spell-out the expressivity of the EDCs with heavy emphasis, as the EI already takes care of the realization of the expressivity feature. To account for the variation between the two speaker groups, I then assume that this configuration allows two realization forms, one using the definite determiner and the other the indefinite one.

(5.121) a. EI+D[*iEx*: INT][*iDef*: –][ϕ: NOM.SG.F] $\Longrightarrow$ EI+die
       b. EI+D[*iEx*: INT][*iDef*: –][ϕ: NOM.SG.F] $\Longrightarrow$ EI+eine

The speaker group that can use both definite and indefinite articles in EDCs, has access to both of these two morphological realization rules. Taken together, the feature combination of [*iEx*: INT][*iDef*: –] can lead to three forms: definite D with emphasis (5.120), EI plus definite article (5.121a), and, for some speakers, EI plus indefinite article (5.121b).[24]

The assumption of the expressive feature not only helps to capture the connection between the expressive-accent DPs and the external degree modification construction, but will also play an important role in addressing the question of why EIs move in the first place.

5.3.5 EIs move to realize expressivity in D

So far, our approach does not feature any reason for the fact that EIs may move to D in the first place. However, the expressivity feature that I used in the previous section to implement the connection between EDCs and expressive DPs with accented determiners provides us with an opportunity for this as well. The main obstacle to providing a formal motivation for EIs to be raised to D° is that this movement seems to be entirely optional, given that speakers are free to chose between internal and external EIs, if we set aside the case of *sau*-type EIs in adnominal use.[25] That is, (5.122a) and (5.122b) can freely be exchanged.

(5.122) a. eine **sau** coole Party
          a   EI   *cool*   *party*

      b. **sau** die coole Party
          EI *the* *cool* *party*

---

[24] Beyond this, there also seem to be some phonological constraints involved that exclude the use of *sau* with the indefinite *ein-*, as this particular form is unavailable also for those speaker who otherwise accept EDCs with indefinite determiners.

[25] That last case will be discussed in the next section.

In order to syntactically regulate EI-raising nevertheless, we therefore assume that there are different features specificiations in D that trigger this movement or not. As I have argued in the previous section, the expressivity features must be realized phonologically in D^0, either by stress on the determiner or by an EI and, as shown by (5.119), these two ways are in complementary distribution. To account for both optionality of the movement and these different ways to realize expressivity in D, I therefore assume that there are different variants of D that come equipped with different features. First, ordinary variants of D do not come with an [*Ex*]-feature at all. Because there is nothing that then forces the movement of a potential EI inside the DP, they surface as ordinary internal EIs with a definite or indefinite determiner, depending on the further specification of D.

(5.123) $[_{DP} [_{D^0} D_{[iDef: +][\phi: \text{NOM.SG.F}]}] [\dots EI_{[iEx: \text{INT}]} \dots]] \Longrightarrow$ die ... EI ...

(5.124) $[_{DP} [_{D^0} D_{[iDef: -][\phi: \text{NOM.SG.F}]}] [\dots EI_{[iEx: \text{INT}]} \dots]] \Longrightarrow$ eine ... EI ...

Beside these simple D-variants, there are also those that carry an expressivity feature. However, the variant assumed so far, [*iEx*: INT], which is realized by the accented determiner, does not trigger anything. In order to account for the case in which there is EI-raising, let us assume that there is also a variant of D that comes with an uninterpretable, unvalued expressivity feature [*uEx*: __]. Recall that in Chapter 3, I adopted the unidirectional, upward-looking version of agreement championed by Zeijlstra (2012), which I labeled ↑Agree$_i$.

(5.125)   **↑Agree$_i$:**   (Zeijlstra 2012: 514)
           α can ↑Agree$_i$ with β iff:
           a. α carries at least one uninterpretable feature and β carries a matching
              interpretable feature.
           b. β c-commands α.
           c. β is the closest goal to α.

Now, the configuration in which there is an uninterpretable [*Ex*]-feature in D and the EI inside the DP carries an interpretable [*Ex*]-feature is none in which ↑Agree$_i$ment could be established, since D (the probe) is above the EI (the goal) and not the other way around as required by ↑Agree$_i$. To bring the two features into a configuration in which ↑Agree$_i$ can be established is what triggers the raising of the EI to D. However, since I assumed that the EI does not move into a position that is above D, but incorporates into D itself, we have to make a small adjustment to the definition and assume that α and β can also ↑Agree$_i$ with each other, if α incorporated into β.

   Equipped with these assumptions, we can see how the raising of the EI with the [*iEx*]-feature to D allows the [*uEx*]-feature of D to agree with its interpretable counterpart and may hence be marked for deletion.

(5.126)   a. **Movement EI to D**

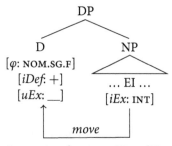

b. **Agreement between EI and D**

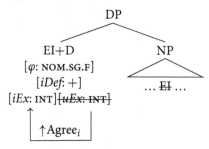

This derivation brings us back to the constellation I assumed in (5.121), which then can be spelled-out as an EDC with a definite or, for some speakers, with an indefinite article.

To sum up, I assume that it is the interplay between the expressive character of EIs and the expression of expressivity in D that is responsible for the EI-movement. In the next section, we will look at another side effect this movement has. This way of thinking about external EIs also has the advantage that it offers a straightforward solution to the question of why ordinary degree items like *sehr* ('very') cannot occur in external position (Q4). They are not expressive and therefore they do not carry the [*iEx*]-feature that would be necessary to trigger the movement, because only the [*iEx*]-feature can be attracted by a corresponding [*uEx*]-feature in D.

5.3.6 *Incorporation with D⁰ is ersatz inflection*

There is a complication to the picture presented so far. As we have seen in Section 5.2.2, and as is summarized in Table 5.2, only *total*-type EIs can actually surface in the Deg_N-position; those from the *voll* and *sau*-group cannot. However, I take the fact that even those EIs can be used adnominally when in an external position as evidence that they are nevertheless adnominal degree elements. But why can't they appear in the internal adnominal position? The key to answering this question lies in another observation presented in Table 5.2: the EIs that cannot be used in internal adnominal position are those that are unable to express φ-features by inflectional morphology, either because the EI has lost this ability (as in the case of *voll*) or never had it to begin with (as in the case of *sau*). However, as can be witnessed by inflectable EIs like *total* (5.127), the Deg$_N$P has to agree in φ-features with D^0 and must overtly express it.

(5.127)   a.   ein   **total-er**   Idiot
              a.NOM.SG.M   EI-NOM.SG.M   *idiot*.NOM.SG.M
              'a EI idiot'

          b.   *ein   **total**   Idiot
              a.NOM.SG.M   EI   *idiot*.NOM.SG.M

Because of this clash between the required overt expression of φ-features and their inability to do so, EIs from the *voll-* and *sau*-group cannot stay in Deg$_N$°. However, the derivation can be rescued if the uninflected EI incorporates into D°. The determiner then functions as a kind of "ersatz inflection." In other words, forming a complex quantifier like *sau+die* 'EI+the' is an alternative way for *sau* to partake in agreement that substitutes for the requirement of expressing the necessary ϕ-features on its own *in situ*.

Some evidence for the fact that the determiner, after incorporation, indeed takes care of the requirement of inflectional morphology is provided by the observation that even EIs from the *voll-*group, which can bear inflectional morphology, receive no additional inflection when they surface in external position.[26] Compare (5.127) to (5.128), where the judgments are reversed.

(5.128)   a.   **total**   der   Idiot
              total   *the*   *idiot*.NOM.SG.M
              'EI an idiot'

          b.   *total-er   der   Idiot
              total-NOM.SG.M   *the*.NOM.SG.M   *idiot*.NOM.SG.M

In addition, this is not only true for EIs, but for other expressions that can occur together with the determiner like some quantifiers. When used inside the DP, such an expression must be inflected, but if it precedes the determiner, it must not carry its own inflectional morphology.

(5.129)   a.   **all-e**   Student-en
              all-NOM.PL.M   *student*-NOM.PL.M
              'all students'

          b.   **all**   die   Student-en
              all   *the*.NOM.PL.M   *student*-NOM.PL.M
              'all the students'

---

[26] This is also observed by Meinunger (2009). In his approach, according to which EIs are adjectives that are base-generated in the external position, they are not inflected because they are merged in a non-inflectional position. In contrast, in our incorporation approach, external EIs are inflected after all, only they use the determiner to do that.

c. *all-e   die   Student-en
   *all-*NOM.PL.M   *the.*NOM.PL.M   *student-*NOM.PL.M

The incorporation-for-inflection approach also provides reasons for the observed definiteness mismatch and for the fact that EIs move in the first place. First, if the determiner is recruited as a means to express the necessary φ−features morphologically, this explains why it does not express its ordinary meaning anymore.[27] In analogy to M. Zimmermann's (2003) analysis of OCs, it also explains why demonstratives, quantifiers, and possessives cannot be used in external EIs, because their additional lexical semantic content would be overridden.

In addition to providing an answer to (Q4), this account also motivates why EIs move at all. While the movement from Deg° to Deg$_N$° is optional from a syntactic point of view, the move from Deg$_N$° to D° is completely driven by syntactic viz. morphological considerations. In the case of EIs of the *voll-* and *sau-*group, it is obligatorily triggered once Deg$_N$° is reached in order to make up for the lack of inflectional morphology that is required in that position. In contrast, whether an EI like *total* moves to D° or remains *in situ* depends on whether or not the suitable inflectional morphology is used in Deg$_N$° or not.

Under this analysis, EI-movement is not only triggered by an uninterpretable expressivity feature in D, but, at least for some EIs in adnominal position, is also a consequence of a EI being in a agreement position but not being able to receive the necessary inflection for ϕ-features in that position. Hence, in some sense, it moves to pick up agreement morphology similar to how a verb moves to pick up its inflection. In this sense, EI-movement complies with the generalization that movement leads to richer morphology even if it *prima facie* does not (Zeijlstra 2012). What is special about this case is that it is a determiner that is recruited to fulfill the role of inflection.

5.3.7 *Intervention effects*

The analysis of EDCs presented here can also explain some additional effects, which, to our knowledge, have not yet been described. The first set of data regards the interaction between adnominal and adjectival EIs. First note that the use of internal adnominal EIs together with adjectival EIs is possible.

(5.130)   ein[$_{Deg_N P}$ **totaler** [$_{NP}$ [$_{Deg P}$ **sau** reicher] Idiot]]
      a   EI   EI   *rich*   *idiot*
      'a total totally rich idiot'

---

[27] This may well also be true for (5.129). However, since a universal quantifier should already be conceived as definite, one cannot really tell whether the CQF with the determiner overrides the D-feature of the determiner.

What is crucial about this constellation is that the adnominal DegN° c-commands the adjectival Deg°. Therefore, an adjectival EI that shall be raised in order to undergo CQF cannot directly be move to D°, because it would cross DegN° and hence would go against the head movement constraint. Instead, it must first move to DegN°. Therefore, an internal adnominal EI is predicted to block an adjectival EI from raising to the external position. As I briefly mentioned above, this is indeed confirmed by the data.

(5.131) ****sau** der **totale** ~~sau~~ reiche Idiot
        EI *the* EI *rich* *idiot*

As is expected as well, adjectival EDCs are not only blocked by adnominal EIs, but also by adnominal size adjectives.

(5.132) ****sau** der **große** ~~sau~~ reiche Idiot
        EI *the* *big* *rich* *idiot*

Of course, the opposite constellation—an internal adjectival degree element and an adnominal EDC—is perfectly fine.

(5.133) **voll** der ~~voll~~ total reiche Idiot
        EI *the* EI *rich* *idiot*
        'a total totally rich Idiot'

In a similar vein, because EIs have to form a complex quantifier with the determiner, the analysis predicts intervention effects if there are other expressions that form complex quantifiers. Again, this is borne out by the data. For instance, consider again the *occasional*-constructions discussed above. As they involve CQF at LF, they interfere with EDCs. As shown by (5.134a) and (5.134b), this holds irrespective of the order in which the infrequency adjective and the DegP hosting the EI are ordered. The same intervention effect can, as expected, be observed with adnominal EDCs, as in (5.134c).

(5.134) a. **Sau der **gelegentliche,** reiche Kunde betrat den Laden.
           EI *the* *occasional* *rich* *customer* *entered* *the* *shop*

        b. **Sau der reiche, **gelegentliche** Kunde betrat den Laden.
           EI *the* *rich* *occasional* *customer* *entered* *the* *shop*
           both intended: 'Occasionally, a EI rich customer entered the shop.'

        c. **Sau der **gelegentliche** Idiot betrat den Laden.
           EI *the* *occasional* *idiot* *entered* *the* *shop*
           intended: 'Occasionally, a EI idiot entered the shop.'

Internal EIs of course do not intervene with infrequency adjectives so that the latter can undergo CQF and the adverbial reading of the OC is available.

(5.135) a. Der **gelegentliche sau** reiche Kunde betrat den Laden.
        the occasional EI *rich customer entered the shop*
        'Occasionally, an EI rich customer entered the shop.'

      b. Der **gelegentliche totale** Idiot betrat den Laden.
        the occasional EI *idiot entered the shop*
        'Occasionally, an EI idiot entered the shop.'

Another set of data that our analysis correctly predicts is provided by similar intervention effects that can be observed for other adjectives that form complex quantifiers with the determiner. For instance, the adjective *ganz* 'whole, intact' can build a complex quantifier roughly paraphrasable as 'all the' (cf. M. Zimmermann 2003: 259, from whom I borrow the following example).[28]

(5.136) Wer hat denn die **ganzen** Punkte hier gemalt?
      who has then the whole dots here painted
      'Who has painted all the dots here?'   (quantificational reading)
      NOT: 'Who has painted the whole/intact dots here?'   (attributive reading)

M. Zimmermann (2003) assumes an analysis for such constructions pretty much like the one he advocates for the OC: the adjective *ganz* LF-moves from its attributive position to D^0 to build the complex quantifier.[29]

(5.137) [DP [D⁰ die+ganzen] [NP ~~ganzen~~ Punkte]]
           the whole   *dots*
     'all the dots'

Taken together with our analysis of EDCs, this assumption predicts that such complex quantifiers also intervene with external EIs, which, as shown by the following examples, indeed seems to be the case.

(5.138) a. ***sau** die **ganzen** reichen Kunden
        EI *the whole rich customers*

      b. ***sau** die **ganzen** Idioten
        EI *the whole idiots*

The fact that the CQF-approach to EDCs can account for these two different kinds of intervention effects 'for free' adds additional empirical support to it.

5.4 Conclusion and outlook

At the beginning of this chapter, I formulated six questions that I took to be the most pressing ones regarding the syntactic analysis of the external degree modification

---

[28] For many more examples, see Pafel 1994.
[29] I changed the analysis slightly to bring it more in line with the present approach.

construction in German. We first described the behavior of four different expressive intensifiers constructions, namely both internal and external EIs in adjectival and adnominal use. From there, we developed an analysis that I think is capable of addressing those questions. The approach is based on two hypotheses. First, all expressive intensifiers are also adnominal degree elements, even those that cannot remain in internal adnominal position (H1). Secondly, from this adnominal position, the external degree modification construction is derived by complex quantifier formation with the determiner (H2). Taken together, these two hypotheses lead to the following answers to questions (Q1)–(Q6).

(A1)   **Relation to internal EIs**
       The EDC is derived from internal EIs by head-movement to D.

(A2)   **Position**
       EIs move to D^0 in order to realize an expressivity feature.

(A3)   **Definiteness mismatch**
       EIs undergo complex quantifier formation with the determiner, which is governed by its own realization rules.

(A4)   **Constraint on EIs**
       Since ordinary degree items lack the expressivity feature, there is nothing that would license their movement.

(A5)   **Different classes of EIs**
       Surfacing in the adnominal degree position requires the overt morphological expression of φ-features. Since EIs of the *voll-* and *sau-*group cannot be inflected, they must not stay in that position. However, incorporating into the determiner serves as ersatz morphology.

(A6)   **Intervention effects**
       Other constructions that involve complex quantifier formation like the *occasional*-construction or quantifiers like *die+ganzen* block EDCs because the determiner can only incorporate with one expression. Internal adnominal EIs or size adjectives block adjectival EDCs, because the $Deg_N{}^0$-position is already occupied and the adjectival EI must not cross it.

However, despite providing answers to these six questions, EDCs pose many more, equally interesting questions for further research which could not be addressed in this chapter. Especially, more work has to be done on the historical development of EIs and their semantic analysis, which we could only touch upon in this chapter. However, with respect to the main hypothesis of this book—the hypothesis of expressive syntax—the upshot of this chapter is that expressivity as a syntactic feature can trigger movement.

5.5 Appendix

TABLE 5.5 Detailed Google hits for the variants in (5.74)

EI	D°	AP	NP	#γ [Def: +]	[Def: −]	EI	D°	AP	NP	#γ [Def: +]	[Def: −]
		coole	} Band	30	0			coole	} Band	1	0
		geile		83	0			geile		106	0
		gute		26	0			gute		9	0
		coole	} Freund	10	0			coole	} Freund	0	0
		geile		58	0			geile		2	0
		gute		4.450	0			gute		206	6
sau	[D]					total	[D]				
		coole	} Freundin	105	0			coole	} Freundin	8	0
		geile		4.410	0			geile		8	0
		gute		6.050	1			gute		6,050	1
		coole	} Idee	79	0			coole	} Idee	474	0
		geile		4.410	0			geile		31,300	1
		gute		5.040	0			gute		5,950	367
		coole	} Party	10	0			coole	} Party	6	0
		gute		2	0			gute		7	0
		geile		1.030	0			geile		1	0
			Σ	30.308	1				Σ	44,128	376

EI	D°	AP	NP	#γ [Def: +]	[Def: −]
		coole	} Band	4.270	0
		geile		25,000	1
		gute		979	0
		coole	} Freund	5,580	21
		geile		5,510	6
		gute		43,900	1,180
voll	[D]				
		coole	} Freundin	24,000	3
		geile		32,600	6
		gute		115,000	574
		coole	} Idee	91,200	7
		geile		161,000	8
		gute		167,000	367
		coole	} Party	1,310	0
		gute		37,600	0
		geile		197	0
			Σ	715,146	2,173

6

Expressive vocatives

6.1 Introduction

The cases studies carried out in the previous two chapters have in common that the two phenomena they deal with—expressive adjectives and expressive intensifiers respectively—are both part of the DP, even if they can be interpreted at a higher position (in case of expressive adjectives) or occur in a seemingly DP-external position (in case of expressive intensifiers).

However, as discussed briefly in Chapter 3, most previous work that dealt with the syntacticization of pragmatic aspects of language concentrated on elements that mainly occur in the left, or sometimes right, peripheral positions (see Section 3.6). With vocatives, this chapter picks up one of these peripheral expressions and, informed by the work carried out in this book so far, offers a semantically-driven perspective on them that also employs syntactic expressivity features.

However, we will see that, even if we start out by looking at the peripheral use of vocatives, that there are also more integrated uses which, as it turns out, have more in common with the more integrated expressives like the expressive adjectives from Chapter 4, coming full-circle so to speak. That this will be the case is because what I am going to investigate in more detail are not stereotypical vocations as in (6.1).

(6.1) **Vocatives**
    a. **Ede**, the pizza is ready.   (Eckardt 2014: 224)
    b. **Angelina**, the sky is on fire.   (Predelli 2008: 97)

Instead, I will focus on a special subset of vocatives which are used for cursing and swearing and which I call expressive vocatives. So what do I mean by this label? First note that standard vocatives like in (6.1) are not really expressive in Bühler's (1934/1982) or Jakobson's (1960b) sense; they arguably instantiate the appealing function of language.[1] For this reason, I will touch upon such plain vocatives for expository reasons only. What I am really interested in are vocative forms like those in

---

[1] They may still be considered to be expressive in the Kaplanian or Pottsean sense in so far as they do not encode truth-conditional content, but instead display some other kind of content (Kaplan 1999; Potts 2005), which certainly is rather use-conditional (Gutzmann 2015b).

The Grammar of Expressivity. First edition. Daniel Gutzmann.
© Daniel Gutzmann 2019. First published in 2019 by Oxford University Press.

(6.2), which consist of a second person pronoun together with a noun. Stereotypical expressive nouns as in (6.2a) and (6.2b) are cases in point, but even more interesting for our purposes is the observation that neutral nouns as in (6.2c) and (6.2d) receive an insult-like interpretation in this construction as well.

(6.2) **Expressive vocatives (eVocs)**
    a. **You idiot!**
    b. **You bastard!**
    c. **You linguist!**
    d. **You philosopher!**

Such vocative constructions are called *evaluative vocatives* (Corver 2008), *exclamatory vocatives* (Welte 1980), or *pseudo-vocatives* (d'Avis & Meibauer 2013) in the literature. And while each of these terms capture an important aspect of their character, I will call them *expressives vocatives*—"eVocs" for short.

The plan for this chapter is as follows. I will begin with standard vocatives, by discussing the data established in the literature and adding a lot of new observations regarding expressive vocatives.

6.2 Standard vocatives

Among the expressions discussed in this book, vocatives, in their simple version, have received the most attention in the syntactic literature (see, amongst others, Haegeman & Hill 2013; Hill 2007, 2014; Welte 1980; Zwicky 1974, and the contributions in Sonnenhauser & Noel Aziz Hanna 2013b), while expressive vocatives ("eVocs") have only received marginal attention (Corver 2008; d'Avis & Meibauer 2013; Welte 1980). Before turning to these, I will first discuss the basic properties of ordinary vocatives.

A precise and general definition of what constitutes a vocative that goes beyond "I know it when I see it" is not easy to come by, since it seems to depend heavily on the theoretical background against which the definition is developed and which languages are studied, as pointed out in detail by Sonnenhauser & Noel Aziz Hanna (2013a).

> Traditionally, and depending to a large degree both on the theoretical approach and the specific language studied, vocatives are classified either in purely formal terms as part of the language system, or as functional structures manifesting themselves in language use only.
>
> (Sonnenhauser & Noel Aziz Hanna 2013a: 1)

For this reason, they decide to use "vocative" only as a "mere label for linguistic addressing phenomena, without any commitment to specific theoretical assumptions or positions" (Sonnenhauser & Noel Aziz Hanna 2013a: 2).

In general, I adopt a similar broad stance here. For instance, a purely morphological definition of vocatives that presupposes that vocatives actually bear vocative case marking is too restrictive for the purposes of this chapter, since I am dealing with vocatives in German and, for comparison and exposition, English, which neither of exhibit vocative case marking. That is, under a more or less theory-agnostic approach, standard vocatives in English or German (6.3) fall under the definition, as do vocative-marked phrases in languages like Sanskrit, Malayalam (Southern Dravidian), or Manambu (Middle Sepik) as in (6.4). Crucially, depending on one's definition of "addressing," some particles and interjections of addressing that often accompany standard nominal vocatives, could also be argued to be vocatives (6.5).

(6.3) a. Ede, the pizza is ready.
       b. Ede, die Pizza ist fertig.

(6.4) a. kany-e   kany-e   kutra-asi
          daughter-VOC *daughter*-VOC *where-be.2.SG.FEM*
          'Daughter, daughter, where are you?'   (Sanskrit)

       b. mooḷ-ee
          daughter-VOC
          'Daughter!'   (Malayalam, Asher, & Kumari 1997: 224)

       c. amæy-a
          mother-VOC
          'Oh mother!'   (Manambu & Aikhenvald 2008: 44)

(6.5) a. hey, ey, hi, hello
       b. he, hey, ey, hi, hallo

However, even if they do not adopt a purely morphological criterion, many definitions one finds in the literature are much stricter than the pragmatic view Sonnenhauser & Noel Aziz Hanna take. According to many definitions, an important property of a vocative is that "it doesn't serve as an argument of a verb" (Zwicky 1974: 787), or, as Schaden (2010: 177, his emphasis) elaborates, that "a vocative does not serve as argument to *any* other element of the sentence." Under this view, the expressions in (6.6) do not qualify as vocatives, as they are the subjects of the sentence and as such serve as an argument to the verb.

(6.6) a. **Du Idiot** sollst   verschwinden.
          you idiot should you
          'You idiot should go away!'

       b. Was   wünscht **die Dame?**
          what wishes   the lady
          'What do you wish, madam?'

However, since the expression in (6.6a) looks just like the eVocs I am interested in, I will not adopt such a strict syntactic criterion for the moment.

    Another property that is often included in the definition of vocatives is that the expression that is used vocatively is a term that "names the addressee explicitly, by using a term referring to and, so to speak, directly acting on them" (Daniel & Spencer

2009: 626). By including this criterion, other forms that address the hearer, like the particles in (6.5) are excluded. For the purposes of this chapter, I will adopt this stance and more or less exlude such vocative particles, even though I briefly consider them when discussion the syntactic position of vocatives later on.

6.2.1 *Building standard vocatives*

The most stereotypical instance of a standard vocative is the use of a proper name in sentence initial position as in (6.7).

(6.7) **Jacquie,** your grammar leaks.   (Zwicky 1974: 787)

But even with this simple pattern, we can observe a lot of variation (cf. Zwicky 1974: 788; some adaptions made for German).

(6.8) a. Petra
          ⟨FIRST NAME⟩

     b. Schumacher
          ⟨LAST NAME⟩

     c. Petra   Schumacher
          ⟨FIRST NAME⟩ ⟨LAST NAME⟩

     d. Professor
          ⟨TITLE⟩

     e. Prof.   Schumacher
          ⟨TITLE⟩ ⟨LAST NAME⟩

     f. Prof.   Petra   Schumacher
          ⟨TITLE⟩ ⟨FIRST NAME⟩ ⟨LAST NAME⟩

     g. Frau   Schumacher
          ⟨PREFIX⟩ ⟨LAST NAME⟩

     h. Frau   Petra   Schumacher
          ⟨PREFIX⟩ ⟨FIRST NAME⟩ ⟨LAST NAME⟩

     i. Frau   Professor
          ⟨PREFIX⟩ ⟨TITLE⟩

     j. Frau   Prof.   Schumacher
          ⟨PREFIX⟩ ⟨TITLE⟩ ⟨LAST NAME⟩

     k. Frau   Prof.   Petra   Schumacher
          ⟨PREFIX⟩ ⟨TITLE⟩ ⟨FIRST NAME⟩ ⟨LAST NAME⟩

     l. Tante   Schumacher
          ⟨KINTITLE⟩ ⟨LAST NAME⟩

     m. Tante   Petra
          ⟨KINTITLE⟩ ⟨FIRST NAME⟩

     n. Tante
          ⟨KINTITLE⟩

While this list may give rise to the impression of "anything goes," there are several combinatoric constraints. For instance, first names cannot be combined with prefixes or titles in German, except for playful contexts in which, say, close friends may use "Prof. Petra" do address her in a jocular or even sarcastic manner.[2] Likewise, combining a kintitle with a prefix or title is rather infelicitous as well.

(6.9) a. *Prof.   Petra
           ⟨TITLE⟩ ⟨FIRST NAME⟩

       b. *Frau   Petra
           ⟨PREFIX⟩ ⟨FIRST NAME⟩

       c. *Tante   Prof.   Schumacher
           ⟨KINTITLE⟩ ⟨TITLE⟩   ⟨LAST NAME⟩

       d. *Frau   Tante   Schumacher
           ⟨PREFIX⟩ ⟨KINTITLE⟩ ⟨LAST NAME⟩

The explanation for such incompatibilities is that these name-based vocatives involve many use-conditions related to the social relation between speaker and addressee, in addition to the use-conditions associated with the vocative itself (to which I will turn later). Together with the distinction between formal and informal second person pronouns, these different choices of vocatives build an intricate honorific-like politeness system in German.

Of course, besides using (possibly extended) proper names as vocatives, the use of a simple second person pronoun is also a stereotypical instance of a vocative. As alluded to in (2.37), German here distinguishes between a familiar and a formal pronoun, whose usage depends on the social relation between speaker and addressee, similar to the constraints on the various extensions of a proper name.

(6.10) a. **Du,**   könnte ich dich   mal   kurz   sprechen?
           *you.*FAMILIAR *could* *I* *you.*FAMILIAR PART   *brief speak*
           'You, could I talk to you briefly?'

        b. **?Sie,**   könnte ich Sie   mal   kurz   sprechen?
           *you.*FORMAL   *could* *I* *you.*FORMAL   PART   *brief speak*
           'You, could I talk to you briefly?'

Interestingly, the use of the formal second person pronoun *Sie* as a pure vocative is slightly more marked when compared to the plan familiar pronoun *du*. However, the reason for this may just be that the contexts that require the use of formal

---

[2] This contrasts with English in which certain aristocratic titles are used with first names only: *Sir John*, *Lord Peter*, as well as some professional titles like *Reverend Henry* (cf. Zwicky 1974: 788).

pronoun generally overlap with contexts in which the use of an extended proper noun would also be almost obligatory. In principle, there in nothing wrong with (6.10b). In a context, where there are multiple potential addresses and the speaker does not know their names, it is fine to address each of them with just *Sie*. Imagine, for example, a context of some health emergency.

(6.11) **Sie**   [pointing to A], bringen Sie   mir ein Glas
        *you.*FORMAL   *bring*   *you.*FORMAL *me* *a* *glass*
        Wasser und Sie   [pointing to B], rufen Sie   bitte
        water *and* *you.*FORMAL   *call* *you.*FORMAL *please*
        einen Krankenwagen!
        a   *ambulance*
        'You, bring me a glass of water and you, please call the ambulance!'

Crucially, using two bare pronouns to address two different persons is only possible if it is accompanied with appropriate eye gazes and/or pointing gestures that make it clear whom the speaker intends to address. This highlights one of the important functions of vocatives (which I will turn to in more detail below): they are use to identify the addressee.

That is, without a clear pointing or gaze that unambiguously expresses the speaker's referential intentions, a pure pronoun is not sufficient to fulfill this function. However, if the pronoun is extended by more descriptive material it can function without a gesture or other extra-linguistic means.

(6.12) ^γSie   mit der roten Mütze. Stehen Sie   auf und
        *you.*FORMAL *with* *the* *red* *hat* *stand* *you.*FORMAL *up* *and*
        helfen Sie   mir.
        help *you.*FORMAL *me*
        'You with the red hat, get up and help me.'
        [https://www.beobachter.ch/prix-courage/zivilcourage-das-experiment]

With adequate linguistic material, two extended pronouns can be used to call to two different addressees, as with the gestures.

(6.13) ^γSie   mit der roten Mütze. Stehen Sie   auf und
        *you.*FORMAL *with* *the* *red* *hat* *stand* *you.*FORMAL *up* *and*
        helfen Sie   mir. Sie   mit der schwarzen
        help *you.*FORMAL *me* *you.*FORMAL *with* *the* *black*
        Lederjacke,   rufen Sie   die Polizei
        leather.jacket *call* *you.*FORMAL *the* *police*
        'You with the red hat, get up and help me. You with the black leather jacket, call the police.'
        [https://www.beobachter.ch/prix-courage/zivilcourage-das-experiment]

Even if there are multiple potential addresses for *Sie* in (6.13), the additional specification can help to single out and thereby set the addressee, as long as there is only one salient potential addressee with a red hat, of course. I will now turn to these functional considerations about vocatives.

6.2.2 *Vocative functions*

Traditionally, the literature assumes a bipartite classification of vocative functions, which according to Zwicky (1974: 799, note 2) goes at least back to Schlegloff (1968). While Schlegloff distinguishes between terms of *address* and *summonses*, it is more common in the literature to use Zwicky's distinction between *addressess* and *calls*. We already encountered instances of the latter in (6.11) and (6.12). A call function of a vocative is "designed to catch the addressee's attention" (Zwicky 1974: 787) and thereby "marks/identifies the selected addressee" (d'Avis & Meibauer 2013: 195). In order for this to be successful and the vocative therefore to be felicitous it is important that the speaker chooses an expression with a content that can unambiguously identify the addressee (or the group of addressees, to be precise). Otherwise, pointing gestures or other extra-linguistic means (like gazes, head nods, etc.) have to be employed to ensure the identification of the addressee.

Calls often co-occur with vocative-like particles like in (6.5), which also function to draw attention, but which do not fix the addressee on their own. These "attention-getters" (Zwicky 1974: 797) precede the vocative when they co-occur.

(6.14)   a. **Hey Ede**, the pizza is ready.
         b. **Hey Ede**, die Pizza ist fertig.

Due to their addressee-fixing function, calls usually can only occur in a pre-sentential position, because their function would be diminished if they occur, say, at the right edge of the sentence.

(6.15)   a. *The pizza is ready, **hey Ede**.
         b. *The pizza, **hey Ede**, is ready.

(6.16)   a. *Die Pizza ist fertig, **hey Ede**.
         b. *Die Pizza, **hey Ede**, ist fertig.

However, as Zwicky observes, calls can occur sentence-internally if one discourse interrupts another (Zwicky 1974: 797).

(6.17)   As I was saying—**Oh Sharon!** Come here and let us see that marvelous new dress!—you can't believe a thing you read these days! In addition, calls can occur sentence-internally, if subparts of an utterance target different addressees.

(6.18)   a. (Hey) **Ede**, here we have coffee and (hey) **Carla**, here, we have tea, and (hey) **Donna**, here we have soda.

b. (Hey) **Ede**, hier gibt's Kaffee und (hey) **Carla**, hier gibt's Tee und, (hey) **Donna**, hier gibt's Cola.

Since the utterances in (6.18) can, however, be understood as three more or less independent information units, it is not completely surprising that they can be targeted at different addressees. Crucially, for each of the three vocatives in (6.18a) and (6.18b), the restriction to precede that information holds.

(6.19)   a. *Here we have pizza, (hey) **Ede** and here we have coffee, (hey) **Carla**, here we have Döner, and (hey) **Donna**.

b. *Hier gibt's Pizza, (hey) **Ede**, und hier gibt's Kaffee, (hey) **Carla**, und hier gibt's Döner, (hey) **Donna**.

Because it is the function of a call to identify the addressee and get their attention, it follows that bare pronouns are not good as calls, if their content is not enriched by some kind of deictic pointing, as shown in (6.11). In addition, this function also explains why quantified DPs are not suitable to be used as calls, as they do not identify a specific individual (or group).

(6.20)   a. ***Somebody with a black shirt**, here I also have a black hat for you as well.
b. ***At least two women**, can you help me carry this box upstairs?

(6.21)   a. ***Jemand mit einem scharzen T-Shirt**, hier habe ich auch eine schwarze Mütze für Dich.
b. ***Mindestens zwei Frauen**, könnt ihr mir helfen, diese Kiste nach oben zu tragen?

The sole exception here is the use of universally quantified DPs, which can be used as calls (Schaden 2010: 177).

(6.22)   a. **Everyone who has a dog**, you need a dog permit!
b. **Jeder der einen Hund hat**, ihr braucht eine Hundelizenz!

That these are really call-vocatives can be illustrated by the fact that they are fine with attention-getting particles of address. In addition, that these quantifiers really target the audience is shown by the possibility of inserting a context-referring expression like *hier* ('here') into the restrictor of the quantifier.

(6.23)   a. Everyone **here** who has a dog, you need a dog permit!
b. Jeder **hier** der einen Hund hat, ihr braucht eine Hundelizenz!

However, it is no surprise that universally quantified DPs can be used here, since it is not uncommon that they can be shifted to type *e* and hence be interpreted as an expression referring to the group of addressees (Eckardt 2014: 226; Portner 2007: 411).

Besides the call function, vocatives can also be used to "confirm the addressee-status of the person spoken to" (d'Avis & Meibauer 2013: 197). That is, the addressee is already established in the utterance situation but its status is kept active by this use of vocatives. That is, even if it is clear to whom the speaker of (6.24) is talking to, she can still use a vocative in order "to maintain or emphasize the contact between speaker and addressee," as Zwicky (1974: 797) puts it. Unlike calls, such vocatives can occur in sentence-internal or -final positions.

(6.24) Kannst du, **Birgit**, mir mal   die Fernbedienung geben?
        can   you Birgit   me PART the remote-control give
        'Can you, Birgit, give me the remote control?'

(6.25) Kannst du   mir mal   die Fernbedienung geben, **Birgit**?
        can   you me PART the remote.control give   Birgit
        'Can you give me the remote control, Birgit?'

Assuming that (6.24) is uttered in a one-to-one situation in which it obvious that Birgit is the addressee, the speaker can still use the proper name *Birgit* as a vocative to confirm and emphasize Birgit's status as the addressee. Zwicky calls such uses *addresses*, while d'Avis & Meibauer call them *A-confirmations* to emphasize the fact, that they confirm an already established addressee.

Even though regarding their syntactic position, addresses seem to be freer than call-vocatives, they are generally much more restricted than calls. Many expressions that seem to be fine as calls, are rather infelicitous as addresses or, if possible at all, seem to be rather rude (Portner 2007: 410).[3]

(6.26) a. **Cabby**, take me to Carnegie Hall.   (Zwicky 1974: 790)
        b. *I don't think, **cabby**, that the Lincoln Tunnel is the best way to go to Brooklyn.

(6.27) a. **Bedienung**, wir würden gerne   zahlen, bitte.
            service   we would gladly pay   please
            'Waiter, we would like to pay, please.'

        b. *Was   können sie heute empfehlen, **Bedienung**?
            what can   you today recommend service
            'What could you recommend today, waiter?'

---

[3] Antonio Fortin (p.c.) suggested that the perceived rudeness of (6.26b) is more a function of the speaker criticizing the driver and not so much of the use of *cabby* as a call. I do not have good intuitions about the English data, but at least the German example in (6.27b) is rude even if the host utterance itself is completely neutral.

Moreover, while quantifiers are ruled out in addresses like they are in calls, even the shiftable *all* and *every* are impossible in addresses.

(6.28) a. *Can you help me with this box, **all strong women here**?

  b. *Könnt ihr mir mit dieser Kiste helfen, **alle starken Frauen hier**?

That is, addresses are much more restricted with respect to the expressions that can fulfill this function. In fact, Zwicky puts forward the hypothesis that addresses are a subset of calls:

(6.29) All address forms are usable as calls.   (Zwicky 1974: 791)

The two-part distinction between addresses and calls is an often used one, but as argued by Schaden (2010), it does not capture all relevant differences in vocative uses. Instead of just differentiating between calls and addresses/A-confirmations, Schaden suggests a tripartite distinction. He claims that vocatives have three basic functions (Schaden 2010: 182; he calls it the "IPA hypothesis" of vocative meaning).

(6.30) (I) **Identification**: identify the addressee(s) out of a possibly bigger group of potential addressees

  (P) **Predication**: globally predicate some property onto some already constituted set of addressees

  (A) **Activation**: activate the addressee

Identificational vocatives are more-or-less what we called *calls* before: their function is to identify and thereby establish the addressee. In contrast, predicative and activational vocatives both presuppose that the addressee (or group of addressees) is already established. They both are akin to the category of *A-confirmations* then. The crucial difference, though, is that predicational vocatives are used to predicate some property onto the addressee whereas activational ones do not do this; they merely just activate the addressee. A clear example for an activational vocative is the use of a proper name (as an A-confirmation) as in (6.24) and (6.25) above: the addressee is already established and, clearly, the speaker does not want to express that she considers the speaker to be called Birgit. This is just assumed and not predicated.

A good example for predicational vocatives are expressions involving terms of politeness and approbation or—and this will be main topic of section—disrespect and negative evaluation.

(6.31) a. Wir haben großes Dinge erreicht,   **werte Kollegen**!
    we   have   big   things   accomplished valued colleagues
    'We accomplished great things, valued colleagues!'

  b. Runter vom meinem Grundstück, **Arschlöcher**!
    down   of   my   property   assholes
    'Get off my lawn, assholes!'

On the one hand, such expressions do not function well as identificational vocatives/calls. In (6.31), the speaker does not intend to only address the subset of her colleagues that she values, but addresses her colleagues as an entire group and (holistically) predicates this value judgment onto them (without discriminating between more and less valued colleagues). Similar considerations apply to (6.31b): the speaker does not restrict the set of addressees only to the set of persons she despises. That is, the uses in (6.31) cannot be identificational and therefore, the addressees must already be established. However, the content of the vocative is clearly predicated over the (set of) addressee(s) and does not just activate them again.

Figure 6.1 summarizes Schaden's (2010) "IPA"-taxonomy of vocative uses. Just like the two-way distinction between calls and addresses, Schaden's (2010) distinction can explain some of the observations about the uses of vocatives in different functions. For instance, as we already observed above in (6.11), bare pronouns are not good as calls in situations in which there are multiple potential addressees.

(6.32)   [Multiple people standing in front of the speaker:]
?**Sie,**   bringen Sie   mir   bitte   eine   Glas   Wasser.
*you.*VOC.FORMAL   *bring   you.*FORMAL   *me   please   a   glass   water*
'You, please bring me a glass of water.'

This is because the only content that is arguably conveyed by second persons is that their referent is the addressee, which is obviously not helpful in figuring out who the addressee actually is. Therefore, bare pronouns without any further ado are not suitable for identificational vocatives (calls). However, when accompanied with pointing gestures or recognizable eye gazes, they become felicitous (cf. Schaden 2010: 183).

(6.33)   [Multiple people standing in front of the speaker:]
Sie+[gesture toward A], bringen Sie   mir   bitte eine   Glas
*you.*VOC.FORMAL   *bring you.*FORMAL *me   please a*
Wasser.
glass   water
'You, please bring me a glass of water'

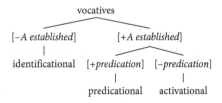

FIGURE 6.1 Schaden's (2010) "IPA"-taxonomy of vocative uses

It should be noted that whatever vocative function a certain form fulfills depends on the context, so that many vocatives, when looked at in isolation, can be interpreted in more than one way. Take for instance, the vocative *werte Kollegen* ('valued colleagues') in (6.31a). I presented that as a case of a predicational vocative, because the speaker does not intend to single out just colleagues she values from a bigger set of colleagues. However, if we assume a context of a more public speech in which the speaker is not just speaking to her colleagues but there are also some guests, the use of *werte Kollegen* ('valued colleagues') can be used as an identificational vocative/call.

(6.34) **Werte Kollegen**, wir haben große Dinge erreicht!   **Liebe**
        valued colleagues we   have   great   things accomplished dear
        Gäste, heute präsentieren wir Ihnen die Ergebnisse unserer
        guests today present   we   you   the   results   our
        Arbeit.
        work
        'Valued colleagues, we accomplished great things! Dear guests, today, we present you the results of our work.'

In such a context, where there are potential contrasting sets of addressees, it is perfectly fine to use *werte Kollegen* ('valued colleagues') to identify the colleagues as the addressees in contrast to the guests (which can than be identified as the addressees of the following utterance). However, note that it is the descriptive content of *Kollegen* ('colleagues') that contrasts with the descriptive content of *Gäste* ('guests') that makes this identificational use possible in such a context. Crucially, the more expressive content of *werte* ('valued') and *liebe* ('dear') cannot really figure into this. This is also the reason why it is much harder, and almost impossible, to use a purely expressive expression as in (6.31b) as an identificational vocative: such "vocatives carrying heavy loads of politeness or disrespect are not very amenable to discriminating between groups of potential addressees" (Schaden 2010: 182). According to d'Avis & Meibauer (2013: 205) this is due to the subjective character of such evaluative expressions: since the evaluation is relativized to the speaker and hence does not objectively establish a set of denotations, potential addressees cannot know if they belong to that set or not. Vocatives with expressive like in (6.31b) will of course be looked at more closely later in this chapter. But first, let us look at the general semantic properties of vocatives.

6.2.3 *Semantic properties of vocatives*

Having distinguished two (Zwicky 1974) or three (Schaden 2010) uses of vocatives, let us now turn to the more general semantic properties of ordinary vocatives. There is not much literature on this issue, but the small set of proposals seem to agree that the content of vocatives is not ordinary truth-conditional content (Eckardt 2014;

Portner 2007; Predelli 2008). First, using a "wrong" vocative can never render an utterance false.

(6.35)   [Talking to Klaus:]
          #**Ede**, the talk tonight has been canceled.

The utterance in (6.35) is true, as long as the talk in question has been canceled. The fact that the speaker is mistaken regarding her addressee does not make the sentence false. The use of the inappropriate vocative only makes the utterance infelicitous, but it is nonetheless true in case of a cancellation of the talk.

The non-truth-conditionality of vocatives is also supported by the fact that one cannot reject an utterance simply based on the wrongly applied vocative.

(6.36)   A: **Ede**, the talk tonight has been canceled.
          B: #No, I'm Klaus!

Vocatives can also not be negated or targeted by other semantic operations. For instance, the negation in (6.37) only targets the propositional content that the talk has been canceled and leaves the vocative content unaffected.

(6.37)   The talk tonight has **not** been canceled, **Klaus**.

That is, an utterance of (6.37) would still be infelicitous if it were uttered to someone other than Klaus; the presence of negation does not help here. Similar considerations apply to other semantic context like conditionals or embedding under speech reports.

(6.38)   If I see you here again, **Giorgione**, I will call the Police.

If the speaker utters (6.38) to a person A and falsely thinks that A is called *Giorgione* (maybe because of his size), this does not enter the content of the antecedent. That is, the content of the antecedent of (6.38) can be paraphrased by (6.39a) and not by (6.39b).

(6.39)   a. c_S sees c_A again at c_L
          b. c_S sees c_A again at c_L and c_A is called *Giorgione*

That is, the fact that the speaker is mistaken about A's name does not automatically render the antecedent false.[4]

The following example illustrates that vocatives cannot be embedded under a speech (or attitude) reporting verb (Eckardt 2014: 225).[5]

---

[4] Similar considerations apply if ones tries to put the vocative content into the consequent.

[5] While this seems true for English and German, I do not know if it holds cross-linguistically. But for example, Aikhenvald (2008: 487) reports that vocatives in Manambu occur in direct and semi-direct speech reports, but not in indirect ones.

(6.40)   a. *Luigi said that, **Ede**, the pizza is/was ready.
      b. *Luigi hat gesagt, dass, **Ede**, die Pizza fertig ist/sei.

An utterance of (6.40) does not mean that Luigi said that the pizza was ready and that he said that to Ede (even if it is of course possible with such a situation). If at all interpretable, the vocative has to be interpreted at the root level and hence (6.40) must be uttered to Ede in order for the vocative to be felicitous. All this shows that the content of the vocative cannot be located at the ordinary truth-conditional level.[6]

Although this is not explicitly discussed in the literature, I think is easy to show that the content of vocatives does not give rise to presuppositions. For the sake of illustration, let us assume that a vocative presupposes that the referent of the vocative is the addressee; otherwise it is just an identity function on the sentence's propositional content.

(6.41)   Ede, the pizza is ready.
      a. PRESUPPOSITION: $c_A = $ Ede
      b. ASSERTION: The pizza is ready.

Given that vocatives are hardly embeddable, it is hard to use projection tests to establish whether the vocative content is presupposed. However, conceptually, there does not seem to be a dependence between the asserted content and the vocative content: even if the content of the vocative is no satisfied in the utterance context, this does not seem to bear anything on the asserted content. As we already saw above, if the speaker of (6.41) does not talk to Ede, the utterance is still true, as long as the pizza in question is ready. A false vocative does not affect the asserted content in any way. However, some dependence between the presupposition and the asserted content is the hallmark of presuppositions. That there is no such dependency can also be shown by examples like the following.

(6.42)   Ede, I am talking to you.

Pragmatically, the vocative in (6.42) is a perfect call: it is used to attract Ede's attention, and so does the asserted content (its semantic content is rather trivial, since it is true by virtue of its character alone). However, if the semantics of the vocative presupposes that Ede is the addressee, there are two cases. First, the speaker of (6.42) actually is talking to Ede. In this case, the presupposition is fulfilled and, by the same token, the asserted content also comes out as true. However, if the assumed presupposition of the vocative is not fulfilled, the content of assertion should—depending on your preferred theory of presupposition failures—turn out to be undefined or unable to be

---

[6] Of course, the non-embedding behavior all could be due to the non-integrated syntactic position of the vocative. But the argument from the truth-conditions still holds even if the syntax is responsible for the fact that they cannot be targeted semantically.

accepted as an update to the common ground. In fact, none of this is the case. It is perfectly fine to accept the asserted content while explicitly rejecting the content of the vocative. This is true for (6.42) but also for more usual cases like (6.35).

(6.43)   A: Ede, I am talking to you.
        B: Yes, you are, but I am not Ede, I am Klaus.

(6.44)   A: Ede, the talk tonight has been canceled.
        B: Yes, it has been, but I am not Ede, I am Klaus.

Crucially, this move of accepting the assertion while rejecting the other content is not possible for standard presuppositions, like the complements of factive predicates such as *to know*, or definite descriptions.

(6.45)   A: Peter knows that the talk had been canceled.
        B: #Yes, he knows that, but the talk has not been canceled.

(6.46)   A: The king of France likes pizza.
        B: #Yes, he does, but there is no king of France.

This should be enough to show that thinking of the semantic content of a vocative as presuppositional is highly implausible. In addition, thinking a moment about the more pragmatic function of vocatives, especially calls, makes this view even more implausible. If a vocative presupposed that the referent of the vocative is the addressee, why use a vocative in the first place? If one of the main vocative functions, the calling function, is to ensure that the intended addressee is correctly identified, the use of a vocative is more like to happen if the speaker can*not* presuppose that the intended addressee is singled out by the context alone. That is, in a context in which there is more ambiguity regarding the identity of the addressee, the use of a call makes much more sense than in a context in which makes one addressee highly prominent. This contrasts again with presuppositions. Think about definite descriptions: if the speaker thinks that the existence of the referent may not be known to the interlocutors, the use of a definite description without any additional introduction is less likely than in a context in which the referent is clearly known. So vocatives show the reverse pattern to what we would expect from a presupposition.

In addition, as discussed by Potts (2005: 33–4) presuppositions are backgrounded and therefore the same presupposition can be triggered even if its content is already established. Again, definite descriptions illustrate this nicely.

(6.47)   I bought a <u>new computer</u> and **it** is very cool. **The machine** has a super bright screen and a nice keyboard. **This computer** is the best I ever had.

The highlighted expressions—a pronoun and two definite descriptions—all presuppose a suitable referent and its existence. However, there is nothing redundant in this, even if all expressions trigger the same, or a very similar, presupposition. Even if the presupposed content is explicitly introduced, one can still use an expression that happens to presuppose exactly that content again, with no feeling of redundancy (Potts 2005: 34).

(6.48)   The earth is a sphere. And for a couple of centuries, most of us have known that the earth is a sphere.

However, this is certainly not true for vocatives. Repeating them becomes socially awkward very fast in most contexts.

(6.49)   **Ede**, the talk has been canceled. (#**Ede**,) what should we do instead? (#**Ede**,) I guess we could work on that problem of the interpretation of proper names. (#**Ede**,) what do you think?

Only if Ede's attention fades from the conversation after each utterance, the use of the vocative would be licensed. However, this would then be a context in which the identity of the addressee *cannot* be presupposed.

In a very similar vein, if is already clear in the discourse context, who the addressee is, using a call is ruled out as well (d'Avis & Meibauer 2013: 195–6).

(6.50)   A to Ede: **Ede**, the talks tonight has been canceled.
          Ede: Oh, that's a pity.
          A to Ede: (#**Hey Ede**,) what should we do instead?

However, if a presuppositional approach to vocatives were on the right track, a context as in (6.50) would be one in which a vocative should be licensed.

Given all these observations, it is safe to conclude that vocatives do not convey presupposed content. And given that we saw above that neither can it sensibly be viewed as being asserted, an analysis of vocatives as carriers of expressive, or use-conditional meaning does suggest itself. Therefore, it comes as no surprise that the few semantic analyses of vocatives all assume that the vocative content is located at a rather independent level of meaning. And even if Portner (2007), Predelli (2008), and Eckardt (2014) use slightly different terminologies and architectures, they all basically assume that vocatives are similar to expressives in this respect (and all of them even explicitly mention this). Moreover, in one way or the other, they all end up using some kind of multidimensional semantics to implement this formally. However, as I will discuss later, there are some problems with their respective approaches. Before that, however, let us turn to the particular properties of expressive vocatives.

6.3 Expressive vocatives: the data

As introduced at the beginning of this section, expressive vocatives ("eVocs") are vocatives that contain a second person pronoun as well as a nominal element, as illustrated by the examples in (6.2), which I repeat here for convenience.

(6.51)   **Expressive vocatives (eVocs)**
    a. **You idiot!**
    b. **You bastard!**
    c. **You linguist!**
    d. **You philosopher!**

Usually, the nominal element is an expressive as in (6.51a) or (6.51b). That expressive elements in general can be used in vocatives is already observed by Zwicky (1974: 791–2), who puts forward the following hypothesis (in addition to the one mentioned in (6.29)).

(6.52)   a. All evaluative nouns can occur as vocatives.
    b. All disparaging names for racial or national groups can occur as vocatives.

Under "evaluative nouns" he basically includes expressive nouns, but also other negatively connoted or at least often negatively used mixed nouns like *punk, slowpoke* or *fatso*. As mentioned in (6.52b), the same holds for racist slurs like *Kraut, Honkie,* or *Frog* (cf. Zwicky 1974: 792).

(6.53)

$$\text{Hey you} \left\{ \begin{array}{c} \text{fatso} \\ \text{punk} \\ \text{slowpoke} \\ \vdots \end{array} \right\}, \text{you don't belong in this class.}$$

(6.54)

$$\text{Hey you} \left\{ \begin{array}{c} \text{Frog} \\ \text{Honkie} \\ \text{Kraut} \\ \vdots \end{array} \right\}, \text{get your ass off that bench!}$$

A little more surprisingly, eVocs can also feature nouns that on their own are purely descriptive elements as in (6.51c) and (6.51d). Crucially, even such neutral nouns receive an expressive interpretation when used as part of an eVocs (d'Avis & Meibauer 2013). That is, an innocent expression like *linguist* in (6.51c) receives an expressive flavor and has to be interpreted as some kind of insult similar to the use of a proper expressive like *idiot* in (6.51a). Here are is another example to illustrate this crucial observation.[7]

---

[7] Since eVocs with neutral nouns are not really acceptable in English, I include an expressive adjective in parentheses in the translation to get the reading of the German example across. Just keep in mind that there actually is no expressive adjective in these eVocs with neutral nouns.

(6.55) **Du Student** hältst den Zustand sicher für angemessen.
    you student hold the state surely as adequate
    'You (damn) student surely consider the state as adequate.'

(d'Avis & Meibauer 2013: 210)

Of course, the negative attitude expressed by this eVoc may not be as strong as the one that would be convey by an eVoc containing a genuine slur, like *du Arschloch* ('you asshole'), but even *student* inherits an expressive, slur-like flair when used in an eVoc. d'Avis & Meibauer (2013) compare the expressivity of such usually neutral items in eVoc with the alternative *du als X* ('you as X') construction. In these constructions neutral expressions do not become an expressive undertone at all.

(6.56) **Du als Student** hältst den Zustand sicher für angemessen.
    you as student hold the state surely for adequate
    'You, as a student, surely consider the state as adequate.'

(d'Avis & Meibauer 2013: 210)

While in such constructions, a neutral noun like *student* does not undergo any change in expressivity, this contrasts with (6.55), in which it is very hard *not* to associate the use of *student* with some kind of negative attitude (*pace* Rauh 2004). This is one of the observations an analysis of eVocs should account for.

6.3.1 *Expressive vocatives and vocative functions*

Interestingly, we encounter vocatives containing expressive elements already in Schaden's (2010) tripartite distinction of vocative functions. As he observed, vocatives with expressive elements cannot be used identificationally, as their expressive content is not suitable to single out one specific addressee or subgroup of addressees from a larger group of potential addressees. That is, if the communicative situation is not yet established and the intended addressee does not yet know that she is being talked to, trying to identify her with a very subjective and even negative expression is not a good way to achieve that, because the addressee most likely does not self-subscribe to that characterization (d'Avis & Meibauer 2013: 205). Therefore, eVocs cannot be used as calls, which seems to run counter Zwicky's (1974) hypothesis in (6.29) that all vocatives can be used as calls; this is why d'Avis & Meibauer (2013) call them "pseudo vocatives": they cannot fulfill the most general vocative function.

In Schaden's ipa-terminology, if eVocs are not used for identification, are they then predicational or activational vocatives? In one sense, they seem to be clearly predicational as the expressive is somehow predicated of the addressee by the speaker. However, in another sense, they are not just plainly predicational, as the way the expressive content is applied to the addressee is not the same as with more descriptive expressions. One aspect that shows this is that, if used felicitously, eVocs and plain predicational vocatives give rise to different inferences. Consider the following example.

(6.57) Heute, **Freunde und Kollegen**, präsentiere ich euch die
      today   friends   and   colleagues   present   I   you   the
      Ergebnisse meiner Arbeit.
      results   my   work
      'Today, friends and colleagues, I am going to present to you the results of my work.'

If (6.57) is used felicitously, one can infer that the speaker is going to present the results of her work to some colleagues and friends. That is, the existence of friends and colleagues (as the audience) can be inferred from a felicitous use of (6.57).

    With this in mind, consider the following utterance involving an eVoc.

(6.58) Heute, **ihr Idioten**, präsentiere ich euch die Ergebnisse meiner
      today   you   idiots   present   I   you   the   results   my
      Arbeit.
      work
      'Today, you idiots, I am going to present to you the results of my work.'

From a felicitous utterance of (6.58), we cannot infer that the speaker is going to present the result of her work to some idiots. Neither can we infer the existence of some idiots (as the audience). What can be inferred is just that there is a group of addressees that the speaker feels negatively about.

    This difference between eVocs and plain predicational vocatives stems presumably from the expressive nature of eVocs. Nevertheless, there is also a structural difference between the two. Recall that we observed that even neutral nouns receive an expressive, derogatory interpretation inside eVocs. However, such neutral nouns can be used in ordinary predicational vocatives and remain neutral. So what exactly is the difference between neutral predicational vocatives and eVocs when the latter do not contain an expressive noun, but a neutral one? As I discuss in more detail below, it seems that there is a structural difference. This difference can mostly be seen in the observation that the expressive interpretation of a neutral noun seems mostly to require the presence of a second person pronoun in addition to the nominal element. Predicational vocatives, in contrast, are perfectly fine without one. Compare the examples in (6.31a) and (6.58) just given. This contrast seem to be even stronger in case of singular addressees, as witnessed by (6.59) and (6.60).

(6.59) Heute, **Professor**, habe ich meinen Aufsatz mitgebracht.
      today   professor   have I   my   essay   with.brought
      'Today, professor, I brought my essay with me.'

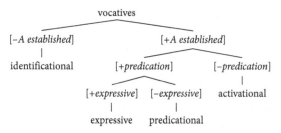

FIGURE 6.2 A four-way taxonomy of vocative functions

(6.60) Heute, **Sie**   **Professor,** habe ich meinen Aufsatz
       *today, you.*FORMAL *professor,* *have I   my   essay*
       mitgebracht.
       with.brought
       'Today, you (damn) professor, I brought my essay with me.'

While the vocative in (6.59) is perfectly fine and even respectful, the vocative in (6.60) cannot be interpreted as a normal predicational vocative. It is rather disrespectful and the noun *professor* can hardly be interpreted in a title-like way and tends to receive a negative and maybe even non-literal interpretation.[8] That is, the presence of the pronoun seems to make a difference here. We will return to this.

The analysis that will be developed throughout the remainder of this chapter will further elaborate on the differences between eVocs and other vocatives. But for now, let us assume that they seem to constitute a fourth vocative use, extending Schaden's (2010) taxonomy. This is illustrated in Figure 6.2.

6.3.2 *Structural types of eVocs*

Having established eVocs as a fourth type of vocative, let us now have a closer look at the structural properties of eVocs. We begin by distinguishing three different contexts in which eVocs can occur.

First, there are the stand-alone, autonomous uses of eVocs like *Du Idiot!* ('You idiot!') as in in (6.2), which I used to introduce the phenomenon and which were repeated in (6.51) above.

(6.61) **Autonomous eVocs**
       Du Idiot!
       'You idiot!'

Besides such autonomous eVocs, which are studied in more detail by Welte (1980), there are also two uses of eVocs together with other linguistic material. First, like the

---

[8] For instance, it can be used sarcastically toward a person that is not actually a professor but, in the speaker's opinion, acted like a smartass, giving it a square-quote like reading, as in *Today, you "professor," I brought my essay with me.*

other types of vocatives, they have an unintegrated use, in which they do not serve as an argument to any other expression. They can either occur in a left- or right-peripheral position or in so-called parenthetical niches (Altmann 1981; d'Avis 2004; d'Avis & Meibauer 2013).

(6.62)   **Parenthetical eVocs**

    a. **Du Idiot,** morgen   hat die Post doch geschlossen!
      you idiot tomorrow has the post PART *closed*
      'You idiot, the post office is closed tomorrow!'

    b. Morgen   hat die Post doch geschlossen, **du Idiot!**
      tomorrow has the post PART *closed*   *you idiot*
      'The post office is closed tomorrow, you idiot!'

    c. Morgen,   **du Idiot,** hat die Post doch geschlossen!
      tomorrow, you idiot, has the post PART *closed*
      'The post office, you idiot, is closed tomorrow!'

Both structural contexts comply with the stricter view on vocatives that requires that they are independent elements that do not serve as the argument to a verb (or noun) in the sentence. However, the reason I did not adopt this strict view is that as a third possibility, expressions that look like *bona fide* eVocs can occur in argument positions as well in German.[9]

(6.63)   **Integrated eVocs**

    a. Hast **du Idiot** schon   wieder vergessen, das Licht
      have you idiot already again   forgotten the light
    auszumachen?
      out.to.switch
      'Did you idiot forget to switch off the light again?'

                                    (d'Avis & Meibauer 2013: 206)

    b. **Du Arschloch** hast mir mein Frühstück geklaut!
      you asshole   has me my   breakfast stolen
      'You asshole stole my breakfast!'

In (6.63), the expression *du Idiot* ('you idiot') serves as the subject of the sentence and therefore is integrated, in contrast with the non-integration that the stricter requirement on vocatives would demand. However, since for all intents and purposes, there do not seem to be any *prima facie* differences between *du Idiot* in (6.63a) and (6.62), I will include them in the present investigation. The similarities and differences between such integrated eVocs and the parenthetical ones that we will discuss will

---

[9] Since eVocs in argument position are almost ruled out in English, it is not easy to give a good translation for them that also shows their argument status, I will just pretend that they are possible in English for the sake of the paraphrases in this chapter.

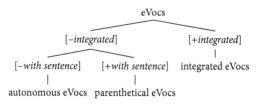

FIGURE 6.3 Structural types of eVocs

guide us as to whether they should finally be counted as vocatives or not. The three structural types of eVocs are summarized in Figure 6.3.

6.3.3 No embedding of eVocs

All structural types of eVocs show strong resistance against syntactic and semantic embedding and modification.

Autonomous eVocs interact neither with negation (6.64), modal adverbs (6.65), nor propositional attitude predicates and indirect speech reports (6.66). As the different variants illustrate, this is not a matter of word order.

(6.64) a. *Nicht du Idiot
      b. *Not you idiot!
      c. *Du Idiot nicht!
      d. *You idiot not!
      e. *Du nicht Idiot!
      f. *You not idiot!

(6.65) a. *Vielleicht Du Idiot!
      b. *Perhaps you idiot!
      c. *Du Idiot vielleicht!
      d. *You idiot perhaps!
      e. *Du vielleicht Idiot!
      f. *You perhaps idiot!

(6.66) a. *Maya {dachte/sagte}, dass Du Idiot!
      b. *Maya {thought/said} that you idiot!

Note that there are certain readings of some of the orders in (6.64) and (6.65) that are grammatical, but not under the intended reading with the eVoc targeted by the negation/modal. For instance, (6.64a) and (6.64c) are fine if they are read as parenthetical vocatives to an elliptical sentence from which only the negation remains. The following example illustrates this.

(6.67) Nicht [den Kaffee auf den Laptop stellen,] **du   Idiot!**
      not   the   coffee   on   the   laptop   put   you   idiot
      'Don't [put the coffee on the laptop], you Idiot.'

Similarly, there are readings of some of the strings of (6.64) and (6.65) in which the eVoc is interpreted as an integrated one, but the negation or modal modifies the sentence into which the eVoc is integrated but which has been elided. Again, one example should be sufficient to illustrate this.

(6.68)   A: Wer hat das Licht schon wieder an gelassen?
         who has the light already again on left
         'Who left the lights on again?'

      B: **Du Idiot** [hast das Licht] vielleicht [wieder angelassen].
         you idiot has the light perhaps again on.left
         'You idiot [left the light on again] perhaps.'

However, what is crucial with these readings is, first, they seem to be phonologically very different from the direct modification attempted in (6.64) and (6.65): the eVoc is intonationally set apart from the negation or modal in (6.67) and (6.68) by so-called "comma intonation" (Potts 2005), whereas a direct modification of the eVoc should result in a single phonological phrase. And, maybe even more important, in (6.67) and (6.68) the negation/modal does not even target the eVoc, so that its content remains untouched by this semantic operation.

Of course, the fact that autonomous vocatives cannot be semantically embedded by negation, modal adverbs, or propositional attitudes, is not surprising to begin with. Even though autonomous eVocs are independent utterances, they are not really sentential and therefore it is to be expected that they cannot appear with sentential negation, sentence adverbs, or sentence-embedding predicates.

As already shown by the considerations regarding the elliptical utterances in (6.67) and (6.68), both parenthetical (6.69) and integrated eVocs (6.70) can co-occur with such semantic operators, of course.

(6.69)   a. Du hast das Licht **nicht** ausgeschaltet, **du Idiot!**
        you has the light not off.switched you idiot
        'You didn't switch off the light, you idiot!'

      b. **Vielleicht** hast du das Licht ausgeschaltet, **du Idiot!**
        perhaps has you the light off.switched you idiot
        'Perhaps you switched off the light, you idiot!'

      c. **Maya sagt**, dass du das Licht ausgeschaltet hast, **du Idiot!**
        Maya says that you the light switched.off has, you idiot
        'Maya says that you switched off the light, you idiot!'

(6.70)   a. **Du Idiot** hast das Licht **nicht** ausgeschaltet!
        you idiot has the light not off.switched
        'You idiot didn't switch off the light!'

b. **Vielleicht** hast **du** **Idiot** das Licht ausgeschaltet!
perhaps   has   you idiot   the   light   off.switched
'Perhaps you idiot switched off the light!'

c. **Maya sagt,** dass **du** **Idiot** das Licht ausgeschaltet hast!
Maya says   that you idiot   the   light   switched.off   has
'Maya says that you idiot switched off the light!'

However, in all these cases the content of the eVoc is semantically not affected by the presence of these semantic contexts. In each case, the speaker is invariably conveying a negative attitude toward the addressee. One notable exception is the case of an integrated eVoc inside the clausal complement of an attitude or speech report as in (6.70c). This example has one reading in which the negative attitude expressed by *du Idiot* ('you idiot') is interpreted as part of Maya's beliefs, not the speaker's. I will return to this issue, but let us already take note of the observation that this pretty much looks like the case of an expressive adjective inside a speech report as discussed in Section (2.8).

(6.71) Maya sagt, dass der **Idiot Peter** das Licht ausgeschaltet hat.
Maya says that the idiot Peter the light off.switched has
'Maya says that the idiot Peter switched off the light.'

6.3.4 *The pronominal element of eVocs*

In the discussion regarding the differences between eVocs and ordinary predicational vocatives in Section 6.3.1, we already saw that one aspect that distinguishes the two is that eVocs seems to require a pronoun, whereas this is banned from standard predicational vocatives. I illustrated this with the contrast between *Professor* and *Sie Professor* ('you professor') in (6.59) and (6.60). Here is another minimal pair to highlight this contrast.

(6.72) Heute beginnen wir ein neues Kapitel, **meine Schüler.**
today start we a new chapter my students
'Today we start with a new chapter, my students.'

(6.73) #Heute beginnen wir ein neues Kapitel, **ihr Schüler.**
today start we a new chapter you students
'Today we start with a new chapter, you students.'

Whereas the DP in (6.72) is a neutral and simply predicational use of a vocative, the one in (6.73), which features a second person plural pronoun (instead of a possessive pronominal determiner), is marked as a plain vocative. This is because *ihr Schüler* ('you students') gives rise to a negative expressive interpretation. However, this feels somewhat at odds with the teacher–student context implicit in (6.73). However, if we change the example that makes a negative speaker attitude toward students more plausible, the use *ihr Schüler* as a vocative is perfectly fine, which shows that (6.73) is only marked because of our knowledge that teachers usually do not disdain their students.

(6.74) Runter   von   meinem   Rasen,   **ihr Schüler!**
        down   from   my   lawn   you students
        'Get off my lawn, you students!'

It therefore seems that the pronoun is a crucial ingredient of eVocs, which sets it apart from descriptive predicational ones.[10] The presence of a pronoun is even a test used by Welte (1980: 12–13) to check whether an eVoc-like expression actually is a vocative rather than an interjection. For instance, English *man* has an interjection-like use (McCready 2009) that is not a vocative, as it cannot be used with the second person pronoun.

(6.75) a. Nonsense, **man!**
        b. *Nonsense, **you man!**

The use of *you man* in (6.75b) may only possible if *man* is intended to function as a derogatory expressive for men and not with its intensifying and strengthening function. Similar observations can be made about the use of *Mensch* ('human') or *Junge* ('boy') in German.

(6.76) a. **Mensch,** kannst du   mich mal   alleine lassen!?
            human   can   you   me   PART   alone   leave
            'Man, can you just leave me alone!?'
        b. *****Du Mensch,** kannst du   mich mal   alleine lassen!?
            you human   can   you   me   PART   alone   leave

(6.77) a. **Junge,** war   das   ein   Spiel!
            boy   was   that a   game
            'Boy, what a game that was!'
        b. *****Du Junge,** war   das   ein   Spiel!
            you boy   was   that a   game

We can therefore conclude, that eVocs seem to involve a pronominal argument in addition to their expressive component.

However, things are actually a bit more complicated, since in parenthetical eVocs, the pronoun can be omitted so that just the expressive noun is used.

---

[10] Note that in identificational vocatives, i.e. calls, pronouns can occur under certain circumstances without rendering the vocative into an expressive one.

(i) Hey, **ihr Schüler** (da),   könnt ihr   mir   mal   mit   dieser Kiste helfen?
     hey   you   students   there   can   you   me   PART   with   this   box   help
     'Hey, you students (over there), could you help me with this box?'

(6.78) a. Wir sind in den falschen Zug eingestiegen, **du Idiot.**
              we   are   in   the   wrong   train   in.gotten   you   idiot
              'We got on the wrong train, you idiot!'

      b. Wir sind in den falschen Zug eingestiegen, **Idiot.**
              we   are   in   the   wrong   train   in.gotten   idiot
              'We got on the wrong train, idiot!'

(6.79) a. **Du Idiot,** wir sind in den falschen Zug eingestiegen.
      b.   **Idiot,** wir sind in den falschen Zug eingestiegen.

(6.80) a. Wir sind, **du Idiot,** in den falschen Zug eingestiegen.
      b. Wir sind,   **Idiot,** in den falschen Zug eingestiegen.

There does not seem to be any difference between the (a)- and (b)-variants in (6.78)–(6.80); they still express the speaker's negative feelings toward the addressee.

   In light of this observation, can we still maintain the hypothesis that the pronoun is a necessary ingredient of the structural makeup of an eVoc? I think we can. First, I am not aware of any eVocs in which you cannot use an explicit pronoun. That is, using a pronoun is always possible with eVocs. Secondly, even without the pronoun, the expressive still expresses the speaker's attitude toward *the addressee*. That is, it cannot target a third person:

(6.81) a. Markus ist in den falschen Zug eingestiegen, **Idiot!**
              Markus   is   in   the   wrong   train   in.gotten   idiot
              'Markus got on the wrong train, Idiot!'

      b. **Idiot,** Markus ist in den falschen Zug eingestiegen!

      c. Markus ist, **Idiot,** in den falschen Zug eingestiegen!

Even if these examples make it clear that Markus did not have his brightest moment, the expressive can still only target the addressee. That is, all three variants in (6.81) imply that the speaker has negative feelings toward the hearer, not necessarily toward Markus, even if that is possible of course as well; it is just not encoded linguistically.

   There is one possibility in which the parenthetical eVocs in (6.81a) can be understood as targeting Markus, namely if they are interpreted as stand-alone utterances of the expressive. Trying to bring this intuition onto paper, we could indicate this with a full stop, instead of the commas that are usually used with vocatives.

(6.82) Markus ist in den flaschen Zug eingestiegen. **Idiot!**

The relation of eVocs and expressives that target a third person will be discussed in more detail below. For now, it is important that a pronounless eVoc usually cannot be interpreted as being aimed at a third person.

   In a similar vein, we can also observe that eVocs without pronouns cannot be interpreted as targeting the speaker herself. This may be a bit surprising, as there is an eVoc-like use of first person pronouns with expressive nominals in German (d'Avis & Meibauer 2013: 206–7).

(6.83) **Ich Idiot!**
        I   idiot
        'Stupid me!'

(6.84) **Ich Idiot** habe schon   wieder vergessen, das Licht auszumachen
        I   idiot   have   already again   forgotten   the light out.to.switch
        'Stupid me, I forgot to switch off the light again.'

These constructions are perfectly fine in German, but they do not have a direct equivalent in English; even with a dative/accusative first person pronoun (Welte 1980: 15).

(6.85) $*\left\{\begin{array}{c} \text{I} \\ \text{me} \end{array}\right\}$ Idiot!

However, as noted by Welte (1980: 15), the use of the first person pronoun with an expressive in German cannot be reduced to just the expressive, in contrast to the second person pronoun. And, to relate this to the discussion regarding the missing third-person interpretation, a third person pronoun is not possible with *Idiot* to begin with (and therefore *Idiot* alone cannot be derived for that either).

(6.86) a. du Idiot ⇒ Idiot
        b. ich Idiot ⇏ Idiot
        c. *er Idiot

Given all these observations, I think it is safe to assume that even if there is no overt second person pronoun, the argument slot of the expressive part of the eVoc somehow still gets filled by a covert second person pronoun, which is why it cannot be recovered with a different interpretation, even if the context could license it (which is to say that it is not ellipsis that is going on here).

In addition, there are some further arguments that call into question whether these pronounless eVoc-like expressions are genuine eVocs at all. One hint that they may not be is given by the following observation. When bare expressives (i.e. with no pronoun) co-occur with ordinary vocatives, like proper names, the vocative must precede the expressive, when they occur at the right edge of the utterance.

(6.87) a. **Du** bist in den falschen Zug   eingestiegen, **Hans. Idiot!**
            you   are   in the wrong   train in.gotten   Hans   idiot
            'You got on the wrong train, Hans! Idiot!'

        b. *Du bist in den falschen Zug eingestiegen, **Idiot. Hans!**

The same is also true for full eVocs with a pronoun, although the contrast is less strong: they tend to precede the purely expressive insult.

(6.88) a. **Du** bist in den falschen Zug eingestiegen, **du Depp, Idiot!**
you are in the wrong train in.gotten you dork idiot

 b. ?Du bist in den falschen Zug eingestiegen, **Idiot, du Depp!**

Taken together, this may suggest that the pure insults do not really belong to the clause and should be considered less integrated than full eVocs. Therefore, they may not be even vocatives at all. However, more evidence may be needed and I will leave this question open for the purposes of this book.

There is, however, another important observation regarding the pronoun in eVocs, which may also call into question the status of the pronounless pseudo-eVocs. In contrast to parenthetical (and autonomous) eVocs, the pronoun cannot be omitted in integrated eVocs.

(6.89) a. **Du Idiot** bist in den falschen Zug eingestiegen.
you idiot are in the wrong train in.gotten
'You idiot got onto the wrong train.'

 b. *****Idiot** bist in den falschen Zug eingestiegen.

Whatever the mechanism that restricts the argument slot of the expressive in pronounless eVocs to the second person, it does not seem to work in case of integrated eVocs. The reason for this is maybe that, using the terminology introduced in Chapter 2, integrated eVocs are mixed expressives that also carry descriptive content in the form of their referent (see Amaral to appear): while the nominal element provides the negative attitude to the expressive meaning dimension, the pronoun is still needed to fill the argument slot of the verb at the truth-conditional tier. This, however, renders the relation between the pronoun and the expressive nominal in integrated eVocs equivalent to the relation between other expressives, like expressive adjectives and epithets, and their arguments. Let us therefore have a closer look at integrated eVocs and such epithets. This will also help shape how a semantic analyses of eVocs, in general, and integrated ones, in particular, may look like.

6.3.5 *Integrated eVocs and epithets*

The integrated use of eVocs is insofar interesting, as it is not entirely clear if really should be considered together with parenthetical and autonomous eVocs. And even if it looks a lot like an expressive vocative and, in many ways, behaves like one, there are at least two important differences. First, integrated eVocs are the only variant that do not fit the stricter vocative requirement of not being the argument of any other expression in the sentence. If integrated eVocs turn out to not be vocatives after all, this would allow us to adopt the stronger definition of vocatives, which would be desirable. So let us have a closer look at integrated eVocs.

The first thing to note is that, given their argument status, integrated vocatives are expected to be able to show different case marking than their non-argumental peers. This is indeed the case (pun intended), as shown by the following minimal pairs.

(6.90) a. **Du**   Idioten   bist in den falschen Zug eingestiegen!
            *you.*NOM *idiot.*NOM *are in   the   wrong   train in.gotten*
            'You idiot got onto the wrong train!'

        b. *****Dich**   Idioten   bist in den falschen Zug eingestiegen!
            *you.*ACC *idiot.*ACC *are in   the   wrong   train in.gotten*

(6.91) a. Ich kann **dich**   Idioten   nicht mehr ertragen!
            *I   can   you.*ACC *idiot.*ACC *not   more   bear*
            'I can't put up with you idiot anymore!'

        b. *****Ich kann **du**   Idiot   nicht mehr ertragen!
            *I   can   you.*NOM *idiot.*NOM *not   more   bear*

In (6.90), the eVoc fills the subject slot of the verb and, hence, should carry nominative marking (or, more precisely, null-marking). Using accusative marking leads to ungrammaticality here. In contrast, the eVoc is the direct object of verb in (6.91) and hence it must show up with accusative marking. Using the nominative/null marking is not an option here. Since case is clearly active here, this shows that integrated eVocs are a proper syntactic constituent of the sentence in which they occur (and not just semantically integrated). And this is true for both the nominal element and the pronoun that accompanies it: both parts of the eVoc must inflect according to their syntactic context. As the ungrammatical variants in (6.92) and (6.93) show, it is not sufficient that one part is inflected; both constituents must show the correct case marking.[11]

(6.92) a. *****Dich**   Idiot   bist in den falschen Zug eingestiegen.
            *you.*ACC *idiot.*NOM *are in   the   wrong   train in.gotten*

        b. *****Du**   Idioten   bist in den falschen Zug eingestiegen.
            *you.*NOM *idiot.*ACC *are in   the   wrong   train in.gotten*

(6.93) a. *****Ich kann **du**   Idioten   nicht mehr ertragen.
            *I   can   you.*NOM *idiot.*ACC *not   more   bear*

        b. *****Ich kann **dich**   Idiot   nicht mehr etragen.
            *I   can   you.*ACC *idiot.*NOM *not   more   bear*

An interesting exception to the strict agreement between pronoun and expressive nominal in eVocs is provided by the politeness form of the second person

---

[11] The variant in (6.93b) is good under the assumption that *Idiot* is actually an accusative with accusative zero marking, something that can be acceptable in spoken language.

TABLE 6.1 The German
pronoun system

	singular	plural
1	ich	wir
2 familiar	du	ihr
2 formal	Sie	
3	er/sie/es	sie

singular German. In contrast to languages like French, that use the plural version
of the second person pronoun as the polite version of the second person singular,
German uses the *third* person plural pronoun. It is used for second person singular
and plural alike, so that we have the following forms of second person pronouns in
German. Table 6.1 gives an overview over the German pronoun system. As one can
see, there is syncretism between the formal second person pronouns and the third
person plural.[12]

Irrespective of the fact that, semantically, the formal second person pronoun is
both singular and second person, subject verb agreement is solely determined by its
grammatical form. That is, the verb has to be in third person plural. Using second
person inflection on the verb is ruled out.

(6.94) a. **Sie**   **haben**   gute Arbeit geleistet.
            you.2.FORMAL *have.3.PL* *good* *work* *performed*
            'You did good work.'

       b. *****Sie**   **habt**   gute Arbeit geleistet.
            you.2.FORMAL *have.2.PL* *good* *work* *performed*

       c. *****Sie**   **hast**   gute Arbeit geleistet.
            you.2.FORMAL *have.2.SG* *good* *work* *performed*

But when it comes to eVocs, we can observe that only the pronoun and accordingly
the verb are used in the plural variant. The nominal part of the eVoc must remain in
singular.

(6.95) a. **Sie**   **Idiot**   sind   in den falschen Zug
            you.2.FORMAL *idiot.SG* *are.3.PL* *in* *the* *wrong* *train*
            eingestiegen!
            in.gottten
            'You idiot got onto the wrong train!'

---

[12] In written German, the formal second person pronoun is written with a capital, while the third person
plural pronoun is written in lowercase. I will stick to this convention in the examples I give, even if we still
think of *sie* ('you') as being systematically ambiguous.

b. *Sie   Idioten   sind   in   den   falschen   Zug
    you.2.FORMAL   idiot.PL   are.3.PL   in   the   wrong   train
    eingestiegen!
    in.gottten

That is, in case of eVocs, number (and person) agreement only holds between the pronoun and the verb. Crucially, this is not due to some more general constraint against plural marking on the nominal in eVocs. In case of an ordinary (familiar) second person plural pronoun, the nominal appears in plural as expected.

(6.96)   a. **Ihr**   **Idioten**   seid   in   den   falschen   Zug   eingestiegen!
            you.2.PL   idiot.PL   are.2.PL   in   the   wrong   train   in.gottten
            'You idiots got onto the wrong train!'

        b. *Ihr   Idiot   seid   in   den   falschen   Zug   eingestiegen!
            you.2.PL   idiot.SG   are.2.PL   in   the   wrong   train   in.gottten

This shows that while the rest of the clause (i.e. the verb) agrees with the formal appearance of the pronoun, the nominal part still seems to treat it as singular.

I will not got into the details of this, but a speculative reason for this may be that whereas the plural on the nominal has a semantic effect—that is, it is an interpretable feature—the plural of the verb is purely formally/morphologically motivated. That is, arguably the pronoun stands in a morphological agreement relation to the verb, while it established a semantic agreement relation with the nominal (P. W. Smith 2015).

Now, while eVocs use second person pronouns—otherwise it would be hard to think of them as vocatives in the first place—we already observed in (6.82) on page 197 that there is a very similar construction involving a first person pronoun (d'Avis & Meibauer 2013; Rauh 2004). Here is another example.

(6.97)   a. **Ich Idiot** bin in den falschen Zug eingestiegen.
            I   idiot   are   in   the   wrong   train   in.gotten
            'Stupid me, I got in the wrong train.'

        b. **Wir Idioten** sind in den falschen Zug eingestiegen.
            we   idiots   are   in   the   wrong   train   in.gottten
            'We idiots got onto the wrong train.'

Like eVocs, such *ich Idiot* constructions not only have integrated uses an in (6.97), but also autonomous ones, as already shown in Section 6.3.2, as well as parenthetical ones, as illustrated by the following examples.

(6.98)   a. **Ich Idiot**, das ist der falsche Zug!
            I   idiot   that   is   the   wrong   train
            Stupid me, this is the wrong train.

b. Ich habe leider,   **ich Idiot**, den falschen Zug genommen.
I   have unfortunately I   idiot the wrong   train taken
'Unfortunately—stupid me!—I took the wrong train.'

c. Mist, das ist der falsche Zug, **ich Idiot**!
shit   that is   the wrong   train we idiots
'Shit, this is the wrong train, stupid me!'

However, third person pronouns are excluded from this. This holds both for singular and plural pronouns, as well as for autonomous and integrated eVocs.

(6.99) a. *{**Sie, er, es**} Idiot!
she he it   idiot

b. ***Sie** **Idioten**!
they idiots

(6.100) a. *{**Sie, er, es**} **Idiot** ist in den falschen Zug eingestiegen.
she he it   idiot is in the wrong   train in.gotten

b. ***Sie** **Idioten** sind in den falschen Zug eingestiegen.
they idiots   are in the wrong   train in.gotten

This is not only true for third person pronouns, but also for propers names: they can also not show up as the anchor part of an eVoc.

(6.101) ***Hans Idiot** ist in den falschen Zug eingestiegen.
Hans idiot is   in the wrong   train in.gotten

Now, there is of course a way to use an expressive nominal for a third person, namely by just using a simple determiner or demonstrative article.

(6.102) {**Der, dieser**} **Idiot** ist in den falschen Zug eingestiegen.
the   that   idiot is   in the wrong   train in.gotten
'That idiot got onto the wrong train.'

In a similar vein, one can use an expressive with a proper name, if the expressive is in prenominal position. However, then it also requires a determiner as in (6.103a). As shown by (6.103b) and (6.103c), it is really the combination of both that enables the construction; just using the article is not enough and neither is just having the expressive in prenominal position.

(6.103) a. {**Der, dieser**} **Idiot Hans** ist in den falschen Zug
the   that   idiot Hans is in the wrong   train
eingestiegen.
in.gotten
'That idiot Hans got onto the wrong train.'

b. *Idiot Hans ist in den falschen Zug   eingestiegen.
   idiot Hans is in the wrong   train in.gotten

c. *{Der, dieser} Hans Idiot ist in den falschen Zug
   the that   Hans idiot is in the wrong   train
   eingestiegen.
   in.gotten

Now, constructions like those in (6.102) and (6.103) are obviously not vocatives—they do not relate to the addressee—but so-called (expressive) epithets, which are one of the main phenomena dealt with in Potts 2005. Therefore, it is not surprising that the structures in (6.102) and (6.104) really look more like the DP-internal expressive adjective construction discussed in Chapter 4 and not so much like an eVoc proper.

(6.104) {Der, dieser} verdammte Hans ist in den falschen Zug
         the that   damn   Hans is in the wrong   train
         eingestiegen.
         in.gotten
         'That damn Hans got onto the wrong train.'

Despite these similarities, I think there is something going on with eVocs that goes beyond the expressive modifications in (6.103) and (6.104). First, note that only second person eVocs can be used with vocative particles like *hey* or *hallo* ('hello'). This is not possible with the three non-second person constructions.

(6.105) a. Hallo, du   Idiot!
            hello you idiot
            'Hello, you idiot!'

         b. *Hallo, ich Idiot!
            hello I   idiot

         c. *Hallo, dieser Idiot!
            hello that   idiot

         d. *Hallo, dieser Idiot Hans!
            hello that   idiot Hans

         e. *Hallo, dieser verdammte Hans!
            hello that   damn   Hans

In addition, only proper second person eVocs allow what may be called 'vocative doubling'.

(6.106) Du Idiot, du!
         you idiot you
         'You idiot, you!'

This is strictly excluded for third person expressive structures and only marginally possible with first person constructions, which, however, give the impression of self-talk and hence may be (non-canonical) vocatives after all.

(6.107)   a. ?Ich   Idiot,   ich!
              I   *idiot*   *I*
              'Stupid me!'

      b. *Dieser   Idiot,   dieser!
            that   *idiot*   *that*

      c. *Dieser   Idiot   Hans,   dieser!
            that   *idiot* *Hans*   *that*

      d. *Dieser   verdammte   Hans,   dieser!
            that   *damn*   *Hans* *that*

I will discuss such vocative doublings in a bit more detail below. But for now, we take the data in (6.106) and (6.107) as additional evidence that the second person pronoun in eVocs behaves differently than the first person pronoun and the articles/demonstratives in (6.107). However, the third person pronoun structures will be particularly helpful for developing our analysis later. Without giving too much away, the main idea will be that eVocs are actually a combination of ordinary vocatives and expressive modification structures like (6.102), (6.104), and (6.104).

6.3.6 Vocative doubling

We ended the previous section with the observation that only proper eVocs can involve what I dubbed *vocative doubling*, that is, the seemingly doubling of the pronominal element of an eVoc after the expressive nominal. For the familiar pronoun *du* ('you') we thus end up with a *du-X-du* schema, where X is the expressive nominal element of the eVoc. I repeat the example from above.

(6.108)   Du   Idiot,   du!
            you *idiot* *you*
            'You idiot, you!'

The question is what the structure of such doubling constructions is. First, note that is seems that strings like (6.108) are not really just one constituent, which is also hinted at by the possibility of having a major intonational break between *du idiot* and the second *du*, as reflected by the comma in written language. Instead, it can be assumed that the second of the second person pronouns is a vocative *du* ("you") on its own, while the second is part of the eVoc.

If this hypothesis is true, it predicts that the second *du* can be substituted by proper names or other ordinary vocative expressions, while the first one cannot. This is indeed the case.

(6.109) a. Du   Idiot, Hans!
             you idiot   Hans
             'You idiot, Hans!'

         b. Du   Idiot, Schiri!
             you idiot   ref(eree)
             'You idiot, ref!'

(6.110) a. *Hans   Idiot, du!
             hans   idiot   yozu

         b. *Schiri   Idiot, du!
             ref(eree) idiot   you

That is, the pronoun doubling observed in (6.108) is not actually a doubling of the pronominal element of the eVoc, but rather consists of an ordinary vocative that follows the eVoc.

(6.111) $\underbrace{\text{Du Idiot,}}_{\text{eVoc}} \underbrace{\text{du!}}_{\text{Voc}}$

That one *du* in our initial doubling constructions in (6.108) is part of the eVoc and the other is a vocative by itself also explains the fact that there can only be two second person pronouns if the first one is part of the eVoc and thus accompanied by a nominal expressive. That is, just using two bare *du*'s is impossible.

(6.112) a. Du Idiot, Du!
         b. *Du, Du!

In the autonomous use of the eVoc, the order is not fixed to the one in (6.112), as the ordinary vocative can also precede the eVoc, as illustrated in the following variants of (6.109).

(6.113) a. Hans, du   Idiot!
            hans   you   idiot
            'Hans, you idiot!'

         b. Schiri,   du   Idiot!
            ref(eree) you   idiot
            'Ref, you idiot!'

Even more surprisingly, standard vocatives can occur before *and* after the eVoc simultaneously. It can be the same expression, but also different expressions can occupy the two positions, so that all of the following variants are possible.

(6.114) $\underbrace{\left\{ \begin{matrix} \varnothing \\ \text{Du} \\ \text{Hans} \end{matrix} \right\}}_{\text{Voc}}, \underbrace{\text{du Idiot,}}_{\text{eVoc}} \underbrace{\left\{ \begin{matrix} \varnothing \\ \text{Du} \\ \text{Hans} \end{matrix} \right\}}_{\text{Voc}}$

To account for this distribution will be one of the aims of the analysis of the syntactic aspects of (expressive) vocatives that we will develop later.

This ends our discussion of the intriguing data of eVocs in German. Before moving on to the discussion of previous analyses of vocatives, it may be helpful to take stock of the main empirical observations that our analysis should account for.

(6.115)   a. eVocs consist of a second person pronoun and an expressive nominal.
       b. There are three structural kinds of eVocs: integrated, parenthetical and autonomous ones.
       c. eVocs are bad as calls.
       d. Neutral nouns may occur in eVocs, but only with an expressive interpretation.
       e. Third person pronouns are excluded from eVocs, as are proper names.

This list will serve as a test pattern to check our analysis against later on.

6.4 Previous semantic approaches to vocatives

Having discussed some general properties of vocatives, the basics of vocative functions, and then dived deeper into the special properties of eVocs, let us now take a broader picture again and look at some previous approaches to vocatives, as this may prove valuable for developing an analysis of eVocs, ideally by reusing or extending the existing approaches. I will start with the semantic approaches, as most of them already involve some syntactic considerations which we can then build upon when dealing with previous analyses of vocative syntax.

As far as I am aware, there are three formally oriented semantic approaches to the meaning of vocatives. As already alluded to earlier in this chapter, all three—Eckardt 2014; Portner 2007; Predelli 2008—assume some kind of multidimensional framework to account for the non-truth-conditional character of vocatives. Interestingly, the three approaches can be ordered with respect to how explicitly they build the compositional machinery that derives the separation of the vocative meaning from the meaning of the rest of the sentence, as well as how explicitly they deal with the syntax of vocatives. I will discuss them in ascending order.

6.4.1 Predelli 2008

Although he does not use this terminology, Predelli (2008) analyses vocatives as contributing use-conditional content (he calls it "contextual bias"). His main idea is that each sentence S is associated with a class $CNU(S)$: the class of *contexts of non-defective uses* of S. To express this in my terminology, we can think of $CNU(S)$ as the use-conditions for S and S is felicitously used in a context c, if $c \in CNU(S)$. The set of non-defective uses of a sentence contains, for instance, general conditions that apply to, say, assertions, but also more basic ones that there is a speaker in the first place.[13] Vocatives, according to Predelli, then put additional constraints on this class of contexts in which the sentence can be used felicitously. Using *voc(NP)* for the vocative NP and *T* for its sentential complement, we can formulate this as follows.

(6.116)   For any sentence *S* of the form *voc(NP)(T)* and any context *c* with contextual addressee c_A: $c \in CNU(S)$ iff

  (i) $c \in CNU(T)$ and
  (ii) $c_A = [\![NP]\!]^c$.

To illustrate how this idea works, let us apply this schema to the following, simple example.

(6.117)   Angelina, the sky is on fire.   (97)Predelli 2008.

In this utterance, *Angelina* is the vocative NP, corresponding to *NP* in the schema in (6.116), while *the sky is on fire* corresponds to the sentence *T*, so that we end up with the following Predelli-structure for (6.117).

(6.118)   *voc(Angelina)(the sky is on fire)*

Plugging in the parts from (6.118) into the appropriate slots in (6.116), we get the following use-conditions for (6.117).

(6.119) $c \in CNU(voc(Angelina)(the\ sky\ is\ on\ fire))$ iff
  (i) $c \in CNU(the\ sky\ is\ on\ fire)$ and
  (ii) $c_A = [\![Angelina]\!]^c$.

That is, an utterance of "Angelina, the sky is on fire" is felicitous in a context *c*, if *c* belongs to the set of non-defective uses of "The sky is on fire" and if the addressee of that utterance is Angelina.

Regarding the truth-conditions of a sentence containing a vocative (or, as Predelli calls them, its "satisfaction conditions"), he assumes that the meaning of the vocative is, irrespective of the context, just the identity function on truth-values (cf. Predelli 2008: 103).

(6.120) $[\![voc(NP)]\!]^{t,c} = \lambda p.p : \langle t, t \rangle$

To bring this more in line with the other approaches to be discussed, we can intensionalize this as the identity function on propositions instead.

(6.121) $[\![voc(NP)]\!]^{t,c} = \lambda p.p : \langle \langle s, t \rangle, \langle s, t \rangle \rangle$

Given this, the truth-conditional content of an utterance containing a vocative is not affected by the presence of the vocative. This fits the data.

---

[13] Predelli (2008: 102) distinguishes between contexts of use (CU), *general* contexts of non-defective use (CNU*) and contexts of non-defective use (CNU). The specific differences do not matter for the discussion in the main text, so that my use of *CNU* encompasses CNU* and CU.

Note that so far, Predelli's analysis is only compositional on the truth-conditional layer. At the level of use-conditions, we only have the construction specific-schema in (6.116). To define the meaning of the vocative on the use-conditional level, Predelli (2008: 102) assumes that it is a function that takes the set of contexts of non-defective uses and restricts it further by adding the restriction that the referent of the vocative NP equals the contextual addressee. Deviating a bit from Predelli's formulation, we can use the following definition of the use-conditional content of the vocative, where U is a variable over set of contexts, i.e. type $\langle c, t \rangle$, which I rendered as type u in Gutzmann 2015b: the type for use-conditions.

(6.122) $[\![voc(NP)]\!]^{u,c} = \lambda U.\{c : c \in U \wedge c_A = [\![NP]\!]^{t,c}\}$

That is, the meaning of the vocative is the function that takes the use-conditions of its complement clause—the $CNU(T)$ in (6.116) and maps it to a set that inherits all the use-conditions of the complement clause and adds the addressee-restriction, so that we end up with a most-likely smaller set and hence with more specific use-conditions (only if the addressee-condition was already part of $CNU(T)$, the set does not shrink; it then just remains unchanged).

Abstracting away from the vocative NP, we can then get to the meaning of just the vocative operator voc. Its truth-conditional and use-conditional content can then be given as follows.

(6.123)   a. $[\![voc]\!]^{t} = \lambda x.\lambda p.p : \langle e, \langle \langle s, t \rangle, \langle s, t \rangle \rangle \rangle$
            b. $[\![voc]\!]^{u} = \lambda x.\lambda U.\{c : c \in U \wedge c_A = x\} : \langle e, \langle u, u \rangle \rangle$

This seems to be a good way to capture the main intuitions about vocatives: (a) The truth-conditional content is not affected by the vocative (that is, neither the NP nor the vocative operator contribute anything interesting to the truth-conditional content); (b) The vocative adds the additional use-condition that the referent of the NP is the addressee, to the already-existing use-conditions of the complement sentence.

From Predelli's (2008) approach, or at least from this more explicit version, it also follows that vocatives cannot involve quantified DP, as discussed on page 181. Since the vocative condition involves the subformula $c_A = x$ and since c_A is an individual, it follows that the DP argument of the vocative operator must also be an individual and hence of type e. Therefore, quantified DPs, which are of type $\langle \langle e, t \rangle, t \rangle$, are already ruled out on the type level. Only those quantified DPs that can be shifted to type e, like universally quantified DPs, can be used vocatively, which is also the case as shown by (6.22).

There are, however, some gaps in Predelli's approach. First note that, while the meanings given in (6.123) are compositional on their own, it is not entirely clear how the calculation of an entire sentence works in his system. To be fair, this is not something Predelli aims at, but since coming up with a compositional syntax-semantics interface for expressive vocatives is the main goal of this chapter, we may justifiably wonder how compositional his system is. There are two pertinent questions that Predelli does not address. First, it is not clear how the use-conditions of the sentence without the vocative are calculated in the first place. Somehow, one must get the class of contexts of non-defective use for the vocative-less sentence in order to feed that set as an argument to the vocative. However, these use-conditions should include, for instance, general conditions of, in our case, assertions. In Predelli's system, how these are calculated is left open. Secondly—and this seems to be the more serious problem—Predelli remains silent as to how the two meaning dimensions are calculated with respect to each other. They cannot be completely independent from each other, as witnessed by the fact that the *use-conditional* content of the vocative operator takes the *truth-conditional* content of the vocative DP/NP as its argument (see (6.123b)). Therefore, there must at least be some interdimensional interaction going on, like in Potts's (2005) system for expressives in which expressives take their argument from the truth-conditional dimension. In contrast, note that the second argument of (6.123b) is the use-conditional content of its sentential argument. However, such use-conditional modification is usually excluded in approaches that deal with expressive/use-conditional content.[14] If it were not, it should be possible to have expressions that directly modify use-conditions by (the use-conditional equivalents of) negation, embedding, conditionals and so on. For instance, an expressive negation *negex*, could easily be stated as follows (Barker, Bernardi, & Shan 2010: cf.).

(6.124)   a. $[\![negex]\!]^t = \lambda p.p : \langle\langle s,t\rangle, \langle s,t\rangle\rangle$
       b. $[\![negex]\!]^u = \lambda U.\{c : c \in U\} : \langle u,u\rangle$

When applied to a sentence, this hypothetical expression does not change the truth-conditional content, since it is defined as the identity function of propositions. This is harmless. On the use-conditional level, though, it takes the set of contexts of non-defective uses of the sentence and returns its complement, which corresponds to a use-conditional kind of negation. This expression could, for instance apply to a sentence containing a vocative.

(6.125)   *negex*(*voc*(Angelina)(the sky is on fire))

A vocative utterance that is modified by *negex* would be true, if the sky is on fire. And it would be felicitous in exactly those contexts in which "Angeline, the sky is fire" would be infelicitous. That is, (6.125) would be felicitous if the addressee were not Angelina (or the conditions on asserting "The sky is on fire" were not met). Similar considerations apply to utterances containing other expressives, like expressive adjectives.

---

[14] Such a "principle of non-interaction" (Barker, Bernardi, & Shan 2010) is built into the system of Giorgolo & Asudeh 2012; McCready 2010; Potts 2005 and, at least at the level of full use-conditions, Gutzmann 2015b.

(6.126) *negex*(the damn dog peed on the couch)

Again, the truth-conditions of (6.126) are not touched by the presence of *negex*, but its use-conditional are "negated."

However, an expression like *negex* does not exist and therefore, allowing an expression like Predelli's (2008) *voc* would open the floodgates for a lot of other unattested expressions. This is undesirable.

Note, however, that this problem is specific to Predelli's rendering of *voc* as a function that takes use-conditions as its argument and *modifies* them. However, his core idea—that the vocative imposes *additional* conditions on the felicitous use of an utterance—does not depend on such an implementation, that is based on modification. Instead, if the vocative just expresses the use-condition that the referent of the vocative DP is the contextual addressee and this condition is then merged with the use-conditions expressed by the host sentence *by the compositional system*, this would be a way to end up with the same result but without wading into the dangerous realms of *negex*.

Another gap in Predelli's (2008) account is that he does not address the various vocative functions discussed in Section 6.2.2 at all. Again, it is clear that diving into the different vocative functions is not what his paper sets out to do—it is only eight pages long to begin with—but these omissions lead to some interesting consequences. Using *you* as a vocative is a case in point.

(6.127) *You, I need some water.

As discussed in Section 6.2.2, using *you* without any additional pointing gestures or gazes to identify an addressee is not really felicitous. Under Predelli's approach, though, it should be perfectly fine to always add a second person vocative, because it just condition that $[\![you]\!] = c_A$, which is rather trivially fulfilled because it is to pick-up the contextual addressee is precisely the indexical meaning of the second person pronoun.

(6.128) $[\![voc(you)(I\ need\ some\ water)]\!]^u = \{c : c \in [\![I\ need\ some\ Water]\!]^u \wedge c_A = c_A\}$

However, we cannot just freely add second person pronouns as vocative to our utterance without any change in felicity. The following examples, a variant of (6.49), illustrate this forcefully.

(6.129) #**You**, the talk has been canceled. #**You**, what should we do instead? #**You**, I guess we could work on that problem of the interpretation of proper names. #**You**, what do you think?

We can therefore conclude that Predelli's (2008) approach, while providing a good starting point that captures some core properties of vocatives, faces some problems regarding the compositional details, as well as the more fine-grained meaning contributions of vocatives, and their different functions. Finally, he does not address the syntax of vocatives in any meaningful way. To be fair again, that was not the goal of his paper, so we have to see what the other two approaches have to offer in this respect.

6.4.2 Eckardt 2014

Building on Predelli's (2008) approach, Eckardt (2014) provides an elaborated account for vocative semantics. Her main goal is to derive the observation that vocatives are banned from indirect speech reports. We already saw that vocatives cannot be embedded in indirect speech, but we illustrate it here again.

(6.130) a. *Luigi said that, Ede, pizza was ready.

      b. *Luigi sagte, Ede,   die Pizza sei   fertig.
         Luigi said   Ede.voc *the pizza be*.subj *ready*

Moreover, as example (6.131) illustrates, vocatives are also ruled out in free indirect discourse, something that Eckardt also aims to derive from the vocative semantics.

(6.131)   Yesterday, Luigi welcomed me warmly. Today was his lucky day, *dear friend.

We are not interested in this restriction for the purposes of the present study. Therefore, allow me to just sketch the core idea of Eckardt's proposal. Just as in her other work on free indirect discourse (Eckardt 2012, 2015), she assumes that free indirect discourse involves two kinds of contexts: the main context of utterance C, the "external context" between speaker and hearer or narrator and reader, and an "internal context": the context of the story that is told. Against this background, Eckardt (2014: 231–2) assumes that "vocatives do more than ensuring the correct kind of addressee": they also indicate that the sentence in which they occur is "intended as a message from the actual speaker to the actual addressee (as specified in the vocative phrase)." Therefore, they are ruled out in indirect speech reports as well as in free indirect speech, because these sentences are intended precisely as utterances made by the speaker of the external context C to the hearer of C, and not the speaker/hearer of the context c.[15]

What is of more interest for our present purposes, however, is the semantics and syntax Eckardt (2014) assumes for vocatives. First, in contrast to Predelli (2008), she provides some details about the syntax of vocatives. She assumes that even run-of-the-mill vocatives involve a (covert) second person pronoun that is the head of the vocative phrase. This vocative head then selects for a vocative NP.

---

[15] Things get a bit more complicated when one takes direct speech reports into account as well, because they license vocatives just fine. Of course, we could just argue that direct speech is the (sole) construction that shifts the external context, which can be witnessed by the fact that proper indexicals are shifted to the reported context as well.

(6.132)

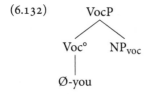

Crucially, Eckardt (2014: 227) assumes that the nominal part of the vocative is a predicate on the referent of the silent pronoun Ø-*you*. Therefore, the NP$_{voc}$ is of type $\langle e, t \rangle$. In order for proper names to be able to function as an NP$_{voc}$ they are type-shifted to type $\langle e, t \rangle$, using a type shifter that shifts an individual to the property of being identical to that individual.

(6.133) $[\![\uparrow^=]\!] = \lambda x \lambda y . x = y$

Applying this type shifter to a proper name, like *Ede*, using the result for NP$_{voc}$ then gives us the semantic representation for an ordinary vocative.

(6.134)   Ede!

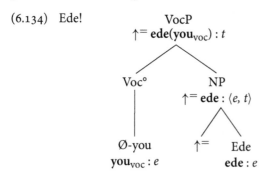

Interpreting the outcome of this tree, we get the following meaning for this vocative phrase.

(6.135) $[\![\uparrow^= \mathbf{ede(you_{voc})} : t]\!]^c = 1$, if Ede $= c_A$

The vocative phrase *Ede!* therefore expresses the proposition that the addressee is (identical to) Ede. Without further ado, this is of course inadequate for a couple of reasons. First, we have already observed that vocatives do not express ordinary propositional content. Secondly, the vocative somehow must be combinable with a host clause. And finally, the semantics of (6.135) does not implement Eckardt's (2014) idea that a vocative encodes the fact that the utterance should be made from the speaker to the addressee.

For these reasons, Eckardt amends the basic structure and semantics of the vocative. First, she follows Predelli (2008) and also assumes that the vocative content is not part of the ordinary truth-conditional content of an expression. In contrast to Predelli, she is a bit more explicit regarding the multidimensionality of this distinction and provides the meaning of an expression as a tuple: ⟨asserted content; additional content⟩. Even though Eckardt (2014: 242, Fn 10; 226) remains neutral regarding the precise nature of the additional content, she suggests that it may best be thought of as expressive/use-conditional meaning. This is precisely how we are going to think of it here, bringing her two-dimensional representation very close to the core idea of hybrid semantics, as sketched in (2.3) in Chapter 2. Secondly, the simple semantic composition in (6.134) is modified so that the vocative also takes a sentential complement. So far, the only reason for this is to distribute the propositional content of the host clause and the content of the vocative into the two meaning dimensions. In order for this to work compositionally, the order of application is reversed: the (covert) pronominal vocative head is type raised so that it now takes the nominal part as its argument.

(6.136) $[\![\mathbf{you_{voc}} : \langle\langle e,t\rangle, \langle\langle s,t\rangle, t\rangle\rangle]\!] = \lambda P \lambda p.\langle\, p; P(c_S)\,\rangle$

Note that in Eckardt's proposal, the content of vocative plus NP, in the second dimension, is still a truth-conditional expression, because the NP still is of type $\langle e,t\rangle$. I will come back to this below.

If the two-dimensional semantics in (6.136) is applied to both a noun and a sentence, we get the following structure and semantics.[16]

(6.137)   Ede, the pizza is ready!

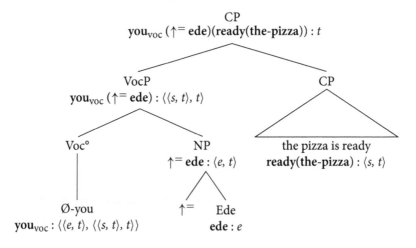

---

[16] Note that Eckardt (2014) does not specify in her paper what the syntactic status of a vocative phrase plus its host clause is. Here, I just assume that the vocative adjoins to the CP without any change in syntactic status. I will discuss some more elaborated syntactic proposals later in Section 6.5.

Interpreting the semantics representation of this modified vocative structure provides the following two-dimensional interpretation.

(6.138) $[\![\text{you}_{\text{voc}}(\uparrow^=\text{ede})(\text{ready}(\text{the-pizza}))]\!]^{c,w}$
$$= \langle\text{The pizza is ready in } w; \text{Ede} = c_A\rangle$$

According to this, a sentence containing a vocative is true, just in case its propositional content is true. This correctly captures the observation that vocatives do not affect truth-conditional content. Moreover, the vocative also expresses that the addressee equals the referent of the vocative NP, but this is communicated expressively. Even though Eckardt does not use explicit use-conditional types here, the fact that she puts it into the second dimension basically does the same job.[17]

The third and final extension Eckardt (2014: 242) applies to the vocatives semantics is that she builds the utterance boundedness of the vocative—the fact that it cannot be shifted by indirect speech reports or free indirect speech—right into its semantics. For this, she adds a predicate MESSAGE to the expressive component of the vocative that sets the utterance parameter to the contextual speaker and addressee. That is, MESSAGE(c_S, c_A, p) says that the utterance is intended as a message with content from the speaker c_S to the addressee c_A. This constraint is just added to the second meaning dimension.

(6.139) $[\![\text{you}_{\text{voc}} : \langle\langle e,t\rangle,\langle\langle s,t\rangle,t\rangle\rangle]\!] = \lambda P\lambda p.\langle p; P(c_S) \wedge \text{MESSAGE}(c_S,c_A,p)\rangle$

Feeding the appropriate parts into this expression leads to the following two-dimensional meaning for the entire vocative.

(6.140) $\langle\text{The pizza is ready in } w; \text{Ede} = c_A \wedge \text{MESSAGE}(c_S,c_A,p)\rangle$

Still, a sentence with a vocative is true if the content of the sentence without the vocative were true. And the sentence is felicitous if the addressee is, in our case, Ede, and the utterance is made by the speaker to the addressee (both of the utterance situation), with the content that the pizza is ready.

All this seems on the right track. So is there anything missing from Eckardt's (2014) proposal? I think there is. While her proposal is much more explicit regarding the syntactic and semantic composition than Predelli's (2008) account, it still is not entirely worked out. First, even if Eckardt (2014: 245) follows the basic, idea as laid out in Potts 2005, that "only the asserted part of content contributes to the meaning of higher operators [while the] commentary contents are projected upward," she does not make explicit how this works in detail; for instance if there already was some use-conditional content. And what if an expression whose second dimension still needs an argument is combined with another that already contains a fully saturated

---

[17] Eckardt remains rather vague regarding how the two meaning dimensions compose with each other (see, for instance, Eckardt 2014: 245).

use-conditional proposition? For the purposes of her paper, whose main aim is to derive the ban against vocatives in indirect speech, it is of course perfectly reasonable not to get into these details and just hint at previous work. For the purposes of this chapter, we would like to investigate this a bit more thoroughly. Fortunately, her ideas can be transferred rather straightforwardly into the compositional system employed in this book. However, I will postpone this until the detailed analysis of expressive vocatives below.

The second gap in Eckardt's (2014) analysis, which she inherits from Predelli's (2008) approach, is that she does not take the different vocative functions into account. As with Predelli 2008, this makes her proposal a bit too weak. With regard to the use conditions given in (6.140), they are just that the referent of the vocative is the addressee and that the utterance is a message from the speaker to the hearer. However, both conditions are rather trivially fulfilled in stereotypical face-to-face contexts. We already illustrated this in (6.129): you cannot just add vocatives to your utterances. Even if Eckardt (2014: 226) acknowledges that the "use of vocatives requires a theory of common ground that can model context changes and the shift from one speaker/addressee to another"—which would certainly also provide a way to account for the different vocative functions—she does not provide something like that in her paper and hence, the vocative functions and the additional constraints they impose on the use of vocative phrases are not reflected in her system. Let us therefore have a look at the third approach to vocative semantics, which—as we will see—does actually attempt to account for (some) vocative functions.

6.4.3 *Portner 2007*

Of the three approaches discussed, Portner's (2007) is the most explicit and elaborated one regarding both the syntactic structure he assumes and the semantic machinery that takes care of how vocative meaning composes with the meaning of the rest of the sentence.

In his article, that besides vocatives also deals with the use-conditional meaning of topics and sentence mood operators, Portner (2007) uses a reformulated, compositional version of Potts's (2005) original system.[18] He assumes that each expression comes with a truth-conditional and an expressive (or use-conditional, as I prefer to call it) component. The semantic composition of the two meaning dimensions is then driven by two composition rules, which are similar in spirit to Potts's (2005) two rules, but are compositional in both dimensions. Portner (2007: 413) provides the following definitions.[19]

---

[18] For a discussion of Portner's system, see Gutzmann (2015b: 108–11).

[19] Portner (2007) uses different variables in the definitions than I do. Furthermore, I correct here an error that was produced by the typesetting of Portner's error-free manuscript version of that article.

(6.141)   **Ordinary functional application**
For all nodes $\alpha\beta$, if $[\![\beta]\!]^t$ is in the domain of $[\![\alpha]\!]^t$, then
a. $[\![\alpha\beta]\!]^t = [\![\alpha]\!]^t ([\![\beta]\!]^t)$
b. $[\![\alpha\beta]\!]^u = [\![\alpha]\!]^u \cup [\![\beta]\!]^u$

(6.142)   **Expressive functional application**
For all nodes $\alpha\beta$, if $[\![\beta]\!]^t$ is in the domain of $[\![\alpha]\!]^u$, then
a. $[\![\alpha\beta]\!]^t = [\![\beta]\!]^t$
b. $[\![\alpha\beta]\!]^u = \{[\![\alpha]\!]^u ([\![\beta]\!]^t)\} \cup [\![\beta]\!]^u$

The first clauses of (6.141) and (6.142) define the composition of the truth-conditional content. For ordinary functional application, the truth-conditional dimension is calculated by just that, functional application. For expressive application, the truth-conditional meaning is just the meaning of the argument β, which means that in case of expressive application, the truth-conditional component of the argument is just returned unmodified (similar to what happens in Potts's system). The second clauses in (6.141) and (6.142) in turn regulate the composition of the expressive dimension. In case of ordinary functional application (6.141b), the use-conditional dimension is simpled merged by union. That is, the expressive dimension of the function and its argument are put together and passed along. In case of expressive functional application (6.142b), what happens is that the expressive content of the function is applied to the truth-conditional content of its argument and (the singleton set of) the result is then merged with whatever the expressive component of the argument was. All this is pretty similar to the composition rules I laid out in Chapter 2.

Now let us take a look at Portner's analysis of vocatives. Let us start with his syntactic analysis. Following Zanuttini (2008), he assumes that vocatives occur in a special syntactic addressee phrase whose function is to represent the addressee in the syntax (Portner 2007: 409; expressions added, D.G.).

(6.143)

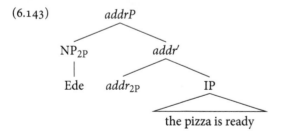

Portner does not provide many details and motivation for his adoption of this structure. The idea behind it, though, is that the head of the addressee phrase carries a second person feature and that the vocative nominal, which stands in a specifier-head relation to the addressee phrase head, also carries such a feature (Portner does not specify whether the nominal already carries this feature or if it is assigned by some agreement process). On the vocative NP, the second person feature has a semantic affect: it presupposes that the denotation of the vocative NP (or more generally XP) equals (the set of) addressee(s). The meaning of a vocative NP is hence defined as follows (see Portner 2007: 409), where the underlined part is the presupposed content.

(6.144) $[NP_{2P}]^{t,c} = \lambda w \lambda x.\{y:\ \underline{[NP]^{t,c}(c_w)(y)\} = addr(c)}.[NP]^{t,c}(w)(x) = 1$

On its own, a vocative NP therefore presupposes that the (set of) addressee(s) is given by the denotation of the NP. If this is fulfilled, the NP has its ordinary predicative meaning. However, the meaning that Portner assigns to the head of the addressee phrase ensures that this ordinary meaning does not play a role in the determination of the truth-conditions of the sentence: it is basically an identity function on propositions, one that also takes the vocative meaning as an argument, but only to ignore it.

(6.145) $[addr_{2P}]^{t,c} = \lambda p \lambda Q.p$

Given these two definitions, we get the following presuppositional and asserted content for a vocative. Note that proper names are presumably type shifted to properties, just as in Eckardt's (2014) proposal.[20]

(6.146)   Ede, the pizza is ready.
      a. PRESUPPOSITION: $\{w:\ \{y:\ y$ is Ede in $w\} = \{c_A\}\}$
      b. ASSERTION: $\{w:\$ the pizza is ready in $w\}$

Despite differences in the assumed syntactic underpinnings, the outcome of this proposal is rather similar to the one suggested by Eckardt (2014). The primary meaning dimension (the assertion here) contains just the propositional content of the sentence, while the vocative meaning introduces a secondary dimension (here a presupposition), the condition that the reference of the vocative NP equals the addressee. The main difference is that Portner renders the addressee constraint as a presupposition, whereas Eckardt suggests that it is more akin to expressive meaning. We already discussed the problems of a presuppositional analysis of the meaning of vocatives, so we just assume at this point that an expressive view on the addressee-constraint is more adequate.[21]

    In contrast to Eckardt (2014), Portner 2007 does not stop with this, but also tries to capture the additional vocative functions—their "pragmatic contribution" (Portner 2007: 409)—which are also not addressed by Predelli (2008). It is with this, that the actual two-dimensional system introduced above kicks in. Portner (2007: 412) is explicit about the fact the he suggests "that the meaning of vocatives be formulated as expressive content in the sense discussed recently by Potts." Focusing on the call

---

[20] I write "presumably" because Portner (2007) does not provide an explicit example.
[21] Another difference with Eckardt is that Portner does not build the utterance-boundedness of vocatives into their semantics.

function, Portner assumes that the additional function of a vocative is to request the addressee's attention. For an utterance like (6.147a), Portner (2007: 414) gives the paraphrase in (6.147b)

(6.147) a. John, your dinner is ready!
            b. 'I hereby request John's attention.'

The idea is then that vocatives in call function involve an expressive operator CALL that takes an individual argument and expresses the (expressive) proposition that the speaker requests that individual's attention. Crucially, Portner (2007: 414) assumes that this operator only has expressive content and is not in the domain of the truth-conditional interpretation function.[22]

(6.148) a. $[\![\text{CALL}]\!]^{u,c} = \lambda x \lambda w.c_S$ requests x's attention in w
            b. CALL is not in the domain of $[\![\cdot]\!]^{t,c}$.

The second clause here ensures that the vocative composes with its argument via the rule for expressive functional application as given in (6.142).

However, I have to admit that it is not entirely clear to me how this expressive operator actually fits into the syntactic and semantic structure given above, because Portner (2007) does not provide any details. He writes that the call operator "takes the referent of the vocative as argument, saturating x in [(6.148a)], and produces an expressive proposition" (Portner 2007: 415). Given the semantic types of the expressions involved, the only sensible option to include the call operator is as an argument to the vocative NP, but only if it is of type e, before it is type-shifted to type $\langle e, t \rangle$ (in order to fit the type required by the addressee head for its first argument). So we arrive at the following syntactic structure.

(6.149)

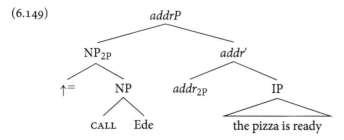

Crucially, since CALL is not in the domain of $[\![\cdot]\!]^{t,c}$, it combines with *Ede* via expressive functional application, which will ensure that the truth-conditional content of CALL **Ede** is just what the proper name *Ede* alone would express.

---

[22] Again, superscripts are adopted to be more in line with the format used in this work.

(6.150) $[\![\text{CALL } Ede]\!]^{t,c} = [\![Ede]\!]^{t} = \text{Ede}$

In the expressive dimension of the vocative NP (before the type shift), we then apply the meaning of CALL to Ede, yielding the use-conditional proposition that the speaker requests Ede's attention.

(6.151) $[\![\text{CALL } Ede]\!]^{u,c} = \{[\![\text{CALL}]\!]^{u,c}([\![Ede]\!]^{t,c})\} \cup [\![Ede]\!]^{u,c}$
$= \{\lambda w.c_S \text{ requests Ede's attention in } w\}$

The two application rules in (6.141) and (6.142) will then ensure that this condition percolates up the semantic composition.

Let us further assume that the meaning of the second person feature on the vocative NP does not presuppose that the addressee equals the referent of the vocative NP, but adds this as an additional use-condition, while not altering its truth-conditional content.

(6.152)   a. $[\![[2p]]\!]^{t,c} = \lambda p.p$
b. $[\![[2p]]\!]^{u,c} = \lambda p.\{c_A\} = p$

Combining this with the type shifted vocative NP and the rest of the sentence, we get the following two interpretations for the overall meaning of the sentence.

(6.153)   a. $[\![(6.149)]\!]^{t,c} = \lambda w.\text{the pizza is read in } w$
b. $[\![(6.149)]\!]^{t,c} = \{\{Ede\} = \{c_A\}, \lambda w.c_S \text{ requests Ede's attention in } w\}$

This basically sums up Portner's (2007) proposal to analyze vocatives and their "pragmatic" function in a multidimensional, expressive semantic framework, or, at least, my interpretation of it. Portner (2007: 415) ends his remarks with possible paraphrases for what he calls tags and addresses, which can be viewed as subclasses of what we called activational vocatives. Tags can be thought of as just activational, whereas addresses contain an additional performative component that expresses the social form of address.

(6.154)   **Tags**   (Portner 2007: 416)
a. What are you doing, John?
b. 'I hereby reiterate that John is my addressee.'

(6.155)   **Addresses**   (Portner 2007: 416)
a. I don't know, my lord, if we have any potted meat in the house.
b. 'I hereby reiterate that my lord is my addressee.'
c. 'I hereby address you as my lord.'

Portner (2007: 416) admits that these are just initial thoughts about other vocative function, but disentangling the addressee constraint from the "pragmatic" vocative functions allows his approach to easily include a variety of vocative functions.

6.4.4 Comparison of the three approaches

How do the three semantic approaches to vocatives discussed in this section compare to each other? First, whereas in Predelli's approach, which really only considers vocatives with proper names, the vocative nominal is of type e, Eckardt assumes they are of type $\langle e, t \rangle$ and proper names are type lifted. Similar considerations apply to Portner's approach insofar as proper names are (presumably) shifted as well. However, this only applies to the addressee constraint; the operator for the CALL function needs an individual type argument and hence must apply to the proper name before it is shifted. For this, it is predicted that calls can only be used with proper names and other referential expressions, like second person pronouns. However, as we saw, calls are fine with proper names, but bare second person pronouns are rather marked.[23] Speaking of pronouns, it can be noted that bare pronouns (without any nominal part), which are of type e, are allowed in Predelli 2008, but excluded in Portner 2007 and Eckardt 2014. In Eckardt's approach, this is because the (covert) vocative Ø-*you* needs a nominal argument (which has to be of type $\langle e, t \rangle$), while in Portner's approach the (covert) *addr*-head selects for a type $\langle e, t \rangle$ predicate, just to discard it; compare (6.139) and (6.145).

Regarding how the addressee constraint is conceptualized, there are a few differences between the three approaches. In Predelli's approach, vocatives contribute to the conditions of "non-defective use," i.e. they can be viewed as use-conditional/expressive content. This is very similar to Eckardt's suggestion to analyze the content of vocatives as expressive meaning using a multidimensional system, even if Predelli does not render his approach explicitly in multidimensional terms. In contrast, the addressee constraint in Portner 2007 comes as a presupposition, although it can easily be implemented as multidimensional, expressive content as well. And for the call function, this is what Portner explicitly suggests.

Discounting differences in how explicit their approaches are and what labels they use for their respective syntactic analyses, the accounts by Portner and Eckardt are not that different from each other. Both use some kind of covert form of addressee representation: the *addr*-head in Portner 2007, the Ø-*you* in Eckardt 2014, which takes the vocative nominal and the host clause as their arguments. The difference is that Portner builds the addressee constraint into the nominal—or, more precisely, into the second person feature that the nominal gets assigned by the *addr*-head— whereas Eckardt puts everything into the meaning of the covert vocative pronoun. The postulation of the *addr*-head also makes Portner's approach the only one that assume some special syntax that goes beyond a special category for the vocative phrase.

---

[23] Maybe bare pronouns can be ruled out in Portner by assuming that they cannot easily be shifted by to type $\langle e, t \rangle$.

TABLE 6.2 Comparing the three approaches to vocative meaning

	Predelli 2008	Eckardt 2014	Portner 2007
Addressee constraint	yes	yes	yes
…meaning type	expressive	expressive	presupposition
Nominal is of type…	e	$\langle e,t \rangle$	$\langle e,t \rangle/e$
Vocative involves two parts	no	yes	yes
Vocative functions	no	no	yes
Special syntax	no	no	yes
Covert addressee representation	no	yes	yes
…in form of	—	covert *you*	addr-head

Regarding the meaning aspects of vocatives, neither Predelli (2008) nor Eckardt (2014) implement the vocative functions that go beyond the addressee constraint, something that Portner (2007) does. On the flip side, Eckardt is the only one who accounts for the utterance boundedness of vocatives in a direct way. The comparison of the three approaches is summarized in Table 6.2.

6.5 Previous syntactic approaches to vocatives

While the three approaches discussed in the previous section provide many details of how a semantic analysis of vocatives might look, they do not dive deeply into questions about their syntax. Predelli (2008) and Eckardt (2014) just assume that vocatives are vocative phrases that take a sentential argument. Since they do not got into the details, I assume that take these vocative phrases to just adjoin to a CP. And while Predelli does not say much more, Eckardt (2014: 243) provide at least a few details about the internal makeup of these vocative phrases: they consist of a covert second person pronoun and a (type-shifted) proper name.

(6.156)

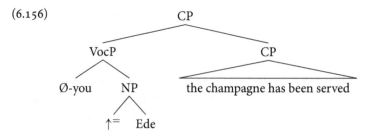

In contrast, Portner (2007) assumes that vocative phrases are merged in the specifier position of a special addressee phrase, which selects the IP and therefore—presumably—can be considered to be part of a more detailed CP-layering, as in the

cartographic tradition (Cinque 1999; Luigi Rizzi 1997). According to Portner's (2007: 409) analysis, the vocative NP itself is not a special kind of phrase, but a simple (though maybe type-shifted) NP. What is special though is that it carries a second person feature, which it gets assigned from the head of the addressee phrase, presumably via some kind of specifier-head-agreement (again, we are not provided many details). In addition, it can be inferred that the vocative NP also involves the call function. That is, from Portner, we get the syntactic structure in (6.149) above, which I repeat here.

(6.149)

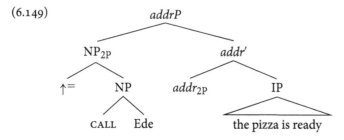

Portner does not discuss this structure, which he adapts from Zanuttini's (2008) proposal for how to represent the addressee in syntax. However, as I already alluded to at various points, in contrast to expressive adjectives (Chapter 4) and expressive intensifiers (Chapter 5), vocatives have received at least some attention in the syntactic literature. I will sketch the main ideas of some of these proposals here, since they provide us with a starting point for our own analysis. However, this is not meant to be an exhaustive discussion of all the previous literature, mostly because they do not address eVocs at all, the one exception being Corver (2008).

6.5.1 *The speech act phrase approach*

The most influential approach regarding the syntactic analysis of vocatives is based on Speas & Tenny's (2003) idea to represent the conversational setting of speech acts in the syntax, as sketched in Chapter 3. As also discussed there, their orginal proposal has slighly been modified by Hill (2007, 2014) and Haegeman & Hill (2013), leading to the following structure (see also Miyagawa 2012 and Zu 2018).

(6.157)

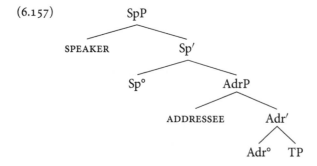

With this structure, Hill (2007, 2014) and Haegeman & Hill (2013) can account for the syntactic constraints on ordering of vocatives and some other discourse particles. On the basis of Romanian, for instance, they argue that the Adr-head can be realized by the particle *hai*. According to Haegeman & Hill (2013: 378), who refer to Tchizmarova 2005, the particle "*hai/haide/hadeţi* is a verb-based particle, which is said to be derived from the frozen imperative form of Turkish *(h)ajde* ('go!'; 'let's go!')." However, despite the fact that it acquired person and number agreement inflection in Romanian, it is not a verb anymore. Instead, it functions as a speech act particle. What is important for our purposes is, however, that this particles selects vocatives as its "indirect object." Crucially, other discourse markers or interjection-like elements like the "lamenting marker" *vai* ('ah') have to precede the vocative (Haegeman & Hill 2013: 380).

(6.158) Romanian   (Haegeman & Hill 2013: 380)

　　a. **Vai Dane**　　hai　că　nu　te　cred.
　　　　INT *Dan*.VOC PART *that not you believe*.1SG
　　　　'Ah, Dan, c'mon, I don't believe you.'

　　b. *****Dane,**　　vai hai　că　nu　te　cred.
　　　　Dan.VOC INT PART *that not you believe*.1SG

However, since such elements can be reasonably assumed to be speaker-oriented expressions, the order restriction follows directly from (6.157), if *vai* is hosted in Sp[0] and the vocative in Adr[spec].

(6.159)

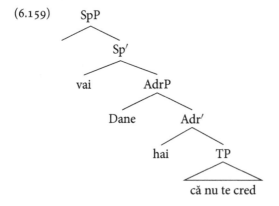

This idea of a speech act phrase that contains a syntactic representation of speaker and hearer is further extended by Haegeman & Hill (2013) and Haegeman (2014). Based on data of West Flemish discourse markers that shows that two speech act markers can co-occur, they propose that there are actually two speech act layers, each consisting of a "little-big" shell (Haegeman & Hill 2013: 386; Haegeman 2014: 135). If we split both into a speaker and an addressee phrase (I am not sure that this is necessary), we arrive at the following extended structure.[24]

(6.160)

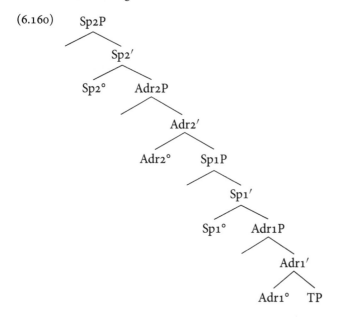

According to Haegeman (2014: 135), the "interpretative properties of the two speech act projections are distinct." What is crucial for our purposes is that this double layering provides an opportunity to represent the different vocative functions syntactically. As Haegeman suggests, the vocatives in the addressee phrase of the higher speech act layer are calls and occur with the discourse particle *né* in West Flemish. In contrast, a lower vocative, which occurs with *wè*, "qualifies or reaffirms the already established relationship with [the] hearer". Assuming that this observation does not just hold for West Flemish, this means that call vocatives reside in a higher position than vocatives with address or activational function. This will be helpful later on.

While the speech act phrase approaches do a good job at capturing the ordering restrictions of peripheral vocatives with respect to other peripheral material (and between different vocative functions), it does not tell us much about the makeup of vocative phrases. That is, a cartographic approach along the lines of (6.160) might be useful for capturing certain aspect of the external syntax of vocatives—in general, but also with regard to eVocs—but does not tell us much about their internal syntax. This is why we will take a brief look at the work by Corver (2008) now, who discusses the syntax of what he calls *evaluative vocatives*.

---

[24] I follow Zu (2018) and use Sp(P) and Adr(P) as labels instead of sa(P) and SA(P).

6.5.2 Corver's analysis of expressive vocatives

Corver (2008) develops a syntactic approach to what he calls "evaluative vocatives," by which he basically means what I dub eVocs. He is mainly interested in their internal structure and focuses firmly on the linguistic variation that can be observed across the Germanic languages. Corver shows, for instance, that besides the German schema of a second person pronoun in nominative case, there are also variants in which the pronoun is accusative (oblique) or in possessive form.

(6.161)   a. Afrikaans   (Corver 2008: 51, citing Ponelis 1979)
              Jou   vark!
              you.ACC/OBL   pig
              "You pig!"

          b. Danish   (Corver 2008: 45)
              Dit   fæ!
              you.POSS   cattle
              "You fool!" (lit. 'Your fool!')

          c. Norwegian   (Corver 2008: 51)
              Din   tosk!
              you.POSS   cattle
              "You fool!" (lit. 'Your fool!')

Based on such variation and other observations about eVocs in Dutch, Corver (2008) develops an analysis that assumes that their underlying structure is that of a possessive noun phrase, and the "surface" structure is derived by leftward predicate displacement. That is, the pronoun is predicative of the expressive noun and not the other way round as I assume.

For the dutch eVoc *Jij app!* ('You monkey'), he provides the following predicative structure as a starting point of the derivation (Corver 2008: 82).

(6.162)

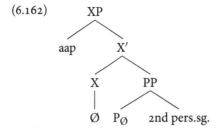

The pronoun starts out a part of a predicate PP with a phonologically empty preposition which is selected by a functional head, which is also covert here and just labeled X. That head selects the nominal element *app* ('monkey') as its "subject". Informally, this base structure could be paraphrased as "(the property of being a) monkey is to you" (cf. Corver 2008: 46).

From the functional phrase in (6.162), the actual DP is derived under Corver's analysis by incorporating the phonologically empty preposition into the functional head X, and then moving the result to a higher D position above the XP, while the pronoun is moved to the specifier position of the resulting DP. A crucial assumption that Corver (2008: 82) makes, is that even if the empty preposition usually assigns dative case, it can no longer do so after incorporation with the functional head X. Hence, the pronoun surfaces in the nominative from. That is, from the structure (6.162), we end up with the following resulting DP.

(6.163)

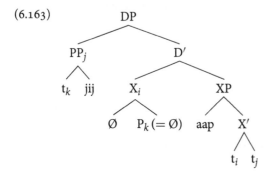

However, although Corver does assume that the pronoun is predicative and the nominal the argument, he mentions at a different point in his paper that there is "a silent/lexical second person pronoun over which the evaluative vocative expression predicates" in addition to the pronoun that is part of the eVoc (Corver 2008: 71).

While Corver's analysis may well be able to capture the variations regarding the concrete structure of eVocs in a variety of Germanic languages, his analysis does not really touch on the questions raised by eVocs that we are interested in for the purposes of this book. First, where does the expressivity of eVocs come from? This is surprising enough in itself, but if we assume with Corver that they are just derived from underlying possessive noun phrases, it is even more puzzling. Possessive noun phrases are not expressive. And certainly, they can feature the most mundane and non-expressive nominals (like *your socks*). So, if eVocs are just derived by a mechanism of predicate displacement, how is it that they are only possible with nouns that are expressives or, if non-expressive nominals are used, they receive an expressive interpretation?

Secondly, the resulting expressions in Corver's analysis are DPs, even if they are derived from a more complex structure. Without any further assumptions then, it cannot be explained based on his syntactic analysis alone, where integrated eVocs get their special behavior from and why autonomous eVocs can be used to make independent and complete utterances. That is, the analysis in (6.163) does not explain the "root-level status" of autonomous eVocs.[25] Corver, to his credit, admits that he

[25] Another gap in Corver's (2008) analysis is that it remains unclear why the complicated predicate displacement takes place to begin with. That is, what triggers it? It seems this would be the right question to ask if one would like to draw the connection to expressivity. I will touch briefly on this below in Section 6.6.5, although I will not adopt Corver's displacement analysis. To consolidate my analysis of eVocs with his idea regarding the variation must be left for future research.

is setting these issues aside in order to concentrate on the variation regarding the internal syntax and while he provides an intriguing analysis of all the different variants of eVocs found in various Germanic (and other) languages, I will take the opposite approach and focus on the expressive character of the eVoc (in German) and set aside deeper questions about their internal makeup and how the cross-linguistic variation is derived. Therefore, I will more or less ignore Corver's analysis for the purposes of this chapter, but I am at least optimistic that his results and the analysis I am going to develop could be brought together, even if this may not be a trivial task.

6.6 Toward an analysis of expressive vocatives

Having discussed a lot of data about (expressive) vocatives and previous approaches to the meaning of (ordinary) vocatives, it is now finally time to come to develop an approach to the syntax and semantics of expressive vocatives, or eVocs, as I continue to call them. As a guide to what follows, let me repeat the list of properties of eVocs from (6.115).

(6.115) a. eVocs consist of a second person pronoun and an expressive nominal.
         b. There are three structural kinds of eVocs: integrated, parenthetical and autonomous.
         c. eVocs are bad as calls.
         d. Neutral nouns may occur in eVocs, but only with an expressive interpretation.
         e. Third person pronouns are excluded from eVocs, as are proper names.

In order to account for these properties, I will go through the three structural types of eVocs one by one, and see how we can capture their similarities and differences. We will first consider the semantic composition, before we have a closer look of the role syntax, and especially expressivity features, plays for eVocs.

But before I start with the development of analyses of eVocs, let us first see if the discussed previous approaches, as they are, can account for them. The first obvious answer is that they cannot account for them at all, because it does not follow from any of the three theories that the structures we dubbed as eVocs exhibit an expressive interpretation. This is just not something that is accounted for in the three approaches we discussed in the previous section. But not only is the expressive semantics unaccounted for; also the structure of eVocs that consists of a pronoun and an (expressive) nominal element is not foreseen by the approaches. First, Predelli (2008) does not discuss the internal structure of vocatives very much but assumes that the overt part of a vocative is a referring NP. So it is not entirely clear how the combination of a second person pronoun and a nominal can fit into that picture even if it is not excluded that this still may be a possibility (more on this later). In Portner's (2007) approach, there is, in contrast, no place for the pronoun, as his structure needs just the nominal. However, one may wonder if the second person pronoun in eVocs is not an instance of his *addr*-head, in which case there would be a natural place to put the vocative pronoun. It would unfortunately then end up in the wrong place, because in Portner's syntactic structure the vocative (including the nominal) dominates and thus precedes the *addr*-head; see (6.143). Finally, in Eckardt's (2014) proposal there is in principle space for both the pronoun and the nominal, but it does not give any expressive meaning and just adds to the addressee constraint. Furthermore, none of the three approaches discusses integrated eVocs or autonomous eVocs.

All this means that we more or less have to start from scratch with the development of an analysis of the varieties of eVocs. However, we build on the insights generated from the three previous approaches and work them into our new approach, which should also be able to account for the difference between eVocs and the other, more ordinary vocative function, which means that we have to keep them in mind as well. Another source of inspiration comes from the well-established semantic analysis of expressives like epithets. This is why I will start the semantic analysis with integrated eVocs: we can build on the analysis of epithets and are not constrained by the ordinary vocative function, because they cannot be used in integrated positions.

6.6.1 *The semantics of integrated eVocs*

In Section 6.3.5 I already discussed the similarities between integrated eVocs and the simple expressive modifications, like those involving expressive nominal or expressive epithets with proper names.

(6.164) a. **Du Idiot** kommst zu spät.
　　　　　　you idiot come　　too late
　　　　　　"You idiot are late."

　　　　 b. **Dieser Idiot** kommt zu spät.
　　　　　　that　　idiot comes　too late
　　　　　　"That idiot is late."

　　　　 c. **Dieser Idiot Hans** kommt zu spät.
　　　　　　that　　idiot Hans comes　too late
　　　　　　"That idiot Hans is late."

Ignoring the syntax of the expressive construction in (6.164c) (especially the demonstrative article), Potts (2005) gives the following, now almost standard way of composing the semantics of expressive modifications of proper names.[26]

---

[26] The semantic types and composition are adjusted to the conventions used in this book, but the overall structure remains as in the original.

(6.165)   Dieser Idiot Hans kommt zu spät. ('That idiot Hans is late')

$$\text{late(hans)} : t \bullet \text{idiot(hans)} : u$$

$$\text{hans} : e \bullet \text{idiot(hans)} : u \qquad\qquad \text{late} : \langle e, t \rangle$$

$$\text{idiot} : \langle e, u \rangle \qquad \text{hans} : e$$

An utterance of (6.164c) therefore has the truth-conditions that Hans is late (as given by the type t expression before the bullet) and the use-conditions that the speaker has a negative attitude toward Hans (as given by the type u expression following the bullet). Note that the local tree for just the DP *dieser Idiot Hans* ('this idiot Hans') already conveys this expressive attitude, while in the truth-conditional dimension it just refers to Hans as if the epithet were not there at all.

(6.166)   dieser Idiot Hans ('that idiot Hans')

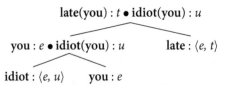

$$\text{hans} : e \bullet \text{idiot(hans)} : u$$

$$\text{idiot} : \langle e, u \rangle \qquad \text{hans} : e$$

Our starting hypothesis is that, in the semantics, integrated, expressive vocatives are just like such structures: they feature an expressive element that combines with a second person pronoun.

(6.167)   integrated eVoc = pronoun$_{2P}$ + expressive modification

The way the pronoun and the expressive nominal are combined is via expressive application. This mode of semantic composition returns the pronoun unmodified at the truth-conditional layer while adding the expressive attitude to the use-conditions of the expression.

(6.168)   Du Idiot kommst zu spät. (lit. 'You idiot are late.')

$$\text{late(you)} : t \bullet \text{idiot(you)} : u$$

$$\text{you} : e \bullet \text{idiot(you)} : u \qquad\qquad \text{late} : \langle e, t \rangle$$

$$\text{idiot} : \langle e, u \rangle \qquad \text{you} : e$$

From this simple assumption about the semantic structure of integrated eVocs, some observations can already be derived. For instance, it directly follows that dropping the pronoun and just using the expressive nominal will not work already in the semantics (not to mention the syntactic problems this would lead to). The problem is that if the pronoun is dropped, the expressive cannot find a suitable type e argument and hence cannot combine in any way with the rest of the sentence.

(6.169) *Idiot kommst zu spät.
        idiot come   too late

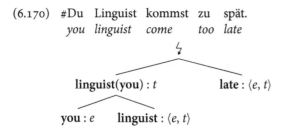

    idiot : $\langle e, u \rangle$ late : $\langle e, t \rangle$

We already saw in Section 6.3.4 that the pronoun plays an essential role in eVocs and, especially in integrated ones, cannot be dropped. So this is nicely captured by the simple hypothesis that integrated eVocs are just second person pronouns plus expressive modification.

Another important aspect that follows from this idea is that we expect only expressive nominals to be part of integrated pronouns. Ordinary nouns—under their plain descriptive standard interpretation—are excluded. Even if they could semantically apply to the pronoun just fine, this would then lead to a type crash in the semantics (in addition to potential syntactic problems).

(6.170) #Du Linguist kommst zu spät.
        you linguist come   too late

        linguist(you) : t late : $\langle e, t \rangle$

    you : e linguist : $\langle e, t \rangle$

Note that the nominal in (6.170) is intended to be completely neutral so that an utterance of (6.170) should mean that the addressee is late and a linguist. However, such a reading is not really possible. This, again, follows from the semantic structure: since the neutral *linguist* is a pure truth-conditional expression it does not pass back its argument unmodified. Therefore, a string as in (6.170) can only be (semantically) parsed if *linguist* is (re)interpreted as an expressive item. If *linguist*, however, worked just like *idiot*, the sentence could be put together semantically. We therefore need a way to shift a neutral noun like *linguist* (type $\langle e, t \rangle$) into a corresponding, expressive counterpart of type $\langle e, u \rangle$. Let us define such a type shifter, which we symbolize with "!".

(6.171) $\lambda p.!p(x) : \langle\langle e, t \rangle, \langle e, u \rangle\rangle$

This, of course, merely defines the semantic combinatorics of this operator and does not tell us anything about its actual semantics and what the conditions are under which it can be employed. I will come back to this. For now, it suffices to see that with such an expressive type shifter *du linguist* ('you linguist') can be interpreted just like *you idiot*.

(6.172)

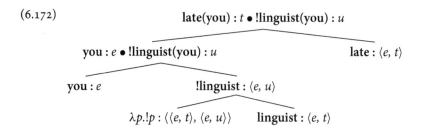

$$\text{late(you)} : t \bullet \text{!linguist(you)} : u$$

$$\text{you} : e \bullet \text{!linguist(you)} : u \qquad\qquad \text{late} : \langle e, t\rangle$$

$$\text{you} : e \qquad\qquad \text{!linguist} : \langle e, u\rangle$$

$$\lambda p.!p : \langle\langle e, t\rangle, \langle e, u\rangle\rangle \qquad \text{linguist} : \langle e, t\rangle$$

Just from the semantics, we would assume that integrated eVocs behave just like ordinary pronouns (with an additional expressive attitude as contributed by the shifted noun). And this seems to be the case. For instance, an eVoc can bind another pronoun, just as ordinary pronouns can.

(6.173) Nur **du**$_i$ **Idiot** hast **deine**$_i$ Hausaufgaben vergessen.
         only you idiot have your   homework   forgotten
         'Only you idiot forgot your homework.'

In this example, the pronoun in the eVoc binds the possessive pronoun, which can be witnessed by the presence of the focus-sensitive exclusive particle *only*. The most salient reading is the one in which, out of the alternative propositions of the form *x forgot x's homework*, only the proposition that the addressee forgot their homework is true.[27] Interestingly, the expressive component of the eVoc does not figure in the alternatives and exclusion introduced by *only* (and the focus). One cannot infer from (6.173) that there are no other people the speaker has negative feelings about; the expressive proposition is not targeted by *only*. This is predicted by the multidimensional analysis of eVocs: the expressive part is, so to speak, invisible for the focus alternatives; something that I have been illustrated for other expressive items (Gutzmann 2007, 2015b).

There is one constraint on integrated eVocs that cannot be derived from the semantic structures we sketched here. If the pronoun in an integrated eVoc is of type e, and the expressive nominal of type $\langle e, u\rangle$ modifies it non-restrictively, why can proper names or third person pronouns, which are also of type e, not occur in eVocs. From the semantics alone, this should be possible. Hence, there must be something more going on with eVocs. I will come back to this when we discuss the syntax of eVocs in Section 6.7 below because, as we will soon see, the same issue applies to the other structural varieties of eVocs.

6.6.2 *The semantics of parenthetical eVocs*

Having sketched a simple analysis of integrated eVocs as pronouns plus expressive nominals, let us now turn to parenthetical eVocs and how that approach can be

---

[27] The one non-bound reading in which nobody except for the addressee forgot the addressee's homework is rather unlikely given our world knowledge about forgetting homework.

transferred to them. Note that I will concentrate on parenthetical eVocs at the sentence periphery. However, the analysis should be directly applicable to parenthetical eVocs in sentence-internal occurrences.

It should be rather obvious that a direct transfer of our analysis of integrated eVocs to parenthetical ones is a non-starter. The following attempt at a semantic derivation illustrates why.

(6.174) **Du Idiot,** du bist zu spät!
　　　　you idiot you are too late
　　　　'You idiot, you are late!'

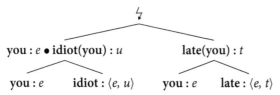

There is an important difference between parenthetical and integrated eVocs with respect to how the pronoun behaves. In case of integrated eVocs, it fulfills a double function: it serves as the argument for the expressive nominal and simultaneously functions as an ordinary pronoun with respect to the host clause. This is not the case for parenthetical eVocs. Here, the pronoun is confined to the context of the vocative and does not serve any role for the purposes of the host clause. This is why a simple "pronoun plus expressive modification" analysis as in (6.174) cannot work. As detailed in Chapter 2, an expressive of type $\langle e, u \rangle$ combines with their argument in a *non-resource-sensitive* way: it leaves its argument back for further use in the semantic derivation. This, however, is precisely not what we want in the case of parenthetical vocatives. They just express an expressive attitude toward the addressee in the expressive meaning dimension, without also referring to the addressee in the truth-conditional level. The contrast is nicely illustrated by the two examples we used for the (attempted) semantic derivations.

(6.175) a. **Du Idiot** bist zu spät!
　　　　　　you idiot are too late
　　　　　　'You idiot are late!'　　　　　　　　　　　　　　　　　　(integrated eVoc)

　　　　b. **Du Idiot,** du bist zu spät!
　　　　　　you idiot you are too late
　　　　　　'You idiot, you are late!'　　　　　　　　　　　　　　　(parenthetical eVoc)

Since the pronoun of the integrated eVoc in (6.175b) remains available after the expressive nominal is applied to it, it can serve as the argument to the main predicate. However, in case of the parenthetical eVoc in (6.175b), the argument slot is already filled by the ordinary pronoun inside the host clause and thus the parenthetical eVoc cannot (only) involve expressive application, because otherwise, the pronoun would be dangling around, as in (6.174), unable to combine with the host clause.

Therefore, there must be something else, or more, going on with parenthetical eVocs. What could this be? I think the key to answering this question lies in the fact that parenthetical vocatives exhibit the utterance boundedness that Eckardt (2014) observed. That is, parenthetical vocatives cannot be interpreted other than relating to the utterance situation and therefore never receive an embedded interpretation. For plain sentential embedding, this of course is also due to their parenthetical status, but as discussed above, Eckardt (2014) shows that vocatives cannot receive a shifted interpretation in free indirect speech either, something that is perfectly fine for other parentheticals, like non-restrictive relative clauses or appositives, and even expressives (see, for instance, Kaiser 2015).

(6.176)   Lisa glared at Jon angrily. He was finally home, three hours late. Yet again, **the idiot** had missed the train. How on earth could someone be so disorganized? Did he not realize that other people were depending on him?

(Kaiser 2015: 357)

In (6.176), the expressive *the idiot* is (most likely) be interpreted with respect to Lisa, not the speaker/narrator. This is also true for expressive content of embedded eVocs. However, due to the presence of the second person pronoun, we cannot just insert an eVoc into any free indirect discourse and be done with it. Attempting to do this with (6.176) fails miserably.

(6.177)   Lisa glared at Jon angrily. He was finally home, three hours late. #**You idiot**, he had missed the train. How on earth could someone be so disorganized? Did he not realize that other people were depending on him?

(Kaiser 2015: 357)

Since the second person pronoun, like the first person one, does not receive a shifted interpretation in free indirect discourse (otherwise we would have an instance of some kind of direct discourse), we need a narration that involves not just a narrator but also some kind of (fictitious) reader to which the pronoun can refer. So let us first transform the narration from (6.176) into a first person narrative including a reader. For instance, a variant of (6.176) that is written from a friend of Lisa's, say Nelson, to Jon in order to explain to Jon why Lisa left in anger.

(6.178)   Lisa was really angry. You were finally home, three hours late. You had missed the train. How on earth could someone be so disorganized? Did you not realize that other people are depending on you?

This still invokes a free indirect discourse insofar as the two (rhetorical) questions at the end are most likely not Nelson's questions to Jon, but attributed to Lisa. With this, we can now try to insert eVocs. First, let us try this with an integrated one. Since those are not good in English to begin with, let us change the example to an analogous German one.

(6.179)   Lisa war wirklich wütend. Du warst endlich zu Hause, drei Stunden zu spät. **Du idiot** hast den Zug verpasst. Wie zur Hölle kann jemand so unorganisiert sein? Merkst du nicht, dass andere Leute auf dich zählen?

This seems perfectly fine. Crucially, the expressive attitude the eVoc conveys in (6.179) is not (necessarily) hold by Nelson, but it is attributed to Lisa, just as with the content of the (third person) epithet in (6.176). Now, let us use a minimal variant of (6.179) that uses a parenthetical eVoc. Here we can give an English and German variant.

(6.180)   Lisa was really angry. You were finally home, three ours late. **You idiot**, you had missed the train. How on earth could someone be so disorganized? Did you not realize that other people are depending on you?

(6.181)   Lisa war wirklich wütend. Du warst endlich zu Hause, drei Stunden zu spät. **Du idiot**, du hast den Zug verpasst. Wie zur Hölle kann jemand so unorganisiert sein? Merkst du nicht, dass andere Leute auf dich zählen?

While inserting a parenthetical eVoc in these narrations is still fine, the expressive attitude is not attributed to Lisa anymore. Instead it reads like an evaluation from the speaker/narrator, i.e. Nelson in our case.

Note that there is a reading of (6.180) and (6.181) under which the expressive attitude conveyed by *you idiot* is attributed to Lisa. However, this would then be something more like free direct discourse (Chatman 1978: 181–5, Leffel & Short 2007: 258–9). But if we alter the example a little bit, we can work out the contrast between the integrated and parenthetical cases.

(6.182)   Lisa was really angry. You were finally home, three hours late.
   a. **Du Idiot** hast sie   wieder im   Stich   lassen.
      you idiot has   her   again   in.the twitch left
      'You idiot, you left her in the lurch again'
      (lit.) 'You idiot left her in the lurch again.'

   b. **You idiot**, you left her in the lurch again.
   How on earth could someone be so disorganized? Did you not realize that other people are depending on you?

Since the target sentences now contain a third person pronoun referring to Lisa, rendering them as free direct discourse is ruled out. And while the expressive component of (6.182a) can either be attributed to Lisa or the narrator, it is linked to the narrator in (6.182b).

This utterance boundedness of the expressive part of peripheral vocatives is not the only aspect that distinguishes them from the integrated ones. Although it is a bit more subtle, this difference may even be more important for what we are interested in here. Recall that usually, expressives can be repeated without redundancy (Potts 2007: 182).

(6.183)   **Damn**, I left my **damn** keys in the **damn** car.

This is also possible with integrated eVocs. Using several of these in a discourse does not seem redundant and may just emphasize the speaker's heightened emotional state. Let's switch back to a German example.

(6.184)   **Du Idiot** bist mal   wieder zu   spät. Glaubst **du   Idiot** etwa,
           you idiot are PART *again   too late   believe you   idiot* PART
           dass es   mir Spaß macht, dauernd   auf **dich Idioten** zu warten?
           that it   me   fun   makes   constantly on you   idiot   to wait
           'You idiot are late again. Do you idiot really think that it is fun for me to wait
           for you idiot all the time?'

Admittedly, the small discourse in (6.184) would be a bit more natural if the expressive nominal part of the eVoc varied a bit (*idiot, ass, fool*).

(6.185)   **Du Idiot** bist mal wieder zu spät. Glaubst **du Arschloch** etwa, dass es mir
           Spaß macht, dauernd auf **dich Deppen** zu warten?
           (lit.) 'You idiot are late again. Do you ass really think that it is fun for me to
           wait for you fool all the time?'

The same is true for (6.183).

(6.186)   **Shit**, I left my **fucking** keys in the **damn** car.

What is crucial here is that integrated eVocs can basically be used at every position at which a bare pronoun would be possible. But this is not true for parenthetical eVocs. Repeating them at such frequency seems rather odd.

(6.187)   **Du Idiot**, du   bist mal   wieder zu   spät. (#**Du Idiot**), glaubst
           you idiot   you are PART *again too late   you   idiot   believe*
           du   etwa, (#**du Idiot**), dass es   mir Spaß macht, dauernd   auf
           you PART *you   idiot   that it   me   fun   makes   constantly on*
           dich zu   warten, (#**du Idiot**)?
           you to   wait   you   idiot
           'You idiot, you are late again. (#You idiot), do you really think, (#you idiot),
           that it is fun for me to wait for you all the time, (#you idiot)?'

That it is not the expressive part of the parenthetical eVoc that makes this awkward is shown by the fact that switching the nominal, as we did in (6.185), does not remove the oddness.

(6.188)   **Du Idiot**, du bist mal wieder zu spät. (#**Du Arschloch**), glaubst du etwa, (#**du Depp**), dass es mir Spaß macht, dauernd auf dich zu warten, (#**du Wichser**)?
'You idiot, you are late again. (#You asshole), do you really think, (#you fool), that it is fun for me to wait for you all the time, (#you fucker)?'

This is very much reminiscent of the awkwardness induced by repeating ordinary vocatives. This was illustrated by (6.49), which I repeat here for convenience.

(6.49)   **Ede**, the talk has been canceled. (#**Ede**,) what should we do instead? (#**Ede**,) I guess we could work on that problem of the interpretation of proper names. (#**Ede**,) what do you think?

So it must be the fact that, in contrast to integrated eVocs, parenthetical eVocs have some true vocative function and this is what makes repeating them infelicitous. That this is on the right track is further corroborated by the observation that (6.188) remains marked if we drop the expressive nominal and end up with plain pronominal (activational) vocatives.

(6.189)   **Du**, du bist mal wieder zu spät. (#**Du**), glaubst du etwa, (#**du**), dass es mir Spaß macht, dauernd auf dich zu warten, (#**du**)?
'You, you are late again. (#You), do you really think, (#you), that it is fun for me to wait for you all the time, (#you)?'

This leads me to the following simple hypothesis. Parenthetical eVocs are vocatively-used pronouns that are expressively modified by the nominal part. To put it simply:

(6.190)   parenthetical eVoc = vocative + pronoun$_{2p}$ + expressive modification

Comparing this to the hypothesis about the structure of integrated eVocs given in (6.167), parenthetical eVocs contain one additional ingredient in the form of the vocative function.

Having three parts, we then have to decide how they combine with each other. We already saw in the discussion at the beginning of this section, that the expressive modification is non-resource-sensitive and thus gives back the pronoun unmodified, something that is not desired for peripheral vocatives. A structure in which the vocative function first combines with the pronoun and then is modified by the expressive is therefore not adequate. Instead, I assume that the pronoun first combines with the expressive nominal. Since, as we saw, the pronoun remains available after that, the vocative function can then apply to it in a second step. Since "pronoun plus expressive modification" is just the structure we assumed for integrated eVocs, we can say that, semantically, parenthetical eVocs are like integrated eVocs but with a proper vocative function attached to them.

(6.191)   parenthetical eVoc = vocative + $\underbrace{\text{pronoun}_{2p} + \text{expressive modification}}_{\text{integrated eVoc}}$

Putting this hypothesis into a proper semantic representation, I assume for the moment that we can have a vocative function operator that applies to the pronoun that is passed back after the expressive modification. Crucially, this expression should not pass the pronoun back unmodified and should also take the host clause as an additional argument, very much as in Eckardt (2014) analysis of plain vocatives. This sentential argument, however, must be passed back. The following expression does this job.

(6.192) $\lambda x \lambda p.\text{voc}_{\text{act}}(x)(p) : \langle e, \langle \langle s, t \rangle, u \rangle \rangle$

This expression first takes an individual argument: the pronoun passed back from the expressive nominal. In a second step, the resulting expression applies to the propositional content of this host clause. This then results in a completely saturated use-conditional proposition (type u) and its propositional argument is passed back. The following semantic tree shows how the composition proceeds.

(6.193)   Du Idiot, du bist zu spät. 'You idiot, you are late.'

$$\text{late(you)} : \langle s, t \rangle \bullet \{\text{voc}_{\text{act}}(\text{you})(\text{late(you)}) : u, \text{idiot(you)} : u\}$$

$$\text{voc}_{\text{act}}(\text{you}) : \langle \langle s, t \rangle, u \rangle \bullet \text{idiot(you)} : u \qquad \text{late(you)} : \langle s, t \rangle$$

$$\text{voc}_{\text{act}} : \langle e, \langle \langle s, t \rangle, u \rangle \rangle \qquad \text{you} : e \bullet \text{idiot(you)} : u$$

$$\text{you} : e \qquad \text{idiot} : \langle e, u \rangle$$

In order to make the compositional structure clearer, let us strip (6.193) down to its essentials. This nicely illustrates the interplay between the expressive and the vocative component of a parenthetical eVoc.

(6.194) $$\text{prop} \bullet \{\text{voc(pro)}, \text{ex(pro)}\}$$

$$\text{voc(pro)} \bullet \text{ex(pro)} \qquad \text{prop}$$

$$\text{voc} \qquad \text{pro} \bullet \text{ex(pro)}$$

$$\text{pro} \qquad \text{ex}$$

What we get from a sentence containing parenthetical eVoc is three things. First, in the truth-conditional dimension, we get the propositional content of the host clause, just as if the eVoc never had been there. In the use-conditional dimension, we get two different use-conditional propositions. First, we have the use-conditions provided by the expressive nominal and secondly, we have the use-conditions as contributed by the vocative operator.

This two-step interpretation accounts for the fact that the pronoun in parenthetical eVocs does not play any role for the truth-conditional dimension, which is also precisely the reason why they are parenthetical and not integrated: the pronoun cannot fill an argument slot. This is another aspect that renders parenthetical eVocs more vocative-like than their integrated variant.

However, the composition alone does not really explain why parenthetical eVocs are marked when repeated at high frequency, whereas integrated ones can basically be used whenever the corresponding bare pronoun could be used, as long as the speaker bears the adequate expressive attitude, of course. Therefore, as already hinted at above, this must come from the vocative function itself, which is also suggested by a similar ban against (fast) repetition of ordinary vocatives. I propose that the vocative operator active in parenthetical eVocs is just one of the ordinary vocative functions. But which one? We can rule out the identificational or call function for two reasons. First, as observed by d'Avis & Meibauer (2013) and discussed above, eVocs in general are bad as call. Furthermore, the vocative function active in parenthetical eVocs has to be usable with pronouns alone (because this is fundamentally what is going on in eVocs, given the structure I proposed) and calls/identificational vocatives are not good with pronouns (except for when there is a pointing gesture). We can also rule out predicational vocatives. Even if the expressive part of an eVoc is predicated upon the addressee, the vocative function itself does not see the expressive and only applies to the pronoun. And second person pronouns cannot be used as predicational vocatives. This leaves us with activational vocatives. This will not come as a surprise, since I already gave that away by the subscript I used on the vocative operator above. Therefore, I will assume that the vocative part of parenthetical vocatives gives rise to use-conditions that capture what the vocative literature assumes about their function (Zwicky 1974: 187; Portner 2007: 415; Schaden 2010: 182; d'Avis & Meibauer 2013: 197). Note that propositional argument does not figure in the meaning of the vocative, but has to be there for combinatoric reasons.

(6.195) $[\![\text{voc}_{\text{act}}]\!]^u = \lambda x \lambda p.\{c : c_S \text{ wants to maintain that } x \text{ is the addressee}\}$

Even if this is a bit vague and could and should surely be developed in more detail, I think it is sufficient for our current purposes, because it is able to rule out fast repetitions on pragmatic grounds. Of course, wanting that the current addressee remains the addressee is nothing strange, but *expressing* this desire repeatedly is rather awkward. This is also witnessed by the following variation on example

(6.188), in which other means of "addressee maintenance" are used at a rather high frequency.

(6.196) **Du hörst mir jetzt mal zu.** Du bist mal wieder zu spät. (#**Hörst du?**) Glaubst du etwa—(#**hallo!**)—dass es mir Spaß macht, dauernd auf dich zu warten, #**ja?**
'You are going to listen to me now. You are late again. (#Are you listening?) Do you really think—(#hello!)—that it is fun for me to wait for you all the time, (#do you)?'

Trying so hard to maintain the addressee's attention is only felicitous if she is really distracted and the speaker is afraid that she might stop listening at any moment. However, in such a (hopefully non-standard) situation, the use of multiple parenthetical eVocs would also be much better. This shows that the constraint against repeating is due to pragmatic reasoning and not just baked into the semantic contribution of the vocative.

What the preliminary semantics for the activational vocative function does not include yet is the utterance boundedness, the second factor that distinguishes parenthetical from integrated eVocs. Here, I follow Eckardt (2014) and use her MESSAGE function; see (6.139). This also gives an additional reason for the presence of the propositional argument for the activational vocative, beside just combinatoric reasons.

(6.197) $[\![\text{voc}_{\text{act}}]\!]^u = \lambda x \lambda p.\{c : c_S \text{ wants to maintain that } x \text{ is the addressee}$
$\text{and MESSAGE}(c_S, c_A, p)\}$

Let us take stock. According to the present proposal, integrated eVocs are, after all, not very vocative-like. Instead, they are pronouns modified by expressive nominals. This is also a part of parenthetical eVocs, which in addition also feature the activational vocative function just defined. This function applies to the pronoun, which is still available after the expressive applied to it. However, the vocative function does not give the pronoun back after the application. Therefore, the pronoun can fill a slot in the host clause in the case of integrated eVocs, but not so in parenthetical ones. Moreover, the specific semantics of the activational eVoc makes a frequent repetition of parenthetical eVocs rather odd, whereas integrated ones can be repeated whenever the pronoun can be used. Finally, due to the utterance boundedness ensured by the vocative function, parenthetical eVocs cannot receive a shifted interpretation in free indirect discourse, while integrated eVocs, which are lacking the vocative operator and thus the utterance boundedness, can.

For one restriction mentioned in the discussion of the behavior of eVocs, we do not have an explanation yet: eVocs cannot be used as calls. We gave a functional explanation above. Due to their subjective nature, eVocs are bad as calls, because they are not well suited to uniquely identify an addressee. However, I think there is also a more semantic, combinatoric reason of why eVocs are bad as calls. In order to illustrate that, we first must have a closer look at the call function of vocatives. However, before we do that, let us first end our exploration of the semantic analyses of eVocs with discussing the semantics of autonomous eVocs.

6.6.3 *The semantics of autonomous eVocs*

Autonomous eVocs are so called because they appear without any host clause with whom they interact.

(6.198)   Du Idiot!
        'You idiot!'

A first hypothesis for these eVocs would be that they are the same as parenthetical ones, which syntactically are not fully integrated into their host clause as well. However, directly adopting the analysis of parenthetical eVocs as a pronoun plus expressive modification plus vocative function as in (6.215) cannot work. The first obvious reason is that the activational vocative function in parenthetical eVocs needs a propositional argument that is absent from autonomous eVocs (which is exactly what makes them autonomous). Therefore, the semantic derivation can not be completed.

(6.199)

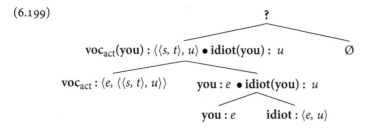

Of course, one could stipulate that autonomous eVocs combine with a covert, trivially true proposition. The semantic derivation given in (6.199) would then be able to be finished. However, recall that the vocative function in (6.197) involves the utterance boundedness property which is ensured by the use-condition that the utterance is meant to be a message from the speaker of the utterance to the hearer of the utterance *with propositional content p*. That is, when we stipulated some trivially true proposition, say "When it rains, it rains," the utterance of *Du Idiot!* ('You Idiot!') should be understood as a message with that propositional content. Which, of course, is not what such an utterance is about. It has no ordinary propositional content and stipulating it just for combinatoric reasons is not a good idea.

Maybe it could be feasible to assume a variant of the vocative function in (6.197) that does not need a propositional argument. However, I will skip this attempt, because there is another reason for not using the activational vocative function for autonomous eVocs. Recall that this vocative function involves two parts: besides the utterance boundedness, there is the addressee maintenance, which captures the (re)activational nature of such vocatives and constraints the frequency of their repetition. However, a closer look at autonomous eVocs shows that this constraint does not hold for them: repeating autonomous eVocs does not seem to be marked.

(6.200)   Du Idiot! Du Arschloch! Du Wischer!
        'You idiot! You asshole! You fucker!'

It seems that, in contrast to integrated eVocs, autonomous eVocs involve neither part of the vocative function in (6.197).

Let us then explore the alternative hypothesis that autonomous eVocs are like integrated eVocs. These can also be repeated and do not need a propositional argument, because they lack the activational vocative operator. So maybe autonomous eVocs are like them and only consist of a pronoun and the expressive nominal. However, this is also not an adequate way to think about the semantic makeup of autonomous eVocs. The following derivation shows why.

(6.201) $\text{you} : e \bullet \text{idiot(you)} : u$

       $\text{you} : e \qquad \text{idiot} : \langle e, u \rangle$

The problem here is that the pronoun is still present at the truth-conditional layer, which means that an utterance of *You idiot!* should refer to the addressee and be an expression of type e. However, this is just not the meaning of such an expression, as has already been observed by Potts & Roeper (2006). Therefore, autonomous eVocs can not just combine a pronoun with an expressive nominal and be done with it.

So, what are our options here? Maybe an autonomous eVoc really is an underlying sentence? According to this idea, an utterance of *Du Idiot!* would actually be a shortened version of (6.202).

(6.202)   Du bist ein Idiot!
        'You are an idiot!'

However, there are several reasons why this is not a viable option either. First, as noted by Potts & Roeper (2006), a full statement like (6.202) seems to be a more general statement and overall characterization of the addressee, while (6.198) can be characterized more in terms of the expression of the speaker's (current) heightened emotions.

The difference between the full, predicational copular sentence and the autonomous eVoc becomes even more apparent when we take usually neutral expressions into account. Compare the following two examples.

(6.203)   a. Du bist ein Linguist.
          'You are a linguist.'

       b. Du Linguist!
          'You linguist!'

In most contexts, an utterance of (6.203a) neither implies any emotional state nor any negative attitude toward the hearer or linguists on its own. It is first and foremost a descriptive statement about the addressee's profession. This is in contrast to (6.203b), which is about expressing a heightened emotion (most likely but not necessary) and not so much about the fact that the addressee is a linguist. Actually, the fact that the addressee is a linguist is rather taken for granted by an utterance of (6.203b). I avoid the technical term *presupposition* here, because it is not easily testable if the addressee being a linguist is actually presupposed or entailed by some other inference. I will briefly touch on this later. For now, it is sufficient to note that the fact that the addressee is a linguist is not at-issue in (6.203b) while it is in (6.203a). For instance, one cannot answer a question about the addressee's profession with the eVoc, in contrast to (6.203a).

(6.204) A: Rate mal, als was ich arbeite.
             guess PART *as what I   work*
             'Guess what I do for a living?'

         B:' #Du Linguist!
             'You linguist!'

         B: Du bist ein Linguist.
             'You are a linguist.'

This points us toward the following conclusion: autonomous eVocs are purely expressive statements that do not have any descriptive/truth-conditional content. Therefore, any analysis that tries to reduce them to something that also has truth-conditional content—like integrated eVocs or copular clauses—is a non-starter. However, analyzing them as parenthetical eVocs, which do not contribute any truth-conditional content, is not an option, as we just saw.

So where should we go from here? I think the best way to approach autonomous eVocs is by taking their purely expressive character seriously. This is in contrast to integrated and parenthetical eVocs, whose expressive content, so to speak, sits parasitically on top of the descriptive content, which is the primary focus of the utterance. However, with autonomous eVocs, displaying the emotional attitude is the primary function of the utterance (since it is the only one). This makes autonomous eVocs similar to other expressive utterances like *wh*- or *how*-exclamatives (Castroviejo Miró 2006; d'Avis 2013; Rett 2012) or expressive *much*-questions (Gutzmann & Henderson 2015).

(6.205) [Seeing many guitars in a store:]
         How many guitars they have!

(6.206) [Seeing many guitars in a store:]
         Guitars, much?

While, in some sense, both of these utterances convey that the speaker considers the amount of guitars they are seeing to be huge, this happens in a non-descriptive way. Neither utterance can be used to answer a question about the amount of guitars in the shop.

(6.207)   A: Are there many guitars in the shop?
           B: #How many guitars they have!

(6.208)   A: Are there many guitars in the shop?
           B: #Guitars, much?

Other tests, like denial in discourse or embedding under semantic operators, would also show that (6.205) and (6.206) do not have truth-conditional content. In this respect they resemble our autonomous eVocs. Especially the connection to exclamatives may be revealing here, as Welte (1980) already called such eVocs "exclamatory vocatives".

So what we need is an operation that combines the expressive nominal with the pronoun to yield the expressive attitude, but only that; it should not pass back the pronoun to the truth-conditional layer. More precisely, we do not want anything in the truth-conditional dimension. What we need is therefore a *shunting* expressive in the sense of McCready 2010. Shunting expressives are expressions that take a truth-conditional argument and map it onto an expressive/use-conditional expression, but do not pass the argument back. (They "shunt" their truth-conditional argument away into the use-conditional dimension.) In McCready's 2010 original system, shunting expressives receive a designated semantic type (indicated by a superscripted s) and there are special composition rules that refer to these shunting types. We can easy implement this into our system by introducing a shunting use-conditional type, let's call it u^s to mirror McCready's system, which is interpreted the same way as u but is composed differently. Applying an expression with a shunting output type to a suitable argument does not then pass the argument back, but like a pure truth-conditional expression, "consumes" its argument. So we would have a derivation as follows.

(6.209)   idiot(you) : u^s

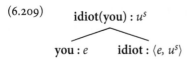

     you : e idiot : $\langle e, u^s \rangle$

However, I think this analysis gets it a bit backwards. It uses a different lexical item in order to account for the stand-alone use of an expression that for all intents and purposes looks like the integrated version. And thinking about the interfaces, such an analysis assumes that the syntax already knows that the expression will be used autonomously when the pronoun and the expressive are merged. I think that conceptually, it would be more honest to just start with the same structure that integrated eVocs have—a pronoun and a standard expressive—and then assume a mechanism that kicks in when the eVocs is used autonomously. So let us do just that. Taking the similarity between autonomous eVocs and the exclamative utterances mentioned above seriously, I assume that the autonomous use of eVocs is enabled by a D(P)-exclamation operation, alluding to Welte's (1980) notion of "exclamational vocatives". Basically, what this does is to get rid of the truth-conditional content of a DP. In semi-formal terms, this be formulated as follows.

(6.210)   **D-exclamation**

A DP with semantic content $\langle p, q : u \rangle$ can be uttered as an exclamation. The resulting D-exclamation has only use-conditional content $q : u$.

We can define a corresponding semantic operator EXCL that takes the two-dimensional meaning of a DP and gives back an empty first dimension, while leaving the second dimension untouched.

(6.211)   a. $[\![\text{EXCL}(\alpha)]\!]^t = \emptyset$
          b. $[\![\text{EXCL}(\alpha)]\!]^u = [\![\alpha]\!]^u$

We can represent this operator in the syntax, which I will do, but not much hinges on this for our purposes. One reason to opt for this, though, is that it can provide a syntactic explanation for why such exclamations do not embed with other syntactic material: we assume that the exclamation operator takes up a very high position in the sentence (where, for instance, other speech act operators could also be located).[28]

(6.212)

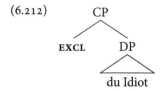

What is crucial here is that the EXCL-operator only takes DP complements and not entire TPs, because these could not just be used as exclamations.[29]

I admit that it is maybe a bit strange to assume that autonomous eVocs are CPs and not just exclamatorily used DPs. However, if we go down this route and represent the exclamation syntactically, the high C-domain seems a natural place for it and, maybe more importantly, this gives us an actual empirical advantage when compared with a completely non-syntactic approach. If we assume that the exclamation operator is located in a high position (as for speech act markers) but below the position for vocatives in call function, we can derive the vocative doubling structures discussed in Section (6.107) from this. Recall that an autonomous eVoc can be preceded by a call vocative and followed by an activational one. Assuming that an activational vocative is a parenthetical vocative that can adjoin at every "parenthetical niche" we

---

[28] It should be noted that banning embedding can already be achieved on semantic grounds since type u expressions cannot be the input for other expressions, as discussed in Section 2.3. But double insurance is of course not a problem here.

[29] Other expressive DPs can also be used as exclamations like *Shit!* or *Asshole!*, which shows that this expressive D-exclamation is not just a stipulation for autonomous eVocs.

can propose a structure roughly along the following lines, where the dashed line indicates parenthetical attachments.

(6.213)

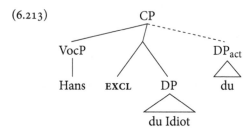

However, spelling this out does require some additional investigations into the syntax of parentheticals that I cannot follow here.[30] Nevertheless, this illustrates how the syntactic assumptions of the EXCL-operator may help cover this data. But again, we could also assume that the operator just adjoins to a DP without changing its syntactic status, which also sounds very intuitive.

Yet another alternative route is to connect these thoughts to the idea of speech act phrases developed by Haegeman (2014); Haegeman & Hill (2013); Hill (2014) and discussed in Section 6.5.1. If there are two speech act phrases, we could assume that the exclamative operator resides in the lower speaker projection, while the call vocative is hosted in the higher addressee phrase. Following Haegeman (2014: 135), we can then assume that activational vocatives are in the lower addressee phrase. And, to complete the picture, interjections like *Oh!* that precede all vocatives (in fluent intonation) occur in the higher speaker projection. The one (admittedly rather strong) stipulation we have to make for autonomous eVocs is then to assume that they have an empty TP argument. This results in the following structure.

(6.214) Oh Hans, du Idiot, du!
         oh hans you idiot you
         'Oh Hans, you idiot, you!'

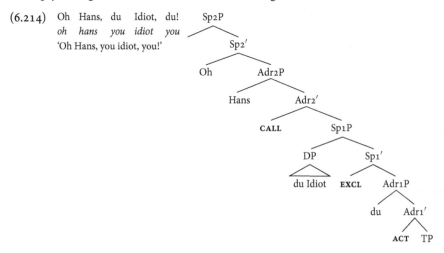

[30] See, for instance, Busch & Schumann 2016; Espinal 1991; Griffiths & Vries 2013; Haegeman 1988; McCawley 1982; Peterson 1999; Potts 2002; Vries 2006, 2012 or the contributions in Dehé & Kavalova 2007, and many others. Regarding parentheticals in German particular, see, for instance Hoffmann 1998; Kügelgen 2003; K. Pittner 1995.

It is an interesting question to decide between the three possible routes. However, since this would lead us a bit too far astray, I will leave this to future research. The crucial part for us here is that autonomous eVocs involve some kind of exclamation component. Summarizing this analysis, we can say that they are like integrated eVocs but used as exclamations.

(6.215)   autonomous eVoc = exclamation + $\underbrace{\text{pronoun}_{2p} + \text{expressive modification}}_{\text{integrated eVoc}}$

This concludes our semantic analysis of the three different structural kinds of eVocs. As it turns out, autonomous eVocs are not core vocatives, just like integrated ones, since they do not involve a dedicated vocative function, in contrast to parenthetical eVocs, which involve the activational function. However, there are still some aspects to be taken care of. First, why are eVocs bad as calls? Secondly, where does the expressive interpretation of descriptive nouns in eVocs come from? And, finally, what role does syntax play in the restrictions observed for eVocs. Let us tackle these questions one after the other.

6.6.4 *The semantics of calls*

There is one constraint that holds for eVocs that I have not discussed on the basis of the proposed semantic and structural makeups of the different kinds of eVocs. As discussed above, eVocs cannot be used as calls.

So far, I have only hinted at a functional explanation for this, based on the subjective nature of the evaluation component of eVoc that is not well suited to ensure the identification of the addressee. However, with the analysis so far, we are in a position to establish why eVocs cannot be used as calls. To explain this restriction, we have to think about the semantics of the calling function. Recall from our discussion of the vocative functions that calls try to establish the addressee by picking out some property that can single out the addressee. For instance, professions are good calls (but bad as activational vocatives).

(6.216)   **Fahrer,** halten Sie   bitte   an der nächsten Ecke.
          driver stop   you.FORMAL *please* at the next   corner
          'Driver, please stop at the next corner.'

Crucially, bare second person pronouns are not good as calls, at least if they are not accompanied by some deictic gesture or additional linguistic material. When they are supplemented like this, they are fine.

(6.217)   a. #Du, komm her   und hilf mir!
             you   come here and help me

          b. Du+[gesture toward A], komm her   und hilf mir!
             you   *come here and help me*
             'You+[gesture toward A], come here and help me!'

c. $^{\gamma}$Du mit   der blauen Kappe, komm her   und hilf mir!
  you with the blue   hat   come   here and hel   me
  'You with the blue hat, come here and help me!'
  [http://forum.fc-saarbruecken.de/index.php?page=Thread&threadID=426]

Since bare second person pronouns are most likely of type *e*, I take this restriction at face-value and assume, that the calling function does not take type *e* arguments. Instead, I assume—loosely following Portner's (2007: 409) addressee constraint— that the vocative call operator takes a predicate as its argument and conveys the use-condition that the set of addressees is given by the (contextually restricted) denotation of the vocative expression. I also add the additional requirement that the speaker actually requests the attention of the addressee, as formulated by Portner (2007: 414) and given above in (6.148a).

(6.218) $[\![\mathbf{voc_{call}}]\!]^u = \lambda P \lambda p.\{c\colon P = c_A \text{ and } c_S \text{ requests } c_A \text{ attention and}$
$$\text{MESSAGE}(c_S, c_A, p)\}$$

The attention request for calls confines their use to contexts in which either the addressee is not yet set or to those in which the addressee is known but their attention has drifted away from the conversation. Like activational vocatives, repeating calls is odd if one already successfully has the addressee's attention.

In (6.218), I also included Eckardt's (2014) MESSAGE constraint that ensures that the sentence the call combines with is intended as a message from the actual speaker to the actual addressee, thereby correctly blocking a shifted interpretation of calls.

From this semantic representation of the call operator it directly follows that a simple second person pronoun (of type *e*) cannot serve as the argument of the call function. Therefore, we also have a combinatoric reason to rule these out from functioning as calls, besides the functional explanation.

(6.219)

$$\overset{\text{\textbareh}}{\overbrace{\hspace{6cm}}}$$

$\mathbf{voc_{call}} : \langle\langle e, t\rangle, \langle\langle s, t\rangle, u\rangle\rangle$ **you:** *e*

With this, let us assume that additional material that modifies a second person pronoun, as well as deictic means like gestures or intentional pointing gazes, can shift the type *e* pronoun into a property. For instance *du mit der blauen Kappe* ('you with the blue hat') can be rendered as the property of being the addressee and being an individual with a blue hat.

(6.220) $[\![\mathbf{with\text{-}a\text{-}blue\text{-}hat(you)}]\!]^u = \{x\colon x = c_S \text{ and } x \text{ has the blue hat}\}$

As a brief detour, although I stipulate this here, an analysis of the modification of the second person pronoun along these lines can be backed up by other data. For instance, such post-nominal modification can also be used with proper names as well.

Interestingly, this also seems to turn the entire modified name semantically into a property and syntactically into an NP.

(6.221)   Der Daniel mit   langen Haaren ist Semantiker, aber der Daniel
          the   Daniel   with long   hair   is   semanticist but   the Daniel
          mit   kurzen Haaren ist Syntaktiker.
          with short   hair   is   syntactician
          'The Daniel with long hair is a semanticist, but the Daniel with short hair
          is a syntactician.'

We could analyze those DPs very similarly to the modification of the second person pronoun. There are two options. We could assume that both occurrences of *Daniel* are represented by the same semantic constant which is shifted to the property of being called *Daniel* or, which is more akin to (6.222), we can assume that homophonic proper names are distinguished in the semantics and are understood as the property of being identical to their respective referent.

(6.222) $[\![\textbf{with-long-hair}(\textbf{daniel}_b)]\!]^t = \{x: x = \text{Daniel B. and } x \text{ has long hair}\}$

Of course, this may leave a lot to be desired, but at least it illustrates that assuming the semantics in (6.222) for the pronoun modification is not a completely unreasonable assumption.

   Let us come back to vocatives with call function. Shifting the pronoun from having an individual denotation to denoting a property enables it to be an argument to the call operator, which then can be applied to the propositional content of the host clause (simple symbolized by p here).

(6.223)

$$p : \langle s, t \rangle \bullet \text{voc}_{\text{call}}(\textbf{with-the-blue-hat}(\textbf{you})) : u$$

$$\text{voc}_{\text{call}}(\textbf{with-the-blue-hat}(\textbf{you})) : \langle \langle s, t \rangle, u \rangle \qquad\qquad p : \langle s, t \rangle$$

$$\text{voc}_{\text{call}} : \langle \langle e, t \rangle, \langle \langle s, t \rangle, u \rangle \rangle \qquad \textbf{with-the-blue-hat}(\textbf{you}) : \langle e, t \rangle$$

$$\textbf{you}: e \qquad \textbf{with-the-blue-hat} : \langle e, \langle e, t \rangle \rangle$$

A semantic analysis like this gives us the propositional content of the host clause just as it was without the calling vocative. In the use-conditional level, however, the vocative introduces the following set of contexts of felicitous use.

(6.224) $[\![\text{voc}_{\text{call}}(\textbf{with-the-blue-hat}(\textbf{you}))]\!]^u = \{c : \{x : x = c_S \text{ and } x \text{ has the blue hat}\} = \{c_A\} \text{ and } c_A \text{ requests } c_A\text{'s attention and MESSAGE}(c_A, c_S, p)\}$

That is, using a call with a host clause with content p, is true if p is the case and, leaving other potential use-conditions aside, it is felicitous if i) the addressee is the addressee and has the blue hat and ii) the speaker requests the addressee's attention and iii) the utterance is a message with content p from the speaker to the addressee.

Calls are also possible with proper names, of course. Following Eckardt (2014), I assume that they are shifted to the property of being identical with their referent (see (6.133)). Then, they can combine with calls just fine.

Having this analysis of calls in place now, we can easily see why eVocs (of any sort) are rather bad as calls. They involve a second person pronoun of type e which cannot be modified to become a property because the expressive nominal needs an argument of type e. Therefore, the call operator cannot apply here, just as is the case with bare pronouns.

(6.225)

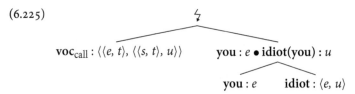

Since all kinds of eVocs involve an unmodified pronoun, the call function cannot apply to them, making them bad calls. Again, we now have a combinatoric explanation in addition to the functional one given by d'Avis & Meibauer (2013).

6.6.5 *Where does the expressivity of eVocs come from?*

For the most part, I used examples of eVocs that involved a proper expressive nominal, like *idiot*. However, I already briefly touched on the surprising observation that even neutral nouns like *linguist* receive an expressive interpretation when used in an eVoc.

(6.226)   Du Linguist! 'You linguist!'

In order to account for this, I introduced the type shifter "!" that shifts a descriptive property of type $\langle e, t \rangle$ into an expressive predicate of type $\langle e, u \rangle$. I repeat from (6.171).

(6.171) $\lambda p.!p(x) : \langle \langle e, t \rangle, \langle e, u \rangle \rangle$

This type shifter does what is needed for using a descriptive predicate like *linguist* in an eVoc, as has already been illustrated in (6.172). However, (6.171) only tells us something about the combinatorics, but remains rather shallow with respect to what is actually going on semantically. To remedy this, let us have a more detailed look at what is going on when a descriptive noun is used in an eVoc, beyond the shift in semantic type.

One aspect that we already briefly looked at is that the meaning of descriptive nouns in eVocs is not conveyed in the usual way. Rather, it is presupposed or otherwise backgrounded; see the discussion on below (6.203). Another question we have to ask is what the target of the expressive attitude of an utterance of (6.226) is. Is it only the addressee? Or is it the group of linguists? According to my intuition, it is both, but the attitudes are conveyed differently. An utterance of (6.226) is (most likely; see below) an insult to the addressee, but at the same time, it would be odd if the speaker generally thought highly of linguists. Why would she use that noun as an insult then?

I think this observation, that eVocs with descriptive nouns express some kind of double attitude, ties in nicely with the previous observation that the fact that the predicate (in its neutral reading) applies to the addressee is taken for granted. Taking inspiration from Hom's (2008) analysis of racial slurs, I assume that an expressively shifted noun expresses a negative attitude toward its arguments *because* the argument falls under the denotation of the (neutral noun). For the expressively shifted *linguist*, we therefore have something along the following lines.

(6.227) $[\![!\text{linguist}]\!]^u = \lambda x.\{c: c_S \text{ has negative feelings toward } x \text{ because } x \text{ is a linguist}\}$

With this, we can give a semantically more substantial definition for the expressive type shifter.

(6.228) $[\![!]\!]^u = \lambda P.\lambda x\{c: c_S \text{ has negative feelings toward } x \text{ because } x \text{ is } P\}$

This captures the two observations made above. First, the negative attitude targets the speaker but, a bit more indirectly, the group of linguists as well. Only if the speaker has some negative associations with linguists, can she have negative feelings about the addressee because he is a linguist. Of course, this does not have to be a general negative view of linguists; it can be just due to some contextual specifics. For instance, the speaker may be rather neutral toward linguists, but in the context be mad about the addressee because the addressee inappropriately behaved like a linguist in a way that annoyed the speaker.[31]

Secondly, since the fact that the addressee is a linguistic is part of the causal explanation of the negative speaker attitude, it is presented as taken for granted and not introduced as new information. Whether we would like to think of this as a presupposition or not, the fact that expressive content may come with its own secondary content is nothing peculiar to eVocs. This holds, for instance, for the expressive adjectives when they target the entire event, as discussed in Chapter 4, or evaluative adverbs like *unluckily* (Liu 2012).

(6.229)   a. **Damn**, the dog peed on the couch!
          b. **Unluckily**, I spilled my coffee on my computer.

In (6.229a) the attitude that the speaker feels negatively about the dog's peeing on the couch is presupposed by the expressive, as is the fact that the speaker spilled coffee on

---

[31] All this is completely hypothetical and rather unlikely, of course.

her computer in (6.229b). Of course, this presupposition is not really important since it corresponds to the truth-conditional content of the respective sentences. But still, this shows that not just the truth-conditional but also the expressive dimension may come with presuppositions (Gutzmann to appear).

To conclude, the semantics of the expressivizer "!" does not just transform a descriptive predicate into an expressive one by a mere change in semantic type; it also establishes a causal link between the expressed attitude toward the addressee and their membership of the shifted nouns denotation.

Up to now, the type shifter has just been there to rescue the semantic composition. However, there are currently no restrictions in place, regarding when the expressivizer can be introduced. This is problematic, as it predicts neutral predicates to be usable in places where they actually cannot be. If the expressivizer can be freely introduced just for combinatoric reasons (like other type shifters), it should be possible, for instance, to get an expressive reading for neutral nouns modifying a proper name as in (6.230).

(6.230) ^{y}... der Sprachwissenschaftler Klaus von Heusinger wurde im
              the linguist   Klaus von Heusinger became in
         vergangenen Jahr misstrauisch.
         last   year suspicious
         'The linguist Klaus von Heusinger became suspicious last year.'
         [http://www.schwaebische-post.de/918115]

The modificational use of *Sprachwissenschaftler* ('linguist') in (6.230) is neutral and there is not really an expressive reading available. However, without further restrictions, using the expressivizer "!" here to transform *linguist* into an expressive should be possible here, just as it is with descriptive nouns in eVocs, as in the following semantic tree for just *Sprachwissenschafter Klaus von Heusinger* ('linguist Klaus von Heusinger').

(6.231) klaus-von-heusinger : e • !linguist(klaus-von-heusinger) : u

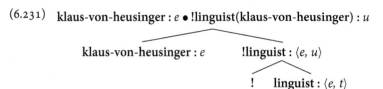

Since the expressive version of *linguist* passed back its argument *Klaus von Heusinger*, it and can semantically be combined with the rest of the host clause. This would then give rise to the use-condition that the speaker of (6.231) has a negative attitude toward Klaus because he is a linguist. However, such a reading is usually not available for (6.230).

In order to exclude false predictions like this, we therefore need some restrictions on when the use of the expressive type shifter is actually licensed. Even though this chapter focused mostly on the semantic side of eVocs, I think the key to understanding this restriction lies in their syntax. Hence, let us have a closer look at that.

6.7 Expressivity and the syntax of expressive vocatives

In contrast to the previous two case studies, this chapter was a bit light on the syntactic part. The reason for this is that, as we have seen, a huge part of the special behavior of eVocs can be attributed to their semantic composition and the way the components—pronoun, expressive nominal, and vocative operators—interact with each other. However, we just saw that a pure semantic approach cannot rule out unattested expressivizations of descriptive nouns. However, there are some additional restrictions that the semantic analysis does not address. As has been discussed in Section 6.3.5, eVocs are restricted to second person pronouns (and marginally first person ones; I will more or less ignore these at this point, however). Third person pronouns like *sie, er, es* ('she, he, it') are excluded, as are proper names. Let me repeat two relevant examples again.

(6.232) a. **{**Sie, er, es**} **Idiot** ist in den falschen Zug eingestiegen.*
        she he it   idiot is in the   wrong   train in.gotten

     b. ******Hans Idiot** ist in den falschen Zug eingestiegen.*
        Hans idiot is in the wrong   train in.gotten

Given that third person pronoun and proper names are individual denoting expressions, our semantic analysis of eVocs does not rule out such examples. Again, a minimal semantic parsetree illustrates the problem.

(6.233) **hans** : e • **idiot**(hans) : u

                         ⌒

     hans : e **!idiot** : $\langle e, u \rangle$

As shown in Section 6.3.5, proper names are only possible with expressive nouns in the presence of a determiner or demonstratives and if the expressive precedes the noun. Third person pronouns can never occur with expressive nominals. What is possible, however, is to have a determiner or demonstrative with the nominal instead (and no proper name).

(6.234) a. {der, dieser} Idiot Hans
       the   that   idiot   Hans

     b. {der, dieser} Idiot
       the   that   idiot

So where should we go from here? I think it could be enlightening to take the superficial similarity between (6.234b) and the version with a pronoun seriously.

Recall also that, at least in German, there is also the variant with the first person pronoun. If we treat them on par, we have a full paradigm for all three persons.

(6.235) $\left\{\begin{matrix} \text{ich} \\ \text{du} \\ \text{der} \end{matrix}\right\}$ Idiot

So, what if the first and second pronouns in such constructions are not pronouns or articles? Or, the other way round, what if the article in the third person were a determiner? This would then unify the three constructions.

Indeed, it has actually been argued on both theoretical and typological grounds, that personal pronouns and definite articles can be unified, based on conflation of the grammatical features of person and definiteness.[32] Some evidence for this move is provided by the fact that cross-linguistically, pronouns and articles tend to have similar expression, as well as by the existence of what Lyons (1999: 142–5) calls *personal determiners*. These are relevant for the present discussion because they are personal pronouns that are used like articles, as in the following examples.

(6.236)   a. We linguists love languages.

   b. Ich Linguist liebe Sprachen.
       I   linguist   love   languages
       'I as a linguist loves languages.'

   c. Ngarka njuntu ka-npa   purlami.
       man   you.SG AUX 2SG   shout
       'You, a man, are shouting.'   (Walpiri, Lyons 1999: 142)

There are some language-specific restrictions on this article-like use of personal pronouns. While English is rather restricted, German or Walpiri are less constrained in this respect. Languages may also differ with respect to whether they impose restrictions on specific lexical forms of the pronouns or articles. For instance, while *the* in English must subcategorize for an NP and hence cannot be used as traditional pronoun, the definite article in German doubles as a bare demonstrative personal pronoun.

(6.237)   a. *The is a linguist.

   b. Der ist ein Linguist.
       the is   a   linguist
       'That is a linguist.'

---

[32] See, e.g., Lyons 1999 or, more recently, Am-David 2013. Vater 2000 provides some arguments for German, and Gutzmann & McCready (2014) use this idea for a use-conditional approach to definite descriptions.

A proposal to unify pronouns and determiners along such lines has been put forward by Vater (1998, 2000), who suggests that both are elements of D. He suggests to differentiate between a transitive and intransitive use of these elements, which he calls *Determinantien*. The intransitive use then corresponds to traditional pronouns and the transitive use corresponds to determiners. Some expressions, like the German definite determiner, can have both transitive and an intransitive use; compare (6.237b) to (6.238).

(6.238)   Der   neue   Kollege   is   ein   Linguist.
        the   new   colleague   is   a   linguist
        'The new colleague is a linguist.'

For Vater (2000), the fact that some D-expressions have both a transitive and an intransitive, and some are restricted to one or the other, is not a reason for him to think of the intransitive/pronoun use and the transitive/determiner use as two different parts of speech. He draws a parallel to verbs, which can be transitive or intransitive and some can be both, in which case we would not think about assigning different syntactic categories to them (Vater 2000: 194). A very similar consideration to unify pronouns and determiners is proposed by Sternefeld's (2008: 152) who analyses pronouns as "intransitive determiners." That is, instead of thinking about pronouns vs. determiners, we should rather think about transitive vs. intransitive D-elements.[33]

Crucially for our purposes, Vater (1998: 15, 2000: 193) provides examples of eVocs in order to illustrate that (first and) second person pronouns also have the transitive/determiner use. He even goes on to note that this transitive use is only licensed if the nominal is an expressive or at least can be construed as such. He also attests our observation that third person pronouns cannot have an intransitive use, even with expressive nominals; see (6.232). Vater does not really give an explanation for these restrictions. However, I think if we connect his ideas with the restrictions observed for eVocs and the idea about expressivity as a syntactic feature, we can make sense of the data in a rather straightforward way.

The key to a feature-based explanation of the data is to build on the hypothesis from the previous chapters, that D is a place of expressivity in German. And as has been the case with the expressive intensifiers discussed in Chapter 5, the form of the D-element may be shaped and/or constrained by the presence of expressivity features. Now, recall from the discussion so far that the second person pronoun can only be used as a determiner-like element when the noun gets an expressive interpretation. On the other hand, ordinary articles can be used with either neutral or expressive nominals, yielding a corresponding interpretation. In light of all this, I propose the following: the second person pronoun can only be used as a transitive D-element,

---

[33] Although I adopt this view, I will keep calling the intransitively used D-elements *pronouns* and the transitively used ones *determiners*.

when it selects for an expressive complement. The definite article, on the other hand, can come in both an expressive and a non-expressive variant.

Let us flesh out this idea in more detail. I will follow Sternefeld's (2008) convention to formulate selection restrictions by means of a syntactic feature of the form [* α *]. An expression that carries such a feature selects for an expression that is either of category α or itself carries the syntactic feature [α], in which case it does not matter whether that feature is interpretable or valued. I will summarize selectional features by shortening [* α *][* β *] to [* α, β *]. Equipped with this, the restriction for second person pronouns to only select for expressive nominals can be formulated as follows.

(6.239)

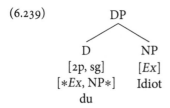

Crucially, in German, selection for an NP and selection for an expressive argument are tied together with the second person feature of D. That is, there is no D-element in German that carries both [2p] and just [* NP *]. In contrast to the selectional features of D in (6.239), the standard intransitive pronoun use of *du* ('you') does not carry any selectional features and therefore is used without any NP complement.

(6.240)   DP
            |
            D
         [2p, sg]
            du

This gives us a syntactic formulation for the restriction of second person determiners to expressive nominals. And if a noun itself is not lexically specified as being expressive, I assume that the cover expressive type shifter "!" gives the entire NP an interpretable expressivity feature—written [*iEx*] as in the previous chapters—so that the shifted NP then fulfills the selectional restrictions of transitive *du*.[34]

Third person pronouns can be prohibited in this system by assuming that they are invariably intransitive. That is, they never come with a [* NP *]-feature. If a third person feature is connected with a selectional requirement for an NP, it is a standard

---

[34] I leave to further research exactly how this operator is located in the syntax. It could be in a dedicated functional phrase inside the NP, a covert expression in (some) specifier position of the NP, or just merged directly with N°. This is indeed an interesting question and the different options may make different empirical predictions regarding the makeup of the NP. I cannot unfortunately delve deeper into this issue for the purposes of this work.

definite or indefinite determiner. But crucially, no third person D-element seems to come with a requirement for an expressive complement. Therefore, standard transitive determiners can come with either a neutral or expressive complement, as long as it is an NP.

Interestingly, even though this syntactic approach only aims to give a uniform account of articles and pronouns, it can also explain why eVocs are impossible with proper names. Even if a proper name like, say, *Petra* is semantically of type *e* (just like a pronoun like *you*), a proper name is not a D-element in German, but a noun (that projects an NP), which may arguably come with a covert determiner. That this is not a far-fetched assumption is shown by fact that in many varieties of German, proper names can be used with definite articles without any change in meaning.[35]

(6.241)   a. Wo   ist denn Petra?
               where is   PART Petra
               'Where is Petra?'

          b. Wo   ist denn die Petra?
               where is   PART the Petra
               'Where is Petra?'

When a proper name is an NP or (with an overt or covert article) a DP, one cannot just use it as a D-element that selects for a expressive NP. What is possible, however, is to have prenominal modification inside the DP (in which case proper names need some kind of D-expression in all variants of German) or a postnominal appositive-like modification, which then must have DP-status. This gives us the two structures we already observed.

(6.242)   a. *Wo   ist denn Hans Idiot?
               *where is   PART **Hans** idiot?*

          b. Wo   ist denn der **Idiot** Hans?
               *where is   PART the idiot **Hans***
               'Where is that idiot Hans?'

          c. Wo   ist denn Hans, der   Idiot?
               *where is   PART the   idiot **Hans***
               'Where is **Hans**, that idiot?'

Before we conclude, there is the question of why we implement the dependency between a second person D-element and expressivity by a selectional restriction

---

[35] Note that proper names do not always come with a (covert) determiner. In some syntactic contexts, one actually cannot insert an overt article without affecting meaning. Cases in point are introductions like *Meine Name ist Petra* ('My name is Petra'). Even in dialects of German in which proper names with overt articles are completely unmarked, one would never say **Meine Name ist die Petra*.

and not by an agreement mechanism as we did in the previous two case studies. The "problem" is that the upwards-looking mechanism of ↑Agree*ᵢ* that we used before is of no help to us now. While it made sense for the expressive adjectives to assume that they cannot be interpreted at their syntactic position, that is no problem for the expressive nominal of eVocs. Moreover, the expressive nominal in eVocs can only be interpreted *in situ* and cannot, for instance, receive a sentence-level interpretation. Consider, for example, the following instance of an integrated eVoc.

(6.243) Ich habe **dich Idioten** nicht gesehen.
       I   *have* *you* *idiot*   *not* *seen*
       'I didn't see you, you idiot.'

Crucially, (6.243) semantically only encodes a negative attitude toward the addressee. It does not have a reading under which the speaker is only mad about the fact that she did not see the addressee. Contrast this with the following sentence containing an expressive adjective.

(6.244) Ich habe den **verdammten Peter** nicht gesehen.
       I   *have* *the* *damn*   *Peter* *not* *seen*
       'I didn't see that damn Peter.'

As discussed in Chapter 4, a sentence like (6.244) is ambiguous between a reading under which the expressive on the object targets the object or the entire sentence.

This shows that the expressive nominal is interpreted where it occurs, which makes an agreement approach based on ↑Agree*ᵢ* rather implausible. However, I think that an agreement-based approach does not even make much sense conceptually here, as the relation between the pronoun and expressivity seems to really be a matter of a selectional restriction and not one of feature agreement and valuation. For these reasons, building the analysis on feature selection instead of agreement seems to be more adequate for this data set.

Of course, all these considerations about the different selectional restrictions of different pronouns and determiners does not really explain *why* the selectional patterns in German are as they are. And I am not going to give one here. However, we have seen that there seems to be a lot of cross-linguistic variation with respect to which D-elements are transitive and which are intransitive—that is, if they can, cannot or may select for an NP complement—and if the complement must be expressive or does not need to be. All this raises a deeper question about a potential deeper connection between the syntactic category of D and expressivity, a suspicion that all three case studies in this book give rise to. However, I am afraid that this question is only addressable with many more cross-linguistic comparisons, so that I have to leave this to future research.

6.8 Summary

When I planned to include a case study on (expressive) vocatives in this book, I didn't expect it to become the longest of the three case studies. Standard vocatives are pretty interesting in and of themselves but when one adds all the intricate data about eVocs, they become a really diverse and maybe surprisingly deep topic that touches upon a lot of important questions. I hope that at least I managed to show that with this case study. So, before zooming out to a broader picture for the concluding chapter of this book, let me summarize the most important observations made and analyses developed throughout this chapter.

After I gave a brief introduction of standard vocatives and introduced two respectively three vocative functions (Zwicky 1974 vs. Schaden 2010), I introduced expressive vocatives. These consist of a second person pronoun and an expressive nominal, usually a genuine expressive, though descriptive nouns are also possible if they can be forced contextually into an expressive interpretation. I furthermore distinguished three structural types of eVoc that vary with respect to how they interact (or not) with surrounding linguist material: integrated, parenthetical, and autonomous types. Having discussed the behavior of eVocs in much detail, I turned to previous approaches to ordinary vocatives. Although I drew a lot of inspiration from them for the later analyses, none of them offered a direct route to account for the expressivity of eVocs. This is why I developed my own approach to the three kinds of eVocs. As it turned out, integrated eVocs do not have many vocative-like features after all, which rendered them more like epithet constructions or other kinds of expressions that are modified expressively. In contrast, I argued that parenthetical vocatives involve the activational vocative function, together with the ingredients of the integrated eVocs. Finally, building on parenthetical eVocs, autonomous eVocs receive a slightly different analysis, since they do not occur with any other material and constitute full utterances on their own. In a nutshell, the three analyses can be summarized as follows.

(6.245)   integrated eVoc $=$ pronoun$_{2P}$ $+$ expressive modification

(6.246)   parenthetical eVoc $=$ vocative $+$ $\underbrace{\text{pronoun}_{2P} + \text{expressive modification}}_{\text{integrated eVoc}}$

(6.247)   autonomous eVoc $=$ exclamation $+$ $\underbrace{\text{pronoun}_{2P} + \text{expressive modification}}_{\text{integrated eVoc}}$

Based on these assumptions, I then provided a semantics for the call function of vocatives in order to explain why eVocs cannot be used as calls. This basically comes down to a problem of semantic composition. The call function needs a type $\langle e, t \rangle$ argument, which is not available in eVocs. I then went into a bit more detail about the semantic mechanism that shifts neutral nominals into expressive ones. Formally, this is done by an expressive type shifter, that shifts a neutral property into an expressive attitude which is causally linked to the denotation of the neutral expression. However, it was clear that freely inserting this expressivizer overgenerates and that, in the end, we need a syntactic motivation for the type shifting mechanism. In the final section of this chapter, I therefore investigate the relation between expressivity of the noun and the pronoun. Building on the assumption that the second person pronoun in eVocs is akin to a determiner, I assume that this transitive use of the pronoun comes with a selectional restriction to expressive nominal phrases and that it is this selectional restriction that can license the use of the expressive type shifter. This hints at an interesting connection between the syntactic category of D and expressivity as a syntactic feature, just as in the previous two case studies. However, with respect to the main hypothesis of this book—the hypothesis of expressive syntax—the upshot of this chapter is that expressivity as a syntactic feature can be selected for.

7

Looking back and looking ahead

7.1 Introduction

For this short, concluding chapter, I decided against summarizing each chapter. Instead, I will discuss the one main hypothesis I tried to argue for in this book:

(7.1) **Hypothesis of expressive syntax**
Expressivity does not only play a role for semantics and pragmatics, but it is a syntactic feature.

I will first illustrate how each of the three case studies independently provided evidence for this hypothesis being true. I will go through the different ways, each chapter does that, before giving a brief outlook for future research.

7.2 Expressivity as a syntactic feature

According to the hypothesis of expressive syntax, expressivity is a syntactic feature, on par with other syntactic features like tense, gender, person, or case. If that is the case, we expect that the assumed expressivity feature is involved in syntactic operations like other features, like partaking in agreement relations, triggering movement, or being selected for by other expressions. The three case studies have shown that this indeed seems to be the case.

7.2.1 Expressivity can agree

The upshot of Chapter 4 for the hypothesis was that expressivity can be involved in agreement. The analysis I developed for the puzzling phenomenon of argument extension provide indirect evidence for this idea. Argument extension describes the observation that in a sentence like (7.2), the expressive adjective inside the DP does not take its NP sister as its argument but can (at least) take the entire DP (which it is part of) or the entire CP as its argument, thereby extending its argument to a larger constituent.

The Grammar of Expressivity. First edition. Daniel Gutzmann.
© Daniel Gutzmann 2019. First published in 2019 by Oxford University Press.

(7.2)   Gestern   hat   der   verdammte   Hund   den   Kuchen   gefressen.
         yesterday   has   the   damn   dog   the   cake   eaten
         'Yesterday, the damn dog ate the cake.'
         a. ☺(the dog)
         b. ☺(the dog ate the cake)

Given that this is impossible for descriptive adjective, this observation is surprising. However, once we assume that there are uninterpretable and interpretable expressivity features in syntax and combine it with an upwards looking understanding of agreement Zeijlstra (2012), which I called ↑Agree$_i$, argument extension does not seem so puzzling anymore. The basic solution is the insight that lies at the core of many agreement phenomena: the places where a syntactic feature is phonologically realized does not necessarily match the place where it is semantically interpreted. Following this insight, I assume that an expressive adjective like *damn* in English or *verdammt* in German is just the realization of an expressivity feature, which, however, cannot be interpreted. It therefore must find a corresponding interpretable counterpart with which it can agree. The place where this interpretable expressivity features is located then gives us the place where the expressive attitude is interpreted. If it is located in D^0, the target of the expressive attitude, if it is located in C^0, the entire sentence is evaluated negatively. These two readings can be traced back to a syntactic ambiguity, because the two readings correspond to two different structures that only differ with respect to where the interpretable expressivity features are located, something that does not have a reflect at the phonological realization of the sentence.

(7.3)   [$_{CP}$ Gestern hat der Hund [$_{DP}$ den$_{[iEx]}$ verdammten$_{[uEx]}$ Kuchen] gefressen]

(7.4)   [$_{CP}$ Gestern hat $_{[iEx]}$ der Hund [$_{DP}$ den verdammten$_{[uEx]}$ Kuchen] gefressen]

What is crucial here is that the puzzle of argument extension is solved by the simple assumption that expressivity is a syntactic feature that, like most other features, comes in an interpretable and uninterpretable variant and which can occur in more than one syntactic location, coupled with the upwards looking view on agreement ↑Agree$_i$, which has been independently argued for and perfectly fits the discussed data. That is, we just transferred an already-developed approach to the data observed about expressive adjectives and the problem almost solved itself. In this respect, we may even conclude, that the way argument extension works supports evidence for ↑Agree$_i$.

7.2.2 *Expressivity can trigger movement*

Another way in which syntactic features can make themselves visible to the syntactician's eye is that they sometimes lead to operations of internal merge, or, as it is traditionally called, movement. We have seen this with expressive intensifiers in Chapter 5. Again, we were faced with a puzzling phenomenon. Expressive intensifiers in German, when used with a DP, usually occur in the expected degree position (either with adjectives or with gradable nouns). However, in case of indefinite DPs, they can also precede the determiner in a position that ordinary degree expressions are excluded from.

Again, this puzzle can be solved by assuming that expressivity is a syntactic feature. However, this time, we do not just deal with agreement, because the intensifiers moves. In addition, it can only move if we have a DP that is interpreted as indefinite, even though the determiner may surface as a definite one. We bring these two special facts about expressive intensifiers together and assume that expressive intensifiers carry an interpretable expressivity feature (in contrast to expressive adjectives like *damn*, which are uninterpretable). Hence, they are interpreted where they are originally merged. The reason that they move is that in that case, there is an uninterpretable expressivity feature on an indefinite D-head. However, since I adopted ↑Agree$_i$ in this book, this is the wrong configuration for agreement, since the needy element is above the needed one. In order to rescue the derivation, the expressive intensifier can move to D° where it incorporates with the indefinite article, thereby entering an agreement relation with it, so that the uninterpretable feature will not make any problems at the interface. The entire string "EI+D" then surfaces as a definite article (for most speakers) or indefinite one (possible for some speakers).

(7.5)   a. **Movement of EI to D**
   $[_{DP} [_{D°} D_{[uEx: \_\_][iDef: -][\varphi: \text{NOM.SG.F}]}] [_{NP} \ldots \text{EI}_{[iEx: \text{INT}]} \ldots]]$
   ↑————————— *move* —————————|

   b. **Agreement between EI to D**
   $[_{DP} [_{D°} \text{EI+D}_{[iEx: \text{INT}][\overline{uEx: \text{INT}}][iDef: -][\varphi: \text{NOM.SG.F}]}] [_{NP} \ldots \overline{\text{EI}} \ldots]]$
   ↑↑Agree$_i$|

Again, the fact that syntactic features can trigger movement in order to establish the proper configuration is nothing new to this analysis of the movement of the intensifier to D°. We just transferred what has been argued for for other phenomena to the puzzling data about expressive intensifiers. And since this worked, it can be viewed as (indirect) evidence for the idea that expressivity is a syntactic feature.

7.2.3 *Expressivity can be selected for*

The last case study on expressive vocatives, carried out in Chapter 6, was a bit less syntactic than the other ones—I was first concerned with getting the semantics right for the different contextual uses of expressive vocatives—but nevertheless contained an additional phenomenon that can be observed with syntactic features. Recall that one of the main challenges raised by expressive vocatives is that we need to explain why they can only be used with expressive nouns and why even neutral nouns are interpreted as expressives. The core idea for the analysis is the idea that pronouns are basically articles (or the other way around) and that the second person pronoun in expressive vocatives is more like a determiner. However, and this is where the hypothesis of expressive syntax kicks in, this second person article cannot select any argument DP. At least in German, it is constrained to expressive DP. Now, according to the model of grammar assumed here, syntax cannot know about the meaning of expressions and therefore, syntax is blind to the fact that a DP is expressive. That is, unless one assumes that expressivity is represented in syntax as, you guessed it, a syntactic feature. And syntactic features can be selected for, since they are proper syntactic objects.

(7.6)

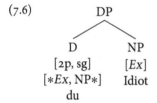

Therefore, expressive vocatives check the last box of the syntactic mechanism that are associated with features: agreement, movement, and selection. Thereby, even the syntactically rather innocent looking vocatives contribute evidence toward the hypothesis of expressive syntax.

7.3 A future for expressive features

Having looked back on the main results, the three case studies delivered for the idea of expressive features in syntax, let me now look a little ahead and conclude this work with some speculative ideas for what question to tackle next. I will only address some rather broad ones and will not repeat the open questions I raised throughout this book.

7.3.1 *Why adjectives?*

It is very interesting that expressive adjectives show this split between where they are realized and where they are interpreted. This is especially surprising given the fact that expressive epithets like *bastard* in *that bastard Kresge* have semantically been analyzed in the same way as expressive adjectives. However, they do not show argument extension at all. Why should this be? What is special about adjectives and their place inside the DP that they behave in this way, whereas nominal elements do not seem to behave in a similar way?[1]

7.3.2 Expressivity and its relation to D

In all three case studies, it turned out to be the case that the category of D played an important role. It was a place to host interpretable and uninterpretable features, and the category that selected for expressive complements. This of course raises the question of why this should be? Is that just an accident caused by the selection of phenomena I happened to investigate (expressive adjectives, for instance, showed that expressive features can also be located on C) or does it hint a deeper connection between this category and expressivity?

7.3.3 Cross-linguistic variation

The three case studies mostly involved German data, with some support from English. This of course raises the question of how stable the patterns that we observed in the three chapters are cross-linguistically. I am pretty sure that expressive intensifiers do show the same ability to occur in an external position in most languages. But what is it about expressive adjectives? Is argument extension a phenomenon that is always associated with expressive adjectives or is that something that is particular about German and English? And with respect to expressive vocatives, we already saw that in German, they can occur in argument position, which is not possible for English, Dutch, or Swedish, according to Corver (2008: 53–4). In addition, the approach I developed in this book should consolidate Corver's analysis of the cross-linguistic variation of the internal syntax, which I have ignored in my case study. Another respect in which the study on vocatives hinted at some variation is which pronouns can be used as articles within expressive vocatives. While in German, the person singular pronoun can be in expressive vocatives, this is not true for English. Getting a better picture of all these points of variation could provide us with a better view on the general role played by expressivity in syntax.

7.3.4 Diachronic development and acquisition

These are two diverse topics, but let me lump them together because they somehow go hand in hand. First, from a diachronic question, one may ask how expressive items come into existence. For all expressions discussed in this book, it is known that they have some descriptive origin that, via some pragmatic bridging inferences, developed into expressive items.[2] However, if we take the view argued for here, this is not merely a semantic change, but one that should come with a syntactic change. The question of course is then if there is a stage in which expressive adjectives are like expressive

---

[1] Thanks to Heidi Harley for pointing this puzzle out to me.
[2] See Davis & Gutzmann 2015 for a type-theoretic view on such diachronic developments.

epithets and only have a local interpretation. And only at a later stage do they become associated with uninterpretable features. Or does this change come automatically with the semantic change? And asking more broadly, was there a stage in the history of German (or other languages), in which expressivity was not a feature, but it became one. Similar considerations apply to language acquisition. When and how do children acquire expressive features? Once they learn expressive language is there a stage at which they acquire, say, expressive adjectives but do not yet have the interpretable–uninterpretable feature split we assumed for adult grammar? I think these are all exciting questions to ask, even though I guess it is really hard to find answers.

References

Abney, Steven. 1987. *The English Noun Phrase in its Sentential Aspect*. PhD thesis. Cambridge, MA: MIT.

Abusch, Dorit & Mats Rooth. 1997. Epistemic NP modifiers. *Proceedings of Semantics and Linguistic Theory (SALT)* 7.

Adger, David. 2003. *Core Syntax. A Minimalist Approach*. Oxford: Oxford University Press.

Aikhenvald, Alexandra Y. 2008. *The Manambu Language of East Sepik, Papua New Guinea*. Oxford: Oxford University Press.

Altmann, Hans. 1981. *Formen der "Herausstellung" im Deutschen. Rechtsversetzung, Linksversetzung, Freies Thema und verwandte Konstruktionen* (Linguistische Arbeiten 106). Tübingen: Niemeyer.

Amaral, Patrícia. Forthcoming. Descriptive pronouns. The semantics and pragmatics of side issues. In Daniel Gutzmann & Turgay (eds.), *Secondary Content*, Leiden: Brill.

Amaral, Patrícia, Craige Roberts, & E. Allyn Smith. 2007. Review of *The Logic of Conventional Implicatures* by Chris Potts. *Linguistics and Philosophy* 30(6). 707–49. DOI: 10.1007/S10988-008-9025-2.

Am-David, Assif. 2013. *The Distribution of Definiteness Markers Across Languages. A Semantic Typology*. PhD thesis. University of Frankfurt.

Ameka, Felix. 1992. Interjections: The universal yet neglected part of speech. *Journal of Pragmatics* 18(2–3). 101–18. DOI: 10.1016/0378-2166(92)90048-G.

AnderBois, Scott, Adrian Brasoveanu, & Robert Henderson. 2015. At-issue proposals and appositive impositions in discourse. *Journal of Semantics* 32(1). 93–138. DOI: 10.1093/jos/ffto14.

Anderson, Stephen R. 1992. *A-Morphous Morphology*. Cambridge: Cambridge University Press.

Androutsopoulos, Jannis K. 1998. *Deutsche Jugendsprache. Untersuchungen zu ihren Strukturen und Funktionen*. Frankfurt: Lang.

Asher, Ronald E. & T. C. Kumari. 1997. *Malayalam*. London: Routledge.

Bach, Emmon. 1967. Have and be in English syntax. *Language* 43(2). 462–85. URL: http://www.jstor.org/stable/411547.

Baker, Mark C. 2008. *The Syntax of Agreement and Concord*. Cambridge: Cambridge University Press.

Barker, Chris, Raffaella Bernardi, & Chung-chieh Shan. 2010. Principles of interdimensional meaning interaction. *Proceedings of SALT 20*. 109–21. URL: http://elanguage.net/journals/salt/article/view/20.109.

Bayer, Josef. 2012. From modal particle to interrogative marker: A study of German *denn*. In Laura Bruge, Anna Cardinaletti, Giuliana Giusti, Nicola Munaro, & Cecilia Poletto (eds.), *Functional Heads* (The Cartography of Syntactic Structures 7), 13–28. Oxford: Oxford University Press.

Bayer, Josef & Hans-Georg Obenauer. 2011. Discourse particles, clause structure, and question types. *The Linguistic Review* 28. 449–91. DOI: 10.1515/tlir.2011.013.

Bayer, Josef & Andreas Trotzke. Forthcoming. The derivation and interpretation of left peripheral discourse particles. In Josef Bayer, Roland Hinterhölzl, & Andreas Trotzke (eds.), *Discourse-oriented Syntax*, Amsterdam and Philadelphia: John Benjamins.

Beck, Sigrid. 2012. Comparison constructions. In Klaus von Heusinger, Claudia Maienborn, & Paul Portner (eds.), *Handbook of Semantics*. 2nd ed. Vol. 2 (Handbücher zur Sprach- und Kommunikationswissenschaft (HSK) 33.2), 1341–90. Berlin and New York: de Gruyter. DOI: 10.1515/9783110255072.1341.

Bhatt, Rajesh. 2005. Long distance agreement in Hindi-Urdu. *Natural Language and Linguistic Theory* 23(4). 757–807. DOI: 10.1007/s11049-004-4136-0.

Boeckx, Cedric & Kleanthes K. Grohmann. 2007. Remark: Putting phases in perspective. *Syntax* 10(2). 204–22. DOI: 10.1111/j.1467-9612.2007.00098.x.

Bolinger, Dwight. 1967. Adjectives in English: Attribution and predication. *Lingua* 18. 1–34.

Borer, Hagit & Yosef Grodzinsky. 1986. Syntactic cliticalization and lexical cliticalization. The case of Hebrew dative clitics. In Hagit Borer (ed.), *Syntax and Semantics*. Vol. 19: *The Syntax of Pronominal Clitics*, 175–217. New York: Academic Press.

Bošković, Željko. 2003. Agree, phases and intervention effects. *Linguistic Analysis* 33. 54–96.

Bošković, Željko. 2004. Object shift and the clause/PP parallelism hypothesis. *Proceeding of WCCFL* 23. 101–14.

Bošković, Željko. 2007. On the locality and motivation of move and agree: An even more minimal theory. *Linguistic Inquiry* 38(4). 589–644. DOI: 10.1162/ling.2007.38.4.589.

Bošković, Željko. 2011. On valued uninterpretable features. *Proceedings of NELS* 39.

Bošković, Željko. 2012. Phases in NPs and DPs. In Ángel J. Gallego (ed.), *Phases. Developing the Framework*, 343–83. Berlin and New York: de Gruyter. DOI: 10.1515/9783110264104.343.

Bowers, John. 2002. Transitivity. *Linguistic Inquiry* 33(2). 183–224. DOI: 10.1162/002438902317406696.

Breindl, Eva. 2009. Intensitätspartikeln. In Ludger Hoffmann (ed.), *Handbuch der Wortarten*, 397–422. Berlin and New York: de Gruyter. DOI: 10.1515/9783110217087.397.

Brody, Michael. 1997. Perfect chains. In Liliane Haegeman (ed.), *Elements of Grammar*, 139–67. Heidelberg: Springer. DOI: 10.1007/978-94-011-5420-8_3.

Bühler, Karl. 1934/1982. *Theory of Language. The Representational Function of Language*. Trans. by Goodwin, Donald Fraser. In collaboration with Achim Eschbach. Amsterdam and Philadelphia: John Benjamins.

Bühler, Karl. 1934/1999. *Sprachtheorie: Die Darstellungsfunktion der Sprache*. Stuttgart: Fischer.

Burger, Harald. 1980. Interjektionen. In Horst Sitta (ed.), *Ansätze zu einer pragmatischen Sprachgeschichte. Zürcher Kolloquium 1978*. (Germanistische Linguistik 21), Berlin and New York: de Gruyter.

Busch, Jerra Lui & Felix Schumann. 2016. Unspecific indefinites and (non-)restrictive relative clauses. *Lingua*. DOI: 10.1016/j.lingua.2016.04.005.

Carston, Robyn. 2016. The heterogeneity of procedural meaning. *Lingua* 175–6. 154–66. DOI: 10.1016/j.lingua.2015.12.010.

Castroviejo Miró, Elena. 2006. *Wh-exclamatives in Catalan*. PhD thesis. Barcelona: University of Barcelona. URL: http://semanticsarchive.net/Archive/mU5NDRmM/wh-exclamatives-in-Catalan.pdf.

Chatman, Saymour. 1978. *Story and Discourse. Narrative Structure in Fiction and Film*. Ithaca: Cornell University Press.

Chomsky, Noam. 1981. *Lectures on Government & Binding. The Pisa Lectures*. Dordrecht: Foris.

Chomsky, Noam. 1992. A minimalist program for linguistic theory. *MIT Occasional Papers in Linguistics* 1.

Chomsky, Noam. 1995. *The Minimalist Program*. Cambridge, MA: MIT Press.

Chomsky, Noam. 2000. Minimalist inquiries: The framework. In Roger Martin, David Michaels, & Juan Uriagereka (eds.), *Step by Step. Essays on Minimalist Syntax in Honor of Howard Lasnik*, 89–156. Cambridge, MA: MIT Press.

Chomsky, Noam. 2001. Derivation by phase. In Michael Kenstowicz (ed.), *Ken Hale, a Life in Language*, Cambridge, MA: MIT Press.

Cinque, Guglielmo. 1994. On the evidence for partial N-movement in the Romance DP. In Guglielmo Cinque, *Italian Syntax and Universal Grammar*, 287–309. Cambridge: Cambridge University Press. DOI: 10.1017/cbo9780511554261.011.

Cinque, Guglielmo. 1999. *Adverbs and Functional Heads. A Cross-linguistic Perspective*. Oxford: Oxford University Press.

Citko, Barbara. 2014. *Phase Theory. An Introduction*. Cambridge: Cambridge University Press.

Claudi, Ulrike. 2006. Intensifies of adjectives in German. *Language Typology and Universals* 59(4). 350–69. DOI: 10.1524/stuf.2006.59.4.350.

Collins, Chris & Edward Stabler. 2016. A formalization of minimalist syntax. *Syntax* 19(1). 43–78. DOI: 10.1111/synt.12117.

Coniglio, Marco. 2011. *Die Syntax der deutschen Modalpartikeln. Ihre Distribution und Lizenzierung in Haupt- und Nebensätzen*. (Studia grammatica 73). Berlin: Akademie Verlag.

Constantinescu, Camelia. 2011. *Gradability in the Nominal Domain*. PhD thesis. Leiden: Rijksuniversiteit Leiden. URL: http://hdl.handle.net/1887/18248.

Corbett, Greville G. 2006. *Agreement*. Cambridge: Cambridge University Press.

Corver, Norbert. 1997. The internal syntax of the Dutch extended adjectival projection. *Natural Language and Linguistic Theory* 15(2). 289–368. DOI: 10.1023/A:1005846812956.

Corver, Norbert. 2008. Uniformity and diversity in the syntax of evaluative vocatives. *Journal of Comparative Germanic Linguistics* 11(1). 43–93. DOI: 10.1007/s10828-008-9017-1.

Cruse, David Alan. 1986. *Lexical Semantics*. Cambridge: Cambridge University Press.

Cruse, David Alan. 2004. *Meaning in Language. An Introduction to Semantics and Pragmatics*. 2nd ed. (Oxford Textbooks in Linguistics). Oxford: Oxford University Press.

Daniel, Michael & Andrew Spencer. 2009. The vocative—an outlier case. In Andrej Malchukov & Andrew Spencer (eds.), *The Oxford Handbook of Case*, 626–34. Oxford: Oxford University Press.

d'Avis, Franz Josef. 2004. Über Parenthesen. In Franz Josef d'Avis (ed.), *Deutsche Syntax: Empirie und Theorie*, Göteborg: Acta Universitatis Gothoburgensis.

d'Avis, Franz Josef. 2013. Exklamativsatz. In Jörg Meibauer, Markus Steinbach, & Hans Altmann (eds.), *Satztypen des Deutschen*, 171–201. Berlin/New York: de Gruyter Mouton.

d'Avis, Franz Josef & Jörg Meibauer. 2013. *Du Idiot! Din idiot!* Pseudo-vocative constructions and insults in German (and Swedish). Addressing between system and performance. In Barbara Sonnenhauser & Patrizia Noel Aziz Hanna (eds.), *Vocative!*, 189–217. Berlin and New York: de Gruyter.

Davis, Christopher & Daniel Gutzmann. 2015. Use-conditional meaning and the semantics of pragmaticalization. *Proceedings of Sinn und Bedeutung* 19. 197–213.

Dehé, Nicole & Yordanka Kavalova (eds.). 2007. *Parentheticals* (Linguistik Ak-tuell/Linguistics Today 106). Amsterdam and Philadelphia: Benjamins.

Doherty, Monika. 1985. *Epistemische Bedeutung* (studia grammatica 23). Berlin: Akademie-Verlag.

Döring, Sophia. 2013. Modal particles and context shift. In Daniel Gutzmann & Hans-Martin Gärtner (eds.), *Beyond Expressives. Explorations in Use-Conditional Meaning*, 95–123. Leiden: Brill. DOI: 10.1163/9789004183988_004.

Drożdżowicz, Anna. 2016. Descriptive ineffability reconsidered. *Lingua* 177. 1–16. DOI: 10.1016/j.lingua.2015.12.011.

Drummond, Alex, Norbert Hornstein, & Howard Lasnik. 2010. A puzzle about P-stranding and a possible solution. *Linguistic Inquiry* 41(4). 689–92. DOI: 10.1162/ling_a_00018.

Dürscheid, Christa. 2002. "Polemik satt und Wahlkampf pur"—Das postnominale Adjektiv im Deutschen. *Zeitschrift für Sprachwissenschaft* 21(1). DOI: 10.1515/zfsw.2002.21.1.57.

Eckardt, Regine. 2012. Particles as speaker indexicals in free indirect discourse. *Sprache und Datenverarbeitung* 36(1). 1–21.

Eckardt, Regine. 2014. Dear Ede! Semantics and pragmatics of vocatives. In Daniel Gutzmann, Jan Köpping, & Cécile Meier (eds.), *Approaches to Meaning. Compositions, Values, Interpretation*, 223–49. Brill. DOI: 10.1163/9789004279377_011.

Eckardt, Regine. 2015. *The Semantics of Free Indirect Speech. How Texts Let You Read Minds and Eavesdrop*. Leiden: Brill.

Epstein, Samuel David & T. Daniel Seely. 2006. *Derivations in Minimalism*. Cambridge: Cambridge University Press.

Espinal, M. Teresa. 1991. The Representation of Disjunct Constituents. *Language* 67(4). 726. DOI: 10.2307/415075.

Faller, Martina. 2002. *Evidentiality in Cuzco Quechua*. PhD thesis. Stanford.

Farkas, Donka F. & Kim B. Bruce. 2010. On reacting to assertions and polar questions. *Journal of Semantics* 27(1). 81–118. DOI: doi:10.1093/jos/ffp010.

Fiengo, R. & J. Higginbotham. 1981. Opacity in NP. *Linguistic Analysis* 7. 395–421.

Fintel, Kai von. 2004. Would you believe it? The King of France is back! Presuppositions and truth-value intuitions. In Marga Reimer & Anne Bezuidenhout (eds.), *Descriptions and Beyond*, 269–96. Oxford: Oxford University Press.

Fox, Danny & David Pesetsky. 2005. Cyclic linearization of syntactic structure. *Theoretical Linguistics* 31(1-2). 1–45. DOI: 10.1515/thli.2005.31.1-2.1.

Frazier, Lyn, Brian Dillon, & Charles Clifton. 2014. A note on interpreting damn expressives: Transferring the blame. *Language and Cognition* 7. 291–304. DOI: 10.1017/langcog.2014.31. URL: http://dx.doi.org/10.1017/langcog.2014.31.

Frege, Gottlob. 1897/1979. Logic. In *Posthumous Writings*. Translated by Peter Long and Roger White. Ed. by Hans Hermes, Friedrich Kambartel, & Friedrich Kaulbach, 126–51. Oxford: Blackwell.

Fries, Norbert. 1992. Interjektionen, Interjektionsphrasen und Satzmodus. In Inger Rosengren (ed.), *Satz und Illokution*. Vol. 2, 307–42. Tübingen: Niemeyer.

Fuß, Eric. 2014. Complementizer agreement (in Bavarian). In Complementizer agreement (in Bavarian), *Linguistik Aktuell/Linguistics Today*, 51–82. John Benjamins Publishing Company. DOI: 10.1075/la.220.03fub. URL: http://dx.doi.org/10.1075/la. 220.03fub.

Gallego, Ángel J. 2012. *Phases. Developing the Framework*. Berlin and New York: de Gruyter.

Garrett, Edward John. 2001. *Evidentiality and Assertion in Tibetan*. PhD thesis. Los Angeles: University of California.

Gehrke, Berit & Louise McNally. 2010. Frequency adjectives and assertions about event types. *Proceedings of Semantics and Linguistic Theory (SALT)* 19. Ed. by Ed Cormany, Satoshi Ito, & David Lutz. 180–97. URL: http://journals.linguisticsociety.org/proceedings/index.php/SALT/article/view/2523/2271.

Geurts, Bart. 2007. Really fucking brilliant. *Theoretical Linguistics* 33(2). 209–214. DOI: 10.1515/TL.2007.013.

Giorgolo, Gianluca & Ash Asudeh. 2011. Multidimensional semantics with unidimensional glue logic. *Proceedings of the LFG11 Conference*.

Giorgolo, Gianluca & Ash Asudeh. 2012. $M, \eta, *$. Monads for conventional implicatures. *Proceedings of Sinn und Bedeutung* 16.

Grice, H. Paul. 1975. Logic and conversation. In Peter Cole & Jerry L. Morgan (eds.), *Syntax and Semantics 3. Speech Acts*, 41–58. New York: Academic Press.

Griffiths, James & Mark de Vries. 2013. The syntactic integration of appositives: Evidence from fragments and ellipsis. *Linguistic Inquiry* 44(2). 332–44. DOI: 10.1162/ling_a_00131.

Grohmann, Kleanthes K. 2009. *Explorations of Phase Theory. Interpretation at the Interfaces*. Berlin and New York: de Gruyter.

Gutzmann, Daniel. Forthcoming. Dimensions of meaning. In Daniel Gutzmann, Lisa Matthewson, Cécile Meier, Hotze Rullmann, & Thomas Ede Zimmermann (eds.), *The Wiley Blackwell Companion to Semantics*, Oxford: Wiley.

Gutzmann, Daniel. 2007. Eine Implikatur konventioneller Art: der Dativus Ethicus. *Linguistische Berichte* 211. 277–308.

Gutzmann, Daniel. 2009. Hybrid semantics for modal particles. *Sprache und Datenverarbeitung* 33(1-2). 45–59.

Gutzmann, Daniel. 2011. Expressive modifiers and mixed expressives. In Olivier Bonami & Patricia Cabredo-Hofherr (eds.), *Empirical Issues in Syntax and Semantics 8*, 123–41. URL: http://www.cssp.cnrs.fr/eiss8/gutzmann-eiss8.pdf.

Gutzmann, Daniel. 2013. Expressives and beyond. An introduction to varieties of use-conditional meaning. In Daniel Gutzmann & Hans-Martin Gärtner (eds.), *Beyond Expressives. Explorations in Use-Conditional Meaning*. (Current Research in the Semantics Pragmatics-Interface (CRiSPI) 28), 1–58. Leiden: Brill. DOI: 10.1163/9789004183988_002. URL: http://www.danielgutzmann.com/work/expressives-and-beyond/.

Gutzmann, Daniel. 2015a. Continuation-based semantics for modal particles. Deriving syntax from semantics. *MIT Working Papers in Linguistics (MITWPL) 75: Proceedings of MOSS 2: Moscow Syntax and Semantics*. Ed. by Vadim Kimmelman, Natalia Korotkova, & Igor Yanovich. 133–50. URL: http://www.cssp.cnrs.fr/eiss10/eiss10_gutzmann-and-mccready.pdf.

Gutzmann, Daniel. 2015b. *Use-Conditional Meaning. Studies in Multidimensional Semantics* (Oxford Studies in Semantics and Pragmatics 6). Oxford: Oxford University Press.

Gutzmann, Daniel. 2017. Modal particles ≠ modalparticles (= modal particles). Differences between German modal particles and how to deal with them semantically. In Josef Bayer & Volker Struckmeier (eds.), *Discourse Particles: Formal Approaches to Their Syntax and Semantics*, Berlin and New York: de Gruyter.

Gutzmann, Daniel & Hans-Martin Gärtner, (eds.) 2013. *Beyond Expressives: Explorations in Use-Conditional Meaning* (Current Research in the Semantics/Pragmatics Interface (CRiSPI) 28). Leiden: Brill. DOI: 10.1163/9789004183988.

Gutzmann, Daniel & Robert Henderson. 2015. Expressive, much? *Proceedings of Sinn und Bedeutung* 19. 266–283.

Gutzmann, Daniel & E. McCready. 2014. Using descriptions. *Empirical Issues in Syntax and Semantics* 10. Christopher Piñón (ed.). URL: http://www.cssp.cnrs.fr/eiss10/eiss10_gutzmann-and-mccready.pdf.

Gutzmann, Daniel & E. McCready. 2016. Quantification with pejoratives. In Rita Finkbeiner, Jörg Meibauer, & Heike Wiese (eds.), *Pejoration* (Linguistik Aktuell/Linguistics Today 2016), 75–102. Amsterdam and Philadelphia: John Benjamins.

Gutzmann, Daniel & Katharina Turgay. 2012. Expressive intensifiers in German. Syntax-semantics mismatches. In Christopher Piñón (ed.), *Empirical Issues in Syntax and Semantics* 9, 149–66. URL: http://www.cssp.cnrs.fr/eiss9.

Gutzmann, Daniel & Katharina Turgay. 2015. Expressive intensifiers and external degree modification. *The Journal of Comparative Germanic Linguistics* 17(3). 185–228. DOI: 10.1007/s10828-014-9069-3.

Gutzmann, Daniel & Katharina Turgay. 2016. Zur Stellung von Modalpartikeln in der gesprochenen Sprache. *Deutsche Sprache* 44(2). 97–122.

Haegeman, Liliane. 1988. Parenthetical adverbials. The radical orphanage approach. In Shuji Chiba, Akira Ogawa, Yasuaki Fuiwara, et al. (eds.), *Aspects of Modern English Linguistics. Papers Presented to Masatomo Ukaji on His 60th Birthday*, 232–54. Tokyo: Kaitakusha.

Haegeman, Liliane. 2014. West Flemish verb-based discourse markers and the articulation of the speech act layer. *Studia Linguistica* 68(1). 116–39. ISSN: 1467–9582. DOI: 10.1111/stul.12023.

Haegeman, Liliane & Virginia Hill. Dec. 2013. The syntacticization of discourse. In Raffaella Folli, Christina Sevdali, & Robert Truswell (eds.), *Syntax and Its Limits*, 370–90. Oxford: Oxford University Press. DOI: 10.1093/acprof:oso/9780199683239.003.0018.

Haegeman, Liliane & Marjo van Koppen. 2012. Complementizer agreement and the relation between C° and T°. *Linguistic Inquiry* 43(3). 441–54. DOI: 10.1162/ling_a_00096.

Harris, Jesse A. & Christopher Potts. 2009a. Perspective-shifting with appositives and expressives. *Linguistics and Philosophy* 32(6). 523–52. DOI: 10.1007/s10988-010-9070-5.

Harris, Jesse A. & Christopher Potts. 2009b. Predicting perspectival orientation for appositives. *Proceedings of the 45th Meeting of the Chicago Linguistic Society*, Chicago Linguistic Society.

Heck, Fabian, Gereon Müller, & Jochen Trommer. 2009. A phase-based approach to Scandinavian definiteness marking. *STUF—Language Typology and Universals* 62(4). DOI: 10.1524/stuf.2009.0020.

Heim, Irene. 2001. Degree operators and scope. In Caroline Féry & Wolfgang Sternefeld (eds.), *Audiatur Vox Sapientiae*, 214–239. Berlin: Akademie Verlag. URL: http://www.sfs.uni-tuebingen.de/~astechow/Festschrift/Heim-7-6-komplett%20fertig.pdf.

Hill, Virginia. 2007. Vocatives and the pragmatics–syntax interface. *Lingua* 117(12). 2077–2105. ISSN: 0024-3841. DOI: http://dx.doi.org/10.1016/j.lingua.2007.01.002.

Hill, Virginia. 2014. *Vocatives. How Syntax Meets with Pragmatics* (Empirical Approaches to Linguistic Theory 5). Leiden: Brill.

Hoffmann, Ludger. 1998. Parenthesen. *Linguistische Berichte* 175. 299–328.

Hom, Christoper. 2008. The semantics of racial epithets. *Journal of Philosophy* 105. 416–40.

Horn, Laurence R. 2008a. I love me some him. The landscape of non-argument datives. In O. Bonami & P. Cabredo Hofherr (eds.), *Empirical Issues in Syntax and Semantics 7*, 169–92.

Horn, Laurence R. 2008b. On F-implicature. Myth-analysis and rehabilitation. Ms. New Haven, CT. URL: http://www.eecs.umich.edu/~rthomaso/lpw08/Horn_LPW.pdf.

Horn, Laurence R. 2013. I love me some datives: Expressive meaning, free datives, and F-implicature. In Daniel Gutzmann & Hans-Martin Gärtner (eds.), *Beyond Expressives. Explorations in Use-conditional Meaning* (Current Research in the Semantics/Pragmatics Interface (CRiSPI) 28), 151–99. Leiden: Brill. Chapter 5 of this volume.

Jacobs, Joachim. 1991. On the semantics of modal particles. In Werner Abraham (ed.), *Discourse Particles*, 141–62. Amsterdam: Benjamins.

Jacobs, Joachim. 2019. Why the meaning of discourse particles is separated from focus-background structure. In Daniel Gutzmann & Katharina Turgay (eds.), *Secondary Content. The Linguistics of Side Issues*, Leiden: Brill.

Jakobson, Roman. 1960a. Linguistics and poetics. In Thomas A. Sebeok (ed.), *Style in Language*, Cambridge, MA: MIT Press.

Jakobson, Roman. 1960b. Linguistik und Poetik. In Roman Jakobson (ed.), *Poetik. Ausgewählte Aufsätze 1921–1971*, 83–121. Frankfurt: Suhrkamp.

Jay, Timothy & J. H. Danks. 1977. Ordering of taboo adjectives. *Bulletin of the Psychonomic Society* 9. 405–8.

Jay, Timothy & Kristin Janschewitz. 2007. Filling the emotion gap in linguistic theory. Commentary on Potts' expressive dimension. *Theoretical Linguistics* 33(2). 215–21. DOI: 10.1515/TL.2007.014.

Jayez, Jacques & Corinne Rossari. 2004. Parentheticals as conventional implicatures. In Francis Corblin & Henriëtte de Swart (eds.), *Handbook of French Semantics*, 211–29. Stanford, CA: CSLI.

Kaiser, Elsi. 2015. Perspective-shifting and free indirect discourse. Experimental investigations. *Proceedings of SALT* 25. 346–72.

Kallulli, Dalina & Antonia Rothmayr. 2008. The syntax and semantics of indefinite determiner doubling constructions in varieties of German. *Journal of Comparative Germanic Linguistics* 11(2). 95–136. DOI: 10.1007/S10828-008-9019-z.

Kaplan, David. 1999. The meaning of *ouch* and *oops*. Explorations in the theory of meaning as use. 2004 version. Ms. Los Angeles.

Kayne, Richard S. 1994. *The Antisymmetry of Syntax*. Cambridge, MA: MIT Press.

Kayne, Richard S. July 2005. Prepositions as probes. In *Movement and Silence*, 85–104. Oxford: Oxford University Press. DOI: 10.1093/acprof:oso/9780195179163.003.0005.

Kennedy, Christopher. 1999. *Projecting the Adjective: The Syntax and Semantics of Gradability and Comparison*. New York: Garland.

Kennedy, Christopher. 2007. Vagueness and grammar: The semantics of relative and absolute gradable adjectives. *Linguistics and Philosophy* 30.1–45. DOI: 10.1007/s10988-006-9008-0.

Kennedy, Christopher & Louise McNally. 2005. Scale structure, degree modification, and the semantics of gradable predicates. *Language* 81(2). 345–81. DOI: 10.1353/lan.2005.0071. URL: http://dingo.sbs.arizona.edu/~hharley/courses/PDF/KennedyMcNallyScales.pdf.

Kirschbaum, Ilja. 2002. Schrecklich nett *und* voll verrückt. *Muster der AdjektivIntensivierung im Deutschen*. PhD thesis. Düsseldorf: Heinrich-Heine-Universität. URL: http://deposit.d-nb.de/cgi-bin/dokserv?idn=969264437&dok_var=d1&dok_ext=pdf&filename=969264437.pdf.

Kramer, Ruth. 2009. *Definite Markers, Phi Features and Agreement. A Morphosyntactic Investigation of the Amharic DP*. PhD thesis. Santa Cruz: University of California.

Kratzer, Angelika. Mar. 26, 1999. "Beyond *ouch* and *oops*. How descriptive and expressive meaning interact." *Cornell Conference on Theories of Context Dependency*. Cornell University. Ithaca, NY. URL: http://semanticsarchive.net/Archive/WEwNGUyO/.

Kubota, Yusuke & Wataru Uegaki. 2011. Continuation-based semantics for conventional implicatures. The case of Japanese benefactives. In Ed Cormany, Satoshi Ito, & David Lutz (eds.), *Proceedings of Semantics and Linguistic Theory (SALT) 19*, 306–23. eLanguage. URL: http://elanguage.net/journals/index.php/salt/article/view/19.18/1394.

Kügelgen, Rainer von. 2003. Parenthesen—handlungstheoretisch betrachtet. In Ludger Hoffmann (ed.), *Funktionale Syntax. Die pragmatische Perspektive*, 208–30. Berlin and New York: de Gruyter. DOI: 10.1515/9783110907278.208.

Kuno, Masakazu. 2011. Separating feature interpretability from feature values. Evidence from negative condord in Japanese. *Generative Grammar in Geneva* 7. 23–32.

Laenzlinger, Christopher. 2010. The CP/DP Parallelism Revisited. *Generative Grammar in Geneva* 6. 49–107. URL: http://www.unige.ch/lettres/linge/syntaxe/journal/Volume6/laenzlinger_final.pdf.

Lahne, Antje. 2008. *Where There is Fire There Is Smoke. Local Modelling of Successive-Cyclic Movement*. PhD thesis. Universität Leipzig.

Lambert, Silke. 2007. Pragmatic and stylistic relevance of free datives in German. Manuscript. Buffalo, NY.

Larson, Richard K. 1999. Semantics of adjectival modification. LOT Winterschool Class Notes, Amsterdam.

Lasersohn, Peter. 2005. Context dependence, disagreement, and predicates of personal taste. *Linguistics and Philosophy* 28(6). 643–86. DOI: 10.1007/s10988-005-0596-x.

Leech, Geoffrey N. & Michael H. Short. 2007. *Style in Fiction*. 2nd ed. London: Pearson Education Limited.

Leffel, Timothy James. 2014. *The Semantics of Modification: Adjectives, Nouns, and Order*. PhD thesis. New York: NYU.

Legate, Julie Anne. 2005. Phases and cyclic agreement. In Martha McGinnis & Norvin Richards (eds.), *Perspectives on Phases*, 147–156. Cambridge, MA: MIT Working Papers in Linguistics.

Lindner, Karin. 1991. "Wir sind ja doch alte Bekannte"—the use of German *ja* and *doch* as modal particles. In Werner Abraham (ed.), *Discourse Particles*, 303–28. Amsterdam: Benjamins.

Liu, Mingya. 2012. *Multidimensional Semantics of Evaluative Adverbs* (Current Research in the Semantics/Pragmatics Interface (CRiSPI) 26). Leiden: Brill.

Lyons, Christopher. 1999. *Definiteness* (Cambridge Textbooks in Linguistics). Cambridge: Cambridge University Press.

Matushansky, Ora. 2000. The instrument of inversion. Instrumental case and verb raising in the Russian copula. *Proceeding of WCCFL* 19.101–15.

Matushansky, Ora. 2002. *Movement of Degree/Degree of Movement*. PhD thesis. Cambridge, MA: MIT.

Matushansky, Ora. 2005. Going through a phase. In Martha McGinnis & Norvin Richards (eds.), *Perspectives on Phases*, 157–81. Cambridge, MA: MIT Working Papers in Linguistics.

Matushansky, Ora & Benjamin Spector. 2005. Tinker, tailor, soldier, spy. *Proceedings of Sinn und Bedeutung* 9. Ed. by Emar Maier, Corien Bary, & Janneke Huitink. 241–55.

McCawley, James D. 1982. Parentheticals and discontinuous constituent structure. *Linguistic Inquiry* 13(1). 91–106.

McCready, E. 2009. What man does. *Linguistics and Philosophy* 31(6). 671–724. Doi: 10.1007/S10988-009-9052-7.

McCready, E. 2010. Varieties of conventional implicature. *Semantics & Pragmatics* 3(8). 1–57. DOI: 10.3765/sp.3.8.

McCready, E. & Magdalena Schwager. 2009. Intensifiers. Talk given at DGfS 2009.

Meinunger, André. 2009. Leftmost peripheral adverbs and adjectives in German. *Journal of Comparative German Linguistics* 12(2). 115–35. DOI: 10.1007/S10828-009-9028-6.

Merchant, Jason. 2011. Aleut case matters. In Tista Bagchi Etsuyo Yuasa Yuasa & Katharine P. Beals (eds.), *Pragmatics and Autolexical Grammar. In Honor of Jerry Sadock*, 382–411. Amsterdam and Philadelphia: John Benjamins.

Mildenberger, Carl David. 2017. Expressives, majoratives, and ineffability. *Kriterion – Journal of Philosophy* 31(2). 1–16. URL: http://www.kriterion-journal-of-philosophy.org.

Milsark, Gary. 1977. Toward an explanation of certain peculiarities of the existential construction in English. *Linguistic Analysis* 3. 1–29.

Miyagawa, Shigeru. 2012. Agreements that occur mainly in the main clause. In Lobke Aelbrecht, Liliane Haegeman, & Rachel Nye (eds.), *Main Clause Phenomena. New Horizons*, 79–111. Amsterdam and Philadelphia: Benjamins.

Morzycki, Marcin. 2009. Degree modification of gradable nouns: Size adjectives and adnominal degree morphemes. *Natural Language Semantics* 17(2). 175–203. DOI: 10.1007/S11050-009-9045-7. URL: https://www.msu.edu/~morzycki/work/papers/deg_nouns.pdf.

Morzycki, Marcin. 2012. The several faces of adnominal degree modification. In Jaehoon Choi, E. Alan Hogue, Jeffrey Punske, et al. (eds.), *Proceedings of Proceedings of the West Coast Conference on Formal Linguistics (WCCFL)* 29, 187–95. Somerville, MA: Cascadilla Press.

Morzycki, Marcin. 2013. Modification. Book draft.

Morzycki, Marcin. 2014. The landscape of nonlocal reading of adjectives. Talk given at University of Maryland, December 5, 2014.

Müller, Gereon. 2004. Phrase impenetrability and wh-intervention. In Gereon Müller, *Minimality Effects in Syntax*, 289–326. Berlin and New York: de Gruyter. DOI: 10.1515/9783110197365.289.

Müller, Gereon. 2011. *Constraints on Displacement*: Amsterdam and Philadelphia: Benjamins.

Müller, Sonja. 2017. Alte und neue Fragen der Modalpartikel-Forschung. *Linguistische Berichte* 252. 383–442.

Munaro, Nicola. 2010. On the edge-feature of particles, interjections, and short answers. In Anna Maria Di Sciullo & Virginia Hill (eds.), *Edges, Heads, and Projections*, 67–86. Amsterdam and Philadelphia: John Benjamins. DOI: 10.1075/la.156.07mun.

Munaro, Nicola & Cecilia Poletto. 2003. Ways of clause typing. *Rivista di Grammatica Generativa* 27. 87–105.

Munaro, Nicola & Cecilia Poletto. 2004. Sentential particles and clausal typing in the Veneto dialects. *ZAS Papers in Linguistics* 35(2). Ed. by Shaer, Benjamin, Werner Frey & Claudia Maienborn. 375–97.

Murray, Sarah E. 2017. *The Semantics of Evidentials*. (Oxford Studies in Semantics and Pragmatics 9). Oxford: Oxford University Press.

Nübling, Damaris. 2004. Die prototypische Interjektion. Ein Definitionsvorschlag. *Zeitschrift für Semiotik* 26(1–2). 11–45.

Os, Charles van. 1989. *Aspekte der Intensivierung im Deutschen*. (Studien zur deutschen Grammatik 37). Tübingen: Narr.

Oyharçabal, Beñat. 1993. Verb agreement with non arguments: On allocutive agreement. In José Ignacio Hualde & Jon Ortiz de Urbina (eds.), *Generative Studies in Basque Linguistics* (Linguistik Aktuell/Linguistics Today 105), 89–114. Amsterdam and Philadelphia: John Benjamins.

Pafel, Jürgen. 1994. Zur syntaktischen Struktur nominaler Quantoren. *Zeitschrift für Sprachwissenschaft* 13. 236–75. DOI: 10.1515/zfsw.1994.13.2.236.

Pesetsky, David & Esther Torrego. 2007. The syntax of valuation and the interpretability of features. In Simin Karimi, Vida Samiian, & Wendy K. Wilkins (eds.), *Syntactic Derivation and Interpretation. In Honor of Joseph E. Emonds*, 262–94. Amsterdam and Philadelphia: Benjamins. DOI: 10.1075/la.101.14pes.

Peterson, Peter G. 1999. On the boundaries of syntax. In Peter Collins & David Lee (eds.), *Studies in Language Companion Series*, 229–250. John Benjamins Publishing Company. DOI: 10.1075/slcs.45.16pet.

Pittner, Karin. 1995. Zur Syntax von Parenthesen. *Linguistische Berichte* 156. 85–108.

Pittner, Robert J. 1991. Der Wortbildungstyp "Steigerungsbildung" im Deutschen. In Eberhard Klein, Françoise Puradier Duteil, & Karl Heinz Wagner (eds.), *Betriebslinguistik und Linguistikbetrieb. Akten des 24. Linguistischen Kolloquiums, Universität Bremen, 4–6. September 1989*. Vol. 1. (Linguistische Arbeiten 260), 225–31. Tübingen: Niemeyer.

Pittner, Robert J. 1996. Der Wortbildungstyp Steigerungsbildung beim Adjektiv im Neuhochdeutschen. *Sprache & Sprachen* 19. 29–67.

Polinsky, Maria & Eric Potsdam. 2001. Long-distance agreement and topic in Tsez. *Natural Language and Linguistic Theory* 19(3). 583–646. DOI: 10.1023/a:1010757806504.

Ponelis, Friedrich Albert. 1979. *Afrikaanse Syntaksis*. Pretoria: J.L. van Schaik Akademies.

Portner, Paul. 2007. Instructions for interpretation as separate performatives. In Kerstin Schwabe & Susanne Winkler (eds.), *On Information Structure, Meaning and Form*, 407–26. Amsterdam: Benjamins.

Potts, Christopher. 2002. The syntax and semantics of as-parentheticals. *Natural Language & Linguistic Theory* 20(3). 623–89. DOI: 10.1023/A:1015892718818.

Potts, Christopher. 2005. *The Logic of Conventional Implicature* (Oxford Studies in Theoretical Linguistics 7). Oxford: Oxford University Press.

Potts, Christopher. 2007. The expressive dimension. *Theoretical Linguistics* 33(2). 165–97. DOI: 10.1515/TL.2007.011.

Potts, Christopher & Tom Roeper. 2006. The narrowing acquisition path. From declarative to expressive small clauses. In Ljiljana Progovac, Kate Paesani, Eugenia Casielles-Suárez, & Ellen Barton (eds.), *The Syntax of Nonsententials. MultiDisciplinary Perspectives*, 183–201. Amsterdam: John Benjamins. URL: http://semanticsarchive.net/Archive/WZkOTVkY/.

Predelli, Stefano. 2008. Vocatives. *Analysis* 68(2). 97–105.

Preminger, Omer. 2014. *Agreement and Its Failures*. Cambridge, MA: MIT Press.

Rauh, Gisa. 2004. Warum "Linguist" in "ich/du Linguist" kein Schimpfwort sein muß. Eine konversationstheoretische Erklärung. *Linguistische Berichte* 197.77–105.

Recanati, François. 2004. Pragmatics and semantics. In Laurence R. Horn & Gregory Ward (eds.), *The Handbook of Pragmatics*, 442–62. Oxford: Blackwell.

Rett, Jessica. 2012. Exclamatives, degrees and speech acts. *Linguistics and Philosophy*. 1–32. DOI: 10.1007/S10988-011-9103-8.

Rice, Keren D. 1986. Some remarks on direct and indirect speech in Slave (Northern Athapaskan). In Florian Coulmas (ed.), *Direct and Indirect Speech*, 47–76. Berlin and New York: de Gruyter.

Richards, Norvin. 2001. *Movement in Language. Interactions and Architectures*. Oxford: Oxford University Press.

Rizzi, Luigi. 1990. *Relativized Minimality*. Cambridge, MA: MIT Press.

Rizzi, Luigi. 1997. The fine structure of the left periphery. In Liliane Haegeman (ed.), *Elements of Grammar: A Handbook of Generative Syntax*, 281–337. Dordrecht: Kluwer.

Roberts, Ian. 2001. Head Movement. In Mark Baltin & Chris Collins (eds.), *The Handbook of Contemporary Syntactic Theory*, 113–47. Oxford: Blackwell.

Romero, Maribel. 2013. Modal superlatives: a compositional analysis. *Natural Language Semantics* 21(1). 79–110. DOI: 10.1007/S11050-012-9090-5.

Ross, John Robert. 1970. On declarative sentences. In Roderick A. Jacobs & Peter S. Rosenbaum (eds.), *Readings in English Transformational Grammar*, 222–72. Washington, DC: Georgetown University Press.

Schaden, Gerhard. 2010. Vocatives: A note on addressee management. *University of Pennsylvania Working Papers in Linguistics* 16(1). 176–85.

Schlegloff, Emanuel A. 1968. Sequencing in conversational openings. *American Anthropologist* 70(6). 1075–95.

Schlenker, Philippe. 2013. Supplements without bidimensionalism. Ms. Expanded version. Institut Jean-Nicod and New York University. URL: http://www.semanticsarchive.net/Archive/jgwMjNmM/Supplements_without_Bidimensionalism.pdf.

Schwarz, Bernhard. 2005. Modal superlatives. *Proceedings of SALT* 15. Ed. by Effi Georgala & Jonathan Howell. 187–204. URL: http://journals.linguisticsociety.org/proceedings/index.php/SALT/article/view/3094/2817.

Schwarz, Bernhard. 2006. Attributive wrong. *Proceeding of WCCFL* 25. Ed. by David Montero, Donald Baumer, & Michael Scanlon. 362–370. URL: http://www.lingref.com/cpp/wccfl/25/paper1469.pdf.

Sigurðsson, Halldór Ármann. 2004. The syntax of person, tense, and speech features. *Italian Journal of Linguistics / Rivista di Linguistica* 16(1). 219–51.

Sigurðsson, Halldór Ármann. 2011. Conditions on argument drop. *Linguistic Inquiry* 42(2). 267–304. DOI: 10.1162/ling_a_00042.

Simons, Mandy, Judith Tonhauser, David I. Beaver, & Craige Roberts. 2010. What projects and why. *Proceedings of SALT* 20. 309–27. URL: http://elanguage.net/journals/index.php/salt/article/viewFile/20.309/1326.

Smith, Peter W. 2015. *Feature Mismatches: Consequences for Syntax, Morphology, and Semantics.* PhD thesis. Storrs: University of Connecticut.

Sonnenhauser, Barbara & Patrizia Noel Aziz Hanna. 2013a. Introduction: Vocative! In Barbara Sonnenhauser & Patrizia Noel Aziz Hanna (eds.), *Vocative! Addressing Between System and Performance*, 1–23. Berlin and New York: de Gruyter.

Sonnenhauser, Barbara & Patrizia Noel Aziz Hanna (eds.). 2013b. *Vocative! Addressing Between System and Performance.* Berlin and New York: de Gruyter.

Speas, Peggy & Carol L. Tenny. 2003. Configurational properties of point of view roles. In Anna Maria Di Sciullo (ed.), *Asymmetry in Grammar*, 315–44. Amsterdam and Philadelphia: Benjamins. DOI: 10.1075/la.57.15spe. URL: http://dx.doi.org/10.1075/la.57.15spe.

Stechow, Arnim von. 2009. Tenses in compositional semantics. In Wolfgang Klein & Ping Li (eds.), *The Expression of Time*, 129–66. Berlin and New York: de Gruyter.

Stechow, Arnim von. 1984. Comparing semantic theories of comparison. *Journal of Semantics* 3(1–2). 1–77. DOI: 10.1093/jos/3.1-2.1. URL: https://unstable.nl/andreas/ai/emplex/vonstechow%20-%20comparing%20semantic%20theories%20of%20comparatives.pdf.

Stechow, Arnim von. 2003. Feature deletion under semantic binding. Tense, person, and mood under verbal quantifiers. *Proceedings of NELS* 33. Makoto Kadowaki & Shigeto Kawahara (eds.).

Stechow, Arnim von. 2004. Binding by verbs. Tense, person and mood under attitudes. In Horst Lohnstein & Susanne Trissler (eds.), *The Syntax and Semantics of the Left Periphery*, 431–88. Berlin and New York: de Gruyter.

Steele, Susan. 1978. Word order variation: A typological study. In Joseph H. Greenberg, Charles A. Ferguson, & Edith A. Moravcsik (eds.), *Universals of Human Language. Syntax*, 585–623. Stanford: Stanford University Press.

Sternefeld, Wolfgang. 2008. *Syntax. Eine morphologisch motivierte generative Beschreibung des Deutschen.* 3rd ed. Vol. 1. Tübingen: Stauffenburg.

Stevens, Christopher M. 2005. Revisiting the affixoid debate. On the grammaticalization of the word. In Torsten Leuschner, Tanja Mortelmans, & Sarah De Groodt (eds.), *Grammatikalisierung im Deutschen*, 71–83. Berlin and New York: de Gruyter.

Stjepanović, Sandra & Shoichi Takahashi. 2001. Eliminating the phase impenetrability condition. Paper presented at the workshop *Motivating Movement: Explaining the Displacement Property of Natural Language.*

Struckmeier, Volker. 2007. *Akademie Verlag. Berlin. Attribute im Deutschen. Zu ihren Eigenschaften und ihrer Position im grammatischen System* (Studia grammatica 65). Studia grammatica.

Struckmeier, Volker. 2014. Ja doch wohl C? Modal particles in German as C-related elements. *Studia Linguistica* 68.16–48.

Stump, Gregory T. 1981. The interpretation of frequency adverbs. *Linguistics and Philosophy* 4. 221–57. DOI: 10.1007/BF00350140.

Sudo, Yasutada. 2013. Biased polar questions and Japanese question particles. In Daniel Gutzmann & Hans-Martin Gärtner (eds.), *Beyond expressives. Explorations in Use-Conditional Meaning*, 275–95. Leiden: Brill.

Svenonius, Peter. 2004. On the Edge. In David Adger, Cécile de Cat, & George Tsoulas (eds.), *In Peripheries. Syntactic Edges and Their Effects*, 259–87. Heidelberg: Springer. DOI: 10.1007/ 1-4020-1910-6_11. URL: http://dx.doi.org/10.1007/1-4020-1910-6_11.

Tchizmarova, Ivelina K. 2005. Hedging functions of the Bulgarian discourse marker *xajde*. *Journal of Pragmatics* 37(8). 1143–63. DOI: 10.1016/j.pragma.2005.01.003.

Trabant, Jürgen. 1983. Gehören die Interjektionen zur Sprache. In Harald Weydt (ed.), *Partikeln und Interaktion*, 69–81. Tübingen: Niemeyer.

Travis, Lisa. 1984. *Parameters and Effects of Word Order Variation*. PhD thesis. Cambridge, MA: MIT.

Truckenbrodt, Hubert. 2006. On the semantic motivation of syntactic verb movement to C in German. *Theoretical Linguistics* 32(3). 257–306. DOI: 10.1515/TL.2006.018. URL: http://www2.sfs.uni-tuebingen.de/~hubert/Home/papers/V-to-C.pdf.

Uriagereka, Juan. 1999. Multiple spell-out. In Samuel David Epstein & Norbert Hornstein (eds.), *Working Minimalism*, 251–82. Cambridge, MA: MIT Press.

Uriagereka, Juan. 2012. *Spell-Out and the Minimalist Program*. Oxford: Oxford University Press.

Vater, Heinz. 1998. Determinantien und Pronomina in der DP. In Peter Bassola (ed.), *Beiträge zur Nominalphrasensyxntax* (Acta Germanica 6), 11–43. Szeged: Jate.

Vater, Heinz. 2000. "Pronominantien"—oder: Pronomina sind Determinantien. In Rolf Thieroff, Matthias Tamrat, Nanna Fuhrhop, & Oliver Teuber (eds.), *Deutsche Grammatik in Theorie und Praxis*, Tübingen: Niemeyer.

Vries, Mark de. 2006. The syntax of appositive relativization. On specifying coordination, false free relatives, and promotion. *Linguistic Inquiry* 37(2). 229–70. DOI: 10.1162/ling. 2006.37.2.229.

Vries, Mark de. 2012. Parenthetical main clauses—or not? In Lobke Aelbrecht, Liliane Haegeman, & Rachel Nye (eds.), *Main Clause Phenomena. New Horizons*. (Linguistik Aktuell/Linguistics Today 190), 177–202. Amsterdam and Philadelphia: John Benjamins. DOI: 10.1075/la.190.08vri. URL: http://dx.doi.org/10.1075/la.190.08vri.

Wang, Linton & E. McCready. 2007. Aspects of the indefiniteness effect. In T. Washio, K. Satoh, H. Takeda, & A. Inokuchi (eds.), *New Frontiers in Artificial Intelligence*, 162–76. DOI: 10.1007/978-3-540-69902-6_15.

Wegener, Heide. 1989. Eine Modalpartikel besonderer Art: Der Dativus Ethicus. In Harald Weydt (ed.), *Sprechen mit Partikeln*, 56–73. Berlin/New York: de Gruyter.

Welte, Werner. 1980. Zur Syntax, Semantik und Pragmatik exklamatorischer Vokative. *Indogermanische Forschungen* 85. 1–34. DOI: 10.1515/9783110243277.1.

Wierzbicka, Anna. 1992. The semantics of interjection. *Journal of Pragmatics* 18(2-3). 159–92. DOI: 10.1016/0378-2166(92)90050-L.

Williamson, Timothy. 2009. Reference, inference and the semantics of pejoratives. In Joseph Almog & Paolo Leonardi (eds.), *The Philosophy of David Kaplan*, 137–58. Oxford: Oxford University Press.

Wittgenstein, Ludwig. 1953. *Philosophische Untersuchungen. Philosophical Investigations.* Oxford: Blackwell.

Wurmbrand, Susi. 2012. Parasitic participles in Germanic: Evidence for the theory of verb clusters. *Taal & Tongval* 64(1). 129–56.

Wurmbrand, Susi. 2014. The merge condition. A syntactic approach to selection. In Peter Kosta, Steven L. Franks, Teodora Radeva-Bork, & Lilia Schürcks (eds.), *Minimalism and Beyond. Radicalizing the Interfaces*, 139–77. Amsterdam and Philadelphia: John Benjamins.

Zanuttini, Raffaella. 2008. Encoding the addressee in the syntax. Evidence from English imperative subjects. *Natural Language and Linguistic Theory* 26. 185–218.

Zeijlstra, Hedde. 2004. *Sentential Negation and Negative Concord.* PhD thesis. University of Amsterdam.

Zeijlstra, Hedde. 2008. On the syntactic flexibility of formal features. In Theresa Biberauer (ed.), *Linguistik Aktuell/Linguistics Today*, 143–73. Amsterdam and Philadelphia: John Benjamins Publishing Company. DOI: 10.1075/la.132.06zei.

Zeijlstra, Hedde. 2012. There is only one way to agree. *The Linguistic Review* 29(3). 491–539. DOI: 10.1515/tlr-2012-0017.

Zeijlstra, Hedde. Dec. 12, 2013. Formal vs. semantic features. Talken given at the *New Approaches to the Syntax/Semantics Interface* workshop.

Zimmermann, Malte. 2012. Discourse particles. In Paul Portner, Claudia Maienborn, & Klaus von Heusinger (eds.), *Handbook of Semantics*, 2011–38. Berlin and New York: de Gruyter.

Zimmermann, Malte. 2003. Pluractionality and complex quantifier formation. *Natural Language Semantics* 11. 249–87. DOI: 10.1023/A:1024937316555.

Zimmermann, Malte. 2004a. Discourse particles in the left periphery. In Benjamin Shaer, Werner Frey, & Claudia Maienborn (eds.), *ZAS Papers in Linguistics*, 543–66. URL: http://amor.rz.hu-berlin.de/~zimmermy/papers/MZ2004-ZASPIL-wohl.pdf.

Zimmermann, Malte. 2004b. Zum "Wohl". Diskurspartikeln als Satztypmodifikatoren. *Linguistische Berichte* 199.253–286. URL: http://amor.rz.hu-berlin.de/~zimmermy/papers/MZ2004-LB-wohl.pdf.

Zimmermann, Thomas Ede. 2012. Compositionality problems and how to solve them. In Markus Werning, Wolfram Hinzen, & Edouard Machery (eds.), *The Oxford Handbook of Compositionality*, 81–106. Oxford: Oxford University Press.

Zu, Vera. 2018. *Discourse Participants and the Structural Representation of the Context.* PhD thesis. New York: New York University.

Zwicky, Arnold M. 1974. Hey, Whatsyourname! *Proceedings of CLS* 10(2). Ed. by Michael W. LaGaly, Robert A. Fox, & Anthony Bruck. 787–801.

Author Index

Subject Index

OXFORD STUDIES IN THEORETICAL LINGUISTICS